FUNERARY SYMBOLISM
IN APULIAN VASE-PAINTING

Funerary Symbolism in Apulian Vase-Painting

By
H. R. W. SMITH

Edited By
J. K. ANDERSON

UNIVERSITY OF CALIFORNIA PRESS

Berkeley • Los Angeles • London

University of California Publications: Classical Studies

Volume 12

Approved for publication June 16, 1972

University of California Press
Berkeley and Los Angeles

University of California Press, Ltd.
London, England

PRINTED IN THE UNITED STATES OF AMERICA

Contents

List of Figures

List of Plates

Editor's Preface

IF VIRTUES CAN be carried to excess, Professor H. R. W. Smith's excessive courtesy and modesty may be considered the reasons that his teaching was sometimes hard to understand. During the last thirteen years of his life, which he devoted to the present book, he was always ready to welcome to his office in the University of California Library anyone who came for advice, for help in disentangling a scholarly problem, or for the pleasure of listening to him discussing his own work. He invariably treated the caller as an equal, and launched straight into his own thoughts at the point to which his argument had carried him, without suggesting in any way that his hearer's scholarship or intellectual capacity might be far below his own. It was not until I had known him for some years that I summoned up my courage, or overcame my vanity, sufficiently to admit ignorance; in the meantime that ignorance had at least been diminished not only by listening to his talk but by my own efforts, through subsequent study, to find out what he had been talking about.

As he talked, so he wrote — addressing equals who were familiar with ancient art in all its aspects, who had the classical authors on the tips of their tongues for immediate quotation, and who would instantly understand an allusion to the writings of any modern scholar (including among the moderns not only those still active, with whom his correspondence kept him in constant touch, but men a hundred years in the grave, "the lights of their world in their several generations").

His equals must judge the conclusions that he reaches in this book — or rather the suggestions that he offers; modesty and a just appreciation of the obscurity of the subject held him back from dictating answers to all the questions that he raised. Whether these answers that he does offer finally prove acceptable or no, I believe that the effort of grappling with these problems will be well worthwhile, and trust that the book will be valuable, as a means of self-improvement, to more scholars than are able to pronounce immediate judgment upon it. At all events, let not judgment be hasty. The perceptive reader will find in these pages occasional rejections — some so gentle as hardly to be recognizable as such — of objections founded on ignorance and rashness. Remembering the conversations in which those objections were made, I own that far sterner rebukes, both at the time and now in writing, would have been fully deserved. At least it serves some purpose that objections and answers are contained in these pages.

Confessions of ignorance also served a good purpose, if they persuaded the author to insert numerous references as he proceeded. (Full notes, to follow the text, were intended, but never written.) I have tried to add further references, often on points which Smith himself perhaps regarded as too obvious to require documentation. It would no doubt have surprised him to

1

learn that it took me several evenings' reading to track down a line in a poem by Propertius which he must have known by heart, and to fix a reference to Ovid. Or perhaps, like the father who told his sons to dig for hidden treasure in the field that he left them, he foresaw the pleasure that these labours would bring.

I am aware that I have not provided adequate documentation, as he would have done, and especially that I have fallen short of his intentions in regard to illustration. Through the kindness of many scholars and museum authorities, he had himself provided before his death many of the photographs that appear here, and similar kindnesses have enabled me to find others. In particular, Professor Sir A. D. Trendall, whose generous interest was a constant source of encouragement to the Author, has kindly provided replacements for many photographs of which only inadequate reproductions existed in Smith's files. But I have not always found it easy to divine the Author's intentions; no doubt the order in which I have arranged the material is not what he would have wished; perhaps he would have selected different illustrations of particular pieces. Even after the pictures were collected and arranged, I realized time and again, upon re-reading, that I had inserted the wrong reference into some blank in the text, and that his argument, now better understood, required a different illustration. Sometimes I have been baffled; "see the illustration provided by my Fig. 00" read his text at one point — with a pencilled reminder, "and don't forget to provide it" — but what it was to have been neither his notebooks nor my own wits have disclosed. It was clear that towards the end the Author felt that he was working against time; the last section of the book is not fully reconciled with the earlier part, and is in fact to be regarded as a sketch of new ideas which he was still turning over in his own mind and which he might have eventually discarded. Nor did he spare the time to divide his argument into chapters; such a division was intended, as references to "the next chapter" in the typescript (deleted from the final text) show, but it was not carried out. I have (by request) added headings at intervals, to break up what Smith left undivided and therefore perhaps the harder to penetrate. But the reader is most earnestly warned that these headings are not the Author's own, and may only too often prove false guides to the book's argument. I would have erred more frequently but for the kind guidance of Mrs. G. Schneider-Herrman, Sir A. D. Treadall and the late Professor T. B. L. Webster, all of whom corresponded with Smith during his lifetime and after his death read and annotated his typescripts.

I have not disguised from the reader that difficulties lie ahead. The Author himself had provided the best guide through them in his article "Deadlocks?," published in *BABesch* 45 (1970) pp. 68-85. But a summary may be helpful, though I apologise for doing injustice to theories which I do not fully understand and, even as far as I do understand them, cannot altogether accept. If Smith makes certain assumptions about the nature of Apulian ware which now appear inadmissible, the reader should consider that these assumptions were only in the nature of working hypotheses, which Smith himself was perfectly well aware might be refuted by excavated evidence. His book does not seek to prove these points, but to find significant meaning in aspects of Apulian vase-painting which are sometimes rejected as trivial and meaningless. His purpose is to show that the different objects that are associated (often apparently incongruously) with male and female figures on these vases form part of an elaborate code of "chattel-symbolism," with important bearings on popular religious beliefs.

He began, then, by assuming provisionally that:

1. All Apulian red-figured vases are funerary, even that great majority of apparently festive vases whose decoration does not include tombstones, heroa and "hellscapes."

2. The ware is Italiote Greek. That Taras, whose role in the manufacture he especially stresses, was not the only centre of production, seems now established. He also discusses the manufactures of Heraclea and Meta-pontum – culturally linked to their great neighbour. The main argument does not however depend on these local distinctions.

3. More seriously open to objection is the assumption that the ware was not made for use by the Tarantines themselves. I cannot believe that the Author would have persisted in this had he shared my good fortune in visiting Sala X of the Museo Nazionale at Taranto at the same moment as Sir A. D. Trendall. If the material from Taranto is less impressive than the Jatta collection at Ruvo, the reason is surely in part that conditions in a great modern industrial city allow only sporadic discovery.[1] Nonetheless it cannot be disputed that these vases did form one item in what must have been a thriving trade between the Greek cities of the coast and their inland, Italic, neighbours. Smith suggests that the staple of this commerce was the exchange of raw materials, especially wool, produced by the Messapians of the Murge, for the manufactures of Taras, and shows convincingly that this trade did influence the vase-painters, at least to the extent of making them frequently dress male figures in distinctive, non-Greek, "Apulian" costume. It may also be allowed that a particular vase might have been selected by a bereaved Messapian family to be placed in a particular grave because its picture seemed appropriate to the circumstances of the burial – whatever it may have meant originally to the painter. Smith raises this possibility of "customer's choice" more than once.

---

[1] Of the pieces from the outskirts of Taranto itself that have hitherto been published in *CVA,* the lekythos found in 1935 in the via Ancona would seem most clearly to be open to interpretation according to Smith's theories. A girl (holding a phiale) and a youth (holding an open "jewelry box") are seated some way apart and back-to-back. An "effeminate" Eros (the "Mise" of Smith's pantheon) pulls the girl round and seems to be forcing an introduction (*CVA Taranto* II [Italia XVIII] IV Dr, pl. 33.2-3. Compare also the "Dionysiac Scamper" of pl. 33.3).

It must be allowed that vases with scenes of Bacchic revelry lend themselves to a funerary interpretation — especially in the neighbourhood of Taras. Smith alludes to the Decree of the Roman Senate against the Bacchanals, and to Plato's contempt for charlatans who offered a Paradise of perpetual drunkenness in the next world, to be gained through pleasurable rites of expiation in this. The religious beliefs of the Messapians are less securely established, but Smith argues from inscriptional evidence (doubtful and fragmentary as it is) that they neglected Dionysos in favour of an "Aphrodite of the Underworld." We are invited, then, to see an exchange of religious ideas as well as of goods; the vase-painters introduced the symbols of their own beliefs, but allowed that at least in commercial matters, "the customer was always right," and might even re-interpret a picture of Dionysos among his nymphs and satyrs as a representation of a dead youth in Paradise, or undergoing due preparation in its antechamber.

Preparation in what form, and for what? Bathing, whose instruments, water-jars, lavers, and sluicing-pans, are so often shown on the vases, forms an important part of it, and the end is "Elysian love," blessed re-union for couples who have been parted by death, or union with ideal partners for those who had died young. Of such unions Aphrodite was the proper guardian, though the Tarantines intruded their own Dionysos, his ministers and their instruments, into at least the antechamber of Paradise, and even once gave the god the duty of literally propelling a girl into the arms of her Elysian husband (pl. 8). Whether the god also enjoyed a certain (or, in its extent, uncertain) *droit de seigneur,* or rather whether the dead girls hoped for a period of bliss in his arms before being consigned to their final mates, is a question whose answer remains somewhat doubtful. The place of the Hesperides and their Garden in the Elysian cosmology, and the full symbolism of Sun, Moon, Daystar and Evening Star, are other matters which, though discussed at some length, are not, as it seems to me, finally settled. Some further suggestions — as that the faithful servants of this world might continue, in the guise of satyrs and nymphs, attendance upon their emparadised masters and mistresses — are perhaps not wholly serious.

In this concept of Elysian love, Smith followed, as he repeatedly acknowledges, the theories developed by the late Professor G. Patroni. But in his anxiety to do Patroni justice, Smith was less than fair to himself. No precise reference to Patroni's writings[2] accompanies the frequent mentions of them in this work, and it deserves to be recorded that Smith's rough notes include the warning that "Professing oneself a Patronian is not what a very circumspect person would be in a hurry to do." It was perhaps excessive patriotism

[2] Smith considered (*BABesch* 45 [1970] p. 68, n. 1) that "*Guida Ruesch del Museo Nazionale di Napoli,* 463, gives Patroni's mature view." See also "Questioni Vascolari" in *Rendiconti della R.Accademia dei Lincei* (*Classe di Scienze Morali*) Ser. 5 no. 21 (1912) pp. 545-600.

that made Patroni regard Apulian vases as Italic rather than Italiote, but, setting this great difference of opinion aside, Smith has certainly gone far beyond Patroni and his followers in developing a "chattel-symbolism" which explains, as they could not do, that the apparently "sex-insulting" offering of women's trinkets — mirrors, fans, catch-balls and the like — at the graves of young warriors is not due to want of "subtlety" on the part of the artists. We are to see in these objects gifts, not for the man himself, but for transmission to his Elysian bride.

The coded meanings conveyed by these objects are elaborately worked out. Mirror in girl's hands, strigil or warlike gear in a young man's, are proof of maturity for marriage. Mirrors, balls, or the curious ladder-like "sistro Apulo" that Smith identifies with "the platage of Archytas of Tarentum" may serve in male hands as gifts of wooing. On the bride's side a dowry (contained in a gable-roofed box) will be required, and after the ablutions already mentioned, the wedding dress, conveyed in a wicker "deep cylindrical basket." That the "deep cylindrical basket" is indeed part of the preparations for marriage is confirmed by Attic evidence; compare two vases by the Washing Painter in New York (Richter and Hall, *Red-Figured Athenian Vases in the Metropolitan Museum of Art,* Nos. 144, 145). Another wooden box, strengthened by diagonal supports, may hold provisions for the wedding feast, to which also are brought "bump-cakes" (popana) in shallow dishes. Fans and parasols (if they are not the insignia of Aphrodite herself) may mark the married woman or — again — be presented by her husband, and we are invited to see (pl. 1b) the progress of a single couple from courtship to marriage through a succession of symbols, or (pl. 28b) to observe which of two girls is closer to her wedding. Smith was always ready to allow that this symbolic code could not, in its entirety, be established by direct proof, and might have accepted modifications, had they been urged with a skill and learning equal to his own.

"Chattel-symbolism" is, as Smith develops his thesis, connected with the exchange of religious ideas as well as of material goods between Greeks and Messapians. But the different theories that he combines are not in fact dependent on each other, the snapping of a single thread does not unravel the whole fabric. This is as well, since the reader may well find that the flimsy evidence for Messapian religion has been strained past breaking-point.

On the one hand, Smith suggests, the Greek painters intruded their own Dionysiac notions to the extent of making "Aphrodite of the Underworld" take up the thyrsus (cf. *BABesch* 45 (1970), p. 68 and fig. 1 (here pl. 29b). "Dionysiac Aphrodite escorting dead Apulian to due mate." On the other, Messapian influence changed Greek Eros from a virile, "eugenic" figure to an effeminite transvestite.

This suggestion, to which Smith constantly recurs, derives from the restoration by O. Haas (*Messapische Studien* no. B.1.45) <M>ISAI (dative case) in an inscription painted on the wall of a tomb at Rudiae near Lecce.

Haas's restoration and interpretation — tentatively offered — were seized perhaps too eagerly by Smith as proof that the Messapians worshipped Mise, an obscure deity whose connections with Eleusis, Asia Minor, Cyprus and Egypt are more securely attested. Smith cites the "forty-second Orphic hymn" as evidence that Mise had a dual nature (ἄρσενα καὶ θήλυν) — male and female. Hence, he argues, the "transvestite" Eros of later Italiote vases — no longer Eros but bisexual Mise, was supplied by the vase-painters to satisfy the demands of their customers.

But, even if one allows that this double nature is in fact adequately represented by a boy with hair dressed in a girlish fashion, and accepts Smith's explanation of the appearance of the "new" Eros on other fabrics than Apulian as due to more imitation, there seems little reason for Mise to take over the part of Eros, son of Aphrodite. An unpleasant Alexandrian procuress swears "by the descent of Mise" (Herondas, *Mimiambi* 1.56) but surely this indicates, not that Mise is to play Cupid in love-affairs, illicit or otherwise, but that he/she is a creature of the underworld, and the swearer a witch. The Orphic hymn already alluded to was found inscribed on an altar, probably of the second century after Christ, in the precinct of Demeter at Pergamum, and the Messapian inscription, if Haas's interpretation is to be accepted, would also provide evidence that Mise was associated with Demeter and her search for Persephone. It does not connect Mise with Aphrodite. It is true that the hymn suggests that Mise may rejoice in Cyprus with fair Kythereia — but his/her connection with Dionysos, Euboulos and Iachos at Eleusis and with the mysteries of the Great Mother in Phrygia have first been mentioned. So far from suggesting that Mise is the child of Aphrodite ("of the Underworld" or otherwise) the hymn (line 9) makes "black-robed Isis" her mother. An alternative parentage, from Dysaule, is attested by Harpocration, as is noted by O. Kern, to whose review of the evidence I am much indebted (s.v. *Mise* in Pauly-Wissowa, *Real-enzyclopädie* XV (Stuttgart 1932) cols. 2040-2041).

But we may insist that Eros, however bonneted, is Eros still without necessarily rejecting Smith's views of his functions. In any case, this problem does not necessarily affect that of the "Great Derangement," as Smith describes it.

The reader must for some time have been ready to object that the clearest and most explicit Apulian pictures of the underworld show, not once but repeatedly (pl. 1b; figs. 4, 11 and 17) the sort of Hell that the most superficial acquaintance with ancient literature, from Homer to Horace, would lead one to expect —

> furvae regna Proserpinae
> et judicantem vidimus Aeacum
> sedesque discriptas piorum.

If Orpheus, with musician's robe and lyre, takes, in the vase paintings, the place of the poet's Sappho and Alcaeus, and if the torments of the damned are more emphasised than the abodes of the blessed, this only makes, it would seem, the point more obvious. The palace of Hades and Persephone, the punishment of sinners, among them the Danaids, in whom Smith saw frustrated would-be brides deprived forever of the pre-nuptial bath;[3] judgment; and a paradise to be reached through rituals authorised by Orphic texts — surely this is what South Italy believed? Besides, if the vase-paintings were not enough, are there not the grave-mounds of Corigliano, whose texts point the way to salvation through purgation of sins — including the "original sin" of god-rending Titans?[4] The very objects that have just been given a place in the symbolism of courtship and marriage may seem to belong more properly in the purifying "dismemberment ritual." Balls and mirrors may be intended to entice the infant god; the "deep cylindrical basket" resembles the mystic *cista* of the Athenian coinage (but unlike that *cista* never has snakes emerging from the lid); even the fan may be supposed to produce purifying winds. (Cf. O. Kern, *Orphicorum Fragmenta,* no. 34).

Smith himself raises these objections, and meets them in part through the supposition that the ornate Apulian vases are dated by the representation on at least three of them (cf. fig. 14) of the victory of Alexander the Great over Darius.[5] That is to say, they date from about the time of Alexander's uncle, Alexander the Molossian, brother of Olympias, whose interest in mystery religions (including the worship of Dionysos under "Orphic" auspices) is attested by Plutarch (*Alexander* 2). Certainly we are not to suppose that the Molossian and his northerners brought into Italy any wholly new ideas. Smith draws repeated attention to the evidence that in the previous generation Archytas of Tarentum had attended mystic rites. But that the late fourth century saw a shift in emphasis, to which some of the earlier

---

[3] Professor Albert Henrichs draws my attention to Eva Keuls, "The Ass in the Cult of Dionysus as a Symbol of Toil and Suffering," *Anthropological Journal of Canada* 8 (1970) 26-46, especially pp. 29ff; "The Ordeal of the Sieves and Myth of the Danaids," where it is suggested that in its original form "the ordeal-of-the-sieves served as an initiation rite" — unconnected with the Danaids.

[4] It is to be regretted that Smith did not live to discuss the very different Pythagorean interpretation of these texts put forward by G. Zuntz, *Persephone* (Oxford, 1971) Book III, "The Gold Leaves," pp. 275-393. In Zuntz's view ("Detached Note XII," pp. 411-412) the "gold leaves" reflect an entirely different concept of after-life from that depicted on the vases. The reader should also, perhaps, bear in mind Zuntz's doubts (pp. 355-356) as to the origin of the Petelia text.

[5] Sir A. D. Trendall questions (in correspondence) the validity of this argument. He points out that "S. himself notes the 'notoriously unhistorical beard of . . . Alexander'" and expresses "grave doubts as to whether in fact the scene is anything more than a generic battle between Greeks and Persians." He is therefore very reluctant "to use the vase as a criterion for dating, though on purely stylistic evidence it must in fact belong to about that period (c. 330-320)."

symbolism could readily be adapted, is an idea that deserves careful consideration.

If symbols of marriage are to be found on funeral vases, a further possibility deserves consideration. This is the marriage of living descendants at the tombs of ancestors, "as Electra vowed, as Epikteta willed" (Aeschylus, *Choephori* 486-487, *IG* vii, 3,330,51) — *ELEP* in Smith's "seminar slang." This possibility, raised at the beginning of the book, he laid aside, but took up again in more detail at the end, where he also laid stress on the "cosmetic" functions of Aphrodite, who furnished brides with her own attributes. That one of the functions of "Aphrodite of the Underworld" was to equip dead girls for the "Elysian" marriages is a consistent and logical development from what has preceded. But examination of the attributes, animate and inanimate, of Aphrodite, and a comparison with the objects associated with the figures occupying painted "heroa" on the vases, led Smith to offer, in the last part of the book, a suggestion about these "heroa" which seems neither consistent with the greater part of the book nor acceptable on general grounds. I am sure, from my memory of conversations with him, that some of the speculations presented at the end of this book (from the section now entitled "A new approach; the heroa of the vases — are they real?") only occurred to him in the last months of his life, when, as has been said already, he was conscious that he was working against time. He hastened to commit them to paper, lest they should be lost, but did not have the opportunity to reconsider and re-examine them. Much of what he then wrote he would no doubt have retained, and it would be impertinent to attempt a drastic revision. But the reader must be warned that the Author did not himself revise that part of the book.

Had he done so, I cannot believe that he would have retained the suggestion that the painted "heroa" containing female figures, which are often represented upon Apulian vases, are not grave-monuments, but shrines of "cosmetic Aphrodite." It is to be noted that he resisted in conversation and here in this book, the argument that, if he was to make this new assumption about the female figures, he must also suppose that the "heroa" containing young warriors were shrines of Ares, or of Italic Mars. This he allowed to be unacceptable; but he fell back on the argument that, whereas "heroizing" of dead *men* was traditional, the "heroa" painted on women's funerary vases originally contained no figures, but were filled with a spray of Aphrodite's flowers, soon to be replaced by the goddess herself. Bound up with this theory is the suggestion that the actual grave-monument is not represented by the "heroon" or "shrine," but by the plain stele which so often is shown on the backs of these vases.

I am sure that these views would have been discarded, or at least considerably modified, if Smith had lived to read Trendall's discussion (in *Revue Archéologíque* [1972] pp. 309-316) of Niobe in Apulian vase-painting, in which it is shown that the heroine's transformation into stone is conventionally indicated by the use of white paint. It follows that the white-painted occupants of the "heroa" are also to be thought of as stone, conventionally represented — welcome confirmation of the obvious explanation that these "heroa" are grave-monuments decorated with figures in relief. Here again, I wish that Smith could have been present when the greatest authority on Italiote vase-painting very kindly discussed these points with me in the Museo Provinciale at Lecce — and incidentally showed that the "heroa" filled with flowers are in general comparatively late — not early, as Smith's theory would require.

But the rejection of this theory does not affect the argument of the greater part of the book, where it does not occur, and with which, indeed, it seems to conflict. Nor does it affect the developing view of the relationship between Aphrodite and Dionysos that Smith presents in these last pages — no longer a mere "business partnership" but a true union. Here perhaps he hoped to find the reconciliation not only of "Messapian" and "Tarantine," but of all the conflicts raised by his theories.

In recommending this book to the judgment of its Author's peers, I must not forget that their help gave him constant pleasure and encouragement during the writing of it. Had he lived, he would have thanked them properly; I can do little more than search my memory for, and record, the names of some of these of whom I heard him speak from time to time. To the many to whom I fail to pay their due, I apologise.

Let me then, express thanks on his behalf to Mesdames L. Berge (for whom he named his Holstein-Berge Painter), B. Kingsley, D. Parker, A. Peredolskaya, M. Sagan, G. Schneider-Herrman, and P. Solmitz; and to D. A. Amyx, D. von Bothmer, A. Cambitoglou, J. Fontenrose, C. Greenewalt, D. E. L. Haynes, R. Lullies, L. A. Mackay, A. Oliver, K. M. Phillips, II. Sichtermann, Sir A. D. Trendall and T. B. L. Webster. Obligations for various illustrations are acknowledged separately in the list of plates.

I would like also to acknowledge kindnesses that I have myself received, not only from most of the above, but from Dr. Ann Birchall, D. Adamesteanu, R. Bronson, A. M. Henrichs, R. S. Stroud and G. Uggeri. Mr. J. G. T. Anderson accompanied me on my visits to Italian museums and spared me the burden of carrying round a great mass of notes and typescript, Above all, my thanks are due to Mrs. Adele Smith, for the manner in which she encouraged my study of her late husband's papers, and for the work that she herself put into making that study easy for me. Mr. John M. Smith also gave me every possible assistance and provided me with ready access to his father's books and documents.

My thanks are also due to the University of California for a Regent's Faculty Fellowship, which enabled me to travel in Italy for the indispensable first-hand study of the material in Apulian museums, and (on the Author's behalf) to the Bollingen Foundation, for the grant which made possible the journey to Rio de Janeiro, of which this book is the fruit.

My wife has given me constant sympathy and help in this last service to an old friend whom she also knew and loved.

Abbreviations of Periodicals

AA	Archäologischer Anzeiger
AE	Archaiologike Ephemeris
AJA	American Journal of Archaeology
Annali	Annali dell' Istituto di Correspondenza Archeologica
AntDenk	Antike Denkmaler
AP	Anthologia Palatina
ArchClass	Archeologia Classica
AthMit	Deutsches Archäologisches Institut : Athenische Mitteilungen
AttNap	Atti dell' Accademia di archeologia, lettere e belle arte, Naples
AZ	Archäologische Zeitung
BABesch	Bulletin Antieke Beschaving
BdA	Bolletino d'Arte
BMMA	Bulletin of the Metropolitan Museum of Art
BSR	Papers of the British School at Rome
BullNap	Bulletino archeologico Napoletano
CIM	Corpus inscriptionum Messapicarum, in Ribezzo *La lingua degli antichi Messapii*
CRPétersburg	Compte rendu de la Commission archéologique de Saint Pétersbourg
CVA	Corpus Vasorum Antiquorum
El.Cér.	See under "Lenormant"
FR	Furtwängler, A. and Karl Reichhold, *Griechische Vasenmalerei*
IG	Inscriptiones Graecae
JdI	Jahrbuch des Deutschen archäologischen Instituts
JHS	Journal of Hellenic Studies
MonAnt	Monumenti antichi
MonInst	Monumenti inediti pubblicati dall'Istituto di Correspondenza Archeologica
MonLinc	Monumenti Antichi pubblicati per cura della Accademia dei Lincei
NS	Notizie degli Scavi di Antichita
ÖJh	Jahreshefte des Österreichischen Archäologischen Institutes
REG	Revue des Études Grecques
RendLinc	Rendiconti dell' Accademia dei Lincei
RivIstArch	Revista dell'Instituto di Archeologia e Storia d'Arte
RM	Deutsches Archäologisches Institut : Römische Mitteilungen
StEtr	Studi Etruschi

Smith also frequently abbreviated the names of books in the references that he inserted into the text, and I have attempted to follow his usage. Full titles are given under the Author's name in the Select Bibliography.

Introduction
(by the Editor)

IMMEDIATELY AFTER HIS retirement from the Chair of Classical Archaeology at Berkeley in 1958, the Author was enabled, by the generosity of the Bollingen Foundation, to visit South America. The principal object of his journey was to study the large collection of classical antiquities in the Museu Naçional at Rio de Janeiro, whose romantic history is touched upon in the Appendix.

Among the objects that drew his particular attention was a small bronze pan handle in the form of a nude youth, which seems to have interested him first as providing evidence for the authenticity of those pieces which M. Gjødesen, in his fundamental study,[1] brings together as the "Reggio Group." The handle in Rio de Janeiro is claimed by Smith as "unimpeachable" because it seems to have reached the New World in 1843, as part of the presents sent by Ferdinand II of Naples to his future brother-in-law, the Emperor Pedro II of Brazil. This date would exempt it from suspicion of being a late-nineteenth century forgery.

It is possible that Smith's original intention was no more than to establish this point. His typescript in fact begins abruptly with the words "Museu Naçional 75," and launches straight into the description and discussion now relegated to the Appendix. Unfortunately the only photographs that he brought back with him are inadequate for publication, and I have been unable to procure better ones, but this is of slight importance to the book as it ultimately developed.

Smith was above all a master of what he described as "the art of the bounce-off." He had a vast store of knowledge, which enabled him to associate objects at first sight unrelated, and to draw upon quite unexpected literary sources in order to explain that association. So, in the present instance, he was led from the Rio de Janeiro handle and its group to a discussion of the purpose of all pans with similar anthropoid handles. Having established a case for regarding them as instruments of purification rather than as libation-vessels, he was drawn to consider the rituals in which such rites of purification might play a part, and so to discover and explain the presence of other purifying vessels portrayed on the fourth-century Apulian vases, the symbolism of whose decoration is the real subject of his work.

The argument that these rites of purification are especially connected with marriage — in the next world, for the occupants of the graves in which the painted vases are assumed to have been laid — leads to the consideration of

---

[1] M. Gjødesen, "Bronze Paterae with anthropomorphous handles," *Acta A* 15 (1944) 101ff.

the symbolism of other objects. Fans, baskets, jewelry-boxes, balls, and musical instruments cannot be directly connected with the ritual bath. But Smith linked them with the marriage for which that bath was to be a preparation, or with the courtship leading up to that marriage, and so, as has been said already, was able to find logical reasons for the appearance in men's hands of objects that apparently belong wholly to the world of women. With the examination of the purpose of the bronze pans his own text may therefore begin.

The Purpose of the Bronze Pans?

GREEK PANS WITH anthropomorphic handles are generally explained as vessels for libation, substitutes — more convenient, not just more ambitiously handsome — for the phiale mesophalos, the original and proper libation-dish but less simple to manipulate, having no handle, only a hollow (under its "navel"), for the fingers to catch. It might seem (the signs are not entirely clear) that the Roman equivalent of the phiale, namely the sacrificial patera, did so develop, acquiring a handle and becoming a pan. However, no evidence of a parallel change occurs in Greek representations of libation-pouring.

Indeed, in a recent paper that raises many curious questions in this neighborhood, Mrs. G. Schneider-Herrmann has fully proved that at any rate the pans with human figures for handles so often pictured on late Apulian vases of the fourth century B.C. were not substitutes for the phiale. In those vase-paintings (belonging to the same region as this bronze, if to a very different phase of its art) the pan with android handle does not supersede the handle-less, dish-like, vessel which archaeologists are accustomed to call phiale. It is seen accompanying it, and this quite often, as if their purposes were distinct. For example merely: a figure flanking the heroon on the reverse of the Hades krater in Munich (no. 3297, pl. 1b) holds pan in his right hand, phiale in his left, and there is a parallel duplication in the little Dionysiac picture above: the principal figure (beatified mystes rather than Dionysos himself?) holds a phiale (level), an attendant satyr brandishes a pan, upright (fig. 1b). Add that on the same side of the same vase a third phiale is seen *in use,* in the decoration of the heroon of the large picture: the youth standing there has just filled it from his pitcher and is about to offer it to the older man seated before him. At any rate, the three phialai on the Munich krater seem to have something to tell us about the two pans there — that the latter are vessels of a different function.

And what was that? The question, to which Mrs. Schneider sees no answer quite clear, certainly concerns us, even without our altogether taking for granted, at this start, that the pans represented in Apulian vase-painting of the fourth century — sometimes in a very curious relation to various interesting contexts — were quite identical in purpose with the more or less similar vessels extant in bronze from the sixth and fifth. Besides the interval of time, there will be a certain difference of pattern of which we must take account. At all events, Mrs. Schneider has cut out our proper work, has put us in the main consideration, which is not the Rio handle's recognizable type, nor its guessable date, nor any curious associations in its past as a collector's piece; rather it is the significance of the whole implement it once belonged to, and

15

not merely its intrinsic meaning, in a Greek design for a certain Greek purpose, but also its suggestive value, in any significant bearing it may have on problems besetting the curious pans of vase-painting.

There is to be said at once: however charming we may find the sculptural work in the best of those early bronze pans, in them a certain foible of Greek design reaches a decidedly vicious extreme, *if they are vessels for libation.* Whatever their purpose, they are of course, like many other things great and small (from the buildings constructed with telamons or caryatids to the table-mirrors perched on statuettes and the pitchers with tense tilt-inviting tumblers for handles), illustrations of a peculiarly Greek tendency: an obsessive proneness to smuggle the human form into structure. Others than Greeks have done this now and then; in a well-known class of mirrors Egyptian art of the eighteenth dynasty plays tectonically with anthropomorphism. But of the designers of these Greek pans one may say that anthropomorphism was playing with them — unless we can acquit them of the extreme ineptitude of intending an Atlas-like element to lie down and *be tilted headlong* in the rite of libation. For this would be much more outrageously incongruous than any corresponding manipulation of the Lasa handle (not "atlantoid") of the Etruscan pan which M. A. Johnstone sensibly judged to be not for libation but for sluicing the body in bathing (*StEtr* 11 [1937] p. 392, pl. 49, 1). In defense of those Greeks I am going to suggest that the function for which they designed these vessels was not libation but one in which, at least at the effective climax of the act of use, the Atlas-like figure took its proper posture, *vertical.* More particularly, that the bronze pans with android handles may have been vessels for ablution, as their quasi-counterparts in Apulian vase-painting must have been, according to the use which we shall find made of them in mythography and otherwise. The argument will have to recognize that the pans *depicted* (those surely ablutionary vessels) are not perfect counterparts of the pans *extant;* here a difficult (and I fear intricate) question will be involved, how much or little to make of the one difference amid general similarity, namely in design of the rim. To this part the vase-painters add two looped features (extra handles) which we are not free to imagine on the Rio handle's lost bowl, for there are none on the preserved bowl of the pan in Karlsruhe which belongs to the same Reggio Group. Moreover, though very few of the bronze handles, of any group, have kept their bowl, enough terracotta imitations of bronze models exist in solid completeness to prove a rule of plain rims. It may be that the discrepancy is of no moment, no proof of any difference in function. But that cannot be assumed without further evidence, which will have to come, of course, from the Apulian side, in signs entitling us to question the historic reality of the more elaborate sort of vessel which the artists chose to draw — signs that this is an arbitrary (not necessarily capricious) fantastication of the simpler pattern. And though it is true that no pans of the elaborate pattern with three handles now really exist, a mere argument *ex vacuo* will not do. We must (sooner or later) exact evidence that the vase-painters knew the simpler pattern, in some material (in bronze it was already obsolete); we must come to see why they altered it, and whence and with what special fitness (conserving ablutionary function) they borrowed the features they added. Further, we must be made to feel that the liberty thus taken with reality was not uncharacteristic, not too unlike other licenses of Apulian vase-painting.

But first, where is the proof that the pans of Apulian vase-painting were meant for vessels of ablution or lustration, for washpans in bluntest English? I hope to produce it from pictures of the least inscrutable sort, pictures of a known myth and so more or less self-explaining in their system of detail (if there be an extant play for searching control of detail, so much the better). But meanwhile we are not to forget that the range of those pans' occurrence is much wider than that. It is indeed limited to certain phases, the latest, of what we call Apulian red-figure. But within those is there any category of subject — definitely mythic, or vaguely Dionysiac, or plainly funerary, or seemingly nuptial — in which the thing we are now concerned with fails to turn up? It is a bowl with two looped handles rising from the flat of the rim and also a third longer and straighter handle, this commonly, but not invariably, in the form of a human figure whose raised arms support the bowl. *Support* it; before we turn to anything more particular, there is Mrs. Schneider's accurate generalization to note: if the handle is a figure, the vessel is represented with the bowl upward, whether the handle is shown held in the hand, or propped on a surface, or free in a field. Primarily, this must be artistic scruple, instinctive reluctance to waste paint on a rendering stultifying the Atlas-like posture of the long handle's human form. One of Mrs. Schneider's observations, that the bowl is never used to *fetch* or to *proffer* anything, is all the more suggestive when we recall the way in which almost every other sort of receptacle is overworked in the pious or festive traffic of Apulian vase-painting; not only phialai but even closed boxes and baskets come with a garnish of foliage or a topping of pastry or fruit. But my citing her must not be taken to imply that in her own *Apulische Schalengriffe* there is any special encouragement of the interpretations now to follow. It would be a mistake to begin them without a parenthesis to show how differently she views the three-handled pans as represented on the vases. She holds that (1) it is difficult, on the whole, to see them as libation-vessels (p. 42: one conviction that she and I fully share); (2) the intrinsic, essential, function of those pans (as the Apulian artists understood it) remains an inscrutable matter, though their occasional and merely incidental use in magic might perhaps be guessed from the intentness with which they are sometimes brandished, especially in rites, probably mystic, at heroa or graves (p. 43 or her postscript, *BABesch* 38, p. 95); (3) no difficulty that there may be in understanding the fourth-century representations (either in themselves, or in their relation to the bronze pans of simpler pattern extant from previous centuries) need make us doubt the function of the *latter*: those bronze ones were for libation, she is sure (p. 44).

A Clue to Exploit:
The Pan at Iphigenia's Feet

ONE OF MRS. SCHNEIDER'S well-selected illustrations of the three-handled vessel now in question is taken from a volute-krater in Leningrad, no. 420 in Stephani's catalogue, famous for a picture inspired by Euripides' *Iphigenia in Tauris.* For her purpose (to show us evidence "für den Gebrauch im Tempeldienst," p. 43 and fig. 4 on p. 42) it was sufficient to reproduce a part of A. Reifferscheid's publication of the whole scene in *MonInst* 6-7 (1862) pl. 66; moreover, to have included the rest would have reduced inconveniently the scale of the detail to be emphasized, the pan which stands up in the temple at Iphigenia's feet; so close to her that the rendering of the smaller handles (on the rim) is less distinct than the vase painters usually make it, the farther one being almost lost in Iphigenia's drapery.

Let us now see the rest of the picture, in my fig. 2. It is less definitely dramatic than the version painted on a vase in another Russian collection, the Moscow krater which lets us number the very line illustrated, 745, Pylades' promise to deliver Iphigenia's letter. This scene is vaguer or seems so at first view, with no sign of the catalytic letter, and (taking the nearer man to be Orestes) we can only say now that it would fit any part of the long colloquy of brother and sister, 482-627. But it has its own compensating precision; at any rate, in this ampler, expressively elaborate, composition there is really more of the play. Apulian vase-painting is sometimes accused of mindless padding, but there is none here, even in the margins. Above, the four deities, and their groupings, are just those required for exactly prefiguring the end of it all: Athena with the personification, Nike, of her success *ex machina;* Artemis with the courier, Hermes, of her cult's migration to Halai. Below, in the fringe of Taurians piously festive (one of them inviting the goddess' deer to nibble his holiday wreath), the artist is back at the play's prologue, improvising an ironically dainty variation on Iphigenia's grim reflection (34-36) that what King Thoas got in her — a regular priestess for his goddess — had thenceforth made proper holiday, ἑορτή, of the traditional butchery of strangers. But what concerns us most is the picture's emphasis — part of it obvious at once in the two full lavers and the two empty hydrias — on the theme of ablution, so essentially involved in the play. It is everything to Euripides' version of the story that Iphigenia's priestly skill should be changed from butchery of Artemis' human victims to their purification beforehand. This of course is no mere expurgation of something μιαρόν, dramatically hideous, lurking in the tradition, it is the making of the play; for the trick by which the Greeks escape to the ship begins with Iphigenia's exploiting a professional problem of exceptional impurity and succeeds because of Thoas' trust in the perfection of her lustral science. Surely then, in this faithful picture, the thing at Iphigenia's feet is a lustral vessel? Has not the artist put it there because this is the implement of her particular duty, aspersion? In this, from the laver which other hands have filled, she is to take water and with the proper gesture of aspersion (not lobbing, not spilling, but slinging) moisten the hair of the victim. In fact, this vessel, where it is placed, at Iphigenia's feet and almost touching her but also near Orestes, all but puts words to the picture; his question (line 621)

$$αὐτὴ ξίφει θύουσα θῆλυς ἄρσενας;$$

and her answer (622)

$$οὐκ, ἀλλὰ χαίτην ἀμφὶ σὴν χερνίψομαι.$$

"I am not the killer; I shall only cast the lustral water, over your hair."

I should like to credit Reifferscheid with anticipating this, in the commentary of his publication of the vase more than a hundred years ago. Not altogether; for one difference, he sorted the figures of this picture less confidently, allowing that the youth nearest Iphigenia might by Pylades; but it is fair to suppose that the above interpretation of the thing at her feet is already implicit in his remark (*Annali* [1862] 118): "I vasi sparsi quà e là" ("quà" for the pan, "là" for the two hydrias?) "ci rammentano la frequente menzione delle χέρνιβες presso Euripide, che servivano particolarmente alla funzione speciale che toccava a fare ad Ifigenia" (he goes on to cite the second of the two lines I have just quoted). It is true that Reifferscheid cannot have been in the least concerned with the *form* of the thing he detected as the instrument of Iphigenia's lustrations, and I cannot borrow his authority for my corollary, *deduced from its form,* that the kind of lustral vessel intended by the artist was one for *aspersion.* That is a further step, and might be disputed on two grounds: first, as wishful, and then as out of line with evidence (the solidest possible, on certain reliefs) of the method of lustration for human victims.

The first objection I must admit, but we can ignore – at least in what we are doing, testing a certainly wishful, but reasonably hopeful, hypothesis that the form of the pans with atlantoid handles is not a disgrace to the Greek sense of design. All the evidence so far (beginning with Mrs. Schneider's demonstration that the Apulian vase-painters avoid inverting or even leveling the atlantoid figure) has been favorable, in its suggesting that form was not at odds with function; it has tended to exclude σπένδειν (pouring or spilling from the tilted bowl) and has pointed us instead to βάλλειν, slinging the contents, with an upward sweep of the hand; a manipulation that would bring the arms of the figure above the hand of the holder at the functional moment, the moment of discharge. This in *IT* 58 is Iphigenia's own word, if with a shift of object (to the target of her βολή):

$$Θνῄσκουσι δ᾽ οὓς ἂν χέρνιβες βάλωσ᾽ ἐμαί.$$

With only a little water taken into the vessel, the effect is aspersion, sprinkling; with more water at closer range, it would be sluicing. However, we see nothing like this when we turn to the quite numerous representations, on Etruscan burial "urns," of Iphigenia herself undergoing lustration before the sacrifice at Aulis (H. Brunn and G. Körte, *I Rilievi delle urne etrusche* 1, pls. 35-47). Making her an unwilling victim, man-handled to her doom by Odysseus, the Etruscan sculptors only too plainly advertise their ignorance of Euripides' *Aulidensis*. But they were not so ignorant of Greek ritual; in what their Agamemnon is doing, above his daughter's head, no Greek viewer of their work would have failed to recognize the rite of χέρνιβες, the lustration which precedes the stab. Yet in these reliefs the water is spilled not sprinkled, and the vessel is not what the Tarentine painter of the Apulian krater gave his Tauric Iphigenia; it is a simple bowl with no handle: for any Greek, a φιάλη. We find the same method of lustration, spilling from an inverted bowl, on four urns with a different subject taken from an unrecognizable myth (unless it is a madly addled version of the Tauric story): two youths seated placidly, like trustful customers of a competent barber, for simultaneous sacrifice, a priestess standing by each, busy with her bowl and ready with her knife (Brunn-Körte, 2, pls. 75-76).

Do these reliefs create any real difficulty, either for the hypothesis that the pans with figurine handles are rationally designed vessels for aspersion or sluicing, or for the interpretation which I have just given of a particular example, the pan that I take to be significant detail in a faithful illustration of the *Iphigenia Taurica* painted by an intelligent (if Western) Greek? They lend themselves to this objection, lucid and crisp at any rate: "If, as conceded, a Greek rite of sacrificial lustration can be recognized on the urns, where is your *evidence* of Greek use of a different, aspersive, method? Without it that wishful hypothesis is ignobly dead, crushed under several tons of Etruscan tufo; you will not revive it by wishful embellishment of Reiffersheid's quite sound recognition of Iphigenia's tool of lustration in the pan at her feet on the vase. It is chivalrous of you to canter out on your hobbyhorse of aspersion (or sluicing), to tilt for the honor of Greek design. But what can you have seen, or what can you have read, to fasten on Iphigenia, of the play or of the vase, a method of lustration any different from her father's fill-and-spill in the reliefs?" There is an answer to this, in the least forgettable lines, 44-54, of the prologue of the *Taurica*: nonetheless decisive because of those lines' describing a dream. This has its miracle, the capital of the one standing pillar of Agamemnon's collapsed palace hailing Iphigenia and changing into a head with long fair hair, Orestes' head; it has proper inconsequence with Iphigenia still at home in Argos yet already practiced in her Tauric office, and somehow having its apparatus at hand, and there is a dream-truth in the compulsiveness of her officious lustration of that fair "foreign" hair (53-55; cf. 622). But surely the climax of this convincingly unbridled dream-stuff is vividly simple, without levitation or acrobatics? From *where she stands,* on the terrace, under the pillar, does she not asperse the head high above her?

Can we fit a name, some dignifying Greek word, to Iphigenia's pan on this vase? Only cautiously, for we have not yet examined this feature's further range of contexts in Apulian vase painting; if it has there more than one function, it may, altogether, require more than one name. But if the question is only what word is most proper here, what unspoken syllables came to the present Greek's mind when he turned to put Iphigenia's tool into this illustration of the play, there is surely an answer: χερνίβιον, if not χερνιβεῖον.

The Back of the Iphigenia Krater: Traps and a Paradox— Putting the Clue to Work

IPHIGENIA'S ABLUTION PAN is not the only one on the vase. How many there are on it altogether is a question that really belongs to the problems of the hitherto un-published reverse of this krater, and at this point they are by no means ripe for exhaustive attention. But here is the place to notice that the photograph of the reverse pictures which the late Dr. Peredolskaya has kindly allowed me to include (pl. 2) forces us to question some points of Stephani's description of them. Stephani saw a pan ("eine gelbe Schale mit langem Stiel") in the right hand of the youth seated above the woman who stands to our right of the heroon, the latter holding a garland (or rather cascade?) of large blossoms, and something that might seem less appropriate (if both are for the young warrior portrayed in the monument), namely a fan. As we shall see, the mistaking of pans for mirrors is quite common in the older catalogues; but here for once we seem to be faced with the reverse confusion. If there is an ablution pan in the lower picture, it is the object in the right hand of the woman top left, which Stephani took for a mirror but wrongly, if its projections (upward, not outward, from the rim) are to be seen as like those of the bowl of the object held in the left hand of the nymph in the Dionysiac picture on the vase's neck. We have some right to appeal to the upper picture for help in reading dim details of the lower, for it is evident that the painter of both intended some correlation; is it just accident that in both a male has the tympanon? Strange as the thing may seem in the hands of the young man below, it is only too perfectly appropriate to the young satyr above, though I must not let myself assume that the painter's knowledge of the plot of the *Iphigenia* was matched by knowledge of the text of the *Bacchae,* where he might have learnt (at lines

130f) that the hand-drum was not Dionysiac till satyrs made it so. All things considered (including what the mirror rather puzzlingly seen in the hands of Nike on the obverse does to establish that this painter's mirrors were of the simplest possible type, their disks being without side-wings), we seem to have the right to relate some of the objects in the four hands of the pair of women below to what the nymph above has room for in her two; the latter's pan settling that what the upper woman of the lower picture has in her right hand is not a mirror, since it is so plain that the nymph's *fan* is intended be in correspondence with the one held by the lower woman. What, then, was the relation intended between the principals of the two pictures, the youth with the lances in the heroon and the youth with the thyrsus in the open landscape above? For the long and gradual preparation that a considered answer would require this paragraph of course gives no room, but I can at least try to make a beginning – by clearing away two booby traps. The more insidious is in the nearness (in the upper picture) of the calyx-krater of wine to the nymph's pan, for in the other matter the lesson not to see Dionysos in every *thyrsifer* whose rump and ears are normally human is one of the first learnt by the student of Italiote and Siceliote red-figure; that Apulian red-figure has means (longer hair, or ampler headband) of distinguishing Dionysos from emparadised young men is displayed quite early in its Dionysiac eschatography, in works of the Lecce and Hoppin Painters (*CVA* Italy 6, pl. 12, figs. 4 and 8; cf. my pl. 8a and b). There Dionysos, fully characterized, appears as matchmaker (seemingly ultramundane) for a girl and a quite ordinary boy. When on vases a little later than this one finds youths not much less ordinary (at any rate, short-haired, short-tainiaed) but provided with thyrsi, we are never sure of a Dionysos in any one of such figures – since, in a single picture, there may be two or three of them (see fig. 3a from the back of Leningrad St. 1427; for a single group which includes three *thyrsiferi*, all unbestial though all cannot be Dionysos, I might cite the colossal mug in West Berlin, accurately described, no. 3383, in Furtwängler's catalogue). For the present let us save our eyes for the things just behind the young man in the Dionysiac picture of the Iphigenia krater, leaving him ambiguous; the question whether he has enough on his head for our passing him as Dionysos might be an affair of laborious collation – comparison with several groupings in the same convention (Dionysiac gatherings on the necks of volute kraters) and with perhaps some others (the triad, *thyrsifera* with man and another woman, on the column-krater Vatican V 44 cannot be quite irrelevant, though the principal of this Dionysiac picture is a soldier, almost as if a comrade-in-arms of the man in the heroon of the Iphigenia vase had managed to climb into its Dionysiac paradise without disarming or divesting, for this helmeted man at the Vatican is getting a not dissimilar reception, though fan and pan and wreath and deep vessel for wine have been reshuffled – see Trendall's *VIE* 2, pl. 32g). The really dangerous trap in the Dionysiac group high on the reverse of the Iphigenia vase, St. 420

in Leningrad, is laid in the deep krater (as, on Vatican V 44, there is one laid in the deep bucket). But it will catch only those who have not quite understood what the wide shallow lavers on the obverse of St. 420 have to do with Iphigenia and who indeed require a lecture, illustrated with curving wine-ladles Greek and Roman, on the difference between ladling and straight scooping. What we have seen held by the rightmost figures of three "Dionysiac welcomes" (the Leningrad nymph, her Vatican counterpart helping to take care of a helmeted soldier, the Munich satyr already shown us in such clear detail by Mrs. Schneider-Herrmann) are all things of functionally the same form — straight, not in the least ladle-like — as the implement given our Iphigenia for her professional specialty of ablution. The myth on a vase to be studied presently, the London amphora F 332 (pl. 5), will so precisely and lavishly exhibit pan and laver as indispensably correlative things that I must excuse myself from labouring the point that what the Leningrad nymph has done or is to do with her pan is neither serving the wine nor a libation of wine nor even (if I may kill a dangerously attractive chimera at birth) a baptism in wine or Orphic milk. Altogether, the lesson of the reverse of the Iphigenia krater is a warning to stick to the plainest mythography if we are seeking none but the best light on this still puzzling object or symbol (if that is a better word for something that, as will be demonstrable, cannot have had quite objective existence). The three-handled variant of a pan properly one-handled is one of the common sights of late Apulian vase-painting: so common that we may presume it to be not separable from the system of chattel-symbolism which, as Furtwängler detected, is the language of this otherwise not very expressive art, its means of having not a little to say even when (as of course is the rule on all but quite large pieces) it has no story to tell. But it is just in those "ordinary" occurrences that the thing is inscrutable, very little less so for our knowing that where it figures between a given pair of lovers, or in a given party of mourners, or at the edge of some Dionysiac vignette, it is a vessel for water and not for wine.

Here at the back of the Iphigenia krater it is worse than difficult: it is troublesome, being involved, by certain other things present, in paradox. The larger picture on this side of the vase is one of those compositions (they are quite numerous) in which things brought to the heroon seem to insult the sex of the hero. Here where the dead is represented as a young knight, standing beside his charger, the clash is extreme: what in the world, his world of the blessed dead, is this lancer to do with the womanish things, the tambourine, the fan, the mirror, that his survivors tender him? Nor is it negligible that the situation presented is appreciably more disconcerting than the text of Stephani's catalogue disclosed. The most unmanly of the things tendered is the object which, in a cross-correction of Stephani's description of the two upper figures in the group flanking the heroon, we had to recognize — in the hands of the *man* — as a mirror. Now, if Stephani's distribution had been correct, a pan to the man and a mirror to the woman, that would have made no trouble, for there would have been no need to suppose that the mirror was an offering to the man of this monument. It is elementary — if one were compiling a key to Italiote chattel-symbolism this would be put at its very beginning — that a mirror is the most proper and sufficient sign of a nubile girl (being for her what a palaestric scraper is for nubile male or a fan is for woman married). Nobody need make a problem of sexual propriety out of a sight to be seen at the back of one or two funerary vases in Apulian red-figure, pair of women each with her mirror, in a sort of race of distress, in seemingly breathless haste to present themselves at a gravestone certified (by the sex of the figure in the heroon opposite) to be for a *man's* burial. To adapt (and clumsily pad) words of an Apulian writing in a later century: *hoc quo tepebant virgines en ut dolent!* Even where we have had to see the mirror of the present picture, at the right with the man and not at the left with the woman, his holding it would make no difficulty if this could be explained as scores, certainly, of mirrors and fans held by men on Apulian vases can be explained, as suitor's or bridegroom's gift. Nor need one have read the will of Theran Epikteta (*IG* xii, 3, 330, 51) to recall a connection between weddings and funerary monuments; that part of Aeschylus' *Choephori* where brother and sister set themselves to arouse their father's ghost, he with a taunt and a threat, she more gently, vowing not to forget Agamemnon's grave at her marriage, is not among the forgettable passages of the play. If only lines 486-487 of that passage, from the fifth century B.C., in a chronologically neat bracket with Epikteta's explicit provision at the turn of the third century for weddings on premises which included a multiple heroon, could have been found to fit the present company on this fourth-century vase just a little more exactly, then in seeing them as a wedding party in its funerary detour we might have helped ourselves to a resolution, welcomely simple, of that double incongruity, a man's mirror for another man. Not least welcome would have been its barring-up that side-turning into which any thinking upon eschatological questions of Italic studies is only too prone to bolt, for unbridled reverie about "Orphism": in this topic of paradoxical mirrors more invitingly open than ever, now that Erika Simon (see *Hommages à Albert Grenier* III) in her attention to the parlor-mysticism of the so-called Campana plaques has shown, incontestably, that the mirrors brandished by satyrs do imply a ritual in which the Titans' trapping of Dionysos with a mirror (and certain toys) was imitated. An affair which those plaques, Roman art of the first century A.D., do not take very seriously: nevertheless agreeing with what those who have improvised the word "Orphism" for a dark and dubious thing suppose to have been that thing's most significant rite.

But can we afford any more time for the back of the Iphigenia krater, its enigmatic (and enigma-breeding?) side? Let me make circumspect preparations, not too hurried but dryly tabular, for leaving it.

Quite the first thing to say is in deprecation of rigid uniformity in interpreting groupings at heroa. I hope it is clear why for the present one I have rejected what, if the driest conciseness is proper, I had best label *ELEP,* interpretation according to Electra's vow and Epikteta's will. Every student of Apulian red-figure must know some compositions (among those centred by graves or heroa) which it would fit well enough, and in any case there cannot be too much insistence on the intrinsic ambiguity of many things that we can expect to see in the ware's funerary pictures, things of nuptial character put there to funerary use. But I have a reason for holding back from the guess that in the present picture certain things of demonstrably nuptial character (the phialai, the fan, the tainiaed sapling, the tympanon, not to mention mirror or pan) are for a wedding of two of these four flankers. This reason is only partly in the relation of this picture, the bigger and mundane one, to the smaller and definitely "otherworldly" picture above it, though certainly it is important that repetition of phialai, fan, tainiaed sapling, tympanon, pan in the Dionysiac picture suggests that below the like things are for consignment to a Dionysiac paradise — whether as tribute to be collected by Dionysos or for some more personal need of the dead lancer was a question left open when provisionally we left undetermined the principal figure of that Dionysiac triad: lancer emparadised, or his Master? Quite half my reason for reluctance to apply *ELEP* was furnished by the man in the heroon of an Apulian volute-krater formerly in Bremen published by H. Schaal (*Abhandlungen und Vorträge herausgegeben von der Bremer Wissenschaftlichen Gesellschaft* 7 Heft 1/2 [1933] pl. 21). There is no question of what is to become of a fan held by a woman at a man's monument, for the man portrayed in the monument himself has the fan, in his right hand; what is to become of it *from there* is no doubt a question that remains, not to be brushed off by imputing exceptional effeminacy to the Bremen "hero" (the grounds that Schaal thought he had for this, in the thing suspended high right in the heroon, were insufficient, for that is not a woman's bonnet, but a conical pilos with chin-strap). Nor by guessing forgery. The Bremen vase must be given full benefit of its relation to a volute-krater in Taranto (61402) from Ruvo (first published by K. Schauenburg, *JdI* 68 [1953] p. 65, fig. 20). In the first place, it is beyond argument that the obverse of the Bremen vase was decorated by the same hand as the obverse of the unimpeachable krater in Taranto; more than that, the composition within the heroon of the Taranto vase seems to furnish a pendant, perhaps an explanatory one, to the surprisingly male fan-holder on the Bremen krater. In the heroon of the Taranto piece there is also a fan-holder: in herself not surprising, if quite sufficiently interesting (having seated herself on one of those "Ionic" kioniskoi of which Patroni made a great deal, as shorthand for gravestones and so symbols of grave transcended; there could of course be other views: altars, marking venerable status? or, as the one *overturned* on an Apulian lid, no. 50630, in the Villa Giulia, suggests, fragments of fallen columns, to mark — like certain rocks which Patroni preferred to interpret as funerary cairns of their sitters? — otherworldly desolation, for are there not several bits of forlorn "architecture" in a famous rendering of that, as Aeneas is taken to the verge of the underworld *perque domos Ditis vacuas et inania regna,* in *Aeneid* vi. 268-281?). What makes the Taranto krater, for any student, a remarkable monument of eschatography, is the woman's attendant, the satyr with pitcher and thyrsus facing this mortal (if I may suppose her to have been so: no Kore? no Libera?) in her heroon. He recalls pictures where a single satyr in attendance upon a company of men and women certifies them to have attained the Dionysiac paradise (for one, the reverse picture of the great Underworld krater, Apulian, in Naples, H 3222 (fig. 11); for another, the Elysian ball-players on a Lucanian lekythos in Munich no. 3270, Jahn's no. 808). But the Taranto krater should be a doubly arresting curiosity to us who have come to it from (1) the main picture at the back of Leningrad St. 420 (pl. 2) by a certain fan-marked route, through (2) the Dionysiac miniature of St. 420, where a nymph partnering a tambourined satyr in attendance on an ambiguously Bacchic youth has taken over the fan held in the picture just below by a woman of another world, our world, paired with a tambourined man in attendance at a soldier's heroon, and (3) another painter's enshrined hero on the Bremen krater, less soldierly but no doubt entitled (by his more or less military pilos) to our belief that he is only trustee of the fan which he handles, for its transmittal finally to (4) that *same* last painter's satyr-attended heroine, or her like. No doubt this is a matter of much hidden difficulty mined with risks of confusion. If I desired to be concise at all costs in analysis of that affair of fan-passing just observed, I should say that we had found a pattern of eschatographical coherence in stuff not really coherent eschatographically. But as anything is better than economy so primly unhelpful, I prefer to make this my opportunity to claim for the inhabitants of Italiote red-figure what, in certain emergencies of our concern with them, may prove altogether helpful, making the difference between meaning and unmeaning, namely an occasional privilege of *oratio recta.* "Don't confuse me with that other woman, holding that other fan and seen with that other satyr in attendance on the young man at the back of the neck of the Iphigenia krater, St. 420; she is only a nymph, in the servant class (like my own little satyr) of our paradise." Space for that warning from the Taranto woman in her heroon was, I am sure, not wasted; the Leningrad man, from his in the larger picture at the back of St. 420, is all the more welcome to reassure us: "in regard to me, don't let it worry you that, unlike the man in the heroon of the Bremen krater of the artist who painted also the Taranto krater but not mine, I am all military, with no fan or any other present for a woman. For that sort of thing my painter, unlike the other, leaves plenty of room outside the heroon; if you care to look there, you will see, in the main picture, three womanish things, fan and mirror and timbrel, among the objects brought by my survivors to my heroon; the smaller picture is, as it were, my receipt for them, given from the threshold or anteroom of the Dionysiac paradise; because it is a small picture, there is only space for two of the three, fan and timbrel. I cannot yet give you evidence of due delivery of the womanish things to any woman, for (as you have just learnt) in my 'receipt' the woman is only a nymph of the place, not my Elysian mate. But it may confirm your trust in my intention of delivering them (anyhow, will continue your education in variety) if you will look first at the pie-like thing which my welcomers have entrusted to me (in the smaller picture) and then at the journey of a similar thing on the reverse of yet another krater, Leningrad St. 424 (pl. 3b), by yet another painter." This third artist, like the painter of the Taranto and Bremen kraters, has no room (at least on this vase) for a regular scene above the heroon in a separate compartment; like the painter of the Iphigenia krater St. 420, he has an Elysian theme, but can only get space for it by allowing no visitors to the heroon. Into the area so cleared the two young men of the monument are allowed to break out, and, sure enough, one of them not only acquires a "pie" (low right) but is seen chiastically (high left) ready to share it with a woman. Are we not now in a better position to seize what is of practical value, either positively or in a cautionary way, in those travels of a fan out of this world and through another? *Positive, and reassuring:* without the impudence of claiming to have solved, in a manipulation of three or four vases, the problem of "sex-insulting" offerings to Italiote or Italic dead, I can suggest that an effort to resolve such incongruities may be worth continuing. We seem now to have three methods of resolution to test, should there be opportunity to apply them all. Already (1) *ELEP's* offer to explain everything by what men take to give women at cemetery weddings may begin to seem less promising than hypotheses of less mundane reference. Namely (2) a tentative eschatology of (re)union (to write it so takes account of what the Attic loutrophoros on a bachelor's grave and Attic choidia in infants' burials will have prepared us to find [H. R. W. Smith *CVA USA* 10, pp. 47-48]), the working of a principle of *compensation* (for the benefit of persons — whether adult or only adolescent — cut off before fulfillment in marriage); or (3) a supposed system of infernal vails (or "tips" or entrance-dues if there be affectation in the neater but old-fashioned word) — I need not depend on Propertius' "three little books" for Persephone (Propertius ii.13, lines 25-26) and Aeneas' golden bough (Vergil, *Aeneid* vi, lines 136ff) for her, for in support of this third hypothesis there are Daunian and Messapian dedications to chthonic goddesses (*Damatria* or *Aprodita*, O. Haas, *Messapische Studien,* pp. 27-33 and 143-150), which seem to be much more exactly relevant, at least in point of date and place. For hypotheses (2) and (3) the cardinal thing is the man formerly in Breman with the fan. Both (2) and (3) would have him ultramundane. But (2) would see him as equipped with this conventionally wifely thing in some connection with his rewedding (or wooing) an Elysian mate (adapting to this an almost forgotten suggestion of P. L. Ciceri, a pupil of Patroni, *RendLinc* [1913], pp. 109-136), while (3) would suppose him to be resting on his way to pay some power of the Underworld her due: this goddess Aphrodite rather than Persephone, for the nuptial associations of the fan make it an attribute of the equipper of brides, Aphrodite. Persephone (of the Apulian vase-paintings) and the goddess whose name is more or less Damatria in the Messapian inscriptions share something else, the cross-headed torch (see the symbol annexed to *CIM* 115; not included in Parlangeli's copy on his *Studi Messapici,* p. 156, but noted by O. Haas, *Messapische Studien,* p. 49, and sketched by Whatmough, *PID* no. 501). *Cautionary:* no scholar who has promised himself the satisfaction of beginning, at least beginning, to master real difficulties of late Apulian vase-painting, namely its apparent contradictions or derangements and its artful ambiguities as history serves them up to us, can afford to make a difficulty of its mere variety, to be understood if possible but anyhow to be accepted, with no effort thrown away in trying, as some have tried, to make monotony of it. Of two points yielded by the comparison just made of three heroa, namely (a) that both the two artists distinguishable have a Dionysiac paradise in mind and (b) that the painter of Leningrad St. 420 did not choose (for he did not need) to have it shown *in* the heroon, point (a) is important, point (b) is negligible. But one consequence or incident of this very variety is that some of the efforts to explain it away are less negligible than others. If Pagenstecher's undertaking to prove the heroa of Apulian red-figure dependent on conventions of funerary sculpture of Athens is one of the former, it is only because a professedly cautionary half-paragraph cannot ignore the disarming plausibility of four or five comparisons with Attic or Boeotian monuments which the wide range of the Italiote material allowed him to make. The illustrations of his *Unteritalische Grabdenkmäler* will always be valuable. But pls. 9-12 need some interleaving, as reminder of how extravagantly far beyond the conventions of Attic or any other Greek stelai behavior in (or rather, on the back walls of) the heroa of Apulian and Apulianizing vases really does go: where a man may lounge at a laver, stand dangling a female mask, sit playing with a swan, sit crouchingly with grapes in one hand and mirror (?) in the other, bend to present a phiale to an invisible person, behave restlessly with something like a thyrsos and something like a ball, peddle (?) fish, enact myth; where a woman may be mysteriously bustling (with wreath and kalathos – for an invisible bride?), or mystically rampant, with thyrsos and an (unaccountable?) alabastron, or even more curiously quiet: deceptively Leda-like as she reposes with water-bird in hand or on lap, or (not quite so deceptively?) recalling the priestess or votary of Fufluns figured on the lid of a famous Etruscan sarcophagus (this because of the fawn which the Italiote woman's left hand is free to pet, her right hand being laden with an open casket and a bunch of grapes): nor really less interesting in a commoner type that is curious chiefly for the impression given of expectancy, those "women at bus-stop" of seminar slang (most deserving that tag when their baggage is too bulky to hold, and is sat on). More positively suggestive was another line of generalization taken, with Patroni's encouragement, by Francesca Vanacore (*AttNap* 24 [1906] 175-196, "I Vasi con Heroon dell'Italia meridionale": especially 184-195). Not, like Pagenstecher's, a line of influence-tracing, but a formula of interpretation, thoroughgoing in its preference for the other-worldly; thus at the back of the Iphigenia vase in Leningrad, St. 420 (fig. 2) the lancer's horse would not be the charger of his military service but a hack supplied for the journey to Elysium; the four persons at his heroon would not be mourning survivors but a party to greet him at the end of that journey. In its polemical aspect, against the contrary formula of J. H. Holwerda (*Die attischen Gräber der Bluthezeit,* pp. 8ff), Miss Vanacore's study was no doubt too much like an invitation to judge between two beds-of-Procrustes, Holwerda's short at the prospective end, hers short at the retrospective and memorial end, of the naturally proper measure of funerary art in a culture not really more optimistic in its eschatology than that of Athens but very much less secretive about it. But here is my place to say that we must be prepared to find scenes at heroa which her formula fits much better than it fits the back of St. 420 or the back of St. 426 (painted by the same hand, pl. 4b). If there is a point to be made against nostrum-peddling and for due recognition of a natural variety, let me make it economically, by reference to the reverse of two vases which lie inevitably ahead, because the mythography of their obverses vary directly concerns the problem of the pan symbol, these both in Leningrad: St. 426 (pl. 4a and b), St. 424 (pl. 3a and b). It is scarcely conceivable that these kraters were painted in different workshops, for the obverses of St. 424 and St. 426 depict successive moments in the elaborately coherent telling of a myth brand-new at the time, doing away with the previous impunity of the Danaids and damning them to an exquisitely ironical penalty of perpetual frustration. But in a quite natural division of labour (natural in the routine of a workshop turning out great monumental pieces richly detailed) the two vases were assigned to different hands. That of the painter of the Iphigenia vase is easily recognized at the back of St. 426, not merely in the style of the drawing there but also in a repetition of the "stratification" of St. 420: below, apparently mundane matter, survivors at a monument; above, an evidently ultra-mundane subject. But of his colleague's work at the back of St. 424 one might say that the picture which its heroon centers is almost as if it had been painted to Miss Vanacore's specification, the only memorial and retrospective part is the group, a pair of young men, within the heroon; the margin is Elysian, *and those same young men can be detected there,* and twice: once as they separate and look around, and again as each finds what he was looking for, a woman ready for him.

The "Pan Symbol" Examined Further:
Dionysos and Aphrodite

IN THIS REGION of incongruity, ambiguity, teasing variety, where – for progress in any good purpose – is there any firm footing to be found?

1. As the Leningrad Iphigenia seems to have promised, there should be some afforded by any *picture of a familiar myth which is telling the story borrows from the ware's code of symbols,* which of course is one of our difficulties, however transparent that code may have been in the fourth century B.C., perhaps to Italic as well as to Greek customers.

2. In starting with the pan symbol, not the least cryptic in the code and likely to prove important if an eschatology of purification is not unlikely to be involved in the eschatography of late Apulian red-figure, we have not made a bad beginning, and pursuit of it through as many myths as use it is the most inexorable of my duties to our subject. But it may have to be last in performance; anyhow, in promising ourselves the excitement of that particular chase (with its climax in this Western symbol's being caught at work in the telling of tales all the more curious for seeming to be Western innovations, about the Danaids' wet hell and the Hesperids' wet limbo respectively) we are not to forget the circumstances which, in allowing us to speak of a "code," exact some methodical curiosity about the whole system of it. Here perhaps there may be more considerations to ponder than the one which is most evidently of practical importance and most in need of immediate emphasis, namely that, if myth is medicine for obscurity or ambiguity of symbols, there are others in not much less need of it than the pan symbol – the boxes and baskets which (apart from a certain small, often open, thing for ribbons and trinkets) defy insight, the domed feature which is sometimes taken for another of those boxes, but looks more like pastry in a pie dish, the ladder-like (or rather, abacus-like?) thing once so variously explained and now passing for rattle or xylophone, without ever (?) its being seen to be used as either: perhaps above all, those rounds (too small to be meant for tympana or phialai) which are most often read as balls to play with but have been taken for folding mirrors or even for purses (and in that last interpretation favouring an idea more upsetting than any "Orphic" corollary of the other two – Macchioro's contention that the stuff of Apulian red-figure, even the latest, just continues the stuff of Attic red-figure, with the latter's mercenary whoredoms available for explaining what the Patronians saw as all-but Swedenborgian "amore elisiaco" [*Orfismo e Paolinismo,* pp. 262ff]). Having allowed myself words possibly demoralizing, "incongruity, ambiguity, teasing variety," I must not delay to mention (and to promise application of) a specific for at least some of those difficulties, the interestingly ironical mythography of Europa (which for any space given

it can render good returns — realization that Apulian red-figure is capable of subtlety, suspicion that perhaps this art is *salted* with it). Just at this point what is more required is some encouraging sense, gotten economically from a sufficient sample of the freshest material, of the pan symbol's palpable nexus — in some line of purpose not the cruelly brief one of Iphigenia's need of the vessel — with other things besides its mere correlatives laver and hydria. "Yes, a system there is, some links of it I can feel even in this dark": when one can say that, he can know himself out of danger of frustration only too exactly comparable to that of the misdirected tourist who drove in to present his reservation (and his license for the hotel's splendid fishing) at what was the local madhouse.

Helpful for this is one of the more recently published examples of the pan symbol in its cryptic use — cryptic for us, with no sidelight from a myth — on the bell-krater shown us by Miss Bianca-Maria Scarfi as principal vase of the first burial of tomb 17 (disturbed) in the necropolis of Monte Sannace between Ionian Taranto and Adriatic Bari (*MonLinc* 45 [1961] 213, figs. 55 and 56; burial of an adult man, with armor and weapons). "Pair of lovers in some 'otherwhere,' one of them with an ablution pan" is a quite frequent composition in late Apulian red-figure. But the present example, though exceptional in its vehicle (krater, not the usual pelike), may perhaps prove the fittest to rank as classic   "classic" in a simply practical sense, the most conveniently central piece in a certain category of pictures of uncommon interest, for there (if anywhere) the "amore elisiaco" of the school of Patroni presents itself for verification. No doubt the lovers from tomb 17, seated together in the open, she rather unsteadily on a pile of rocks, yet able with her free hand to hold up a big box which is garnished with a spray (myrtle? recognizing Aphrodite's part in this, as the suspended leaves of ivy recognize Dionysos part?), her companion more secure on a ledge of ground, brandishing a pan and dangling a bunch of grapes, are all the better as specimens for their having been found in a "sexed" grave in an expertly dug and published cemetery, for the circumstances permit much eye-opening collation. But what I meant especially in those perhaps too flattering phrases was to stress the present lovers' place *midway* in a certain typical affair which begins with encounter (the norm as on Vatican pelikai Z 8 and V 33, Trendall, *VIE* 2, pl. 45a and b: woman on rock, man *standing* with pan); pauses (as here on the M. Sannace krater) for brief dalliance with both seated; then ends (not quite the right word?) in a scampering-off together (M. A. Del Chiaro, *Greek Art in Private Collections of Southern California* [1966] fig. 64, Brundage 3/242); the second and third phases are all the more interesting for their resisting Albizzati's device (as it were, an invisible heroon to drop over the sitter) for reducing emparadised lovers to "dead and survivor."

"Lovers," "emparadised": at the point reached in those words we may well begin to feel the irony of our first understanding of the pan symbol having come by way of a lethal duty of a virgin priestess of a virgin goddess. But for Iphigenia, Euripides' Iphigenia, we should not have known what manner of "wet" thing this constant of lovers' meetings was; either we should have read it as representing a special (nuptial?) kind of libation-spiller, or (with an uncomfortable sense of near-waggery) we should have begun to wonder whether it might not mean some special, spoon-like, drinking vessel. Conversely, in Iphigenia's lesson that it meant a washpan there was no preparation for what we may now begin to expect, a further context of nuptial symbolism. But in the meantime it is quite interesting that the "wet" note in tomb 17 at M. Sannace gets an echo in a woman's grave there, tomb 2; this from a terracotta, Miss Scarfi's no. 2 of fig. 11, col. 157. As Iphigenia's apparatus has already taught us and the infernal bathroom of a London vase (pl. 5a) should in due turn make unforgettable, pan and laver are correlatives, and terracotta no. 2 represents Eros and a woman (the sex is variable from a specimen better preserved) idling at a laver. Terracotta no. 1 from the same grave, woman beating a timbrel, reverberates with mixed suggestions. By reminding us of the big tympanon above the "honeymoon" of Hades and Persephone in the great "Under-world" in Naples (fig. 11) it rather strongly encourages us to find a hint of nuptial bathing in terracotta no. 2. Also it tempts us (in a further rebound) to relate an even more certainly nuptial feature of that Underworld, Persephone's spray-garnished phiale, to the sprayed box of the woman from tomb 17, companion on its krater of the youth whose *pair* of attributes, ablution pan and probably Dionysiac grapes, cannot but remind us of actual ablutions, actual Dionysos, actual nuptials with his blessing, on a much published krater in Lecce, Apulian but of an earlier phase (assigned by Cambitoglou and Trendall to their Hoppin Painter: for P. Romanelli's publication with laconic but epoch-marking comment see his text to *CVA* Italy 6, pl. 12, fig. 8). (Cf. my pl. 8b.) There a woman keeps a man and a god waiting; between bridegroom (with sprayed phiale ready) and Dionysos (who has already lit the nuptial torch) the bride goes on washing her hair. Lecce 620 is an important vase, worth returning to. But it is not "fresh material" and the pan symbol is not to be seen (as we shall find, it was not yet invented). Fresher (of later publication) than the Monte Sannace krater, fragments of a late Apulian lekanis-lid shown in Margot Schmidt's fascicle for Heidelberg (*CVA* Germany 23) demand attention – for the pan at the woman's feet, the rock she, like the mated girl of M. Sannace, is put to sit on, her probably Dionysiac tympanon (no. U9, pl. 78, fig. 7): also for her isolation in one framed segment of this lid, question-posing. Is she, is this *her* narrow 'otherwhere,' expecting a mate? Is it the promise of one that Eros in the opposite segment (*ibid.* fig. 6) has for her, for what he has is a palm branch, sometimes symbol of nuptial fulfillment? What is the relation of this combination of figures to a closer one on a vase longer and better known, the column-krater (583) Pal. 955 in Bologna, in a picture by the artist known (in Berkeley at least)[1] as the Holstein-Berge Painter (*CVA* Italy 12 IV D r, pl. 20, fig. 1)? Something is taking shape, or at very least some knots are being tied, for in the Bologna scamper (woman with pan and spray-garnished box or basket leading, Eros with tympanon and grapes following) it is almost as if the Heidelberg girl were there being steered by the Heidelberg god to her tryst with the M. Sannace man.

3. Anyhow, shaping or knotting, what is becoming more and more observable is a partnership between (Tarentine?) Dionysos and (Messapo-Peucetian?) Aphrodite in their chthonic aspects; an association somehow involving the symbolic ablution-pan, as has been visible ever since Mrs. Schneider enabled one to collate the Munich satyr, holding it at a beatification, with the Geneva Eros, flourishing it at a tomb or tomb-like monument (*BABesch* 37, pp. 44-45, figs. 6 and 7b; 38, p. 95, fig. 5). Its terms (perhaps unstable?) we shall be lucky indeed to discover, but it can hardly be that they now favour Dionysos, unless the change has only been *delegation* of the function we saw him exercising in earlier (Middle Apulian) pictures by the Hoppin and Lecce Painters, as the next world's hearty matchmaker, delighting in personal service.

Eros and "Orphism"

I WROTE APHRODITE just now, not Eros, because in late Apulian red-figure it is so certain on the whole that its Erotes, bonneted, bedizened, are only agents of the goddess, even though we may let them keep a capital letter to mark a vaguely felt difference from the satyrs and nymphs in *their* relation to *their* Master. The point is important, for two reasons so distinct and far apart that my present need to couple them is almost embarrassing. I suppose it could be said that the first is our danger of an excess of Aphrodites (through mistaking bride served by Eros for goddess with dutiful son), the other Aphrodite's danger of altogether losing importance, through our impulsive promotion of Eros to Orphic independence of her – to the point, that is, where (in Guthrie's good phrase) he turns into "one of those who come at

---

[1] Smith named this painter after Mrs. Louise Holstein-Berge, who submitted, in fulfillment of the requirements for the degree of M.A. at Berkeley, a dissertation upon the krater Berkeley 8/2320. Smith attributed a large number of vases to the same hand, which, Sir A. D. Trendall very kindly informs me in correspondence, "are not so. They all come from one workshop (that of the Patera Painter), but in my opinion they are *not* all by the same hand." The reader is therefore warned that the painter repeatedly referred to in the latter part of the book as "my" (i.e., Smith's) "Holstein-Berge painter" is something of a chimera, and to treat with caution the argument, to the extent that it is founded upon the identity of hands. [J.K.A.]

the very beginning of things, not the youthful son of Aphrodite" (*Orpheus* 295). No doubt there is some trace in the earlier catalogues of mischief from the former cause; even now, it is not only in Campanian red-figure of the C A Group that the "doubtful water-bird" (Leda's swan? Aphrodite's swan? symbolic bird of bathed-and-ready bride?) is a pest of hermeneutic scholarship. Yet today there cannot be many students of Italiote pottery, novices even, who on being faced with some smallish Apulian piece, askos or slim oinochoe, with just enough surface for the subject hackneyed on such vases, "Eros with things for this nubile woman," would need to be nudged away from the wrong to the right recognition by a reminder of the half-truth (true for an immense number of Apulian vases) that Eros, in so far as he is Aphrodite's mobile partner in an exceedingly brisk business of service to ripening women and young couples, has no time to waste in her company, making her "presents from stock." That half of the matter is of course itself conducive to an "Orphic seizure"; the women attended by Eros on the great majority of late Apulian vases are not Aphrodites, and moreover the winged daimones who chase or are otherwise concerned with women in Heraclean and early Apulian vase-painting have not even effeminacy to suggest their being subordinate to a goddess; there is no bonnet, no jewelry to say "hang no Orphic alias here." But whereas there is nothing (so far as I recall examples) in that earlier type of Italiote Eros to restrain the whim, (if it should seize one) to surname him Protogonos – Erikepaios – Phanes, and so make him (in the very connection Guthrie had in mind) an ancestor of Aphrodite, at the same time it would be shameful if I could not see how two vase-paintings, right in our own path, discourage the playing of any such trick on the more or less effeminate type; both of them pictures of the sort in which it is natural enough to find Aphrodite and Eros unseparated, mythographies. For one, see the drawing in my fig. 4, clearer than the photograph of pl. 3a in rendering the Olympian level of the obverse painting of Leningrad St. 424. Not everything up there is self-evident. It is not at once plain what interest the adult males, Apollo on the left and Pan(!) on the right have in the Danaids below, brought to judgment but far from understanding their situation (of many signs one is the leading Danaid's ablution-pan, so prominent – whether she has only planted it, casually, on the platform of the royal pavilion, or is bidding for attention with impudent raps of its handle). But it is not in doubt what Olympians the female figures represent, or what they have sides to take in the affair below. The goddess with Apollo is Artemis and she is for the viricides; the goddess with Eros and Pan is Aphrodite, and here she is even more against them than in a famous fragment of Aeschylus. (Fr. 125 Mette, 44 Nauck[2]). An issue quite practical – urgent if one of the best opportunities in a sufficiently resolute confrontation of the difficulties of Apulian red-figure is our chance of doing something toward settling the uncertain relation of its Greek Dionysos (dominant at first?) to its perhaps partly ethnic Aphrodite – obtrudes itself in the question, "how secure, after all, is our right to see a cult of Aphrodite, an encroaching Aphrodite, in all the (suddenly teeming, suddenly so effeminate) Erotes of late Apulian red-figure?." It could be impugned only, I think, by unfair, slyly plausible, manipulation of texts belonging (or more or less fairly annexable) to Orphic literature: one of them a Messapian inscription, Haas B.1.45, from Rudiae-Rugge — finding-place of the momentously Dionysiac work of the Hoppin Painter mentioned just now, p. 32 — the lettering of which has been restored to include the name of the deity, *ambisexual but more Dionysiac than Erotic,* addressed in the forty-second hymn of the collection of Pergamene litanies ascribed to Orpheus, *Mise*; another, the much better-known document from Gurob, Kern *fr.* 31, a papyrus which seems to invoke Erikepaios at line 22, invites restoration of the name Protogonos at line 18 and of the name Phanes at line 23, certainly names Eubouleus and Dionysos at lines 18 and 23 respectively, and can be linked up with Apulian vase-painting, not unplausibly, just where this papyrus becomes for us more than a name-dropping document of the paratheologies ascribed to Orpheus and is suddenly seen to concern a Dionysos-trapping ritual like the one fathered on Orpheus by Onomakritos; the link is that the mirror thrown, with the rest of the bait, into a kalathos or deep work-basket at line 30 can hardly be kept from volunteering an Orphic explanation of the "sex-insulting" combination, mirror and woman's kalathos, put to flank a man's heroon on a loutrophoros in Naples, no. 2251 in Heydemann's catalogue — less simply explicable, we have to grant, than the two mirrors stuck in kalathoi beside the woman's heroon on an amphora in Taranto from Ceglie del Campo, no. 242/7014, *CVA* Italy 15 IV Dr, pl. 14, fig. 1. That is much more than enough to make it quite fortunate that Orpheus himself is the principal figure of the vase-painting, which in my fig. 5 reinforces fig. 4 by an even more intimate pairing of Aphrodite with an even more markedly effeminate Eros, on the volute krater (ex-Caputi no. 270) in the H.A. collection in Milan (*CVA* Italy 49, IVD, pl. 10) (my pls. 11-13). And it is certainly not lucky that there is encouraging orientation in this. At the end of a line, through an avenue of vista of mythographies, which we have already marked for traveling, there is now seen to be waiting a conveniently small "Orphic question," all our own, not very likely (we can hope) to entangle us awkwardly with whatever Father Festugière's battering-ram (*Revue Biblique* 44 [1935] pp. 471ff, and *REG* 49 [1936] pp. 306ff) and Ivan Lindforth's even more ruinous undermining have left to the old big one, more hypothesis really than question, assuming for the fourth and even the fifth century B.C. an ascetic religion of Dionysos, based both theoretically and ritually on a myth of the god's having been trapped and killed and eaten by Titan ancestors of the human race: a religion deriving its authority from scriptures attributed to Orpheus, and so "Orphism" if a name must be coined for it. Our own Orphic question will not be ripe for discussion until we have finished our business with the pan symbol by having done our best to deepen our understanding of its functional correlation with the other "wet" symbols, hydria and laver, through attention to all the six mythographies in which it helps to tell a story or at least to set a recognizable scene. But it is so simple a question in itself, just this: the feature under the laver on the H.A. krater being meant for a conch shell, may we suppose its *position* significant? If it can be rendered likely, on the showing of other works of late Apulian red-figure, that the present shell under the present laver is neither "just scenery" nor some rough fellow's discarded hoot-horn, then and only then there should be some use of the exotic but not very abstruse fact that the Indian conch, *turbinella pyrum,* was and is still a regular vessel of religious ablution. Scale is important. Neither here nor on a vase in Bari (Apulian amphora no. 873) (pl. 23) where such a shell is being *used* by a man in Thracian (or Illyrian?) dress at the edge of a laver in the presence of Orpheus should the object be explained as a murex (source of the saving purple used to dye Cabiric amulets for sailors and their passengers). *"Murex* is quite a little thing," my friend Professor Denis Fox had to remind me, thus killing the impulse (or "Orphic seizure") to refer the subject of the H.A. krater to Orpheus' sojourn and Cabiric initiation in Samothrace (Kern *Test.* 105). We are a long way from the right place for a fuller consideration of the H.A. krater in its interesting bearing on Bari 873. But it is quite to my present point to expose the full badness of a Cabiric interpretation of either, worst in ignoring Aphrodite – present (unmistakably, thanks to Eros) on the H.A. krater, not without representation on the Bari amphora if we may see a sign of her cult in the censer fed by the naked man for whose impending ablution Orpheus is harping. Proof of our right to see one I must leave to the promised "Orphic epilogue." I know that I do not have to labour to prove that in theography the censer is an established attribute of Aphrodite. But for full rigor the argument in this matter will need a third vase, one which offers just the required complement to the Bari picture, a scene in which as at Bari Orpheus is harping for the benefit of a candidate for ablution out of a laver, but (together with the shell) Aphrodite's censer has vanished – to make room for herself (fig. 6).

It would be a bad sign if there were no *shock* in our thus finding (or knowing ourselves to be on the way to find) Orpheus taken over by Aphrodite. Let us make the best of it for present headway and momentum if possible but in any case for its timely analysis now and our better going later. It would have been less conclusive and dazing if it could have been just vicarious: the sympathy which, even without our acceptance of his premises, would have been the right of any friend who had written confidently of "Orphism" as an ascetically mystical religion of Dionysos. One may write as I an now writing without having the slightest stake in "Orphism": having, on the contrary, a decided opinion that it is a chimera, of establishable parentage – result of unguardedly commingling two elements, each well enough attested but quite distinct, belonging to the hugh miscellany of scriptures claiming to be revelations of Orpheus: one ascetic and ethical, contributed by Italiote Pythagoreans (Brontinos and Kerkops, for two), one Dionysiac and concerned with various effective rituals (this other element consisting mainly of Onomakritos' Τελεταί) (Cf. Pausanias viii. 37.5.) What is so confusing but also so interesting (so that the first daze turns to a consuming ache of curiosity about many other shifts and contrasts) is not so much the ravishing of Orpheus away from his Dionysos (Dionysos-Zagreus of our writers about "Orphism," but also Cicero's fourth and Orphic Dionysos [*De Natura Deorum* iii.58]; I would have bundled in "Herodotus' Orphico-Pythagorean Bakchos" had not Ivan Lindforth eroded all faith in the vulgate reading of Hdt. ii.81 [*Arts of Orpheus* pp. 45-46]). Nor is it even this, that Orpheus' career in Apulian red-figure begins so shamefully (butchered by women, on three vases of early style found at Tarentum) and ends so prosperously (as charmer and rite-founder on vases found in regions more properly Apulian). It is not rather this, that the ravisher is the deity for whom (in their funerary inscriptions) the Italic neighbours of Tarentum so conspicuously *slight* Dionysos, namely Aphrodite?

Tarentine Response to Messapian Demand— Alexander the Molossian

WE BEGAN THE last paragraph with a hope of useful considerations. Has it not armed us with at least two? (1) In the review of mythographies proposed for some place in this study we shall need to be more alert to signs of Aphrodite's presence or influence than previous students of the same pictures have been. Nothing is more crudely fatuous than hermeneutic bigotry in the interpretation of funerary vase-painting, for a customer's reading could never be "wrong," however far from the designer's meaning; thus I must acknowledge, for example, that my own preference for Dionysos, if (in a question ahead of us) there is to be naming of the principal person of the strip picture above the Garden of the Hesperides in my fig. 7, is subject to ghostly corrections: "no, you odious man, that is our little Dazimos, in paradise." But while there should be no shrill scolding of the latest interpreter of London F 332 for putting Aphrodite out of the place which Walters allowed her in the first of that series of pan-showing mythographies (pl. 5a), let us not be too set against her readmission, and if we reinstate her let us make the most of any help this "outfitting" Aphrodite can give us with the last and most difficult picture in that series (fig. 8, pl. 15) where a figure who should be some "Mistress of the Robes" — if not a bride on her own boxed belongings? — awaits some affair requiring an ablution-pan, at the very centre of the Garden of the Hesperides. (2) More important practically (if well-characterized figures of a goddess should be trusted to make their proper impression?), have we not just had a sharp reminder — like a bite in the heel — of something which, for all our ignoring it, has been dogging us ever since our collation of a bell-krater from M. Sannace (not too distantly associated with terracottas which, as I might there have said, are independent, notably so, of Tarentine tradition) with a lid of a lekanis in Heidelberg, and so belonging to the very collection of Italiote fragments which, as I had neither room nor reason to say there, caused in Germany notably and certainly influential defection, Pagenstecher's, from the belief there prevailing in the Tarentine origin and continuance of Apulian red-figure. Nor is the lid's relevance merely in some loose association with an apostasy. It is formidable on its own account: the thing we made welcome as late Apulian work, with one more pan for us, is one of the *unprovenienced* items of a collection partly formed by "sherding" at Taranto. It is of course this ware's fundamental problem, our need to make *sure* of its home, that has become suddenly mordant, or (is it time to say?) suddenly clamant. From its obverse side the Archemoros krater in Naples (fig. 9) (just now adduced, in my allusion to the woman-on-wardrobe in its reverse), the side that is sprinkled with good Greek (more and better than is furnished by a vase warrantably Greek, the Heraclean ΣΦIPAN krater in the same collection, K. Kerenyi in *Hommages à Jean Bayet,* pp. 336ff, with references (p. 337, n. 2) to earlier publications) and is famous for its superior mastery of Hypsipyle's story, seems to shout derisive protest against even the thought that its finding place, Ryps-Rubi-Ruvo in the wool-wealthy backland of the Adriatic shore, might perhaps have been the place of its designing and making: "Sad though it was that Pagenstecher, victim of his inability (venial at that time) to distinguish early Tarentine fragments from Attic rf., put the *origin* of 'Apulian' (Tarentine) vase-painting at Ruvo, his theory was not irrational, all things considered (for one thing, a certain consequence of that inability, namely his imagining a great intrusion of Attic craftsmen, from whose competition the Tarentine potters fled to Rubi and Canusium; for another thing, the truth revealed (to you if not to him) in *CVA* It. 6 even before Cambitoglou and Trendall made the world acquainted with the Parasol Painter and his peers, that work provincially feeble is no more lacking in early and middle Apulian vase-painting than it is in the early red-figure of Greek Sicily (*APS* pp. 11-12). But only in some entirely mindless seizure of local patriotism could even a mayor of Ruvo be moved to challenge Tarentum's claim to that thorough miracle of sophistication, economic as well as 'cultural,' the *late* Apulian vases." That is only one voice, against others audible. There was always the pattern of distribution to be explained away, and though new finds have made it less unfavorable to

Tarentum's claims this is perhaps offset by a new objective. Just because the new terracottas from M. Sannace agree so well with the nuptial eschatography of late Apulian vases — the Eros-attending girl at a laver and from the same grave the woman beating a timbrel for that girl's marriage — there might seem to be significance in their clashing with the contemporary typology of Tarentine figurines; this was not in the least concerned with "getting married," being given to another system of funerary symbolism more connubial than nuptial: unmistakably the Panhellenic one which is more fully displayed in the "Totenmahl reliefs," with their intimate banquets of "hero" and "heroine" who are served by children in the presence of pet snakes and in the neighborhood of weirdly eavesdropping horses. (E.g., S. Reinach, *Répertoire de reliefs grecs et romains* II, pp. 45-163, no. 4). But with the closing phrases of that spokesman for Tarentum, about the quality of late Apulian red-figure, we need not quarrel; grateful for the leave to dislike which the prim word displacing "artistic" seems to give, but recognizing in the last phase of Apulian vase-painting a thing portentous — this not so much because capable of the colossal as because nearly incapable of feebleness. It would be flippant, but it would be exactly true, to say that feebleness is the *forte* of such art as is attempted by the Italic (as against Italiote, i.e., Greek) potteries of South-Eastern Italy; the evidence swarms in the forty-two plates of Max Mayer's *Apulien.* At any rate, *demanding to be seen as an event in conditioned history* (and one of some vehemence if not violence), the final reflowering of the principal branch of Italiote vase-painting is a matter asserting many aspects: one even military? At least a faint glimpse of that seems to go with much vivider apprehension of economic aspects, those which are disclosed as it dawns on one that the modern dispute about its home has been a tugging-match between those, not all Italians, who with Patroni sought to tow Apulian red-figure northward to a country which, as it happens, ancient texts warrant wool-*raising*, and those, not all Germans, who with Furtwängler sought to keep it at Greek Tarentum, which, were there no books to tell us so, would be seen to have been wool-*working.*

Looking at coins of Tarentum we are perhaps not sure whether it is a charged spindle or a charged distaff that Taras carries, but we can see that the thing means "bring your clip to us; we'll spin it" — to which Taranto's famous dump of murex waste adds "and we dyed it too." (Cf. C. M. Kraay and M. Hirmer, *Greek Coins,* pp. 314-315, nos. 298-305.) It may turn out that in this evidence of dealing there may be something for mediating the ceramic dispute, or at least for getting a new grasp of its problem. But one of the newest revelations of field archaeology reminds us that while, as boasted by dolphin-riding Taras, Tarentum always commanded the sea quite sufficiently for fetchings and sendings (besides having an incomparably inviting trade-magnet in its great safe dual harbour), it did not equally command the land, at the time important. The stones (Manduria's) could not have more impressively confirmed the records, as one may grant without daring to suppose that it is even knowable whether the stupendous fortifications which the visitor can now see there were raised for, or against, the Greek cause, and without being quite sure that they confirm the identification of Manduria (some thirty kilometers east of Taranto in the direction of Lecce, so anciently Messapian) with Mandonion, where in 338 B.C. a king of Sparta, Archidamos III, was defeated and killed fighting for Tarentum against an enemy called Messapian by Plutarch (*Agis* 3), Lucanian by Diodorus (xvi.62-63). In a quite welcome muddle of the matter — welcome because it passes us from Archidamos to another and slightly later champion of the Italiote Greeks less indirectly relevant to ceramic questions — Pliny the Elder (iii.98) wrote uneasily (suspecting his authority Theopompus of having made a ghost-town) *Mardoniam Lucanorum urbem,* as the place of the defeat and death of Alexander I of Epirus, about 330 B.C. Here seems to lurk some confusing of Alexander's disaster, towards the toe of Italy at Bruttian Pandosia near Cosentia-Cosenza in a fight against Lucanians, with Archidamos' disaster, towards the heel of Italy it rather seems, in a fight with closer neighbours of Tarentum (if Messapians). Anyhow, this Alexander, sometimes distinguished as the Molossian, is sufficiently pertinent: brother of Olympias, who (Kern, *Test.* 206) was devoted to Orphic excesses, uncle (and brother-in-law) of Alexander the Great on whose victory at Issos in November of 333 B.C. our dating of latest Apulian, which thrice took note of the battle, mainly depends:[1] attested ally of the indubitably best *buyers* of Apulian red-figure, the Daunians (who had Canusium-Canosa) and the Peucetians (who had Rubi-Ruvo), and so more than merely the champion of the Greek metropolis, Tarentum, place the most reasonably credited with *making* it. It can only be a guess, but it is no silly one, that in the ware's three pictures of the pursuit of Darius the notoriously unhistorical beard of the greater and unseen Alexander was misapplied from the face well enough known to all parties to late Apulian red-figure. All *three*, if I am not wrong in my count of the factors of this phenomenon — Peucetian wealth and Daunian wealth at their historic acme demanding, Tarentine resources of literary culture and sheer vital dexterity organized at the acme of a long-established industry to supply — all that makes the difference (in emphasis as well as in scale and style) between late and earlier in Apulian vase-painting. With the evidence (in a noteworthy passage of Strabo, vi.280) of a political and military combination correspondingly triple (at just the important time, with intimate bearing on an archaeological problem, the fate of Heraclean red-figure) we shall be concerned before long. It should be pertinent to a question I cannot shirk: "Knowing that the last third of the fourth century,

---

[1] Cf. Furtwängler in FR II, pp. 149ff; H. Metzger, *REG* 80 (1967) 308 offers (as Professors Webster and Trendall point out to me) an easier solution for the bearded Alexander (p. 7n. 5 *supra*) [J.K.A.]

however good for Apulian red-figure, was so bad for Tarentum's relations with neighbours that she had to be rescued thrice from their mortal hostility by champions summoned from Greece (add Kleonymos, rescuer in 303 B.C., to those other two; Diodorus xx.104-105; Livy x.2) can we permit you to offer an assumption of good relations as basis of a theory in explanation of prodigious developments in Apulian funerary pottery during that very period, those 'shifts' and resulting (?) 'contrasts' about which you have owned to being so consumedly curious?"

Already it must seem that this need not be an embarrassing question (I am quite aware of another that, for a time, until mercifully it bows off, self-answered, will really be so — about our right to apply an emphasis of the *Messapian* inscriptions, favoring chthonic Aphrodite at the expense of an all but totally eclipsed Dionysos, to late Tarentine vase-painting for the detection of Greek response to *Peucetian* and *Daunian* preference). But it could be ruinous to our study if I let it pitch us into a chaos of curiosities, with loss of the very direction for which we wish momentum. If an almost chaotic medley of metaphors should be incidental to my preventing that, let me hope to be forgiven it.

Elysian (Re)unions in the Light
of Attic and Other Parallels

IN THE MAIN issue, something is on trial; as has been clear ever since at Miss Scarfi's Monte Sannace we found the pan symbol in which Mrs. Schneider kindled interest (symbol of purification, as we had to find out for ourselves) found it there as a possession of Miss Scarfi's unearthly-seeming pair of lovers. This "something" is a certain idea, the most interesting ever contributed to Italiote studies, if not (so far, in some seventy years of public existence) much in favor, Patroni's *amore elisiaco.* Here (since this bears both on the point of disfavor and on a special importance of Miss Scarfi's exhibit from M. Sannace) it is well to recall the device (invisible heroon for clapping over *sitters*) by which Carlo Albizzati, loyal as well as eminent disciple, sought to clear Patroni's master principle ("keep interpretation of Italiote vases funerary") of a sentimental embarrassment: this without giving any encouragement to V. Macchioro, or to any other inheritor of Heydemann's master principles ("above all, keep the interpretation of Italiote vases unmystical; anyhow keep it mundane"). Albizzati seems to have believed that in Apulian vase-painting there was no "(re)union in Elysium" which could not be broken up into "the dead and dutiful survivor" by reference to more elaborate, less "symbolically idealized," pictures of survivors (posed *standing,* at least in the foreground) doing their duty to the dead person represented (*seated*, as a rule) in a heroon. But on the M. Sannace krater *both* the man with the pan and grapes and the woman with the garnished box were seated, in surroundings desolate enough to be ultra-mundane – by Vergilian standards if these, across a gap of three centuries, were pertinent. Moreover, as was remarked if not developed, what was exampled in that session of two lovers was only the middle stage of an affair in three stages, some ten Apulian vases showing one or another: (1) the pan-holder's finding the sitter, (2) the former's (uncomfortably and briefly?) settling down with the latter, (3) their scampering off, the pan-holder not always leading. Only to the first stage could one even think of applying Albizzati's device for returning to earth one of the lovers, and of course it was altogether ineffective. It would show up that recently displayed impatience for momentum and headway as merely rhetorical puffing and panting if now I could not see and use the practical, course-setting, to some extent program-dictating, importance of Albizzati's failure in his attempt, so well and filially meant, to suppress an idea, "Elysian love," with which our formerly main topic, the pan symbol, is involving itself more and more – fortunately, for it is an idea capable of taking revenge for neglect, or even condescension.

It has done so at least thrice. Except that V. Macchioro, in a hurry as so often, pilloried the wrong culprit, the blunder which read the reunited family (my pl. 1a) of the Underworld krater (3297) in Munich as "Dionysos, Ariadne, and the child" deserved its derisive reception. Though not of that order the traditional explanation of the obverse of London F 332 (*separation,* no solemnized marriage, of Kore and Hades) is no slight mistake, unless I have myself blundered (pp. 37-38, pl. 5a). We, who have entered the difficulties of late Apulian red-figure through the door marked *To The Scandalous Misfits,* are rather well prepared for profitable reflexion on the revenge which was taken on Albizzati himself, for it happened in that very department. Perhaps all the better prepared for having been cautioned, as we went in, not to be scandalized by disconcerting variety; at any rate, Albizzati's trouble was no matter of obscurely recalcitrant exceptions on which the "desentimentalizing machine" would not work. Rather (if I may shift mechanism to the other side), it was as if, on his filing his sober amendment in the proper orifice of the right depository, two arms had clanged out from it to hand him a grim choice of certificates: this one, of his ward's (the ware's) senile derangement, or that one, of his own invincible incuriosity. And as if, thereupon, he had judged it better, better and more stimulating for Italiote studies in the long run, to acknowledge acceptance of both. "Singolare interesse hanno per noi gli oggetti recati dagli offerenti. Uno studio minuzioso mi persuade a fondarmi ben poco sulla rispondenza con il sesso dei defunti. Anche qui, *come sempre* [my italics], gli artefici lavorano senza molto sottilizzare; specchi, ventagli, strigili e cofanetti, sono offerti tanto agli uomini che alle donne" ("Saggio di esegesi sperimentale" p. 163). Surely his having to own himself completely baffled by the "sex-insulting" things to be seen at men's graves or heroa was consequence of his own destruction of the destination, *ultimately* quite fit, which the Patronian eschatology of (re)union had provided for all that kind of thing, those worse than womanish instruments, painfully "gentlewomanish" and *sub*musical, timbrel and so-called xylophone, as well as the fans and mirrors. The passage deserves rumination, more than our present duty of circumspectly launching Patroni's idea into a certain gentle ordeal of testing allows it to have. But let me stress: (1) Albizzati's own words "saggio" and "sperimentale"; criticism must make him every allowance for the hesitations of a tentative approach; (2) the merit, after all, of that word "derangement" — if it does not have to connote unreason; our need of special circumspection, now that we have gained direction, is just because there is not less than that very degree of change in late Apulian vase-painting, to be measured only by looking back, to be explained only after looking round about; (3) that there is a target for indignant polemic in Albizzati's "sempre gli artefici lavorano senza molto sottilizzare," but also that the right to bombard it has to be earned, and for that, without some looking over the hedge and even some climbing of trees, even the most patient quartering and scrutinizing of the field of late Apulian vase-painting is not sufficient. This is, for one reason, because we are concerned with specific appraisal, at this extroversive turn needing criteria of the subtlety which is certainly to be found, if one does not fail to look where it mostly is, (1) in the *composition* of large many-pictured vases, even the shapes of which (volute kraters, panathenaic amphoras) are arrestingly significant (extroversively!) if they betray not only a special link with Attic tradition but a further web of connections: organic relation (of which other signs exist) to the red-figured pottery of a colony of Tarentum, Greek Heraclea, relation also (not organic, merely as model) to imitative wares which as securely "Lucanian" bear a generic name which, just here, is almost bundle-making, knot-tying, we may feel; was it not over Heraclea that Alexander the Molossian quarreled with his allies, Tarentine, Peucetian and Daunian, in a war against Lucanians mainly? (2) in the range and (especially) the levels of *symbolism*. Perhaps some aspects of this double matter would be better treated in other connections. In our inevitable though still distant "avenue of mythographies" there should be some further room for touching on "moral composition." No very happy phrase: but a good and not distracting, in fact even already quite opportune, example of what I mean would be the bitter fantasia on the theme "reunion" worked up on Munich 3297, pl. 1a: (1) happy ending in an anonymous widower's achieving reunion with his family, set off by (2) happy achievement of a homicidal widower, Herakles with Kerberos already mastered and removable, in which the theme of reunion is outrageously mocked because of the presence of the wife and sons he once slaughtered, now ignores, and will never see again,[1]

---

[1] The family of Herakles is expressly identified on the Naples krater, fig. 11. [T.B.L.W.]

with not inappropriate byplay in (3) the happy-unhappy separation of damned inseparables, Theseus and Peirithoos. To keep my words "not distracting" true there must be no asking at this pass — with any hope of an answer! — how the hero of the master theme of the whole pattern of the picture (the widower so publicly and officially reunited to wife and son at the Civic Centre of the Next World, in the presence of its King and Queen and Judiciary and piquantly near its great Penal Institution) is to be related to all the figures, mundane at the heroon, ultramundane in the strip above it, on the reverse of the same piece (pl. 1b): especially, how he is to be related to the principal figure of another happy ending (as it must be, for Nike, personification of such endings, is present with awards to make), which is being celebrated so privately, in Dionysiac seclusion at the back of the vase's neck (fig. 1b). That is a question which, in a study not unconcerned with ablution pans (of which there are two on this vase's reverse, one at the heroon, one in the limbo above) and proposing (p. 30) to be concerned with the limboes of prepurgation, can be trusted to impose itself at its first convenient occasion. Let us keep now to what is so opportune, so directly bearing on the already importunate "platter-problem" (we cannot pretend it is not there, for all questions about Apulian red-figure are served up on it), the problem "Made where, by whom, for whom, when?" That is not a question which can really be shortened to one word, but asked in malice, in the hope of provoking merely subjective vaporing, it might be insidiously snipt to "Greek?"

Mercifully, for us as we stand, with backs only just turned on Albizzati's provoking chalk-up "this is an art without much subtlety," the answer to the short one could be almost wordlessly objective. Not quite and altogether wordless, for (quite apart from some plays of symbolism requiring explanation to such a challenger's inexperience) the question so put would invite our making signs of counter-invitation to come over and read all the Greek words written in the adscripts of late Apulian mythographies, for comparison in respect of quantity, correctness, mythological erudition, with the amount of Greek that, thanks to Trendall's rakings, we have from the rest of Western red-figure. But our luck is in this, that in regard to the actual challenge, on the point of subtlety, there is a quite apposite foil or touchstone, Attic Greek, available (in due course at due interval) in *each* of the two departments, theme-building and ingenious symbolism, for which the actual claim of subtlety sufficiently Greek for Tarentum was made by me. If here I may take "Greek?" less as a question economically posed than as a challenge granted, a challenge in regard to method and expandable to "so you claim some private gift or wizardry for distinguishing Hellenic from Hellenizing!," then that will suit the latter half of a chapter conducive, evidently, to question but essentially concerned with method. If the need of method includes the need of being *seen* to be neither astray nor taking liberties, especially the liberty of unscrupulous shortcuts, it is here that I must show that in some judgments of quality (above, that late Apulian vase-painting was hardly ever feeble; now, that it was not unsubtle) measurement was done, impressions were not passed off as judgments.

It will be of great practical convenience if we may — as far as possible — separate observations not open to question (once observed!) from the problematic questions, thread-menacing and altogether importunate, which must later be placed where at least they can have their right neighbours, all in the territorial and political situation so far as retrievable (we have not done with Alexander the Less, and shortly there may be some need of reference to the truly great Archytas). Here and now, after the promise of foils and measurement just given, what most urgently presents itself for observation is the Attic counterpart in New York to the Apulian "Underworld" in Munich: this is the upper frieze of the Metropolitan Museum's calyx-krater 08.28.21, and of this part my fig. 10 reproduces L. P. Hall's indispensable drawing (Richter and Hall, pl. 135). To put it to temporarily degrading duty as foil to a composition more intricately *felt* as well as more accomplished cannot, of course, detract from the really great importance of the New York Nekyia; it is of singular interest as anticipating, affording prophetic commentary upon, the *locus classicus* of eschatic reunion, a passage (68 A) of Plato's *Phaedo* — this even if with P. Friedländer and Miss Richter one should halve the correspondence registered by P. Jacobsthal, who did not allow the frieze any mundane pocket, and so let us have Plato's reunion of man and boy as well as Plato's reunion of man and woman, which latter is unmistakably prefigured; she, clasping hands with him, has in her free hand the alabastron of her burial (this it must be, for she is still wearing the jaw-strap of her laying-out). No doubt this Attic krater is one of the things most arresting — not less so than St. Jerome's unconcern with Matthew xxii.30 in his letter to the widow of Lucinius, or St. Thomas More's epitaph, hoping that text no bar to reunion with two wives, or the aspirations of Queen Victoria's will, or what my friend Harold Small contributes for climax, Thomas Hardy's lines promising to become better *worth* rejoining — in the heap of evidence which certifies the hope of ultimate reunion to be simply human, simply natural. Evidence indeed which the Patronian eschatology cannot quite afford to scorn, for (as R. Lattimore's *Themes in Greek and Latin Epitaphs* brought out, pp. 247-250, 342), hope of more than tomb-sharing, assurance of a second life together, is not often clear in the Greek and Latin of the stones. In the famous prayer of Furia Spes (*CIL* vi.3.18817) it is of course movingly so; but generally it is no clearer than in the legend THEY WERE REUNITED of a certain firm's cannily mass-produced borders for double graves in Yorkshire churchyards (though the memory of some seven such graves, as opportunely seen round Wragby church by anyone coming from testing Patroni's eschatology by the Italiote vases of Nostell Priory in the same park, is not unlikely to be lasting). But however grateful we may be for this bonus of wider relevance, let us try to hold down the Attic Nekyia of the New York krater to an ancillary role (not the first which it has served in relation to something more powerful, E. Fraenkel having used its principal's handclasp to defend the MSS reading of *Agamemnon* 1559 against the hug substituted by Porson in the terrible passage in which Clytaemnestra sketches the welcome with which Iphigenia, reunited to the father who killed her, will make up for all the heartlessness of his own burial: see pp. 735f in the third volume of his edition). "Try to hold down" I wrote: for indeed the first effect of the New York krater on being brought up to play foil to the obverse of the Munich krater is to arouse feelings — like the protective feelings Miss Richter had, but stronger — which threaten to abort the comparison proposed. The Attic curiosity puts the Apulian masterpiece, puts Albizzati and our business with his "always unsubtle," out of attention in the appeal of its own artlessness — the picture having just enough weak charm to enlist the decently sensitive person for quite hard work in search of points or configurations to respect; we must agree with Miss Richter that there may have been intention, grim wit even, in the misspelt adscript (Talamedes not Palamedes) for the most conspicuous figure in the inward traffic which the wife of Hades is left to watch while her husband concentrates on the task (of separating inseparables) which Hermes and Herakles have just set him: so far there has been no budging Theseus (on the Apulian krater already persuaded to take his freedom). No doubt even the lifelessness of this painter's style is, given the infernal subject of his upper frieze, not a deadly fault, contributing as it does to an effect which Miss Richter appreciates in the aforesaid traffic, "the feeling of mystery . . . as if the figures were indeed ghosts in another world passing noiselessly to and fro." But the nexus of it all? Will a little more patience with the reunion piece of this ἀμενηνός good at ἀμενηνὰ κάρηνα disclose any patterned offering of ideas and feelings creditably comparable with the striking and self-disclosing one in which the Munich reunion is set? Here, with the Apulian term of the comparison asserting itself and setting the standard, is sufficiently objective riddance, once for all, of the slur "Apulian vase-painting is always unsubtle." But it remains so useful that Albizzati thought so. Let us leave the suggestive slur unerased for long enough: until the proper turn (not to be anticipated for fear of chaos, or at least of Orphistic muddle) for confronting with Attic and other foils the trick, in late "Apulian" vase-painting, of salting mythography with a certain group of essentially ambiguous symbols, in the shape of a thing to play with (catchball) or of things to dance to (timbrel; also Archytas' musical rattle?); means of health or cheerfulness, especially subject to wear or soiling, which are only nuptial because on marriage a girl discards her scuffed or otherwise worn (or just grimy!) possession for a new one. On such things will depend our right to retort with contradiction: "Unsubtle? On the contrary, *late* Apulian red-figure, after the ware's development of chattel-symbolism, is an essentially rather subtle art, with an unmatched *delight* in irony." Meanwhile it would be slovenly to drift away from the New York Nekyia with no answer at all to the question asked about its composition, though to our recent situation, challenged as we were ("subtle enough to be Greek?") about late Apulian red-figure in general and the Munich Nekyia in particular, no answer could have been so relevant as the very question whether the Attic foil presented any integration comparable with the powerfully complicated "fantasia on the theme 'reunion'" which (even without attention to the picture's Orpheus) can be savored in the Apulian counterpart. It is safe, I think, to encourage anyone with a palate for "moral composition" to persevere with the New York Nekyia, exploiting with the aid of *Iliad* ix.525-595 and the franker ending of the same story supplied by Pausanias (x.31.3) the significant dejection and *isolation* of Meleager, separated by three figures form the group of veterans of the Trojan war and by four and six figures respectively from Hades and Persephone, to whom his mother (maddened by his slaying her brother in war) prayed for his death — inflicted, after she had forgotten the prayer, by Apollo, who is present on the same side of this same vase in the lower frieze, taking vengeance on Tityos (almost directly below Meleager) for violence to *his* mother (the figure between him and Tityos). It is not quite safe, I fear, to take the further step which would intensify the Attic foil by removing it altogether out of the sphere of the specific goddess, Aphrodite, of Patroni's *amore elisiaco,* and would (if rightly taken) justify the Metropolitan Museum in henceforth giving its Nekyia krater annually on New York's Mother's Day quite special prominence. Nevertheless, since a quite inexorable condition of effective insight in the study of Tarantine and Heraclean pottery is a perpetual readiness to profit by searching comparisons with the parent ware, we may count it a gain (if only a rebound) to know that the more generous opinion (giving this bad draughtsman but good interweaver full benefit of the doubt) will take the man and woman reunited in the upper frieze to be son and mother, not husband and wife.

Aphrodite's Encroachment: Trade, Alliance and Interchange of Religious Symbolism

THERE WOULD HAVE been a bonus of economy if the comparison just made between one of several Apulian "Underworlds" and its interesting but sapless counterpart in Attic red-figure could have been taken in satisfaction of the promise not to leave unjustified the generalization, that *late* Apulian vase-painting is almost incapable of feebleness. But of course it cannot; "almost" is the now important word, for such a rule will be proved only by its exceptions − if these are few in a long count and have some exploitable significance of their own. There will be none, of course, in work merely unfinished (like the intended front of a krater in Sevres, *CVA* France 13, pl. 37, fig. 1), or *merely* haste-hideous (like too many of the heads of women in the rapid daubing-up of small vases; one may not impute to feebleness the runaway chins of a runaway hand, however telling in another connection, Aphrodite's encroachment upon Dionysos, the suddenly multitudinous vogue of such dashed-off heads may be). For the long count, in the present question and others more important to which I must contrive to make it ancillary, and hundreds of late Apulian vases published in catalogues are not quite enough; we cannot dispense with the medleys (of Apulian red-figure with other wares, mostly figureless) offered us in excavation reports, such as N. Gervasio's for Ceglie del Campo (*Iapigia* 1 [1930] 262-272, figs. 3-17). Miss Scarfi's for M. Sannace at Gioia del Colle (*MonLinc* 45 [1961] cols. 145-332 with tomb groups in figs. 9, 30, 54, 55, 63, 71, 85, 92, 108, 129, 132, 141-143), Mrs. A. M. Chieco-Bianchi Martini's for Conversano (*NS* 1964, pp. 100-176, tomb groups in figs. 4, 10, 11, 12, 22, 24, 30, 32, 35, 43, 50, 78, 80). Such need as there may be to catch late Apulian red-figure at its least vigorous should presumably be served by those tomb groups, where nothing expresses a modern collector's taste, though I have other and perhaps really better reasons for judging that string of references to be not too particular for a place in my text. One is that Miss Scarfi and her editor deserve conspicuous acknowledgement and applause for the new standard in ungrudgingly helpful presentation set by the publication of the pottery found at M. Sannace in that excavation outside the walls (1957). Another is in the practical need of emphasizing promptly − for further development later − how lamingly uncircumstantial is the best knowledge we can have of the great majority of even "provenienced" examples of Apulian red-figure, for lack of the whole message of the set or "service" of red-figured vessels to which, underground with the dead, most museum pieces once belonged. There is perhaps less need of laboring to stress the importance of cemeteries such as the three aforesaid for apprehension of *change,* of the sort we are already so deeply concerned with, new turns of funerary art of perhaps richly mixed significance if political as well as religious fluctuation awaits detection there. In *this* regard it would be silly to say that scholarship has any new art of scrutiny to learn; at any rate, even in the hastiest thumbing-through of Miss Scarfi's and Mrs. Chieco-Bianchi's reports anyone can discern a trend which is certainly an encroachment upon Dionysos, though the encroaching force (the bonneted Goddess with her bonneted Son) never quite overcomes him (even in tomb 3 at Conversano, figs. 12-21 of the publication, he lurks in the symbolical grapes and ivy leaf; as again at tomb 3 of M. Sannace, in Miss Scarfi's figs. 39 and 43; in tomb 2 there, a woman's grave which we have already glanced at for some consideration of its "nuptial" terracottas, the principal vase-painting is still overtly Dionysiac, though if we turn from fig. 9 where these satyr-escorted lovers [?] dominate the tomb-group to figs. 13 and 16, Aphrodite and her son seem not far from ready to take over). Ugly — I would not say weak and provincial — heads of Aphrodite in Miss Scarfi's fig. 13 signal that I have not unlimited leave of absence from duty to a certain generalization. If I could have believed their ugliness homemade, M. Sannace's weakly best rendering of its Aprodita's beauty, would these profiles have made sufficiently cogent exceptions in proof of the rule which I have not been afraid to state, that late Apulian red-figure is never really feeble? To have taken them so would have been a blunder, perhaps a colossal one; but I must accept the reminder that proof is required, and can see, from my Tarentinist point of view, that if the proving is to be by exceptions, the ones most interesting should be those happening to be casual imitations of Tarentine work — if I can detect and adduce any; one region for search, sooner or later, should be that peculiar class on which Gervasio's report for Peucetian Ceglie touched incidentally (*Iapigia* 1, pp. 268f reporting tomb 7; fig. 12 on p. 263), though its catering to provincial taste by its shapes (mostly column-kraters and nestorides) and its acquaintance with the high hats and gaudy shirts of provincial costume are quite compatible with its being on the whole Tarentine. Or at least that is so on the hypothesis which I am defending, that late Apulian red-figure is Tarentum's response to a demand made on it by Italic allies and partners, Peucetians and Daunians allied with this Greek metropolis and its outpost Heraclea (that "last ditch") in a league to keep the Lucanians out of south-eastern Italy, but having even more intimate and indispensable ties in trade, growing the wool that Tarentum worked. For the present let us digest Gervasio's observation that the high hat of the man in the gay shirt on the column-krater of his tomb 7 seems to be of lambskin with the wool left on, and returning to the heads let us add to the pool of charmless profiles one from a chous in tomb 4 Ceglie (Gervasio, fig. 9) and another from a platter in the Eros-dominated tomb 3 Conversano (Chieco-Bianchi, figs. 12 and 19). What for the best purpose in present sight (better than any chasing of significant freaks, however necessary that may continue to be), is the best use we can make of their almost routine ugliness, on my assumption that the vase-painter's instructions were "give them their Aprodita"? If I may postpone any excusing or guarding of explaining which that assumption should have, my answer would be this (at first) rather lame one, that if we are hoping to get the Patronian eschatology, not indeed to a throne, but as near as may be to its due place in the respect of scholars, then one condition of that (and of orderly benching of any attendant straggle of problems) is having and practising a keener sense of setting and sequence than either Patroni, ultra-mundanist, or Macchioro, banalizer, brought to their inconclusive, mainly dust-raising, strife. Neither quite understood the topography of Italiote vase-painting, and neither sought to explain (for neither had measured) the break and revolution marked by late Apulian red-figure. Our luck is that our way, taken (for another reason) through certain cemeteries, has just exposed us to a view of the development in which that break and revolution occurred. Moreover, this has happened in such a way as to expose to *us* something at the heart of a whole complex of historical and topographical questions about the vase-painting of south-eastern Italy, namely the need for curiosity about the relation of Heraclean to Tarentine red-figure (Early Lucanian to Apulian, in an older system of labels); the principal vases of two of the earliest tombs at M. Sannace are of the former sort (tomb 20, no. 1, figs. 132, 135, 136, Pisticci Painter, cf. Trendall, *LCS* 1, no. 66; its no. 2, figs. 132-134, Cyclops Painter, cf. Trendall, 1, no. 92; tomb 4, no. 1, figs. 71-74, Amykos Painter, cf. Trendall, 1, no. 129). Is there insight, or only phrase-making, in such an observation as this, "Tarentine skill is the right hand of the Attic tradition, Heraclean the left"? Was rustic reaction to Heraclean offerings felt at Tarentum (and vice versa)? What happened to Heraclea in the Lucanian wars, with what effect on its ceramic art? Our present duty to these topics is to remain aware of them without letting them distract us from the best use there may be for our pool of profiles, which we dare not quit and neglect, if it is possible that these (with countless others, some less ill-favored and some few more so) represent Aphrodite – as indeed A. Cambitoglou, who has studied these dubiously decorative heads for their value in stylometry, did not fail to suspect (*JHS* 74 [1954] 121). My "dare not" is not meant archly, in allusion to formidable aspects of Aphrodite; I have in mind the place, leading place, which O. Haas had to give *Ana Aprodita* in his brief theology of the Messapian inscriptions of South-Eastern Italy (*Messapische Studien,* pp. 27-51, the order not altogether alphabetical). Let me add to the select group which we compiled from the cemeteries a type, "exceptionally clumsy" as Cambitoglou mildly says (p. 116), characteristic of his Group of London F339 (*JHS* 74 pl. 5a and c; p. 115, fig. 5). It is an appreciable reinforcement of the shield we have been given. The uglier they come the more usefully these profiles rebuke glib objection to our allowing them religious importance. One might have some difficulty, or rather one might have to spend some minutes, with a banalizer of the man and woman (emparadised, from Patroni's point of view) on the pelike which is vase no. 10 of tomb 3, for a man, at M. Sannace (Miss Scarfi's fig. 41); his "since when has Watteau been eschatography?" would require at least an invitation to very careful study of the tomb group in her fig. 30. But "just another pretty girl," perhaps riskable for the less often quite charmless heads on late Campanian vases, will never be said of the larger of the two faces on London F339 or its counterpart at Geneva (Cambitoglou's figs. a and c on his pl. 5). From recent need to refer to a whole *corredo* (of tomb 3 M. Sannace, fig. 30) we have incidentally gained something surely of value for any required gauging of development in the religion of cemeteries, in our having seen in that rich tomb how thoroughly, with conspicuous reiteration, the goddess Aphrodite could put her stamp on the Greek provision for an Italic burial. At least threefold, if I am not mistaken, in that tomb-group: we are given the goddess herself on the lekanis of Miss Scarfi's fig. 44 and the platter of fig. 49; her son (in the new, "foolproofed for our neighbors," bonneted and earringed type) on the nuptial lebes of fig. 45 and the skyphos of fig. 47; their swan inside the kylix of fig. 49. Or fourfold? My own reckoning would be more cautious, excluding the two "filles en fleur," one on the neck of the krater, figs. 30 and 37, the other on an alabastron, fig. 36, there are good reasons for guessing that there may be more whimsy than resigned catering to neighbors' religious fads in the heads (sometimes wearing a Phrygian cap, though not at M. Sannace) that erupt from the central flowers of symmetrical tangles of ornament in the naturalistic yet essentially protean and capricious style which is among the innovations of late Apulian vase-painting, inviting comparison with *carparo* sculptures. For me, one of those reasons, perhaps almost as good as the Phrygian caps unbecoming an Aphrodite of ultramundane match-making, is that such heads are infinitely less blighted by boredom, so much so that Miss Scarfi thought two of them worthy of admission to her only colored illustration (her pl. 1), and one of those worthy of repetition there (her figs. 1 and 4).

I must reserve comment on the one flower-borne head which has an adscript; incised, and rather roughly (so by a retailer, or by the purchaser, not in the potter's shop?), but the publication (H. Jucker, "Das Bildnis im Blätterkelch," fig. 127) leaves no doubt of its being the same word, to be translated *Aura*, as is neatly painted on the scarf of personified Sea Breeze, placed opposite Eros on a famous skyphos in Sydney, a vase which to any mind with room for both the story of Prokris and the eschatological association of *refrigerium* must seem to have been given the message "To you where you are, refreshment, with love!" (Trendall, *LCS*, p. 70 Sydney 53.30, pl. 33, 1-2).

Does all this imply that in the profiles blighted, or liable to blight, the Aphrodites as I take most of them to be, there is submalicious intent, comparable with an element detectable on some Attic black-figured vases made for export, in the meaningless inscriptions of cups and other vessels, in the subtler impudence of quite empty mannerism in pictures by the Affecter (for all that, a great favorite abroad, as has been remarked,[1] *Gnomon* 30, 363), and again in the cynically ragged ugliness of the latest black-figured cups? That is not an unwelcome question, giving as it does opportunity for drawing a double distinction (one within another) not unnecessary to the hopeful view of late Apulian red-figure which I am trying to present, my idea that some of its grievous difficulties for scholars (including what is paradoxical in its rarity at Spina and in Spain) almost vanish when the ware is understood as the result of a peculiarly close interdependence of shared prosperity (of course only gradually consolidated) between Tarentum and a few pastoral places of the uplands northward, none more distant than the one, Canusium, which Pliny happens to couple with Tarentum in the context of his tribute to Apulian wool (*laudatissima,* viii.190). On the one hand, in

---

[1] By Smith himself. [J.K.A.]

the last thirty or forty years of the fourth century B.C. the old Attic sport of teasing the unknowable (or should I have said the uncertain?) from a great distance was not for any vase-painter employed at what is now Taranto by a trade which had grown to colossal prosperity by being enterprisingly responsive to the mortuary requirements of exploiters of what is now Le Murge — exploitable (if one must comprehend the whole "symbiosis") on an increasingly great scale only because a great and thriving Greek metropolis (soon to begin its decline, but now at its acme), with command of the lower Adriatic (and more), was in a position to collect, work and internationally sell its wool. At the same time, to complete my distinction, we are not to suppose that everything in this relationship was so congenial to the Tarentine artists as the opportunity to teach (if only fleetingly and piecemeal, to Paucetian and Daunian and some Messapian executors as they buried their dead) all and more than all the mythology so copiously illustrated from "Apulian" vases in our works of reference. The later the phase, the grosser folly it would be to look in Tarentine vase-painting for irresponsibly mischievous sport at the customers' expense; but we may well be alert for interesting symptoms of constraint, sighs of distaste for some imposed preference. These Greeks had had to take some correction from those Italic executors, the formers' theology (and tinge of philosophy?) not having been so perfectly acceptable as their legends. Unless I am mistaken, what the latter rejected was a not quite simple matter; if we had to make a symbol for it this might perhaps be a thyrsos-head crossed with stlengis (strigil, scraper). In part it was an "overpromotion" of Dionysos and his satellites, but in some part too an unwelcome idea or interest which the once Pythagorean atmosphere of Tarentum had fostered there and at Heraclea; pending better explanation I can only call it "eugenic love," republishing in my pl. 6, the most remarkable of several manifestations of it, on a lekythos in Torino (Eros with the switch of a palaestric trainer or umpire, sitting on a block daubed with the Pythagorean sign for health, pentagram, "blessing" a young couple).

Functions of "Greek" Dionysos and "Messapian" Aprodita— the "Bonneted" Eros

BOTH ELEMENTS CAN, be studied in the earlier tomb-groups of M. Sannace and Conversano (*MonLinc* 45, 231-235, *NS* [1964] 137-138), but among the indispensable documents (on the Dionysiac side of this matter) are two stray bell-kraters, Lecce 623 from Carovigno, attributed by Cambitoglou and Trendall to their Lecce Painter (my pl. 8a) and Lecce 620 from Rudiae-Rugge (my pl. 8b) given to their Hoppin Painter. At this first opportunity to notice the snub administered, it will be seen that Patroni's nuptial eschatology of reunion (or simply, union) is not *here* in jeopardy. Far from it: evidently the gravest objection to the earliest funerary vases made at Tarentum or Heraclea for Italic burials was that the function of nextworldly match-making had been denied to its proper goddess (it is piquant that Carovigno is source of an *Aprodita* inscription; Parlangeli no. 5.12 or Haas no. B.1.27, as well as that "objectionable" vase), and made over to Dionysos; an upstart all the worse (from the point of view of a surviving parent or husband) for the bad company he kept. On both these kraters it is Dionysos who "gives away" the bride to her husband, and on the one from Carovigno there is exceptionally firm indication of a Dionysiac paradise; of all the women in Apulian red-figure deposited on rocks to be picked up by a young man is there any who seems more dumped and dazed and altogether disearthed, and of all the rocks so sat on is there any more weedily like that which Dionysos himself occupies in the classic Italiote picture of his thiasos from Ceglie del Campo (Trendall, *LCS* 1, no. 280, pl. 24, by the Karneia Painter, one of the men now thought by T. to have worked both at Heraclea and at Tarentum)? One of the best services of O. Haas to Italiote studies is his having prepared us in the theological section of his *Messapische Studien* for appreciation of the blunder of those Tarentine and Heraclean artists. Haas was aware of the importance of Dionysos at Tarentum (p. 14); believing it scarcely possible that he had none among Tarentum's neighbors, Haas had reserved for him third place (after Aphrodite in the first place and Athena in the second) in his pantheon for the Messapian inscriptions (p. 34ff); but this throne was never really filled, for the best efforts of Haas to find Dionysos named produced only *kretaaihi oikoroihi* – a dubious Zagreus, and only that if the words could be garbled Greek and mean "to Cretan Guardian of the House" (pp. 37-39, his B.1.16, Ribezzo's *CIM* 130; in support of his ignoring B.1.45 see my p. 00).[1] Of course it would be stupid to make too much either of the epigraphic vacuum or of Dionysos' ceramic recession; on the one hand, there can be little doubt that the inscriptions composed in the Messapian language mark (on the map) a pocket of special recalcitrance (against Greek, and later against Latin); in the Peucetio-Daunian region of Tarentum's best customers for its pottery, from Gnathia to Canusium, there is not the dense peppering that darkens the heel of Italy in O. Parlangeli's chart for the Messapian inscriptions (*Studi Messapici*, pl. 1) and it is not even clear (as Parlangeli notes, pp. 11-13) that the language of the comparatively few inscriptions collected for the former region is quite identical with the language of those, further to the South-East, in which a name for Aphrodite is significantly frequent and where the absence of any name for Dionysos is more telling than it is towards the North-West, in the fewer inscriptions of Peucetia and Daunia. And on the other hand, as I have already said, and need now to stress (lest such deposits as those of tombs 3 and 5 at Conversano should make a grossly false impression), Aphrodite

---

[1] Apparently never written. [J.K.A.]

never banishes Dionysos from the funerary vases of Apulian red-figure; she just asserts herself, and of course it is highly interesting that the chthonic goddess thus cropping up is not an Eleusinian divinity corresponding to the goddess conspicuous in the Messapian inscriptions of the North-Western region, *Damatira* at Vieste, *Damatyra* at Rubi-Ruvo (Parlangeli, pp. 33-34, Haas, pp. 44-45, no. B.1.35) and in the South-East sharing importance with Aphrodite (at Uria-Oria, Rudiae-Rugge, also Gnathia-Fasano perhaps: Parlangèli's nos. 9.14 and 9.23, cf. 9.29; 16.15, cf. 16.111; 3.27 and 3.215, perhaps cf. 3.25). In all those mushrooming heads of her, no doubt Aphrodite would have been less surely recognizable without the role which, in significantly close relation to them, in tomb-groups or on single vases, is given to Eros – the new Eros, by no means hermaphrodite but so very carefully distinguished, more by what he is made to wear than by the new hips, from the previous type, that of the too sturdy Eros who pipes for an eugenic affair, stlengis-displaying athlete introduced to girl, on a Heraclean bell-krater by the Cyclops Painter from a burial at Rubi-Ruvo (M. Jatta, *Iapigia* 3 (1932) 244, fig. 27b; Trendall, *LCS*1, no. 93) and of many more Erotes, hulkingly like him, in the same Amycan group. What most distinguishes the new Eros from the old is that, from the neck up, wearing necklace, earrings, and *bonnet*, "he" is indistinguishable (as Cambitoglou noted, *JHS* 74, 121) from the mushrooming heads, which cannot however be meant for his in the absence of some sign of his wings (corresponding to what is required for abbreviations of Nike, as in Cambitoglou's fig. 2). Thus, given moreover that an explicit adscript is not lacking for identification of the new and effeminate type with Eros (*BullNap* 5, pl. 6, fig. 1), it is most unlikely that, if, in those heads which are not obviously Nike's, one of Nike's fellow-goddesses is meant, anyone but the mother of Eros is meant in the heads which (1) seem to have originated on the lids of vases of two sorts belonging to her domain, the nuptial lebes and the lekanis (Cambitoglou and Trendall, p. 48, no. 18, p. 82, nos. 19 and 20); (2) in a still later phase can loom huge on large vases, yet (at least once) with Eros on the back of the piece reminding us of that region of origin (col. kr. Berkeley 8.2320, my pl. 9a and b); (3) are associable with one of the earliest appearance of the bonneted Eros (compare the entries, nos. 19 and 20, just cited for Cambitoglou's Lampas Painter's heads, with the same craftsman's no. 2 as published by C. in *BSR* 19 [1951] pl. 5, 3); (4) are, in the vase-paintings within particular tomb-groups, combined so *systematically* with figures of Eros, the system having more than one thread; the family threading is most unmistakable and significant when the family's pet water-bird supplements mother and son, as in tomb 4 Ceglie (*Iapigia* 1, 257, fig. 9) and tomb 3 M. Sannace (*MonLinc* 45, 181, fig. 30); since we are so much concerned with and for Patroni's eschatology, the nuptial threading should be not less interesting – in both tombs specifically nuptial vessels, a lebes and a lekanis, with Eros on the former and a head of Aphrodite on the latter. But we have reached a point at which a random clotting of topics threatens. In the least I can do to prevent that happening to ideas which have arisen from or have been improved by the opportunity to collate tomb-groups, namely the very minimum of *sorting*, by pairs of at least related topics, I am compelled to take for the first pairing what the Amsterdam pan (pl. 10) forces upon us. For, unless I am mistaken in my impression that in the dead drawing of the Eros inside and the wasting of paint on the android handle there is neither Tarentine work nor modern forgery, we have a bonanza here. In this delighted and (apart from the turning of long streaks of pebbles into short incrustations of jewelry, like pearly roller skates) accurate imitation of the new Eros ("our *Aprodita's* own boy at last, thank you for being so adaptable, thank you for him"), pairing may register the required complement to that boredom of the Greeks with their best customers' call for so much, too much, of his mother. But moreover, in the style is there not something which I may tender in at least partial satisfaction of an offer of proof by exception that Apulian red figure (as we call it) is — at its late acme under a special stimulus — significantly incapable of merely feeble work? Not that this exhausts the promise of help from feeble foils; apart from any further discussion the Amsterdam pan may require, it must be obvious that only through some similar contrast with a really provincial godsend can there be any corroboration of my assumption that we may treat as no less Tarentine than the rest of late Apulian red-figure even the most "locally colored" pieces, having a shape either native (nestoris) to the sheep-raising uplands, or naturalized there (column-krater) in a significant supersession such as Gervasio has illustrated (*Iapigia* 1, pp. 19, 266-269), and giving us pictures of the sheep-raisers, under hats sometimes wooly and in (always prudishly "step-in") shirts commonly gaudy (with Tarentum's murex?). There is material for the requisite contrast, to which I had better refer before going further in precautionary pairing: see pl. 41, top row, of *CVA* France 13, a godsend indeed: the nestoris no. 21 (figs. 2 and 3) Tarentine, the smaller nestoris no. 20 (figs. 1 and 4) provincial imitation; with rejection, be it noted, of any idea of eschatic union such as is lurking, perhaps, in the festive scamper on the other; between the woman and the man it is not "amore elisiaco" but mere "amore funebre," for he, seated on the landscape under a garbled diptych doubly misunderstood — repeated from the diptych's proper place on the vase's other side — is unmistakably dead, *only* he, as the woman's gesture of grief is to tell us. "Campanien" at the foot of that plate is a slip, for everything there is (in the conventional usage) Apulian. But I may count it lucky that opposite, on pl. 40 of the Sevres fascicle, there is a most opportunely Campanian bell-krater, making two islands (figs. 21 and 25) in a sea of Apulian Aphrodite heads? There could be no apter last words for this paragraph than a reference to its relative charm.

Change in Nature of Satyrs
and Nymphs:
Their Relationship to the "New" Eros
and Symbols of "Elysian" Love

MAY I CONTINUE, a procedure that should eventually lead up to topics proposed for later examination, the pairing which began with (1) the Tarentine
and Italic sides of a theological adjustment in the art which Tarentum was
prepared to supply for the funerary demands, becoming immensely lucrative,
of the religion imprecisely Hellenized? Of which it may be said, subject to
proper reserves (for inscriptions not yet dated and for a spatial "extrapolation" already acknowledged), that it had adopted the name of Aphrodite for
its great chthonic goddess without having been effectively schooled to
connect with either power a winged son and agent, and so was not quite
ready for any but the "easiest" (most monstrously Aphrodite-like) Eros; nor
had it been given any inclination to subordinate its great goddess to Dionysos, whose chthonic importance at Tarentum is advertised to us by
funerary terracottas (unless those males, often with his cut of beard and
nearly always with his length of mitra, have been misinterpreted). At such a
place as Rubi-Ruvo Dionysos and all his thiasos may have been very well
known, *visually,* long before the middle of the fourth century B.C., as we
may grant on the general evidence of Attic vases, black-figure as well as
red-figure, in the Jatta collection there (though in antiquity perhaps not long
enough above ground, any single one of them, to stamp an exact impression). But nothing on the Attic imports or on the earliest Italiote vases had
been much preparation for eagerly instant trust in Dionysos for bliss after
death. Some early Heraclean vases had even suggested that a paradise served
by his minions might have its alarms (for one, the principal piece in tomb 4,
M. Sannace, Miss Scarfi's figure 73; the pursuer of the nymph is not
ithyphallic, but a satyr still frankly if puzzlingly so can be caught on a
skyphos from a now famous tomb at Heraclea itself, figs. 27-28 facing p. 11
of what had made it famous, Nevio Degrassi's publication of its vases, some
of them magnificently mythographic, *BdA* 50 (1965) and *RM* Erg. hft. 11,
pl. 71,3. (2) By a natural transition, we are already at another suggestive
pairing in the contrast, needing closer observation than it got in our look at
the Dionysiac triad Pl. 2, of the Iphigenia krater, between the long-tradi-
tional type of satyr just exemplified, quite wild and free save for the duty or
habit of attendance upon Dionysos, and its eventual supplanter in the
funerary vase-painting of more than one region of Southern Italy — the tame

satyr, lackey of the dead, such as passes cakes in the Elysian reverse of the Underworld krater in Naples, and even (on a rather late Lucanian lekythos in Munich) acts as ball-boy in a playground for mixed recreation, an assignment quite in keeping with the provision for ball-playing suspended above men, women and satyrs on a perhaps Campanian pyxis in Lecce (not to mention actual play going on between men and women – the latter in a perhaps even worse than Victorian handicap of dress – in the however satyrless paradise on the wall of a Roman tomb, *AA* [1957] fig. 37).

Like the Italiote catchball when nested in its looped cradle, this is a matter with more than one handle. The best for taking it up should be the observation that this development does not occur in the Dionysiac vase-painting of Athens, since attention to that (what there is required for characterization of Dionysos, what his satyrs and nymphs there have and do, whom D. entertains, especially, all this, in Attic red-figure of the fourth century B.C.) is the beginning of profitably *curious* study of the corresponding department of Italiote vase-painting. The former goes on and on without taking in ordinary mortals on clearly paradisal terms (indeed there is something rather like a counter-development; from the time of Exekias well into the second half of the fifth century, Dionysos is allowed one tailless male attendant with perfectly human ears, nose, and feet; but suddenly the Kadmos Painter is found applying Exekias' adscript for this person, Oinopion, to a regular satyr: Beazley, *ARV²* p. 1184, no. 1). Not that Athens lacked a Dionysiac – at any rate, an Iacchic – paradise, but art was shy of it, and poetry could be ironic. It is an almost indigestibly rich irony of Aristophanes' *Frogs* (and richest for us, so much concerned with the god's importance in the eschatology of the Italiote Greeks and even more concerned with an eschatic need of Italic men and women for each other's company) that Dionysos, entering the roast-pork-scented paradise of the mystai, does not know that he is the Iacchos invoked by this company of blessed men and women nor do they (316-436): the latter with more excuse, for Dionysos should know (and has claimed to know, 75-82) his Sophocles, *who did identify him with Iacchos,* in the very passage which declares him patron of *the Italiote Greeks* (*Antigone* 1115-1152). Perhaps the cream of it is that an effeminate, even bisexual, Dionysos-Iacchos, sponsored by the Orphic Hymn to Mise (no. 42), could have been fetched in from the heel of Italy to impersonate the "new" Eros of Apulian red-figure, if only there had been less risk in O. Haas' (only tentative) restoration of the initial letter required to make *misai* in an inscription of Rudiae-Rugge marked with an Eleusinian symbol and honoring (in any case) one other Eleusinian deity (his B.1.45). But Degrassi's publication of the Italiote vases for a burial at Heraclea (*BdA* [1965] pp. 5-37) happens to offer something of more particular importance: the question whether our present pairing and contrast, of the old with a new type of satyr, can be illustrated in a single grave (and so at a turning-point) from the pair of skyphoi published opposite his p. 11.

There can be no doubt that the ithyphallic one of Degrassi's skyphos no. 12 (fig. 27) is of the old, irresponsible type. About his relation to the athlete on the other side of it (fig. 28) we are not called to rack our brains. But his relation to another satyr (not ithyphallic) capering on no. 11 the companion piece (fig. 25), with tympanon in his left hand and something puzzling in his right, poses a problem really crucial, for Degrassi did well to be dissatisfied with the only guess he printed (p. 19, "piccolo otre?") for the thing in this second satyr's right hand. There would have been no crux, no dilemma threatening Orphic rigmarole, if that object had been even in the least like a wineskin, and therefore readable as contribution of a little drink, to go with provision of a little food brought by the scampering nymph opposite (if nymph she is) in her not very roomy "cofanetto" (fig. 26). Then this creature would have been a satyr of the old sort, ready for some revel — in view of the timbrel in his other hand, one would have specified whatever may be the unaffectedly English equivalent of *gouter dansant*. That may not be, yet to take this stemmed thing as a pan, comparable with one held by the satyr in the Dionysiac vignette above the Munich "Reunion in Hades" (my fig. 1b), would be wrong for the time and the place if I may press my own opinion that the ablution pan (at least as we have already seen it in vase-painting, and as we shall continue to find it there, always with loops sticking up from the rim) is peculiar to late Apulian work.

Likelihood that a mirror is meant in Degrassi's fig. 25 seems to be reinforced by the object, unmistakably a mirror of a certain peculiarly embellished type, held by a satyr standing alone, with a wreath in the other hand, on an earlyish skyphos, Apulian, in Milan (*CVA* Italy 31 IV D, pl. 12, no. 269; on the other side, woman with thyrsos, standing not less quietly than the satyr). Altogether this reminds us of what Miss Erika Simon has quite justifiably made of mirror-brandishing satyrs on Campana plaques some three or four centuries later in date — namely something really Orphic, in the sense at least of reflecting a ritual known to have claimed Orpheus' authority. If that be an unwelcome reminder, we have a choice of two hatches of escape from being forced to recognize, in the mirror of Degrassi's fig. 25, bait for the Dionysos-Zagreus of some passion-charade in which satyrs (like Miss Simon's) were cast for the part of deicidal Titans in ambush. One would be by way of a certain roundabout insistence on the Greekness of Heraclea ("why not *pan after all*? the bowls of all real pans were like that, with plain loopless rims; what need of 'footnotes' — explanatory ex- crescences borrowed from footbasins — in the work of a man addressing Heracleotes, Greeks in spite of the syncopating roughness of ΣΦIPAN on a Naples krater and now ΓΟΣΔΑΝ on the pelike that is no. 8 of the present tomb-group, fig. 38 and p. 15 — not to mention a further contrast with Tarentine accuracy in the female breasts given, as Degrassi noticed, to Sarpedon and perhaps to Glaukos on the hydria no. 1, fig. 5, p. 6?").

I find this not quite satisfying. No doubt there is acuteness in any recognition of the decided *suburbanity* of Heraclea that is also recognition of so much more: for one thing, of a certain gulf between the Sub-Thurian Sub-Tarentine compatriots of Zeuxis, even at their rustiest in what was destined to become a frontier fort, and the chief Italic customers of Tarentine potteries, even at their wealthiest and most educable: suspectable, those latter, of having been the stolidest folk of Southern Italy (on the evidence of their demure best, at Canusium, in the terracottas that teem on the bloated askoi, and in the corresponding wall-painting: the crudest work of the South-*West*, on the wildest Campanian pottery and bloodiest Paestan walls, is more alive and enterprising). Welcome, also, was that incidental grasp of the need of some peculiar and modifying stylization of the pan if its import in vase-painting as a symbol of purification was not to be lost in confusion with a common type of mirror (for which, in catalogues, it has rather often been mistaken, by minds less excusingly ovine than that of a rich Daunian rancher). The ideal stylization for that purpose has, I acknowledge, been hit in the guess that the "explanatory excrescences," the two loops or arches, are an addition to the sluicing-pan borrowed from a type of footbasin. I think that the London "Solemn Marriage of Hades" (pl. 5a), when we come to it, will offer something only a little short of fullest confirmation of that conjecture. Anyhow, those excrescenses would deliver their warning by a license of *excess* pardonable in a symbol of complete purification: pardonable at least in a world that had lost the bronze-age bathtub and now bathed (from head to *foot*) at a pedestaled basin and especially excusable along coasts thereof which research, mainly Austrian, has shown to be relatively spongeless; altogether, the composite says: "lest you should take me for a mirror, I remind you of the *rest* of what is needed (besides high laver and pan) for a thorough bath taken standing." But, with all due gratitude for some profitable considerations aired, and with every hope of making use of them sooner or later, I think I can justify my distrust of the notion that what Degrassi took hesitantly for an askos of wine, in the right hand of the satyr of his fig. 25, should be read as a "realistic" sluicing-pan, dispensing at keen Greek Heraclea with the "footnotes" inserted on the ablution pan held by the satyr in the Dionysiac vignette (my fig. 1b) of the "Underworld" krater in Munich, made at equally Greek Tarentum, but for its trade with dull Daunian Canusium. The risk involved in taking this thing for a *mirror*. namely the risk of encouraging a fantastically Orphistic idea of the whole tomb-group, the view of it that is already invited by the doings with a ball, tufts of wool, and a kalathos in the upper picture (Degrassi's fig. 13) of the fourth of six (!) hydrias in this burial at Heraclea-Policoro, is greatly reduced if we have observed, and now use our right to emphasize, all the play that is made in this tomb-group with the twofold symbolism of nubility: a system already (my p. 24) quite familiar, palaestric scraper for the man, mirror for the nubile woman.

Begin this with the lower picture (Degrassi's fig. 14) of that same hydria;

do not the first three figures (left to right), by affording a key to the puzzles that were set by the skyphoi (D., figs. 25-28), offer to counteract the first impression made by the upper storey (a false impression in my judgment, though ball and unspun wool were Dionysos-bait in the myth, no less than the notorious mirror, and though dropping the bait in a kalathos is attested for a rite based on the myth)? In the lower storey (D., fig. 14) the nubile boy, scraper in his right hand, overtakes the girl thanks to a satyr's checking her flight to put a box into her left hand. But where is the girl's badge of nubility, her mirror to match his stlengis? That is a question which the planner of the whole tomb-group's eschatography may have asked at the counter (if any) of the pottery shop. In any case, I am satisfied that Degrassi's fig. 25 answers it; the satyr who on his side of the skyphos (no. 11) balances the woman (with box!) of fig. 26 is surely another of these abettors of ultra-mundane lovers; his mirror is not for some Orphic mumbo jumbo, nor even for awaking some courtable nymph to her own beauty, for where is there evidence that Dionysiac nymphs so stand on ceremony? The box proffered on the hydria said "now that he has caught you, here's your bridal paraphernalia"; the mirror and the timbrel of the satyr on this first of the two skyphoi say, respectively, "let her take this, and know she is ripe for catching," "rely on me for noisy celebration of the catch." All that is clinched by the second skyphos; in Degrassi's fig. 28 behold (again) the youth of this match-making, scraper in hand, nubile: "admirably so," the satyr of the reverse seems to be telling us, in his conservative idiom. "The old rough stuff": that, or an equivalent phrase, heads a set of cards, I cannot doubt, in the box of every card-filing student of revolutionary change in the religion that is allowed to come to the surface of Italiote and South—Italic grave-gods, in welcome contrast to Attic secretiveness; no doubt also, every such student has had the thought "what a triumph it would be to catch and register the *last* satyr to be ithyphallic in south Italian vase-painting!" Perhaps here, in Degrassi's fig. 27 for this side of the skyphos which is no. 12 in his inventory for this Heraclean grave, we have caught the last in the Heraclean line. But chronometry, awarding of lasts and first, is for the comprehensive stylometrist (Trendall, our master in stylometry, has put both skyphoi in the second of three compartments for vases of that shape in his Reggio Group, *LCS* 1, nos. 310 and 311, without intending any very precise pinning, either in time or in stylistic relation to the Dionysiac paradise which on Degrassi's hydria no. 4 [his fig. 14] shares the new tame, subservient, actually lady's-maiding, type of satyr with the skyphos from the same grave which is Degrassi's no. 11, Trendall's no. 310; Trendall's place for the hydria, at no. 290, acknowledges at least affinity with the style of those skyphoi, which indeed he assigns to the same workshop; see his general remarks on the tomb-group in the introduction to the fourth section of ch. 1 of *LCS* 1. That at any rate there is a satyric *turning-point* to register in this tomb-group needs no more laboring, but as we are at the verge of what needs to be said about the relation of the taming of satyrs to the bonneting of Eros, it is opportune to add that the skyphoi of the Degrassi tomb as it may deservedly be called have, in their Reggio Group, the company of the most wholesomely virile of all Italiote Erotes, with the attribute of a trainer of athletes [switch] and seated on a palaestric block [such as has been found provided, for a privileged spectator of another sort, at Olympia], this bedoodled with the Pythagorean symbol of health; see Trendall's no. 318, squat lekythos Torino 4427, my pl. 6, after *CVA* Italy 32 IV d, pl. 1).

A question of great interest, and perhaps in some fashion answerable, is whether the satyrs and nymphs who wait on the dead in the Dionysiac paradise are beatified servants. It is certainly not a vainly fanciful question, for there are inscriptions to consider. But it must be postponed to its due place after a far more important consideration. For surely the prime importance of the Degrassi grave at Heraclea-Policoro is in doing so much to explain what, to our taste, is the prime abomination, and for our scholarship is perhaps the prime enigma, of late Apulian red-figure, its "new" Eros, like Aphrodite from the neck upward, necklaced, earringed, bonneted, often enough met in visible association with her and unquestionably the agent of her traffic in equipping brides. To some degree, as we have already seen, that effeminate Eros may be Tarentum's concession to dissatisfaction with, or obtuseness in regard to, the older and ephebic type of Eros. "You do not see what those 'athletic louts' can have to do with your great *Aprodita*? Take this then (and may 'he' sicken you)." But still more is it, I judge, the result of horrified objection, by Messapian, Peucetian, Daunian customers of Heraclea and Tarentum, to something in the Dionysiac paradise by no means expurgated (at Heraclea itself) from the Degrassi grave's picture of it, where (low on the fourth of six hydrias, Degrassi's fig. 14) a satyr forces the match and equips the bride of this eschatic union; it is no great mitigation that this satyr has (in his conspicuous thyrsos) a badge of authority, or that he is less indecently cordial than the perhaps epoch-closing satyr on one of the skyphoi of this burial. I must not unduly and confusingly anticipate the correlative "benching" of topics promised for a fitter place. But already, approaching an eschatological frontier, between Dionysos' zone and Aphrodite's, we cannot be too circumspectly and concretely objective and discriminating. It is not irrelevant that of the present (South-Eastern) matter there is a Western annex. *Mutatis mutandis,* spear for scraper as symbol of male nubility, fillet for box or cylindrical basket as the outfitting satyr's present, eagerness instead of an affectation of trapped alarm on the girl's part, patience instead of predatory rush on the man's part, the preliminaries of Elysium on a Campanian hydria that is rather early, being a work of Trendall's Painter of B.M. F63, are a most noteworthy match for the satyr-abetted wooing on the aforesaid Heraclean piece. Especially so if the former (Cambridge, Fitzwilliam Museum no. 248) is allowed its proper supplement, hydria by the same painter in the Museo Provinciale of Salerno, on which a satyr with the like badge of authority (and certain curious trappings) offers a box garnished with little pastries to a girl "holding mirror and fillet" — as Trendall in the commentary for his fig. 8 describes her on p. 37 of the first issue of V. Panebianco's *Apollo;* add, if I am not astray in a mirage of nuptial symbolism, "and small catchball." The Cambridge hydria is very accessible in *CVA* Gr. Br. 6, pl. 44, 1, where it is conveniently near two or three foils, pl. 46, 1 a-b and 2, eschatic courting as late Apulian red-figure has it, not trusting the satyrs of Elysium for any ministrations to women, nubile or renubile — for the first of those two Apulian pelikai is one of many Tarentine vases of this particular shape on which repetition, repetition with an "otherworldly" difference, in the relation of reverse to more mundane obverse hints reunion. But the ideally helpful publication of the Cambridge vase is Trendall's in *Apollo* 1 (1961) pp. 34f, figs. 6f, from which one has only to turn the page to the Salerno hydria in fig. 8; the very large scale of fig. 6 leaves no doubt that the Cambridge satyr has not the trappings which accordingly require us to keep his Salerno counterpart in view for further inspection and comment. The republications in Trendall's *LCS* pls. 124, pl. 125 fig. 1, I have not yet seen. Before returning — if there be opportunity — to the more general question whether our sociologists should be alerted to these Elysian satyrs — if their ministrations imply the beatification, second class, of domestic servants — the Salerno satyr must have the rest of all the scrutiny he deserves. I have said, more than once, that what is most interesting in the revamped Eros of late Apulian vase-painting begins at the neck, in his having thence upwards what his mother has, necklace, earrings, woman's headdress. That ignored all his lower adornments: justifiably, it is now seen, for they were so little (or so loosely) characteristic of Eros that now we find every one of them on this flat-faced and horse-eared satyr: not merely the beady bandolier (which on him could be discounted as Dionysiac διάζωσις, whatever that, in a famous inscription, really may be?), but also the anklets, the bracelets, and the thing I have to call a thigh-garter. I should be the last to claim complete understanding of all this (lower) trumpery, but evidently it has to do with the glitter and pomp of marriage, for one can see almost all of it on figures that appear to be in the situation of a bridegroom, however little their "hardware" might seem to suit intimacies of the bridal night (second figure from the left in the main picture on another Campanian hydria, Trendall's no. 112 at Reggio Calabria from Gizzeria, inv. no. 8781, in his·Kneeling Eros Group, *LCS,* part 1 of book 2 for Campanian, pl. 87, 4-6; compare with him the youth in less mundane circumstances, waiting to claim a rock-sitter on yet another Campanian hydria, *CVA* Romania 1, pl. 38, fig. 2, Bucarest inv. no. 03360, no. 72a in part 2 for early Capuan in the same book of *LCS,* given by Trendall to his Seated Nike Painter). Though there is no satyr on the Capuan vase parenthetically mentioned (Aphrodite, in person, is the match-maker?), that hydria is so curiously a counterpart to the middle-Apulian krater in Lecce (my pl. 8a) on which Dionysos is the match-maker at another pickup from the rocks that it seems to give us leave to attend to the signals of the satyric "lady's-maid" on the Salerno hydria of Trendall's Painter of B.M. F63, though as a Campanian this artist is rather far from the region of our concern with a Peucetio-Daunian rebellion against some ways of Heraclean and Tarentine caterers to luxurious burial. We must not, of course, be dazzled by the luxury of the Degrassi tomb at Heraclea itself into forgetting that (for some time: until the Lucanian menace made it a place of danger?) Heraclea rivalled Tarentum in supplying funerary pottery to the wool-wealthy uplands; Rubi-Ruvo, where the most acclaimed master-piece of early Tarentine ware, the Sisyphos krater, was found yielded also the vase that gave the first of three successive clues by which it was established that the Amykos Painter (a contributor to the splendor of the Degrassi tomb) had belonged, proudly, to Heraclea. Nor must we fail to give due heed to Trendall's recent warning against drawing a line too hard and fast between Heraclean and Tarentine red-figure; the Amykos Painter's heraldic hints seem to tell us "I like it here; I am not sorry to have left Thurii, and I have not the least desire to move on eastward to the Big City," yet he and other Heracleote artists may have been forced to do so, as Trendall acknowledges in the introduction to book 1 of his *LCS* (though I must not claim his blessing for my own inclination to connect this with Tarentum's loss of Archytas, and a weakening of the Western defenses of her little empire after the death of this effective statesman and general about the middle of the fourth century B.C.). But that is in parenthesis, and is not to keep the more eloquent of the two bride-equipping satyrs of the Campanian Painter of B.M. F63 from his message. Best in *oratio recta:* "There was never, for anything from my potter's Campanian shop, the slightest chance of crossing the Apennines, either to please or to shock Peucetian or Daunian or Messapian probatocrats with women to bury. But if you have not understood how the satyrs of Heraclean or early Tarentine red-figure *caused* the effeminate Eros of late Tarentine vase-painting's *adjustment* to Italic disgust, look from Aphrodite to him and from him to me; in what I am wearing, from below my neck to my ankles, I am as much like him as he is like his mother in what he is wearing above his shoulders. His work (with women only) is that half of my work, preparing women for Elysian unions, which the Salerno hydria illustrated; you will find Tarentine satyrs still employed in preparing men."

I take this to be not very far from the truth of the matter. It seems to find illustration in a middle region of Apulian (Tarentine) vase-painting which not long ago (1964) Karl Kerényi explored interestingly. For there the "adjust-ment to Italic disgust" can be seen in process (*Hommages à Jean Bayet,* pp. 334ff, figs. 1-3, 7-13; may I interpolate, before the Bonn pelike of his fig. 7, the Catania chous no. 746 published on pl. 85 of G. Libertini's *Museo Biscari* — for then we shall see, in a painting of almost identical style, the satyr whom the Bonn Eros has displaced from the little procession?). Of course Kerényi's own view of the Heraclean and Apulian part of what he surveyed is not to be reconciled with my championship (for a fair hearing) of Patroni's opinions. Evidence which we might cite as revealing hope of reunion for husband and wife, hope of nuptial fulfilment for even all others, would be for Kerényi (unless I have misunderstood his pρ. 338-341) signs that the vase-painters were indulging women's belief in Dionysos' *ius primae noctis,* his "droit de seigneur," but without much disclosure to them of what was to follow his delightfully exercising it. But we can envy Kerényi his instinctively keen sense for such a field of ore, and should certainly be grateful for the relevance of some of the samples brought up: fig. 1, the Heraclean ΣΦIPAN krater, to show us the arch-lout of the early and hulking Erotes who conceal their relation to Aphrodite, on a vase not worse (in the present connection) than difficult; fig. 3, Tarentine calyx-krater by Trendall's Hearst Painter, classically "disgusting." Or fit to disgust; at Rudiae-Rugge about the turn of the fifth to the fourth century, some Messapian parent or widower found nothing clownishly heartless on it. But the picture on the side republished by Kerényi could be taken farcically, for so indeed it was taken at its publication in the *CVA* (It. 4, IV D r, text to pl. 3, fig. 1): the poor girl, in pitiful contrast to her neighbor in Kerényi's fig. 2 (for whose union or reunion Dionysos himself is holding the torch), can seem, has seemed, to be victim of a practical joke. Kerényi's fig. 2 is of course for the Hoppin Painter's Lecce 620, the bell-krater of my pl. 8b also from Messapian Rudiae, and we have more than one reason to be grateful for the cross-lighting which Kerényi's juxtaposition of that calyx-krater, Lecce 629, has provided. In the first place, if in view of Lecce 620 it is really impossible that the Hearst Painter meant to be heartless on Lecce 629, then after all the subject on the latter is not "girl's nuptial bath comically frustrated, Hermes (thief, *teste Flacco,* from birth) making off with her mantle and shoes (just what she will need for her next step), while that crudely agile bounder of a satyr distracts her attention by offering ointment for those finishing touches to her hair which now, bathed and half-dressed, she is free to give."

Moreover, there is a bearing in which it is not unimportant that on Lecce 629 this must be a serious Hermes, more gravely helpful than the Hearst Painter's jerkily bouncing mannerism quite disclosed, namely Hermes Psychopompos, ready to cloak the dead girl for introduction to some bridegroom not too unlike the Hoppin Painter's youth, who, nubile as his stlengis says, in Kerényi's adjacent fig. 2 watches the girl corresponding (but differently supervised) wash *her* hair, quite ready to marry her (as his phiale with pastries and two sprays and Dionysos' smokily burning torch combine to say). It is momentous that for both pictures, that in which the divine supervisor is Hermes of the Dead and that in which he is Dionysos, we could (if we had the levity for it) write the same title: "hair comes last in the last nuptial toilet." For we needed assurance that the god of Lecce 620 was

Dionysos of the Dead, not Dionysos in an aspect he has on the François vase, taking in a living hero's marriage the interest so perfectly natural to the father of Hymenaios.

Funerary Purpose of Apulian Red-Figured Vases

THIS, IF NOT the most urgent message of Kerenyi's batch of more or less Dionysiac vases (especially since the difference made by Miss Scarfi's raking out for us the pottery of the *inhabited* part of M. Sannace in *NS* 1962, pp. 1-283) is of practical importance. For, however brittle really, one of the sticks most obviously at hand (more than ever, since the excavation of Greek Olynthos) — for trouncing Patroni's theories — is the contention that in very great measure Italiote vase-painting is not even funerary, much less eschatographic: "nuptial, yes and yes, but in the most ordinary and earthly way, to brighten wedding presents." Are we to count the pieces into which Miss Scarfi's two publications, of a cemetery in *MonLinc* 45 and of part of the town-site of M. Sannace in *NS* for 1962, have, or should have broken this? The first work had already warned us (especially by the tomb-groups of her figs. 9 and 30) how fatuous it was to study late Apulian vases, as they stand or lie on the shelves of museums, in complete forgetfulness of their past as grave-goods, and so with no thought of the eschatographic *whole* which the pictures on the smaller vases (of lovers, ministering Erotes, heads of Aphrodite, bird of Aphrodite) had once formed with pictures on larger vases (of tombs or of a Dionysiac union; both, it may be, as arguably in Miss Scarfi's fig. 9). Of course it would be not less fatuous to assume (for some side-issue of connoisseurship) that all the figured vases of one burial must show the personal style of one hand; what matters (for the present question) is their being of one time. With *MonLinc* 45 open at cols. 195-196 to show the pelike of another tomb (no. 3) in isolation (figs. 41-42) from anything larger, one might excusably think "why not a wedding present, long treasured by the dead man? does it have to be paradise when the girl of a pair of lovers sits like that? are there not rocks in only too many Berkeley gardens? are there not some few pelikai with pictures of *earthly* weddings elaborately taking place?" Of those four thoughts the third and (as I judge) the fourth are true. But the first would not survive one's passing, overleaf, to cols. 191-194, for the volute krater of figs. 39-40 from the same tomb is contemporary, and it is not one of those funerary vases (with heroon only, no separate showing of a tomb) which a determined banalizer could imagine standing in a house for years, as a reminder of duties of ancestor-worship.

But what I have just written has full force only for late Apulian vases (and it concedes that even there, at least in the department of pelikai, there are difficult ramifications of the matter; what of redundantly nuptial pelikai, such vases as Torino 4129 and 4149 [*CVA* Italy 32 IV D, pls. 12-15]? reminiscent and earthly on one side, Elysian on the other and more or less rocky one?). I do not think that we can quite afford to dispense with the force, for counter-objection to a rather plausible quibble, which is preciously latent in Miss Scarfi's second study. Until all who should do so have attended to what is set out under her heading *ceramica italiota* in each sounding and each clearance reported in *NS* 1962 (pp. 1-285), her sequel concerned with the fortifications and buildings on M. Sannace and having only accidentally to treat tombs, it may be that the two manifestations of a match-making Dionysos on vases in Lecce will need (no. 620 more than no. 623) the supporting footnote with which a chthonic Hermes, collaborating with a deputy of Dionysos on a third vase there,[1] underwrites a chthonic interpretation of what the Dionysos of those two bell-kraters is doing in person for his two young friends.

The significance of Miss Scarfi's low count of Italiote red-figured fragments from the inhabited area of M. Sannace is of course in relation to the abundance of figured pottery yielded by some inhabited sites in Greece. The very basis of Patroni's nuptial eschatology was his generalization, in his own circumstances almost rash, that Italiote red-figure (in contrast to Attic) was funerary in destination *as a rule*. It is thus a not unacceptable by-product of attention to satyric deputies of nuptial Dionysos that we are in a position to appreciate the disappointment which the report on the walls and settlement has in store for anyone committed, in interpretation of Italiote red-figure, to the kenotic or "cool" tradition of Heydemann, G. Jatta after his conversion by H., and Macchioro. Without being such a banalizer, yet knowing that there were "wedding-presents" (even a lebes gamikos, not just lekanai) among the Attic red-figured vases found in *houses* of Greek Olynthos by D. M. Robinson (*Ol.* xiii, nos. 64, 65; no. 53), any student might begin a rapid perusal of Miss Scarfi's *L'abitato peucetico di Monte Sannace* with the thrilling feeling that his thumb was putting Patroni's hypotheses on trial. And soon enough, before it had gone further than between p. 75 and p. 77, they would seem to be in some danger. But Miss Scarfi's text reveals that the Italiote vases published there in her figs. 64-66 (good, by the way, for contrast of the old and "wholesome" with the new and transvestite Eros) come from graves destroyed in fortifying the place (as other graves were by the construction of a certain public building, causing a vast dispersal of sherds, pp. 126-127). In general, she says on p. 163, "il materiale apulo a figure rosso si può considerare, per gran parte, tombale,; fanno eccezione vasi di uso practico di piccole dimensioni"; while indeed she mentions lekanai

---

[1] No. 629, *CVA* Italia 4, IV Dr pl. 2, 3 and 3, 1). [*JKA*]

together with "skyphoi, lekythoi, piatelli" in her enumeration of types, it perhaps makes no small difference that we are given no reason to suppose that her fragments from vessels of that shape were like the aforesaid Attic lekanai from Olynthos (Robinson's nos. 64 and 65, nuptial fuss and bustle, with and without Eros) in their having themes expressly matrimonial. If I may return to Kerényi, let me acknowledge and try to apply what is perhaps the most practical contribution of his study of a batch of vases important, as we can see, for any future interest in the give-and-take between Greek eschatography and Italic eschatology: namely, the lesson Kerényi sought to give in the value of a sense of series, an eye for threads.

His own particular suggestion, of the need of alertness to the effect of pattern-books, was made without knowing, as a specialist would have known, of great advances made recently in the connoisseurship of personal styles in most branches of Italiote vase-painting. It is of course an acceptable hint, and I hope that my own welcome of it will be evident in what presently has to be said about two kraters in Leningrad, evidently painted up in one and the same shop by two distinct persons briefed (it might seem) to tell successive chapters of the same serial story, a new one, how after all, and to their great surprise, the Danaids discovered that their murderings had been no venial matter. Here and now to the topic in hand, my own application of Kerényi's lesson would be a handing-over, if the connoisseurs of style would consent to put their grasp of personalities, their phaseological acumen and sense of development, to work in making sure of the threads to be traced in this self-education of two sets of inheritors of the Attic tradition, respectively Heraclean and Tarentine, in what the Attic painters of red-figured vases had never been forced to study, the eschatological taste of customers. From the connoisseurs' side, "what, for a beginning, would you have us consider " would be a fair, a necessary question. Let us suppress or postpone "Well, the beginning, the relation of your zero to ours," too pretentious (and cryptic) to be quite the right lead from our side; perhaps our most pressing need of expert verification is in regard to some affinities of one of the vases adduced by Kerényi, from an earlier publication by Ernst Langlotz (*Anthemon,* for Carlo Anti, pl. 4, 1-2; Kerényi's fig. 7), a pelike in Bonn the Eros on which is of momentous importance if I am not misplacing the vase where I would put it, fourth in the following series: (a) The inexhaustibly interesting bell-krater on which a girl washing her hair keeps two persons waiting, one a young man certified by his stlengis as fit to marry, by his phiale and its contents as altogether ready to marry the present girl, and the other a fully characterized Dionysos, with torch lit for their marriage (Lecce 620, Kerényi's fig. 2, my pl. 8b); the experts, Cambitoglou and Trendall, have a place for it, as their Hoppin Painter's no. 3; I put it first in the present list for a succession because it had a narrow escape, eschatographically, from "zero" — without sidelights from other vases, one of them (as we found) the Hearst Painter's Lecce 629, we should not have known that the young graduate from the palaistra was not meant for a living athlete about to contract one of those eugenic unions such as robust Erotes, not Dionysos, are seen blessing in contexts (earthly, to all appearance) which put us in mind not so much of Tarentine Archytas as of his fellow-Pythagorean Okellos (it is a pleasant coincidence, if it is not better than a coincidence, that this man, thought to have preached eugenic marriage, should be sur-named "the Lucanian," thus sharing the conventional label of the vases, Heraclean and Intermediate, on which especially one finds palaestric match-making). (b) Next to that in both scales, of style and of eschatography, another Apulian vase (not quite the only otherˆ) on which Dionysos in person makes the match, Lecce 623 (my pl. 8a). C. and T. assign it to their Lecce Painter, whom they place (pp. 62-63, no. 3) as a follower of the painter of the preceding vase. To that relation (in mere style of drawing) it corresponds, in the subject, that Dionysos is still in charge, not having yet resigned his nuptial function to a deputy, but the effect is now frankly unearthly, not less so than a satyr's intervention would have made it. Desolate situation, strange affair, even if we need not suppose that the position of the god's right hand and the boy's holding his arms open mean that Dionysos is about to push the girl off her weedy rock into the bridegroom's embrace! Instead, of course, the boy's gesture with "sawing" or weaving hands and the god's encouraging pat or grasp (together saying "come to, my dear . . . or can't you read the message of your own reflected faceˆ"") give an object-lesson in the symbolism of the mirror, as concomitant of female nubility. And this is a lesson vastly more important for us than anything noteworthy in suppression of the bridegroom's stlengis or in the indication of a wall pierced by a door. But it is not uninteresting (phaseolog-ically) that the Lecce Painter's development of the affair has taken from this boy that link with life which was retained not only by the Hoppin Painter's youth but also by the impetuous suitor on the fourth hydria of the Degrassi grave, though already (this Heraclean lover) satyr-abetted and deep in para-dise, while certainly it is not regrettable (unless there is a certain cheapness in the assonance) that, phraseologically, my already frequent use of this half-Persian word is now justified — for without a wall such as that door and the many windows of Italiote eschatography imply there can be no "para-dise." There should be no need to revert to the Hoppin Painter's krater (pl. 8b) to borrow — for a hammering-in of the present point — the mirror which is only idle there, hung up. But if need there be, let me do so. In no forthright or meander of our course as at present set must we forget our company, and that what has set our direction is the undertaking to escort Patroni's nuptial eschatology to a position decently unmolestable. The risk meanwhile of molestation is (at least as I judge) less from mere banalism (of which scholarship is already tiring?) than from Orphistic misappropriation of Apulian red-figure's nuptial symbolism, beginning, only beginning, with the mirror (which Miss Simon's satyrs, not to mention contributory factors at

Stuttgart as well as from Policoro, have made it easiest prey). But take now, if this does not break our latest thread, (c) and (d) : respectively the sole picture on the Catania chous 746 (Libertini, *Museo Biscari,* pl. 85) and the obverse one on the Bonn pelike which interested first Langlotz (*Anthemon,* pl. 4,1 and 2) and then Kerényi (pl. 5,7). To the topic which put us to threading the series concluded by the chous and the pelike, namely two contrastable types of Italiote satyr and a certain Italic objection to even the tamed and paradisal type which was met (from the Italiote side) by con-cocting a new Eros only too suitable for part of the latter' work, could there be anything much more relevant than this pair of vase-paintings (unless it spoils everything that the Eros here relieving the satyr is not sickeningly effeminite)? Dionysos having withdrawn from personal service to lovers after (b) of this series, the satyr who is his deputy in continuance of that service in (c) does not last into (d), where Love himself takes over. As to the rest of (d), there is remarkably little difference from (c), either in its drawing or its composition and the attributes which the latter involves — timbrel for the girl to beat in the middle of the scampering procession, wreath for the boy behind her to hold.

Further Considerations on Satyrs and Nymphs in Paradise

WHAT, IN ANY CASE, we can take for the task in hand is an easier transition, by way of some considerations for which the Catania chous gives occasion, to the next in the methodical series of pairings hopefully undertaken. This will be the proper one to follow pairing of contrasted types of satyrs, namely two sorts of Dionysiac grouping, both being stationary gatherings of nymphs and satyrs about an honored figure, but distinguished according to the figure honored, Dionysos (of course always principal, if he is present at all) or not Dionysos. If the triad on the Catania chous should receive (and obey) an order to halt, that would not entitle them to rediscussion in this new collation, for (according to the interpretation which effective stylometry already favors) the girl in the middle belongs not (as nymph) to the satyr in front but (as mate) to the boy behind; on the other hand, for the com-parison we are turning to there certainly will be matter available in the picture (pl. 2) at the back of the neck of the Iphigenia krater — and matter, it may be, for dispute which side should take it, Dionysos' or the other. Transition itself is no great triumph, even in the jungle-hacking of ceramic archaeology, and it was ludicrously maladroit if I slipped into phrasing that seemed to imply blindness to evident gains from my own experiment, that collation of satyrs. It might not have prospered without the fortunate illustration the Degrassi grave at Heraclea-Policoro happened to give it. Not to harp on an incidental though most important gain of light on the pan symbol's strange stylization, vases from that grave were of precisely cardinal importance in exhibiting the very turning point of the change from wild to tame; moreover, there was almost complete illumination of the nature and cause of the change, in what was shown taking place in a section of the Dionysiac paradise sliced for us by Degrassi's fig. 14, leaving us only with almost frivolous questions to ask: "has the present uncouth abettor of an eschatic union any personal interest in it? had he been servant in either family? where, indeed, did good slaves (male and female) go when they died?" To take my last chance of beginning an answer to the most general of these, let my start be the very safe one that scholarship should remain on the watch to catch, especially on Italiote vases retrieved from burial or seclusion, any inscription that would add significance to a small but already suggestive store, as follows: (a) In the picture decorating a red-figured chous from a grave at Taranto (B. Neutsch, *AA* [1956] 209-211, fig. 12 at 214), ΕΥΜΑΣ inscribed on what seems to represent to a tomb; name of the satyr who sits on it? Name, anyhow, that fits him all the better if we may suppose that once, in life, he was the "well-disposed" servant of the young man facing him; as Neutsch notes, it is interestingly near the most honored of all servile names, Eumaios. (b) In the reverse picture (*n.b.*!) of a skyphos (Lucanian of the Heraclean stage, Palermo 961) decorated by Trendall's Palermo Painter (*LCS* book 1, no. 275), the word ΟΝΝΑΣΕΥΑΣ, on a steloid which is a mere label-holder like that for the name of Marsyas on a vase of the same shape decorated by the same hand (Trendall's no. 273); quite certainly designating the satyr whom a piping nymph is entertaining. In their "after-noon off"? That is a question which I cannot take as grossly flippant; it should give us some curiosity about the other side, and from our point of view in the present topic this must mainly be: "what's the level? The same satyric-nymphic, or above?". Trendall's description of it in *LCS* is brief but quite arresting, for it reveals a composition which (but for its lacking the match-making Dionysos) is not unlike that of a classic of eschatography (for such it already is for us, pl. 8a) on the Apulian bell-krater Lecce 623: in his words, but with italics mine: "*youth standing* in front of *woman seated on rock,* looking at her *reflection in a mirror.*" There is a gap I must not minimize. Lecce 623 is "Apulian" and Tarentine (unless this Lecce Painter and his master the Hoppin Painter belong — where Trendall by no means encourages us to put them — to Rudiae-Rugge in the heel of Italy); the skyphos Palermo 961 is "Lucanian" and Heraclean (unless made and painted after the exodus from Heraclea in which Trendall is inclined to believe, with some idea of its direction, to Tarentum first). But perhaps it is a gap between parallels? When we were tracing a development of nuptial eschatography in the school of the Apulian Hoppin Painter we found the line to run: (1) and

(2), Dionysos himself united the pair, mirror-work at a rock not coming in before (2); (3) Dionysos had done his work (or was only doing it through a deputy?): the pair were already together, scampering off somewhere some-whither under the guidance of a satyr who had a bucket of (considerately) mixed wine for their refreshment; for Greek to describe his pace and service we might have prompted ourselves from the satyr's name, Onnaseuas, on the Palermo skyphos; was not the satyr on the Catania chous ONAΣIMOΣ EΣΣYMENΩΣ? Σευίδαι, από τοῦ σεύεω, ὅ ἐστιν ὁρμᾶν, Cornutus explains in a passage of his theological compendium (ND 30) devoted to the origin of species of satyr. Trendall's Palermo Painter having taken the trouble to advertise the one on that skyphos as a *profitable individual* of the "seuid" or rushing kind, let us take grateful advantage of him (if gratitude may begin there, let us be thankful that on this Heraclean piece the Greek of his name is not worse; having one N too many, its venial fault is the opposite of the shrinkage oafish in ΣΦΙΡΑΝ and sinister in ΓΟΣΔΑΝ, which by recalling PAESTVM, the fate of Poseidonia's name, for us presages Lucanization). Here we are not concerned with what was so important before, stage (4) at which some scruple replaced that good and speedy servant by Eros. What matters is, first and less important at present, an impression that the Palermo skyphos stands eschatographically abeam of phase (3) in the Apulian line, which leaves lovers to depend on the satyrs and nymphs of their paradise; second and more directly opportune, that we have something, in the name Onnaseuas, for another and now epigraphic threading: something to go between the name, Eumas, of the "complaisant" satyr (communicating with a surviving master?) on the Taranto chous, and, for (c) of the "small store," an anonymously beatified servant's complaisant good nature (*simplicitas facilis*, line 16 of an inscription, *CIL* iii., 686, famous for a supposed "satyrization"). There is not a little difficulty (result of the Macedonian cutter's own great difficulty in reading the Latin draft?) in the text of this inscription from Doxato near Philippi, which as often taken at lines 17-18 (surviving master addressing dead servant as if he might have turned satyr) would give quite a good match for the pair on the Taranto pitcher. But what is in doubt for us is only how far the qualifying ugliness (line 5) of this child lovely at heart (line 6) is to take him — to become a satyr, if *satyrum* at line 18 is in the accusative singular, or perhaps not quite so far as that (short of a tail and new ears?), if the word is in the genitive plural. I quite understand that anyone citing this Macedonian Latin in a trans-Adriatic connection with Italiote vases of a much earlier time must submit to make very plain what he is about. Its quite explicit attestation of a Dionysiac paradise we do not need, and its eschatology of the sexes we cannot use (this gives Patroni's no support, its all-but-harem of *Bromio signatae mystides* agreeing better with Kerényi's; their making a pet of the satyrized child will not help — I hope it cannot harm — my own notion that a reaction of satyrophobia is to be traced, at least as regards women's burials, in the Italic reception of Italiote eschatography). What most needs light and explanation is the standpoint from which serious interest can be taken, by us must be taken, now at the present stage of a series of hopefully experimental comparisons, in class-distinctions of Dionysos' paradise. With D for Dionysos, s for satyr, n for nymph, this third of the collations undertaken could be dryly formulated as study of the interesting difference between still groups the nucleus of which is $s+D+n$ and groups also still (not "scampers") the nucleus of which is $s+not\ D+n$. In what connection with this, with what gain for the overdue deserts of Patroni's nuptial eschatology or for the exploration of symbolism, was it worthwhile to be so far-fetching, for the sake of a little support of "Eumas's" encouragement to take interest in "Onnaseuas" on the Heraclean skyphos as probably having meaning, unlike the notorious gibberish, *noraretteblo,* in a dramatic picture by a Tarentine contemporary? It is not much of an answer to all this that there was plenty of meaning found, "Giving-'Rush'-Service," as adscript name of the satyr there grouped with the nymph — in the servants' quarters of this skyphos if the Palermo Painter is to have the credit he reasonably should get of intending to integrate this two-sided vase. "Service to whom?" "To the nearest, of course: to the lady and gentleman opposite." Not that, so far as it goes, I have any fault to find with this, and we know that we could ourselves supplement the satyr's *explication du texte:* "who are so like the more privileged lady and gentleman at another rock for whom Dionysos himself turned out, on the Tarentine Lecce Painter's Lecce 623, pl. 8a." The point I have to press is that "What service?," an even more important question, and "service to whom?" have a certain interdependence, and to all our present concerns it must make some difference whether the satyrs and nymphs of the formula $s+not\ D+n$ are deputies of Dionysos whose duty (apart from mere guidance) is to perform rites essential to eschatic (re)union, or old family retainers whose good memory and *simplicitas facilis* are at the service of qualified arrivals in a matter merely of cordiality and comfort. We have been so much concerned with ablution — as organic link between the topic nuptial eschatology and the topic symbolism — that I cannot feel there would be mere levity in letting the figures with sluicing-pans in two such groupings (pl. 2, fig. 1b) remind us of Don Fabrizio's arrival at Donnafugata in the second chapter of Tomasi di Lampedusa's *Gattopardo,* and of the great hot bath in which the master relaxed from traumatic discomforts of a three-day's journey from his Northern to his Southern home (no solemn emphasis should be laid on the numeral coincidence, two the number of required servants, as in the bathroom for Don Fabrizio, so in the Dionysiac strips of the Iphigenia and Nekyia kraters for the youths who have been or who are to be sluiced, no doubt from such a laver as is seen in the similarly Dionysiac but panless strip of my fig. 1c for a picture at the back of the neck of the great "Persians" krater in Naples — to say nothing, for the moment, of a pair of lavers quaintly "his" and "hers" and not without pan for sluicing, in the palatial master-bathplace disclosed by my pl. 5a, Hades' own on the London amphora F 332. But because of the bearing it has on right reading of a vase which may turn out to have some importance to us, the chous published by Miss Scarfi in pl. 62, fig. 1 of *ArchCl* 11 [1959] as a work of her Apulian Snub-Nose Painter, it is worth stressing how intimately nymph and satyr combine as a team, a team for reception as so far I have interpreted it; evidently sluicing is not the satyr's specialty, for the pan which he had at the back of the neck of Munich 3297 [fig. 1b] passes to the nymph in the corresponding triad of the Iphigenia krater St. 420 [pl. 2] and is retained by the nymph of the dyad on the aforesaid chous).

If the chous just mentioned in parenthesis can cut out work for us, so much the better. The nymph and satyr there are less relaxed than Onnaseuas and his piping partner on the skyphos of Trendall's Lucano-Heraclean Palermo Painter (the Snub-Nose Painter's satyr lounges, but erect and with a torch lit — for an impending duty of escort?). One would say that he and she (quite tense, with her pan hoisted and her phiale extended) were waiting for work, not enjoying a rest from service to neighbors, like the other pair; they have no neighbor. But if there is anything for us to use here it will be more in the likeness than in the difference, and a likeness not quite fully seizable on pl. 62 of *ArchClass* 11 begins to develop as soon as one turns to M. Bernardini's publication of the tomb-group to the krater of which this chous was ancillary (*NS* 1957, p. 418 for description of the burial, tomb 12 at Roccavecchia in the then Messapian heel of Italy, on the coast less than fifteen miles to the southwest of Lecce and Rudiae-Rugge; fig. 25 on p. 17 for the obverse of the bell-krater; fig. 27 on p. 418 for the chous; fig. 28 for two gold "leaves" provided with pins; insidiously like fibulae for a woman, but I take them to be for insertion in a headband, part of a set to make it more wreathlike). On the bell-krater of Bernardini's fig. 25, vessel for which the chous is dipper and pourer in one, the team which was idle on the chous has been overtaken by the duty they were waiting for, or some part of it. Here they are in attendance on a seated male whom Bernardini took for Dionysos, perhaps not rightly but not without reason, for his hair is quite long (till we know him better, neither formula of the present collation will do; let us write only *s+X+n,* noting attributes: like some other principals of the triads we are now concerned with, the unknown has phiale as well as thyrsos, having gotten the former from the nymph; of her sluicer there is now no sign, though what she has on the krater of this tomb-group is a crisscrossed box of just the sort carried by the companion of the man with sluicing-pan and bunch of grapes on the principal vase of another burial, t. 17 M. Sannace; the satyr retains the torch he had on the chous, and has picked up a timbrel, which promises movement: perhaps only a dance by the nymph if the recumbent male is Dionysos, a dance on the spot; but it may be that he is not Dionysos, only a mortal recovering from death in the trauma-room, as it were, of Elysium; presently, then, they would be up and away, for this satyr and nymph to find what Onnaseuas and his partner are resting from finding, a rock-perched mate for their young man). However it may be with the matters of that long parenthesis, we have once more, thanks to a planned tomb-group, found a thread of eschatography that we could and did use. To escape something?

No doubt the chous could have been, in isolation, a trap set to give false impressions, one or another: "eschatic mating, second class," or "escort's lounging rudeness to lady departed," or "girl tense with distrust of Dionysos' deputy." But I think that what we have just had is, more positively, a crowning and quite fresh object-lesson in Kerényi's principle "get threads!," his tacit adaptation (to a level a little lower than its honored inventor's) of the Forsterian "Only connect!" In the process of acquiring not less than due respect for Italiote vase-painting there is no little connection demanding to be seen or to be done: from part to part of the vase when it is not (as choes and most pouring vessels are) single-pictured; from vase to vase in the eschatographic meaning of a tomb-group of figured vases; from beginning to end of a painter's career or a school's tradition, if respect is in the least concerned with development to meet such exigencies as history forced on late Tarentine red-figure; last and (I suppose) humblest, if not so humble as to make the above word "crowning" ridiculous, along lines or sweeps of versatility sometimes most respectably subtle (as we shall find certain am- biguities of nuptial symbolism to be), sometimes drawbacks of the scale and intensity of a great industrial enterprise limited in means of expression. The picture on the chous in question could not have been rightly read out of connection with tomb 12 at Roccavecchia and the principal picture on the bowl for which it was dipper there; could not have been understood from any stylometric point of view out of connection with vases by the same hand adduced by Miss Scarfi. But can its very existence be understood out of connection with the class of motive from which it is — by sharpening an ear, blunting a nose, adding a horse's tail — adapted, namely the stereotype, so important in connection with the Patronian eschatology, for which we phrased the formula "pair of lovers in some 'otherwhere', one of them with an ablution pan." The topic that has cropped up, in the midst of an all-but-algebraic collation of the two most interesting schemes of Dionysiac composition, namely the versatility of late Apulian red-figure, must be dismissed as an interruption, retrospectively not unwelcome if it has whetted any insight, or mere curiosity, for future use. The practical turn that its dismissal occasions is, evidently, the need to take some step or stand to reduce the risk of floundering confusion with regard to the female element of Dionysiac groups. A certain stand has already been taken in the notation of our inquiry into the difference to be recognized when an Italiote vase- painter does *not* mean *D*(ionysos) by the figure he associates with *s*(atyr) and *n*(ymph). My *n* respects the Attic origins of Dionysiac red-figure; ΝΥΦΗ or ΝΥΣΗ are generic words, the latter more official (to judge by an inscription in the theatre of Dionysos at Athens), the former recommended by Klitias' use of it. ΜΑΙΝΑΣ is (for vase-painting) only a proper name, a favorite adscript of course, as ΣΙΜΟΣ is for satyrs on Attic vases. (For references, see Charlotte Fränkel, *Satyr und Bakennamen auf Vasenbildern* [Halle, 1912].) But the reason valid for not beginning to call satyrs or silens "simes" stands good for our dropping "maenads," in modern cataloguing quite generally accepted for noting the Dionysiac nymphs of vases but doubly objectionable; first because its generic use is a matter either of ignorance (of the facts of usage as Miss Fränkel troubled to collect them) or of whimsical affectation (excusing itself with "guys," "dolls," "dicks," "tommies," "jocks"). But worse in its indifference to the most humanly interesting thing in the whole course of Dionysiac vase-painting, the gradual divergence from Attic tradition which ends in the Italiote minions of Dionysos being tamed for the service of mankind in its second life. Not, at the stage of Lecce 683 (*CVA* It. 6, pl. 32), too tame for a revel; in our preoccupation with Dionysiac neck-strips of volute-kraters, where the nymphs exhibit no more maenadism than is seen in the routine of a hospital-nurse, we must not forget the livelier Elysium on part (the bowl) of this skyphoid pyxis, no doubt of earlier date (slightly) than those kraters, but with specific bearing on some of their questions; indeed, the first thing to point to if one is challenged about the quartered catchballs and reerected column-tops of paradise, or about the right of Eros to sit where and with whom he is in the picture at the back of the neck of Leningrad St. 426 (figs. 6 and 12, pls. 4b; 6; 17b). But really more important is the impression which only comparison with the rowdiest Attic thiasoi can fully give, that the satyrs and nymphs on the pyxis are not just "being themselves" in natural exuberance: this is a celebration (in the most nearly Latin sense of the word) in honor of mortals certainly present, though not all very easily picked out from the dark photographs without help from Romanelli's text.

Consorts and Companions of Dionysos

AND "ARIADNE"?, There is no doubt of her occurrence in Apulian vase-painting, well acquainted (as B. Neutsch has recently reminded us: *AA* [1956], 209-211) with her desertion by Theseus, to whose story (as may be said for the whole of Greek vase-painting) she properly belongs. Whether we may expect to find here there as what neither Homer nor (surprisingly?) the Attic Kerameikos would allow her to be, the firmly wedded consort of Dionysos, is of no less concern to us than it has been to cataloguers, whose indexing of her makes interesting reading (even Heydemann, who was scolded by Albizzati for being too ready to recognize her, had eight question-marks in his). This question might seem to be part of another, inconveniently large: how

Greek, and cognizant of Homer, were the painters of Apulian red-figure? But it has some opportune relevance to one in particular, whom we cannot avoid considering in our present business with stationary groups.

This is the person known to connoisseurs as the Lycurgus Painter, almost a great figure (in the Italiote scale, at least); no very lively soul (perhaps livelier than he was encouraged to show, his silens hint), but truly an artist, accomplished and ambitious: at any rate, equal to making his gifts for charm and balance tell on a scale which would have been embarrasing to the Lecce Painter. With the latter's instructive eschatography we have not yet finished (not the least discussible of all *not D* triads, reverse for one of the earliest pictures of a heroon, occurs on the vase most citable for his being significantly less ready than his younger contemporary the Lycurgus Painter for the coming surge of monumentality, I mean the calyx-krater belonging to Professor Erich Boehringer and published by him in memory of Erich Pernice in *Greifswalder Antiken*, pls. 49-50). But the "Ariadne question" having arisen in just the right place for it we are not taking the Lycurgus Painter out of turn. Perhaps there could be more than one attitude to it, but certainly the most practical is that which a very effective introduction to the Lycurgus Painter, contributed by Andrew Oliver, Jr., to *BMMA* (Summer, 1962) pp. 25-30, cannot fail to suggest on final reflection, if we have noted, in the first place, that Oliver takes it for granted that Greek Tarentum, not any of the Peucetian or Daunian wool-towns (ill-acquainted with Homer?), was the home of Apulian red-figure (p. 25). And have observed, next, that it never occurred to him even to mention Ariadne in his interpretation of the vase-painting so strikingly published on his next page; this is the obverse picture of the Lycurgus Painter's bucket in New York (56.171.64) from near one of those towns, Ryps-Rubi-Ruvo: a composition which a less extremely circumspect reading than Oliver's might quite well have made out to mean "deserted Ariadne (note phiale and paraphernalia-box of her marriage to Theseus!), having been already discovered by Dionysos' advance party (the satyr who has already set up the krater of the *coming* affair and chous in hand is about to fill its phiale, with [naturally] that satyr's nymph), is now sighted with great surprise and concern by the god himself (guaranteed to be Dionysos by nearly the fullest possible characterization: face turned from profile, long hair, conspicuous headdress, chariot to ride in, griffins to pull it)." There is more Dionysiac matter in the same article, but Ariadne is not to be found there — no more than in a longer work, so excessively abounding in Dionysiac matter that it has even a prayer to waste on Dionysos' mortal enemies, the Titans, namely the Pergamene collection of Orphic hymns (p. 29 Quandt[2], no. 37). Interesting as that double vacuum is, I do not think that the practical point is quite reached until (inevitably) we are driven to ask "if this woman in Ariadne's situation is not Ariadne, who then is she?"

A fair question; in the first place, it is nearly the question which Greek art of all periods was so ready to answer in writing, with — as a rule — any name but Ariadne's as adscript for a woman grouped with Dionysos. Reading *Semele, Thyone* (behind the god in a file) with *Dione* (ahead), *Eriope, Pompe, Eirene, Paideia, Akme,* instead of the expected word, we have to recognize significant evasion. Not of course absolute interdiction, comparable with the sinister blank in the otherwise so inclusive Orphic Hymns; while the *Ariadne* of the Palermo pelike 1109 by the Chicago Painter must be disallowed (her Dionysos being infant fosterling, not lover, *MonInst* 2, pl. 17), a woman with the like adscript on the bell-krater Compiègne 1025 need not be (there companion of an adult Dionysos, *CVA* France 3, pl. 18, 1); both are Attic vases. Altogether, in Greek art the rule as it is set off by rare exception corresponds to, and must be the effect of, the weight of literary tradition, Dionysos of the Odyssey (xi.321-325, tell-tale destroyer of Ariadne; never for a moment her lover?) having been too much for Hesiod's Dionysos (*Theog.* 947-949 gave him Ariadne for ἄκοιτις, by the grace of Zeus made immortal and ageless for him). Part, but only part, of the present relevance of Oliver's introduction to the Lycurgus Painter is then that the not altogether petty question, "any Dionysiac Ariadne in Apulian red-figure?" is pitched into the widest of all laps, that of the ubication question, "and where was Apulian red-figure made?" — this when a specialist of Oliver's experience, having declared for Tarentum as the ware's home, tacitly judges (quite soundly in keeping with his declaration) that there is no Ariadne to be seen even in the Dia-like setting of the obverse of the New York bucket. That I altogether agree with him I scarcely need to say. But until there shall be no one left believing that the Lycurgus Painter was a Peucetian, of the region where the bucket was found, impartial scholarship will need a certain document which shows how much difference, in regard to Ariadne, it could make to have less than a Tarentine's presumable knowledge of the Homeric and most "vulgate" tradition of her relation to Dionysos, and to be ignorant too of the strength of Semele's claim on this "mother's boy" (lines 28-30 of Pindar's second Olympian ode, on the apotheosis of Semele, almost cancelling Hesiod's passage because of their stress on the opportunity made for the son's loving care of her, were for Western ears, and may well remind us of a Greek inscription from far to the west of Tarentum even [*IG*.xiv.205, Akrai] in which the mutilated name of Dionysos' associate in a public cult is certainly not Ariadne's and seems to be Semele's). How far the archaeological document which I have referred to would licence Peucetian liberties I do not exactly know; it is Etruscan, a mirror-engraving with adscripts (Gerhard, *Etr. Spiegel* 4, pl. 299). But at any rate, *Semla's* toleration of a decidedly mature *Areatha's* overtures to a Dionysos (*Fufluns*) not fully grown and holding a schoolboy's lyre could hardly be bettered as an example of what Greeklessness allows. It would be unfair if I failed to mention the fourth figure, *Sime*, for nothing could be more soundly traditional than such a name for any satyr. But can we really feel that there is any but the most emptily nominal link with the two conflicting traditions in a "reconciliation" of them composed as if Semele had just said: "by all means kiss and fondle the lad – but it will cost you a stoop, big girl"? The point for us, I am sure, is that (thanks to a staunch Tarentinist's suggestive reserve in a speciously Ariadnic matter) we can be aware of a connection in which that Etruscan curiousity belongs to at least the background of the ubication problem, of the "where?" controversy. Is it not a nearly indispensable foil to what I may call that controversy's Roscher-Séchan material, meaning thereby the wealth of sound illustration of Greek legend which from "Apulian" vases has been banked in the works of reference for Hellenic studies? It is one of the assumptions, one of the motives, of the present study that, however paradoxical such hydralike vitality may be, a cause of controversy continues to exist. That late Apulian red-figure is Greek and Tarentine we must hold, with Oliver, to be true. But some of the significance of this would be missed in supposing the truth self-evident. It is not, for there have been apostasies, and the standpoint from which these are most interesting is precisely mine, with ground taken that should be firm enough for one's swinging a club of solid history at the hydra-theory of "sheep-clippers'" vase-painting, not to be annihilated with snips of mere banter, sneers at shears. Of those changes of mind not even Watzinger's is more noteworthy than Séchan's. Not many can have noted it; at the back (p. 634) of his *Études sur la tragédie grecque* (which for the question "Greek?" is certainly the most testing concentration of "Apulian" mythography) it is in his ERRATA: "P. 530, 1. 15. Au lieu de *peintre tarentin* lire *peintre apulien*." I am not presenting the Etruscan thing as a knob of that "club" (by which I mean solid comprehension of the art in question as Tarentine response to Apulian demand, in a quite peculiar relation of mutual stimulus and adjustment at a time of economic symbiosis and political alliance). But we may welcome it as a certain extension of our means of objective judgment, a wilder and nuance-making inch or so in expansion of the scale of comparative Hellenism we began to have in Nevio Degrassi's publication of mythographies from merely Sub-Tarentine Heraclea, these impressive in so many respects but not in flow of adscript Greek nor (as Degrassi's noting of muddled sex brought out) in accurate command of their matter.

The Lycurgus Painter's masterpiece, on the front of the New York bucket as published by Oliver on his p. 26 in an expert photograph that does the picture's crisp equilibrium glareless justice, is an only too arrestingly good thing – our best use for this engaging artist being just as a phase-marker of "Apulian" eschatography who is also pace-maker for our business with it. May I even defer attention to the back of the bucket (where there is a challenging $s+x+n$, in Oliver's (fig. 3), that we may take prompter advantage of the most propulsive thing in this person's painting, the reverse decoration (for neck as well as bowl) of the volute krater which is no. 1097 in the collection of the Jatta family at Ruvo (my fig. 7, after *BullNap* NS 5, pl. 13; for a photograph, see M. Jatta's in *Iapigia* 3 [1932] p. 270, 51; Sichtermann

K72, pl. 49)? It would be the archest phrase-making if I said that the Lycurgus Painter was ready to do us a good turn of phase-marking in our very act of passing to this; but it would be a pity for eyes quitting Oliver's p. 26 to take off without seeing the Eros opposite on p. 27, not too unlike the Lecce Painter's type in wing-pattern but already transvestite (bonneted), and with some elements of the later chattel-symbolism round about him (not yet the pan, but its correlative laver is there; also "horned" wreath; para-phernalia-trunk full-size and duly sat on — as another is, so near a pan, in my fig. 8; deep cylindrical basket). If it is progress to be now with a vista ahead let us get the full encouraging sense of it from what the two pictures at the back of the Jatta krater disclose (separately rather than in combination). The smaller picture is the more timely. But before exploiting it let us make at least acquaintance with the Garden of the Hesperides in the larger. If there is any good in a "method of vistas" the best way to do so should be by comparison, the briefest necessary, of my fig. 7 for the Lycurgus Painter's Garden with my fig. 8 for a later version, part of a picture which is at the back of the Archemoros krater from Ruvo in Naples, H 3255. We have not time for more than two combinations of impressions. There should be future advantage in now seizing (1) the different means taken of showing that the Garden is a significantly wet place (in the earlier version a spring-fed pool of water and several waterpots, which make some of the women look like Danaids; in the later one, just an ablution pan, of the same pattern — with the long handle not android — as that of the pan provided, surprisingly, for the Danaids, as in my figs. 4 and 12); (2) the similar self-concern of women in both pictures, though one cannot quite apply to the earlier version "mit der Sorge für Putz und Schmückung scheinen sie ausschliesslich beschäftigt," E. Gerhard's words for the later version (*Gesammelte akademische Abhand-lungen* 1, p. 22).

Given the Dionysiac strip at the top, we can feel that with this we now have quite a gallery of such neck-groups, all from volute kraters, all of satyrs and nymphs met to honor someone of another order, who is always male. In one case, and one only, this person is unquestionably a god: a minor and menial god, Eros rendered according to the transvestite type of him which is so loathsome until one has discovered the historical reason for its indecent but effective emphasis on this minion's complete dependence on a deity adopted, devoutly, by Tarentum's neighbors, Aphrodite, with no importance apart from his role of bearer of what this goddess of cohabitation (cohabita-tion in more than one world?) had to say or furnish to women (Leningrad St. 426, p. 4b; the main picture of the other side is, as it happens, of the second stage in a certain pottery's version [so exceptionally ironical that it will require discussion] of the serial punishment of the Danaids, pl. 4a). Let me at once expose to questioning my own opinion that the principal of the group in the Dionysiac strip of the Jatta krater is also a god, Dionysos himself — a belief not at all obstinately held, much less strong than my belief that the principal of the Dionysiac group at the back of the neck of the Darius Painter's masterpiece (fig. 1c), with even less hair and ribbon on his head than his counterpart on the Munich Nekyia krater (fig. 1b) and holding sapling instead of thyrsos, cannot possibly be meant for Dionysos. As to the groups typologically intermediate, I am almost as confident that *s+not D+n* is the right formulation for the nucleus of the tetrad on the Nekyia krater. I think that it is also right for the triads in the rest of this vista of neck-panels, but what I think about them can be of no interest till justice has been done to features especially vista-causing, the winged figures which in both the Ruvo pentad (fig. 7) and the Munich tetrad (fig. 1b) close the left of the composition.

Dionysos Triumphant and Aphrodite in "Orphic" Eschatology

WE ARE ALL tired of parroting "Nike" for such figures; "Triumph" for a figure attending Dionysos, "Success" or "Happy Ending" for a figure with a crown or any other award for a finally emparadised mortal, would be acceptable changes. Certainly our first observation, to be made before any consideration for antecedents or background, must be that at Ruvo the principal seems to be getting worship from his winged women (divine worship out of a censer, this not, by any sign whatever, the nuptial thurible, and so we may let it recall the pinches of various sorts or blends of incense prescribed to accompany six of the eight hymns to Dionysos in the Orphic collection, nos. 30, 42, 46, 47, 52, 53, meaning of course by those references no encouragement of Orphistic wrenchings) (fig. 1b). At Munich the winged figure offers the principal a wreath first, after that she has a bunch of grapes for him, less wrench-proof, perhaps. But my argument is not that one would not compliment a triumphant Dionysos by handing him the fruit which, torn and eaten, was the very substance of the Titans' triumph over him in the mimicry performed at a rite really Orphic as practised in the time of the Campana plaques, according to Miss Simon's interpretation of one type of these Roman revetments. Indeed, one would not. But, as may be said without too much disdain for the plaques as late and Roman (it being quite credible that there is matter from Onomakritos' Τελεταί in as many as two or three of their subjects), we can be glad that the proper logic of the question at Munich has facts of closer pertinence to work with. In the first place, in the picture of survivors at a heroon on another volute-krater from the very same chamber, apparently, of the same tomb, there is a bunch of grapes (low left) among the offerings of the survivors (reverse of Munich 3296; Millin, *T. de Canosa*, pl. 8). We know, having taken from the back of the Iphigenia krater in Leningrad and from the fronts of kraters in Cologne and Taranto quite a lesson in the facts of addressing and of delivering offerings to the dead, what we should think of anyone's merely impulsive guess "Oh no, that is the young fellow's direct propitiation of chthonic Dionysos; those grapes on 3296, grave-fellow of 3297 which has grapes too, say 'Grape-God down there, be good to my friend'." I should be the last to minimise the intricacy of the problem of "funerary grapes," an important one certainly; I am only too well aware of the concurrence (many more than the several in the vase-paintings from this Monterisi tomb at Canosa; T. Bertocchi, *Pittura Funeraria Apula*, pp. 27-28) which threaten to entangle it with the problem of the washpan, and of others (more than those handled by Eros with grapes and fan for the bride on the solidly real pan in Amsterdam, pl. 10) warning me that from there it may shoot out tendrils to clutch Patroni's "amore elisiaco." If only we can find a way of understanding the grapes as credentials for the dead to keep for presenting, then for addressing the two bunches (and not merely the two or three pans) on the vases of the Monterisi tomb to its dead warrior we shall not have to depend entirely on Cumont's generalization, "the dead are hungry; above all they are thirsty" (*After-Life in Roman Paganism* [1959], p. 50), interesting though that is, and not Orphistically compromised by its illustration in some of the tablets which are so often called "Orphic." Indeed, it is quite to the point to reflect that this would not happen even if proof of their verses' being snippets from the canon of Orpheus' writings should ever let us lift the inverted commas from those among the "Orphic" tablets which stress the thirst of the dead (the Petelia-Pharsalos-Eleutherna group, Kern *Fr.* 32 a-b; N. M. Verdelis, *AE* [1950-1951] p. 99). These are the tablets most adaptable to the very thing we have to defend from heedless contamination with modern Orphism, namely the Patronian eschatology – this because the Petelia and Pharsalos tablets seem to imply a purpose of *reunion* by their directions for recovering memory, to which the Petelia tablet adds a promise of joining company, lines 4 and 9, line 11. At the same time, these are the tablets least annexable by Orphistic speculation, not having the words which in most of the tablets from near Thurii (Kern *Fr* 32, c-e) invite us to see dark allusion to atonement at last made for sin blastably Titanic. There is something here for us to take up, for coming to terms with Orpheus, as we must, for inescapably he sits in wait for us, in my fig. 13, at the end of the "vista" which begins with the embowered Dionysos on the Lycurgus Painter's "Hesperides" krater in Ruvo, fig. 7, takes our eyes past the "happy ending" of a mortal Dionysiast on the "Reunion in Hades" krater (fig. 1b) and other groups with the like nucleus (*s+not D+n*, the "not Dionysos" holding a thyrsos), and has its open ending at the group (fig. 1c) on the "Persians" krater, a gathering which is Dionysiac in a still more diluted degree, *for the principal has lost his thyrsos*. However, the nucleus is still according to the formula *s+not D+n*, for there is a satyr present and two of the females are distinguished as nymphs: this very plainly, for doubly – by their ancillary duties and attitudes as well as by the thyrsos each has. There are moreover links with the "Reunion" krater, Munich 3297; above all with its pan-brandishing satyr, in that pan's correlative thing, the laver against which the third female leans, in an attitude so little *ancillam decente* as to set us wondering who she is, and what we should make of a certain combination of fruit and foliage that presents itself as a *severed* link with Munich 3297. Anyhow, one thought quite unescapable is that the suspended bunch of grapes and the substituted foliage (principal's *sapling*, no longer a thyrsus) are begging us to connect them: is not all this as if the short-haired short-ribboned young man of Munich 3297 had taken quite a step, to a new stage, in the present reappearance on Naples H 3253, and on arrival (across some border?) had filed credentials; had hung up the grapes Happy Ending gave him; had passed to one of the nymphs (on border duty?) the thyrsos he had when we last saw him. I am not suggesting that the "Reunion in Hades" krater has any connection of stylistic identity with the "Persians" krater in Naples (H 3253); Miss Margot Schmidt (*Dareiosmaler* p. 22) has cautioned us against attributing their paintings to one and the same hand. Nor, at this point, can it be more than a guess, hypothesis for the severest possible testing, that grapes, thyrsos and a third thing often seen which is no more thirst-quenching than the second, namely the equally Dionysiac ivy leaf, are all tokens belonging to a traffic, or at all events to some relation of interdependence, between Dionysos and Aphrodite, though it is encouraging already that we have seen in Dionysiac hands (cf. pl. 8a with pl. 8b) one or two symbols that belong to Aphrodite's side of the relation. It would be premature to count the pan among them until we have had firm evidence of its use in a nuptial bath, but let us not quite forget pan-wielding colleagues of the Munich satyr, the Roccavecchia nymph whose manipulation of the thing is so like his (*ArchClass* 11 [1959] pl. 62,1), and the numph at the back of the Iphigenia krater (pl. 2), who has quite a message for us: "if it is premature to relate me and my pan to Aphrodite-*Aprodita*-Libitina, look at a picture by the hand which also painted me, at the back of the neck of Leningrad St. 426 (pl. 4b) where a team like my satyr and me are waiting on the son of Aphrodite, new style, as redesigned for wool-hatted worshippers of *Ana Aprodita* who without his borrowing of her bonnet would not have recognized the connection. But before you look away to them from us note in our picture some things you will not see in theirs; the fan which I will not call mine, though it is in my right hand, and my satyr's relinquished thyrsos, beribboned like mine which is harder to see. Altogether, that will be the best possible preparation for the shock in store for you when you look out of the open end of your tunnel of Dionysiac neck-strips, from the last thing in it (the most diluted, from the neck of the "Persians" krater, where the hero has exchanged thyrsos for simple sapling, and an important-looking woman is lounging against a laver [just right for my pan!], holding a tray of things mostly invisible but with the same garnish of sprays as a nuptial phiale)."

The "shocking" sight visible from the present and latter end of our Dionysiac "tunnel" is the Orphic triad on the late Apulian oinochoe, no. 1554 in the Jatta collection at Ruvo reproduced in my fig. 13 from *BullNap NS* 6, pl. 11. If there was justification for that recent volley of privileged *oratio recta* it was more in the nymph's hint of mitigating continuity than in any need we had to be warned of a sudden and disrupting apparition of Orpheus just at the point where the god thought in modern speculation to be most his, Dionysos, seemed to be in danger of eclipse by the deity who, if only the evidence collected by Kern (*Test. 76-77*) under the heads VENERIS CONTEMPTOR, AMOR PUERORUM, deserved the least respect, might have been reckoned least his. We have had preparation already (p. 37) for the paradox, as it is in some degree, of Aphrodite's appropriation of Orpheus, as well as some introduction to what might be called "banausic ambiguity," a shop's right to profit by leaving a choice open; by which the answer to the question "is the figure behind the man with the harp on the Jatta vase *Aprodita*, or can it be our dear daughter?" is naturally "dear sir, you are paying for the right to settle that." Subject to this (quite important) condition and to what I may as well call the "Roccavecchia lesson" (that pitchers are not safely interpreted out of reference to the krater of their tomb-group), let us accept the woman leaning on the laver behind Orpheus as Aphrodite, having encouragement to do so from the unmistakable presence of Aphrodite above a laver and Orpheus on a krater in the "H.A." collection (pl. 12), and perhaps even from the censer (which could easily be Aphrodite's) between Orpheus and the naked man about to be aspersed or sluiced from a laver on an amphora in Bari (no. 873) (pl. 23). The aforesaid hint of continuity may have been too urgently given, but let us take and use it where it helps – to discourage what one or two of this group of Orphic scenes have in fact undergone, interpretation according to the idea which Ovid and Hyginus got from Phanokles,[1] that Orpheus was the culture-hero, *auctor*, of Priapic love. (F. Gargallo Grimaldi, *BullNap* NS 6 [1858] p. 131; Heydemann, *BdI* [1868] p. 153: against him, G. Jatta, *Vasi italo-greci del Signor Caputi di Ruvo,* ppl 58-59). So taken, the Jatta oinochoe would have little bearing on the eschatology of *amore elisiaco* as Patroni conceived it, for it would show us Aphrodite faint with resentful horror at a defiant Orpheus' evilly Priapic influence on the present young man. The point of the reminder given in the last paragraph was that even from the s . . . . n eschatography at the back of the neck of the Iphigenia krater, just a little more strictly Dionysiac (pl. 2) than a work of the same hand in which we could see at least the *son* of Aphrodite made welcome by two similar minions of Dionysos (pl. 4b), certain threads of connection could be traced as running to the Jatta oinochoe. One surely in the symbolism of fans, whether the fan-holding person to whom Orpheus was turning and talking (not defiantly!) was the

---

[1] Phanokles in I.U. Powell, *Collectanea Alexandrina* 107 lines 9-10; Ovid *Met.* 10.83.

goddess of natural cohabitation (entitled, of course, to appropriate as attribute any article of her business of equipping brides), or "our dear daughter" duly bathed and equipped for the companion she did not live to have but was now winning in the man seen approaching, or "our dear mother" about to be reunited (not without some of the rites and ceremonies of earthly marriage) to "our dear father." Besides that thread from the fan in transit at the back of the Iphigenia krater (in the youth's baggage as taken over by the nymph there) to the fan in possession of the leaning woman or goddess on the Jatta oinochoe, is there not another one running *to* all the ceremonial streamers (two on the sapling, one on the wreath which the bridegroom also carries) of the Jatta vase *from* similar streamers which make banners of the saplings of the satyr and nymph who are entertaining Aphrodite's agent Eros on Leningrad St. 426 (pl. 4b) and even of the thyrsoi (at least sub-gala!) of the more porter-like pair, painted by the same hand, who are taking care of the mortal transient on the Iphigenia krater — himself bridegroom, if the fan twice shown (at his heroon first, before delivery to those "porters") is not less significant than the fan of our man formerly in Bremen.

If all this seems too fine-drawn, let me avail myself of Professor Cedric G. Boulter's kind permission to mention a splendid oinochoe in the Cleveland (Ohio) Museum of Art (no. 28.601). Nothing at all could serve better than this pitcher, of the same ware and no doubt of nearly the same date as the Jatta pitcher but with slimmer neck, to stand as landmark at the foot of the pass we are about to cross. Its single picture is a composition of two figures, Eros and an ambiguous female (for again we have to write "woman or goddess"), whose conspicuous thyrsos (streamered, like others we have just now seen) has a setting of symbolism which without Orpheus' presence contrives to be suggestively Orphic. This, chiefly, by means of three features of the scene. First, a triangular harp in the background: though this is overlapped by the figure (facing left) of the woman or goddess, it can be seen to be significantly like what Orpheus is playing on the Jatta oinochoe, with the inconvenient but eloquent serrations on top and the perhaps not really so eloquent bird in front (the spikes, meant to recall the ridge of the richest form of Thraco-Asiatic headdress, say "quite exotic"; the bird would suggest what in one legend Orpheus himself became if only it were less of a crane and more of a swan). Next, the seated female's fan. But that would arouse no particular curiosity, would mean no more than "wife, if not wife-making goddess," if this "wife," or this Aphrodite, were not sitting on part of a thing like what the fan-holding woman or Aphrodite leans against on the Jatta oinochoe. For it is not the familiar "kionisk of the beyond," the support recognizable (because it is baseless and because the fallen whole does occur in late Apulian red-figure) as just the top of a ruined Ionic column reerected (Paris has it to sit on in his beyond; Elysians have this convenience in their less pastoral one). Though it affords the present sitter more room than would commonly be given, there can be no doubt that what we can see is meant for a shaft of the same function as the based, flaring, fluted pedestal with salient ring and flat top of the laver which, as disbowled in the brawl which cost Thersites his head, is represented on a late Apulian vase, the enormously monumental volute-krater in Boston (03.804) published by James M. Paton in *AJA* (1908) pl. 19.[1] Except the merely ornamental stop-gap, just a rosette, between the sitter's feet and the feet of Eros who stands facing her, nothing in the background of the figure, still less any of their attributes (best enumerated gradually), is quite meaningless. But of the two things suspended the more compact one — plaything; not a purse, not a folding mirror, but a ball — is the more interesting, as perhaps of even double meaning (it will be time to enquire quite fully into that when we shall be offered a third and Orphistic symbolism; but perhaps it is not too early to have warning that when on the London amphora F 332 ahead of us, pl. 5, we have explained Aphrodite's present of a catchball at Kore's finally decent wedding to Hades — as with the help of Kore's Locri plaques should not be too difficult — there will be on that vase one more, suspended like the present ball, still to be accounted for). The wreath shown hung up in the Cleveland scene is merely festal in this "horned" form, though our knowing one or two of this sort as commonplace decoration of a theatre need not prevent the present example from borrowing narrower significance from the presence of Eros holding tainia and *pair* of phialai, if he has come or is about to go on a nuptial errand.

I had several things in mind in using for the Cleveland vase the word which I risked. It will be disappointing if this landmark "at the foot of a pass" and so of transition proves not to be one of those which themselves can afford a view. How badly we seem to need an opportunity for just desultory circumspection, though what we have come through was not quite a tunnel, and what we could observe in that gallery of Dionysiac neck-strips from volutekraters was interesting enough, signs, in what is almost the only part of such a vase that is exempt from mythography, of a further development in chthonic Aphrodite's assertion of herself against chthonic Dionysos: signs of her having come to terms with him. We are reminded that (whatever its acclamation may be worth) the fifty-fifth *Orphic Hymn* hails her (line 7) as majestic sharer of the throne of Bacchos. Perhaps it would be premature, before that opportunity for circumspection which must certainly be made, to settle confidently (subject to his and the purchaser's rights of "banausic" ambiguity) that the Darius Painter must have meant Aphrodite in the figure leaning possessively (?) forward on the laver in the neckstrip of the "Persians" krater (fig. 1c). But with one thing and another — chiefly the principal's exchange here of the usual thyrsus for a sapling (nuptial symbol, as pl. A of Trendall's *South Italian Vase Painting in the British Museum* has

[1] A better publication is in "Greek, Etruscan, Roman Art," p. 151, Fig. 130. [A.D.T.]

recently and sumptuously emphasized, and anyhow seeming to be preparation for the stage which the journeyer with the sapling on the Jatta pitcher
has already entered upon and has perhaps nearly finished, through satyr-free
country which is not Dionysiac at all, Aphrodite and her surprising Orpheus
seeming to control it — was not an impression made of something much
more prospective than was meant in the neckstrip of the Munich "Happy
Ending" krater? There too no doubt some things pointed forward (to a laver
ahead, the satyr's sluicer; perhaps to affairs still further ahead, the satyr's
sapling). Perhaps also, somehow, Happy Ending's provision in reserve, the
grapes. But she herself and her award of a crown set the picture's tone.
Without any implication that Naples H 3253, the "Persians" krater, was
painted by the same hand (telling a serial story), it may be said that at the
back of the neck of the Naples krater some hint seems to be given of a stage
which is altogether to lose the *s . . . . n* element of what we were just now
collating. That is, it could be thought that what was passing between the
principal female and the principal (and only tailless) male was the intimation
"now the really important business — mine with you — can almost begin; if
you would tell that nymph behind you that there is no more need for her
hovering with the crown given you at the beginning of the last stage, the two
girls and their colleague can go back through the dark to Dionysos."

Symbols of Ablution with
Reference to Hesperids and Danaids

THAT IS AN impression which we shall be able in due course to control, by
grave-mates of this vase, and so without any climbing up to pinnacles, such
points of view as may be necessary for our satisfying curiosities now almost
urgent: not only that which was aroused by a glimpse (fig. 7) of signs of a
link (in surprising hydrias) between Hesperids and Danaids but also that
which cannot but fasten on the sudden importance of Orpheus, in some
connection, evidently, with Aphrodite, *Ana Aprodita* of the "woolhats," in
some connection, possibly, with a turn of history which seems to have begun
with a raid on their behalf by a man to whom Plutarch has given a certificate
(*Alexander* 2) of acquaintance with Orphic religion of a certain orgiastic
kind, Alexander the Molossian, Olympias' brother and son-in-law. For (if it is
not affectation to borrow twice from the source of the word just quoted)
may I not say that it would be remiss to ignore "all the King's men," who as
allies in the Lucanian war mingled with Tarentines and with Peucetian and
Daunian friends of Tarentum, partners of the complex economy which its
coins advertise? The course of Alexander's campaign in Italy is not easy to

follow, but if it began at the geographic beginning of his adventure (as Justin says, xii. 2.5) the Daunians of the interior (Canusium) were its first bene-ficiaries, from Alexander's capture of coastal Sipontum; numismatically, it is Peucetian Rubi that (in this pastoral interior) shows most gratitude to Alexander, or most awe of him (P. Wuilleumier, *Tarente*, p. 84). The time of this (334-333 B.C.) fits the style of our Cleveland marker, and also the styles of the three vases which, more explicitly and without the concession to Dionysos which help to make the Cleveland *thyrsigera* a landmark of transition, attribute to Orpheus religious importance, the H.A. krater, the Jatta oinochoe, the Bari amphora (fig. 13, pl. 12), and of all others which show any interest in Orpheus that is above what the earliest Tarentine vase-painting expressed, contemptuous pity for him. I must not begin to write as if this study were turning Western ἐτητύμως, with the views which Dr. Vanacore and Dr. Ciceri helped Patroni to ripen to the maturity of their presentation in *Guida Ruesch*, p. 463, now peering from a stage-coach halted between two alarming notices: "load guns" "unload superfluous baggage." But I could say nothing timelier than that between the subtleties of two confusable symbolisms, that of the latest Apulian vases, that of a certain Orphic ritual, there is a trying defile ahead of us, last stage of my acknowl-edged duty of escorting Patroni's theories to their due place on a plateau of sufficient respect (but with benching for some open questions, where the research of others may pick them up). It will be last stage but one of the whole journey, for this must not end short of all the verification which pictured myths (the Danaids' serial story for one and the Hesperids' setting for another among several) can give of the reading ventured of the laver and sluicer symbols in their meaning as correlatives. Incomplete as our collation of Dionysiac neck-strips was, short perhaps of one of our real needs, need of never *failing* to know the god's presence, it seems to have shown already that these two, in their due conjunction, are the prime symbols of late Apulian eschatography. On the late vases the way to bliss is more of a point-to-point affair than it was (before there had been need, even, of the pan symbol) in the eschatology of the Hoppin Painter, whose chthonic Dionysos could not dispense with ablutions, we saw (pl. 8b), but had by his prompt and personal attention kept the mating of blessed souls quite a simple matter.

It is important, even if it should take quite a wide arc of circumspection, to perceive how the symbolism of purification gained emphasis through the very development which ended by making beatification (with the mating which was essential to it, as Patroni saw) a round-about procedure; circuitous indeed for some souls, if these had not two but three jurisdictions to transverse. My fig. 13 (Jatta pitcher) and pl. 12 ("H.A." krater) are already suggesting that finally, whether or not an influence from across the Adriatic in the last phase of the Apulian vase-painting helped to prompt her, Elysian Aphrodite found the whole mate-mill, mate-water-mill, too much for her and invited Orpheus (the greatest mortal authority on purity and on effective rites) to take over the stream of *men*. It is becoming one of our problems to find that the signs of this are related to signs in a very strange configuration of pictures, some of these showing us the Hesperids' Garden and some perhaps the Danaids' failure to reach it, indicative of a correspondingly separate stream of women. For that problem and doubtless for other questions it will be helpful to note how a symptom of all this elaboration and protraction, the inventing of the pan symbol of thoroughly effective purification, concocted by fusing the two movable things required for a good bath at the fixed thing, happened to provide funerary vase-painting with a system of tenses, nay of moods and tenses. As handled by satyr or nymph of a Dionysiac induction team, this rather bizarre composite of sluicer and footbath is in the future indicative (see the back of the neck of the Munich "Happy Ending"). But as deposited (or as is safer to say, manipulated) with notably proleptic gesture by a survivor (see a flanker of that vases's heroon, pl. 1b), the thing's mood might be parsed, without hair-splitting, as optative. There may be perhaps more subtle employments of this resource. If its being on the ground at the feet of the sitter-on-the-wardrobe in the Hesperides' Garden on the Archemoros vase (fig. 8) means what the like position in Hades' bathroom quite unmistakably meant (pl. 5), then its past tense makes present sense of something which E. Gerhard seems to have found (among other features of the scene) silly and pointless, the alabastron held by the figure standing nearby (Aphrodite, not a Hesperid?) who also holds a fan. Fan, as we know by now, is the final ornament of wifely status, there not quite reached. But the timing of the vial of perfume can be taken to match, neatly enough against Gerhard's censure, that of the alabastron for the already bathed and clothed woman on the Hearst Painter's calyx krater in Lecce (p. 64), which is brought to her by a satyr perhaps opportune in this his present reappearance. Let him be a reminder, good for our sense of gradualness and of overlaps, that even the Lycurgus Painter, whose own and earlier Garden of the Hesperides gives much the same hint of safely segregated facilities for the baths of women in transit to mated bliss (fig. 7), once saw nothing wrong in entrusting such a transient, not yet clothed, to a satyr's care (Anna Rocco, *ArchClass* 3 [1951] pl. 40, 2; especially remarkable because the Lycurgus Painter has made it so plain that the *thyrsigera* sitting naked on her clothes [while that satyr pours her a drink] is destined for the commonplace young man, decidedly no Dionysos, sitting top left, his head and the rest of him turned away from the Dionysiac group). The pictures in Leningrad which refine the punishment of the Danaids into a hellish *disappointment* are to be discussed later in this study. But that would be no excuse for not mentioning here the climax of this grammar of the sluicing-pan, as in my fig. 4 for St. 424; is not the mood of the thing as it is made to stand so very obtrusively there *imperative*, even if we hesitate to imagine that its vertical handle as held by the most forward (in every sense) of the six Danaids is rapping out "give us our baths" on the platform of

Hades' pavilion. Anyhow, fig. 12 for the sequel on St. 426, with the pan cast on the rocks, is anticlimax, even if perhaps its place does not quite make the nearest Danaid's gesture and finger-play tell the Danaid with the mirror "throw it too away; we are not going to get them."

Turning Away from Dionysos: Aphrodite—Her Functions and Relationship to Pan

IF ONLY THE rest of the symbolism which we must master (or at least preserve, from Orphistic confusion) were as lucidly eloquent! But perhaps worst in the fog of ambiguity resulting from the very sophistication of the latest phase of Apulian red-figure is something which is not really a matter of symbolism. Of the three figures of its religion now most important to us, only the last-come, Orpheus, because as a rule he dresses strangely, is nearly always recognizable. It was only because the first of the *s . . . . n* "sandwiches" of a recent collation marked mere zero in a development *away from* Dionysos (substitution of an Elysian transient, at most "Dionysiast," for the god himself) that we were quite justified there (the group above the Lycurgus Painter's Garden on the Jatta krater, fig. 7) in borrowing its principal figure as a Dionysos sure *enough*; he seemed to be getting divine honours, to be embowered and settled (no transient!) and to have not less than the needful minimum of hair and ribbon. He was at least good enough for employment in a demonstration that cropped *passengers* to and beyond a bathe could scarcely be meant for Dionysos. But what have we in the pair top left in the larger picture on the same side of the Jatta krater, just below this "practically sure" Dionysos, in his strip so thoroughly and infectiously settled down that even the artist's favourite deer has caught it, no longer the alert little thing of Oliver's figs. 3 and 4? Is the figure to whom in the big picture Eros is showing something resembling a daisy-chain to be read as Aphrodite, like the figure who *must* be meant for this goddess top right in one of the Leningrad pictures of Danaids (St. 424, fig. 4)? There between this sure Aphrodite and Pan (whatever it may seem that this god of the reeds is so near) we find Eros hovering with a similar chaplet or unfinished wreath and a plaything (whatever it may mean that this, a quartered ball recalling the *pilae pictae* of Ovid's list of things to woo with [*Metamorphoses* X 262], is of the same sort as the plaything hung up above the "Aphrodite or . . ." on a landmark of the present region of excessive subtlety and Orphic complication, the Cleveland oinochoe, p. 84). Or (with fig. 7 for the Jatta krater again before us) is the woman top left in the Lycurgus Painter's Garden to be explained altogether by the waterpot which lies so near her? If the figure in the Cleveland picture, provided with fan and Thyrsos and seated on half a laver near an Orphic harp, was not Aphrodite instructing Eros, then of course this strangely perched and circumstanced person was a woman receiving through him Aphrodite's instructions: "you have already had your bath (evidently, since you have contrived to make a seat of it), and you are provided with the proudest badge of your new (or renewed) wifely state; here now are things for the ceremony, a two-phialai one, just as in my mother's arrangements for Helen and Paris" (Lilli B. Ghali-Kahil, *Les enlèvements et le retour d' Hélène*, pl. 28, 1-2, p. 186 n. 157, Amphora Berlin F 3244; she is not quite sure — "[Helene]" : "[Paris]"). Correspondingly: if the figure facing Eros in the Lycurgus Painter's Garden of the Hesperides is not Aphrodite waiting to reassign an idle hydria then she is a woman receiving through Eros notice of her turn to draw bath-water. The best, or rather the highest, we can make of her is thus a questionable Aphrodite, and let us note at once that she is not our second such, but our third or even our fourth. On the Archemoros krater, with which we have already had a good deal to do, there is an absolutely sure Dionysos with adscript, and the sooner we are free to notice him (on the front, fig. 9 not in the Garden at the back) the better. But (fig. 8) at its back, in its Garden, Aphrodite is surely, nevertheless ambiguously, present, if I am not too sanguine in judging that with the help of two figures on the Lycurgus Painter's namepiece in London and two corresponding figures to support them from part I of the Danaids' disappointment (St. 424) one can establish securely the following dilemma. If on the Archemoros krater Aphrodite is not the female standing ready with the two things respectively last and last but one in bridal preparations, fan and alabastron, then she is that woman's seated neighbor, with a certain consequence for the chest sat on; no longer girl's "hope-chest" (as women tell me the women's magazines used to call it) but now Aphrodite's reserve of supplies for eschatic brides (not only alabastra and fans and phialai, but also the things which so provokingly correspond with objects used in an Orphic ritual, balls and mirrors and work-baskets to cast them in, and other things not much less open to Orphic interpretation, rattles, timbrels, gabled caskets, grapes).

For the operation we need not only fig. 8 and pl. 15 for the chest and the persons on or around it and pl. 2 for the triad in Leningrad, Eros between Aphrodite and Pan, which is so eye-opening when duly compared with a certain triad back of the British Museum's Lycurgus krater F 271, the side from which Oliver's fig. 2 was taken (*BMMA* [Summer 1962] p. 27). A quite necessary supplement is Miss Margot Schmidt's pl. 3 of her *Dareiosmaler*, with a slightly more ample view of that side; hers (top left) sufficiently discloses a figure of Pan, next to the goddess who is sitting (like the principal figure among the women in the later of the two gardens) on a big chest, with Eros for her other neighbor, at this level (he is just above the laver at which a figure of the foreground, Hippodameia, has prepared herself for Pelops, seen sitting close to the spring from which the laver's water was drawn; not in vain this time, for we can see Myrtilos, wheel in hand, setting about the mischief which is destined to balk her father's assurance of its being only one more in a series of mockeries of nuptial bathing. Of course this is work of Eros and his mother, from above. For work of our own, further and very necessary practice in recognizing Aphrodite, we can be glad to have Oliver's encouragement (his p. 25) to find her on the chest between her son and Pan (whom Oliver did not fail to mention, though his fig. 2 did not have room for this Pan's person and could take in only part — the most important part, beribboned tip — of his attribute). This is not where an earlier interpretation put her, at the same level but further to our right, cut off by the shaft of an agonistic monument from the picture's main web of significant relations. It was by the figure of Pan, interested, intrusively leaning in, holding a beribboned sapling, that Walters in the British Museum's *Catalogue* (p. iv, no. F 271) was put off; fitter, he thought, for Pan's neighborhood and Pan's interest would be some nymph of Olympia's valley (a well-watered one, certainly). For my part I can only be grateful to the god in his present company with his present attribute of a wedding-guest for his effect, annihilating, on part of an earlier draft of this study: a passage which purblindly explained as mere space-padding the addition of Pan to another significant grouping of Aphrodite and Eros above another matter of water, the punishment of the Danaids as, with irony which that grouping helps to flavor, it begins on the volute-krater St. 424 in Leningrad (fig. 4). It would be quite exquisitely bad management if, very near the point of greatest need for doggedly objective scrutiny of symbols threatened with Orphistic contamination, I let Pan, Pan with a capital letter, get in the way and block them from sight. And this in a paragraph concerned to establish Aphrodite's presence at the back of the Archemoros krater — with a washpan at her feet, and so one of several Aphrodites in Tarentine vase-painting who (besides any other interest they should have for us) can claim special importance in their having appropriated (or at least attracted) one symbol or another of the disputable code. It needs only a glance at my pl. 23, where in the frieze of Bari 873 such a washpan is seen below what looks like (and in some sense must truly be) its Orphic *aition*, for anyone's grasping how specially exposed that very symbol is to what I have called "Orphistic wrenching"; if now bluntest *oratio recta* is better, say it invites "no, that's for remission of sin; what made you think it could have anything to do with mating (or remating) in a future life?" The briefest (and so here best) provisional answer to that being "ideas which its association with an interracial goddess of mating seems to confirm," perhaps this is just the right dialectical turn for exploring further connections of Aphrodite with the chattel-symbolism of latest Apulian red-figure.

If it is, then that is an enquiry which Pan must not be allowed to interrupt, but is welcome to forward, having — even on his own account —

some claim on our curiosity. There is, in the first place, the question (quite explorable since K. Schauenburg's "Pan in Süditalien" in *AthMitt* 69 (1962), 27-42) how much this Greek god essentially pastoral does in fact matter to a funerary art, which in my theory of it is a catering of Greeks to pastoral neighbors. More important, there is the hint which we have just caught (in one of the pictures of Danaids) of an eschatological relation between chthonic Aphrodite in her well-watered meadow of purification and Pan in that palustrine or riparian aspect of his pastoral essence which he gets from his duty of finding water for stock on the range; a function neatly annotated, as my friend Professor William Hunter Macrea caused me to see, by the "dew-ponds" put down with reeds on winter mud for the sheep of the South Downs of England. In our present concern with an aspect of Aphrodite problematically Orphic (her association with Orpheus undeniable, "Orphism's" right to appropriate her symbols very questionable), the most profitably suggestive Pan is the one in whose company she seems to be on a pelike at what is now officially known as the Hearst San Simeon State Historical Monument, near San Luis Obispo in California (no. 5696 or PC 2817, pl. 16a and b here). "Seems to be" I had to write for two reasons; to recall the principle of banausic ambiguity which applies in the present case, and to emphasize our need (and my purpose) of surer, the surest possible, criteria of Aphrodite. I have myself no doubt that this painter's tidy plan was to confine his mortals to the back of the vase, where I am quite willing to recognize what of course Patroni would have seen there, a pair of lovers in Elysium. For the other side he provided three immortals, natural neighbors as he chose to depict them: Pan not lacking the attribute which most marks him as at home in watery places (fresh and living reed, not the mere reed-pipes held by the Pan who is Aphrodite's neighbor above the Danaids' boisterous demand for bath-water in my fig. 4); Aphrodite and Son not failing to display samples of the stock of the bride-equipping affair which they run at a moist edge of Elysium in the Garden of the Hesperides, which already in the Lycurgus Painter's version of it (fig. 7) was too well-watered for any surprise now at finding Aphrodite's swan perched on the firm's stock-box. If I think it important to allow the artist the following afterthought, or underthought, "all the better, if some Pan-enriched probatocrat's taking my outfitter Aphrodite for his outfitted daughter sells the piece," that is no really fresh point; I hope it has long been clear that I judge nothing more disqualifying for the study of late Apulian red-figure than a certain lack of the lowest grade of imagination, the imagination required for seeing it as a business, seeing it so in vivid detail: in the present connection, Apulian detail relayed through a Tarentine head, this painter's vision of the wool-land warehouse, with the local agent of his pottery steering steeple-hatted survivors through long sheds, with many opportunities of helping choice and of encouraging a rational if expensive taste for sets that (eschatographically) made sense.

If one has not forgotten the iron which Albizzati heated for branding late

Apulian vase-painting "unsubtle," then even the most coarsely canny of its equivocations is interesting and relishable. But the present value of the not quite unambiguous neighbor of Pan in my pl. 16a should be propulsive. She cannot but give a sense of our need of still better Aphrodites: better for decisive help in a dilemma now quite definably embarrassing us. Is the eschatology of the latest Apulian red-figure still "nuptial" and its symbolism still in large part cosmetic (requiring, and able to make, signs for things essential to a bride's full bloom or dignity)? Or does the new prominence of Orpheus, a somehow cleansing Orpheus in evident association with Aphrodite, mark a very great change? A shift, that is, from something not very unlike one of Swedenborg's optimisms, *facultas perpetua amandi uxorem in caelo,* to the eschatology of a religion of guilt and a corresponding symbolism: a code wholly cathartic, yet quite a jumble, consisting partly of old symbols easily converted from cosmetic to cathartic meaning (ablutionary things, laver, sluicer, hydria, alabastron), but partly too of signs having or promising correspondence with objects well known to have been handled in rites of purgation. It is not quite the turn of this second part. But perhaps it is not too soon for a compliment to the modern Orphist on the elegance which his point of view lets him enjoy in a significantly frequent conjunction of two particular symbols, mirror with bunch of grapes. This is a difficulty for the Patronians (mirror for nubility, but what of the rest?). But with mirror recognized as bridge between sects (cosmetic thing turned trap, implement of the deicidal *telete* that is best attested of all the tools, by Clement, by the papyrus ritual, by Miss Simon's Titan-enacting satyrs), and moreover with Dionysos himself recognized (Miss Simon's plaques assisting) in the bunch of grapes, we could be invited to salute a very neat compendium of South Italian Orphism — neatest when the grapes and the mirror are entrusted to an effeminate winged child as on the nuptial lebes F 346 in the British Museum.

"Orphic" Objections; the Purgation of Sins; Counter Arguments for "Nuptial" Eschatology

IT IS PART of a strange pattern of coincidence that for our Orphists this person can instead of an Eros be Mise, that frankly bisexual (not merely διφυής) god identified in his or her Orphic Hymn (no. 42) with Eleusinian Iakchos, whom Sophocles hailed as patron of Southern Italy. The Pan of the San Simeon pelike cannot but remind us of this matter's extravagant ramifications; according to a legend none the worse (in the present context) for being ludicrous the native region of Italiote Pan was the Krathis valley, supposed cradle of Orphism for those who allow themselves this word: source, anyhow, of Corigliano Calabro of the golden tablets which are so different from the Patroni-favoring (because reunion-hinting) tablets from Petelia and Pharsalos; notoriously, they imply a religion of guilt, being certificates of purity through atonement. It is less notorious that one of them (Kern's *Fr.* 32,d) was found in impressive association with someone reported to be only too like Mise, "un Genio alato, *ermafrodito*." The red-figured plate on which this figure could be made out belonged to the third cremation burial of the third *timbone*; though found outside the "cassa sepolcrale" which yielded that tablet and moreover classed "Lucanian" (not "Apulian") by the finder, this piece of evidently late pottery from near Thurii (roughly contemporary with the Molossian's strategic interest in that part of the Krathis valley!) almost deserves to outrank, in the more curious data of the present question, the Messapian inscription in a tomb at Rudiae-Rugge which O. Haas was inclined to read as a mutilated dedication to hermaphrodite Mise (*Messapische Studien,* p. 49, B.1.45). The present question, or sheaf of questions, needs a bow of pink or blue ribbon much less urgently than it needs my making good my word "propulsive" for the San Simeon pelike. But there could hardly be apter decoration of it than that which another red-figured vase with another effeminate Eros offers to give, Verona no. 143 Ce, *CVA* Italy 34 IV D, pl. 13. Somehow adhering to the flying messenger's shanks is a cross-headed torch of the same pattern as the "Demeter-Symbol"[1] recorded by Haas for the (*m*)*isai* inscription at Rugge; hanging somehow from his phiale is a ball, more easily rolled to the Orphistic side of our major problem than the dry skull (ram's, not goat's) seen in the field. Here is a quite pretty, perhaps better than pretty, crux. As part of the apparatus of an Orphic *telete* of purgation mock-Titan's ball is surely attested, only a little less superabundantly so than mock-Titan's mirror. And another thing in this picture, the timbrel hanging from the bonneted boy's right hand would go well enough with an Eros sufficiently effeminate to pass (in just one more mix of convenient syncretism) as Mise-Iakchos, whom the Pergamene hymn makes so adaptable (child of Egyptian Isis by a god whom the Krathis valley tablets mention and most of the others ignore, Eubouleus; but at home with Demeter in Eleusis, with the Great Mother in Phrygia, with Aphrodite in Cyprus). This is hardly yet the place for superimposing the ugly, at any rate cruelly tiresome, crux of Herodotus ii.81 which some relate to an Egyptianizing Orphism in the Krathis valley. But in the Eleusinian connection, was it not with a timbrel that the mother of Eros (after trying cymbals first, if we must slavishly follow lines 1346-1352 of Euripides' *Helen*) succeeded in drumming Demeter out of dislike of her daughter's

---

[1] Haas' phrase connotes this peculiar shape: that his mere "Fackel" implies it for the symbols on B.1.20 and 26 is clear from J. Whatmough, *PIO* 2, 372 and 47.

infernal marriage? However, appreciation of this and a not inelegant corollary (Demeter's cheerful enough application of her cross-headed torch to a conventional duty of brides' mothers, on Geneva 15043, not unrelated to the Bari Orpheus amphora [pls. 14, 23]) must not fail to savor the irony of the ram's skull. Mutton, even sacrificial mutton should have had no place in even Apulia's Orphism, if the "Orphic diet," βίος Ὀρφικός, Plato's phrase in *Laws* vi.782C for the strictest avoidance of meat, was part of it.

Perhaps this should be no stumbling block, for it is a principle of the religious studies, seriously based on common experience, that mere prohibitions should never be given cardinal importance. The world changes, and I shrink from instances modern but perhaps no longer telling; it must suffice for my point that, rightly, the Pythagorean aversion to cremation has never been cited in derision of Macchioro's peopling the *timboni* of Corigliano with Orphico-Pythagoreans out of Herodotus' ii.81 (*Orfismo e Paolinismo*, pp. 274ff). But it may conduce to timely pursuit of Aphrodites if we leave the Verona counterpart of the Corigliano Eros by way of the bridge there is in realizing how useful a commoner stopgap, skull of the vine's devouring enemy, might have been to boldly Orphistic interpretation of the round picture in the Verona cup. I mean such interpretation as, under goat's horns but perhaps even without our making very much of them, is invited by what there is to see on the hydria Lecce 801 (*CVA* It. 6, pl. 42,3).

This is another of the vases related by style of drawing and by conventions of accessory painting (how the white or yellow is put on) to the Orpheus amphora in Bari; besides, its picture's subject, altogether and in detail, is suggestively comparable with the Orpheus oinochoe in the Jatta collection in Ruvo (fig. 13). No Orpheus now on the hydria; but does not the youth, holding tainiaed wreath and tainiaed sapling and seen to be following the woman or goddess, remind us of the enigmatic person — candidate for what? — approaching (with just such things) Orpheus, a laver, and a possible Aphrodite, on the Ruvo oinochoe? Moreover, if lovers now are out and Orphism now is in, a special Orphism adapted to Italic awe of a goddess unquestionably identified with Aphrodite in the same series of Italic inscriptions that (more questionably) offered us Mise-Iakchos and Cretan Zagreus, should not the things carried by the woman (or Aphrodite?) on the Lecce hydria also interest us? Or is that quite the right word for the proper effect of this sluicer and this *popanon* (big pie-like cake in the shape of an Italic cavalryman's shield, round with central cone or boss)? *Arresting*, rather, now; as they should have been (an Orphist might say) from the first acquaintance with them on the Leningrad volute-krater St. 420 (fig. 2, pl. 2), where there were three sluicers (Iphigenia's, and two more on the back) and *popanon* (for the young man attended by satyr and nymph, in readiness for his presentation to much higher authorities of his new world — not at the desk of some matrimonial agency of theirs, but just as an acceptably pure soul?).

"How was it," the Orphist has some excuse for asking, "that all this was not enough to check your rush to embrace, protectively at least, Patroni's sentimentalities? What, in the first place, could be less cosmetic and nuptial, more grimly cathartic, than the tool of lethal lustration inserted at the feet of Iphigenia, spinster darling of two spinster goddesses in that illustration of that story? Of all stories of human affection the least concerned with nuptial love, you might have reflected. But that is by the way; it was your missing, in your fig. 2 for the obverse, the picture's richly Orphic point that was so discreditable and disastrous: its point of acceptable purity in preparation for death. Discreditable, because with some knowledge of the certificates of purity for the Corigliano dead, confessing sin but registering expiation, you had not the gumption to connect it with your knowledge of the plot of the *Iphigenia Taurica*. Disastrous, because your being too dull for any quickening of your appreciation of a play *turning on technicalities of infernal presentability* spoilt your exegesis of the whole vase. The two washpans of the reverse were not put there to be read out of connection with Iphigenia's on the obverse, where the picture is a great classic of funerary vase-painting: not indeed just because of the lethal pan, but because of a certain subtle layering of meaning in the whole consoling theme ("lucky escape of great sinner, greater than you") to which Iphigenia's tool (hinge of her cunning excuses) does not fail to contribute. We cannot help contrasting its routine work (its preparation of past strangers for bloody presentation to Tauric Artemis) with the quite exceptional operation of purging execrably unnatural sin which Iphigenia — in her stratagem for escape — is about to pretend to be necessary before acceptable slaughter of the present matricidal Greeks (*IT* 1191-1195). How did you manage to lose the idea of sin in just a half-turn of this vase, to the side where you could see the same tool of purgation, long-handled sluicer, twice? That is, not only at the monument of the Apulian sinner (sinner in the Orphic sense as at Corigliano, inheritor of an original taint of Titanic deicide), but also in the picture above, which shows a team neatly representative of the Orphic *paredria* of Dionysos and Aphrodite (that satyr and his nymph) inspecting the dead man's credentials of salvation, pl. 2. Naturally, these are things which were used in some saving Orphic *telete*; not necessarily the deicidal one, Orphism having its Eleusinian side, as volute-krater W 4 in the Vatican (Trendall, *VIE* 2, pl. 51) almost trumpets, with an exotic head which should be that of Orpheus (not of an eschatographically worthless Adonis!) above the subject, Triptolemos' mission, of a poem attributed to him (Pausanias, i.14.3; cf. Kern's *Fr.*, 52-53). Being such a zealot for recognition of the Tarentine subtlety of "Apulian" vase-painting, to the point of seeming to want to inject an empathy of it, a sense of the painter's own pleasure in it, please savor now the crowning felicity of the back of the neck of the Iphigenia krater: its triangulation or (to use the better, the Orphic, word) its *triagmos* of the actual instrument of purgation (sluicer, held by the nymph) with two other articles of mystic apparatus which one of the grimmer Fathers, Epiphanius, *packages together* in a list of *Eleusinian* things (timbrel, held by the satyr, bumped cake or *popanon*, held by the saved sinner)."

What we have just been handed is notice that the idea "Mysterienbilder," the death of which at the hands of Heydemann made room for Patroni to develop his "amore elisiaco," has come Orphistically to life again. I cannot grant that this makes it true, believing that in due course, a course which three Aphrodites, at San Simeon as just seen, (pl. 16a) at Naples (fig. 14), at Berlin (fig. 15), are already marking for us like buoys, we shall come to regard that view of late Apulian vase-painting as only a mirage, though a vivid one. Nevertheless, it is of actual importance, in proper justice to some of the freshest material in evidence, that we should not be too impatient to dismiss as a merely rhetorical packet of assonance, as a notoriously harsh prelate's sour jingle, "thump-thing, ay, and bump-thing too," what comes to us with a double ligature of particles when St. Epiphanius (taking, as he chooses to say, a higher tone) passes from Eleusinian *doings* rather like the riskily naked snack on the Lycurgus Painter's krater in the Hieronymites' library in Naples to Eleusinian *things* exactly like some symbols of late Apulian vase-painting; for he begins with τύμπανά τε καὶ πόπανα (*Adversus Haereses* iii.2, 1092 Migne, Kern *Fr.* 34). For evasion of this the line which has sometimes been taken in fighting Orphistic argument, especially with regard to the Corigliano tablets which are addressed to Persephone, namely "don't confuse Dionysos' Orphic with Kore's Eleusinian," is not open any longer. Partly because Dionysos seems now to have relinquished so much of his Orpheus to Aphrodite. But what has mainly restored plausibility (a little more than a little) to the hazily Eleusinian mysteriomania of Böttiger, Gerhard, and Panofka is archaeology's new need to take rather seriously a personification of just such confusion as aforesaid, Mise-Horos-Dionysos-Iakchos-probably Eros-perhaps Attis, addressed in one of the *Orphic Hymns*, the forty-second. It remains to be seen how much interest the bump-cake, more perhaps than in its bearing on the "Orphic diet," should be worth. What we have already seen of Mise has been wildly near nightmare. Out of its Pergamene hymn the monster stepped, both anachronistically and anachoristically; then it went to ground in the field-archaeology of our question at its two poles (at Messapian Rugge in the [*M*]*isai* of an Eleusinian inscription, at Greek Corigliano in the effeminate daimon associated with atonement tablets), after flourishing certificates of various qualifications. Of its being quite Western enough, Sophocles having made Eleusinian Iakchos so Italiote; of its being (for the vases' late Erotes) more than epicene enough; of being, altogether, interchangeable enough, most conveniently so in its status as common pet of all goddesses conceivably concerned, not only Aphrodite and the two Eleusinians but also Egyptian Isis — this conferring on Mise relevance even to the passage of Herodotus (ii.81) which as commonly printed is evidence of the historian's acquaintance (probably near modern Corigliano if it is true that he had land in the Krathis valley as citizen of Thurii) with Egyptianizing Orphico-Pythagoreans whom, somehow, he rated *less Dionysiac* than his own generation supposed them to be.

The first thing that should come of this is a better understanding of the threat — from the ware's own symbolism — menacing an opinion in which we have by now a stake, namely that Apulian red-figure, Tarentum's eschatography on funerary pottery made for her neighbors, continued until its end to be inspired by an eschatology of completion in love. That stake was acquired when the mere feeling that Patroni's hypothesis deserved more patient consideration than it had, on the whole, received was superseded by a conviction, or something very near it, that in regard to a certain stretch of this art's development, from its turning frankly eschatographic in the ultra-mundane subjects of the Hoppin Painter to the point at which (still in that artist's school) authority for reunions and matchmakings seemed to be shifting from Dionysos to Aphrodite, Patroni's view had verified itself. Any more of "fair play for poor Patroni!" would then be affectation? At all events there is something, a nuptial eschatology, sufficiently established for at least hopeful defense against the proposition "yes, but it did not last; in a shift much more cataclysmic than a mere adjustment of theology to please Messapians or Apulians a great flood of holy terror washed all the old cosy things out of funerary vase-painting." I acknowledge, of course, that this attack can be launched, that, moreover, there is need of practical attention to recent reinforcement of its weapon; in "holy terror" is packed not only the conviction of sin which Plato attributes to "Orpheus and company" in *Cratylus,* 400 B-C (the "your body's your penitentiary" passage) but also the more superstitious δεισιδαιμονία of the Eleusinian cult, with mysteries which (as Polygnotos had so graphically advertised to all the world) it was dreadfully dangerous to decline. This extra and Eleusinian charge is a contribution from several sources, and what just now came from St. Epiphanius is no doubt more formidable than the Eleusinian tinge which ingenuity can mix for the effeminate Eros of the late vases out of the *Orphic Hymn* to Mise-Iakchos-and-more and the mention of Italy in the hymn addressed by the chorus of the *Antigone* to a many-named Iakchos (1115-1151). In the first place, just because he is not, like his companions in Kern *Fr.* 34, Clement and Arnobius, an Orpheus-quoter making polemic about the silly toys of of deicidal *telete*, it is important (and a nuisance to Patronians) that things which Epiphanius names in a different and Eleusinian connection — timbrels, *popana* pies umbonate like a cavalry shield, flaring *kalathos* work-basket for wool — are not less conspicuous in the symbolism of the late vases than certain things (mirror and ball) named by Clement and Arnobius as apparatus of the *telete* derided by them, an affair which we need not scruple to reckon Orphic, since Clement and his echo Arnobius tell us that Orpheus did the verses for it. Next, without the Eleusinian coincidence in symbolism (Epiphanius' things turning up on the vases), the other and Orphic coincidence would be less impressive. For quite the acme of curious correspondence with vase-painting is reached when in the Gurob papyrus (Kern *Fr.* 31, reciting Eleusinian names as well as alluding to the Dionysiac *telete* aforesaid), Clement's mirror is flung into Epiphanius' work-basket (lines 27-30), this now making the most remarkable of all the coincidences in its agreeing exactly with what incongruously flanks a youth's heroon on a Naples loutrophoros, no. 2251 in Heydemann's catalogue, mirror stuck in *kalathos.*

"Flood of terror, rather mixed terror" is thus a practically interesting idea, as long as another idea, that the nuptial eschatology did not much outlast the Lecce Painter, is actually entertainable, and such pictures as that on H. 2251 might encourage one to entertain it: "Wedding present for infernal bride, and saying 'keep your beauty but keep busy'? Simpler, saner, more or less directly documented (whether the object in the work-basket by the man's monument be a mirror — instantly recalling that papyrus — or something else conceivably teletic, like the washpan basketed on Jatta *Cat.* 1337), to take it all as 'He's in no danger, he did the saving *telete*'. Like the man in the papyrus he was given objects to discard ($\dot{\alpha}\nu\eta\lambda\tilde{\omega}\sigma\kappa\alpha$) into a thing most aptly like a modern waste-basket. Naturally, we cannot tell whether it was quite the same batch of objects as in the papyrus, where all was standard god-bait, cone-top, rhomb, playbones, mirror, every one of them mentioned by Clement and Arnobius in their citations from an Orphic poem. Arnobius doing us the service of clearing up 'rhomb' (rumbling whirligig, so the thing that on so many late Apulian vases has been taken for a love-charm). But on that vase at Naples you can see the mirror sticking out. What projects from the other *Kalathos* placed symmetrically on the opposite side of the man's heroon is a fan (cf. Vergil's *Aen.* vi.740-741 for the 'dry-cleaning', moral, a teletic fan might do)."

The "Great Derangement";
Orphism and Alexander the Molossian?
Further "Orphico-Pythagorean"
Problems

THIS SHOULD HAVE stopped before its weakest point; we have had our own lesson, solemnly serial, from vases in Leningrad, Cologne, Taranto, on the infernal circulation of women's fans through male hands. Nevertheless, if the more general matter in question has any practical holds — practical for some scarcely shirkable business of making out the historically concrete relations of late Apulian vase-painting — these we have to find.

At any rate, the question concerns a great change — not to be appre-hended, much less understood, without some perception of its setting and factors. But not equally great for both sides of it. For the thorough Patronian, not ready to allow that an extinguisher came down on *amore elisiaco* at about 340 B.C., it is only a change of management, of dispensa-tion. In his reading of the late vase-paintings, as these were still done by and for persons who thought that any bliss to be enjoyed in the next life depended upon the most natural of human companionships, it was only proper that, after a time, Aphrodite the goddess of cohabitation should take over its dispensing from Dionysos; doubly natural and proper if there is not faulty extrapolation from the Messapian inscriptions in judging that among the Apulian customers for Tarentum's funerary pottery the goddess (as *Ana Aprodita*) possessed what the god (under any name) never got, sure standing as a chthonic power. Why those not-Greeks ever put up with the Hoppin-Lecce Group's Dionysos as infernal match-maker the Patronian does not have to explain; I quite agree that he need only point to the fact of it, not more than once or twice (pl. 8a and b should be facts enough; exploration of [stably?] Dionysiac eschatogamy in the afterlife of *Tarentines* is another matter, having much to do with terra-cottas; yet it might begin with the marvelous little *corredo* of grave 47 Tarento, with real and depicted ring and a quaint "before and after" pair of young [very young?] lovers, R. Bartoc-cini, *NS* [1936] 135, fig. 25; it is not unimportant that Cambitoglou and Trendall in assigning both the "before" vase and the "after" vase to their Thyrsus Painter [*APS*, p. 78, nos. 16 and 17] give them derivation from the painters of those "facts").

But certainly the Patronian can be required to have an answer to this challenge: "How do you explain the vases' Orpheus (and their Triptolemos) *away*? Aphrodite's 'take-over' was one observable change. But together with it and apparently in some essential connection there came another, that unheralded emergence of Orphic and Eleusinian personages, Orphic and Eleusinian symbols. If this sudden rash may be diagnosed as symptom of an abrupt seizure of teletic mysticism, the seizure's violence hardly needs explanation, given what Plato wrote earlier in the century (*Republic* i.330 D-331 D; ii.364 B-E) about precisely this king of religion, its promoters' intensive cultivation of natural fears universally strong, lucrative of course for the exploiters but in its incidental mummery and what not 'such delightful fun!' (διὰ παιδιᾶς᾿ ἡδονῖον, ii.364.E) for the exploited. Evidently your view of the matter sees not a seizure but stuffing; in some vague way, for you it is only reinforcement or decoration of the old paradisal pairing that there is, in the first place, suddenly so much of Orpheus, in manifesta-tions which should instead embarrass you, in both their kinds, mundane and inframundane. The former (pls. 12 and 23) show him musically preaching purification or musically presiding at it — if not mystical purification, remission of sin, what other kind? Is the tune, then, 'Bathe, too, you rough, before you marry; *she* will have done so'? The latter kind, of course, shows him in a setting of Eleusinian mysticism, for whatever you make of his being shown always on the right hand of Persephone (chief addresses of the Corigliano certification of purity) you cannot dare to make nothing of the Eleusinian tempering with old justice, packing the bench with Triptolemos in place of Minos. And before your imagination goes after means of making perhaps very little of Demeter's pet's having replaced the most awesome of the infernal judges in both the chief Naples and the only Munich hellscape (fig. 11; pl. 1a) give it the wholesome, steadying, exercise of supposing that the Minos-disqualifying Munich krater, from Canusium at the far end of Horace's Aufidus valley, had been dug up not by Caroline Murat's archaeological miners but by peasants in the poet's lifetime, with himself and his friend Torquatus present, *after* he had written, for that friend,

> cum semel occideris et de te splendida Minos
> fecerit arbitria.

And that is only the half of it. Whatever may remain obscure and difficult in the chattel- symbolism that comes in with Aphrodite's take-over it is not plain that this interpenetration Orphic and Eleusinian extends to it? On the one hand, two of its commonest elements, mirror and ball, are named by both the Orpheus-quoting Christians, Clement and Arnobius, among the things they list for Orpheus' *telete* imitating the Titans' trapping of Dionysos; moreover, since Mrs. Erika Kunze-Götte's publication of the Stuttgart oinochoe KAS 161 in *CVA* Germany 26, pl. 52, figs. 3 and 4 (my pl. 17a and b) these have acquired quite special significance, seeming more teletic than ever, partly because the pelt-clad youth on the Stuttgart vase (who seems to prefigure Miss Simon's mirror-brandishing satyrs in a teletic episode of the Campana plaques) has a slung ball to dangle, partly because that youth's own setting is so bizarre (unhooding of a great speckled egg in an affair requiring a kantharos, etc?). But while there are doubtless on the vases other symbols which one might assign to Orphic mummery or to Orphic purification (to say nothing of all the boxes or closed baskets available for *packing* Orphic symbols named by those two Fathers but not openly shown by our painters), there can be no making real Orphic stuff of the three symbols which are positively and exclusively on St. Epiphanius' Eleusinian list, timbrel, *popanon* cake, open *kalathos* basket (the rumble-wheel, *rhombos* or *volubilis rotula*, is in both listings). You have been seeking 'holds'. Well, now take this one; it comes with a jingle, 'expiation, propitiation', which may help you not to lose it. Certainly you need a practical grasp, good enough for intelligent perseverance with your material, of the historical but not altogether simple fact of this cataclysm of 'holy terror'. That is not too bad a phrase for one aspect of the fact, in its doing some justice to all that is packed in Plato's phrase about remissive *teletai* (*Republic* ii.364E), μὴ θύσαντας δὲ δεινὰ περιμένει "if you grudge what the holy transaction should cost (in meat or money) it will go terribly with you in the end'. But for your own 'historically concrete relations' be ready to shift your attention nearer the home of late 'Apulian' red-figure, Tarentum (the one sign given of your right to the phrase, of your knowing what such "concreteness" should mean, was your allowing that this funerary art got almost all its character from a uniquely initmate correlation of demand and supply between the rustic wealth of Apulia and the metropolitan – not just Greek – sophistication of Tarentum). And you can pitch it nearer than Corigliano-Thurii, which lay over a hundred kilometers to the southwest, important thought it certainly is that all consideration of the tablets from the mounded cremations there should be in properly sharp focus – with clear perception of their difference from the memory-reviving reunion-assisting tablets from Petelia and Pharsalos, and with the right sense of what was *lucky* in the Corigliano find of passport tablets: first, the luck that three of the four were copies, *excessively careless*, of a single text prescribed for making previous expiation *work* (in finally effective propitiation of the Infernal Powers), this with decided gain to our impression of cynically comprehensive quackery recklessly busy; next, the luck of some contraction of that gulf of a hundred kilometers, thanks to the red-figured plate at Corigliano which providentially the great weight of mounded earth failed to smash, sparing its effeminate Eros to forge a link (of surely temporal coincidence at the very least) between all this quackery at Thurii and the 'Great Derangement' of funerary vase-painting at Tarentum. But at Tarentum itself there is better than that, the best possible footnote to Plato's moral disapproval of expiatory *teletai* in *Republic* ii.364E should be the words in which his Tarentine friend Archytas shows scientific interest in them, his taking 'rumble-wheels in *teletai*' (τοῖς ῥόμβοις τοῖς ἐν ταῖς τελεταῖς) for crowningly clear illustration of the rule that slow to fast in movement means deep to shrill in sound (Diels-Kranz, *Fragmente der Vorsokratiker*[6], 1 Archytas Fr. B 1, p. 435, lines 2-5). You have not hesitated to suggest that Archytas at Tarentum (more than his unpolitical fellow-Pythagorean Okellos) was in a position to influence the tone of funerary vase-painting in that very phase of it which the Great Derangement terminated (p. 68). You have not to acknowledge that the teletic quackery which (with the bitter sauce of a bad pun) Plato condemned in *Rep*. ii.364E had established itself in Tarentum in the lifetime of Archytas, and was only too precisely in a position to derange the funerary art of the place after his death, the date of which should be reckoned as after the beginning of 349 B.C. (Cicero in *Cato Major* 41 being credible authority for Archytas' survival till then, even if not so for a last meeting with Plato in 349/348 B.C.), but before Tarentum's crisis of self-defenselessness in 346/345 (Diodorus xvi.61.4; 62.4; 63.1) – if the beginning of its desperate dependence on foreign champions may be thought not unconnected with its loss of a soldier-statesman already aged but not used-up, in his singularly successful experience still invaluable (cf. Aristoxenos in Diels-Kranz[6], Fr. A

1, p. 421, lines 23-24, 34-35; it need not affect this question that his seven successive tenures of supreme command, undefeated, have been conjecturally put earlier, at 367/366 through 361/360, doubtless his prime of life; see P. Wuilleumier's *Tarente*, p. 69)."

"Get yours no less concrete": perhaps that is the best of what this discharge leaves for the Patronian to pick up, to be used as may be in positive improvement of his position. This of course is already entrenched in a conviction that while the Great Derangement quite deserves its capital letters it should not, in spite of some appearances that make unshirkable difficulties, mean quite as much as just suggested, namely a collapse of the old optimism, this undermined as a matter of profitable business by *agyrtai* (to borrow Plato's word for peddlars of atonement and propitiation), with a beggarly exchange of hopes resulting — for the old hope of completion in renewed or fresh companionship this new one, that the price of buying off misery (the money spent, the stock slaughtered, the mumbo-jumbo undergone) would turn out not to have been wasted. "Getting it concrete" should be an affair of seeking comprehension of the whole issue in terms of its things, its persons, its places. A referee of the question would do well to allow some stretch of license in lining up the persons historical to it. Let them be of both sexes: for on the whole it would be unreasonable to disallow Plutarch's credentials for the woman who is more important to us as sister of Alexander the Molossian, the most timely and relevant of those foreign champions of Tarentum and her Apulian allies, than as mother of Alexander the Great, Olympias, certified ἔνοχος τοῖς Ὀρφικοῖς (*Alexander* 2, Kern's *Test.* 206). If there is Orphic religion on the vases made at Tarentum for rich Peucetians or Daunians with dead to bury, it is not of her kind; for that (or much of it, Dionysos, liknon, frantic play with snakes) see instead an Attic piece, more than a century earlier than the climax of Apulian red-figure (S. Aurigemma, *Scavi di Spina*, 1:1, pls. 19-30; Beazley, *ARV²*, p. 1052, no. 25). Nevertheless, she is one of our practical "holds"; less because her son makes chronology for us by winning the battle of Issos (333 B.C., November) on a late Apulian vase of great importance for its light on Aphrodite's dominance of the ware's symbolism (fig. 14), than because she helps to bring the Derveni papyrus to bear on our question by assisting our grasp of a fact which her brother's cognomina tend to make slippery, that this lesser Alexander ("of Epirus," or "the Molossian") should count as Macedonian not less than the dead at Derveni. Space for discussing this earliest of all papyri must be found in due course. For the present I must only make two points: first, that because of a chronological nexus which the aforesaid vase-painting helps to establish it is arithmetically not impossible that Alexander the Molossian and his army of Northerners, from nearer the home of Orpheus than Tarentum's previous champion (Archidamos of Sparta, during 344-338 B.C.), contributed to causing the great upset in the tradition of something in which (as mortal soldiers fraternizing with all concerned) they could not quite lack interest, the mortuary vase-painting of Tarentum done for Alexander's own Apulian allies: that derangement of which the chief symptoms are Aphrodite's rather sudden dominance, Orpheus' quite sudden prominence as somehow her minister, and the emergence of a rich symbolism, some elements of which happen to correspond (delusively?) with symbols of *teletai*, Orphic but also Eleusinian. For the second and my last point: what was only an arithmetical possibility (established by Wuilleumier's correlation of the battle of Issos with the presence of Alexander the Less in Italy, *Tarente* 82) takes on at least a little logical likelihood from the Derveni papyrus, if that roll's scraps show (p. 106) that a Macedonian officer of about that time, buried in a cemetery dated by coins of Olympias' husband and son, was interested in Orpheus as an *authority*, since he prized a dry-as-dust commentary on a cosmogonic treatise of this poet. It may be that I have not sufficiently emphasized that the interest of the Patronian in Orpheus' invasion of the late vases is all but precisely that.

Not quite exactly, because, as two fields for prophetic authority, cosmogony and what is decent and auspicious in nuptial custom are rather far apart. But not much good could be expected of a review, from Onomacritus downward, of the historical figures material to this controversy if it were meanwhile forgotten that the alternative to Orpheus as ordainer of *teletai* (whether for the remission of felt guilt or in prudent cringing to the Queen of uxorious Hades) is Orpheus at one notch back from that, namely in his prime importance as inspired *warranter* of what is proper and effective in religion. That indeed, as was seen in the keenest and deepest of Linforth's insights, is the fundamentally Orphic thing, assumed by, accounting for, all the so miscellaneous scriptures "of Orpheus," all the statements of his instituting religious practices — very many more than the three which are of most obvious interest when in ridicule of a nuptial eschatology the invitation to register Orphic balls and mirrors' Eleusinian pastry and tabourines, is addressed to the student of vases contemporary with the "Titan-flavored" texts from Corigliano and made at no immense distance from that site in Tarentum a Spartan colony: namely the *telete* efficaciously commemorating the Titans' snaring and rending and eating of Dionysos, and the Laconian cults of the two goddesses whom, everywhere, it is convenient to call Eleusinian, at Sparta Demeter as D. Chthonia and Persephone as Kore Soteira, agent of *salvation* after death.

It happens that all three matters come to us in one rather curious basket. It is Pausanias who, having noted that Orpheus' claim to have made the temple of Kore Soteira is disputed (iii.13.2) and having declared his disbelief of the Spartans' tradition of the prophet's founding their cult of Demeter Chthonia (iii.14.5), suppresses his name altogether when it has to be said who wrote the book of the Dismemberment *telete*; in viii.37.5 he attributes it to a writer active at the turn of the sixth to the fifth century B.C., Onomacritus, with as little hesitation as Clement and Arnobius show in their ascribing it to Orpheus. Because Pausanias' attribution hangs such a respectably early date on the Dismemberment *telete*, one that would make it less importable that the Corigliano tablets allude to it, Linforth's invitation to suppose it mistaken (*Arts of Orpheus*, pp. 350-353) would — if only it were not involved in an archaeological problem of enormous difficulty — be most acceptable to any quite obstinately Patronian minimizer of the derangement certainly visible on the late vases. That is, anyone protesting, as to the sudden prominence of Orpheus, "had there not to be authority for the promotion, to please the tune-calling 'woolhats', of Aphrodite at the expense of Dionysos?," and, urging, as to alleged signs of Eleusinian *deisidaimonia* in some of the new symbols as well in conjunctions of Orpheus and Triptolemos with Persephone and Hades, "were not she and Hades (on whatever terms united) archexemplars of the (re)union eschatology?," and finally, daring to retort to the claim of teletic character for the whole symbolism "you only show that you have never troubled to follow it into pictures of simple myth."

If it is still important to have a muster of persons concretely relevant, let Onomacritus remain at the head of a list which I should like to close with Giovanni Jatta, if without seeming to indulge in whimsical disparity I may include a modern, reckoning him a historical figure in right of a monumentally epoch-closing book, *Catalogo del Museo Jatta* (1869). No doubt it is pressing that the "problem of enormous difficulty" should be at least a little unwrapt from its cryptic phrase before I try to explain why Onomacritus (expelled from Athens before the murder of Hipparchus in 514 B.C.) and Archytas (in 348 still alive?) may be put together as persons less neutral in the present question of rival eschatologies than Archidamos of Sparta (in Italy as ally of Tarentum from 344 B.C. or there-about to 338 B.C.) and Alexander the Molossian (in southern Italy between 335 B.C. at the earliest and 330 at latest, as champion of Tarentum and its Apulian allies till they deserted him as too enterprising). But I should despair of making myself understood about the peculiar interlock of Orphic and Eleusinian ideas in the only formidable alternative to the eschatology discerned by Patroni if I were forbidden to exhibit G. Jatta at work quite contrastingly, encouraged by Sophocles (whose Iakchos belongs to "Demeter of Eleusis" yet is an Italiote Dionysos) to explain the theology and symbolism of the late vases altogether by the Eleusinian cult, its mysteries and any legends conveniently — no matter if loosely — related to them. What is most to my point is his independence of the Dismemberment *telete* which Christian Fathers assign to Orpheus but Pausanias to Onomacritus: for Jatta even the balls and the mirrors had nothing to do with the Titans' trap for Dionysos, most examples of the former being for him (as indeed for the Patronian) just a woman's plaything explicable by its context in the picture, while the mirrors are symbols of initiation into mysteries of Demeter, signs of purity and of confidence in it (pp. 66-68, 236-237). But — for us to whom Aphrodite and her belongings, her pet bird only less than her son, are disturbingly important — it is also interesting that Jatta had so little difficulty in finding an Eleusinian coop for swans; any creature that can pass as a goose "forma un' allusione ai misteri di Cerere" (p. 262), this on the basis of the legend recorded by Pausanias in his ix.39.2-3, about Kore's masterly recovery of helpless Herkyna's lost pet (p. 671). No one but a lout who was also an ignoramus would now quote the book to make fun of it, and I must hope that my own need to refer to it is not misunderstood; in a certain stand taken, upon the conviction that the only counter-hypothesis to Patroni's assumptions formidable enough to serve for testing them would be an Orphistic revamping of Böttiger's and Gerhard's mystery-spying, there could be no ignoring the work which happens to present quite the final (as well as the most winningly modest and sober) development of *pure* Gerhardism; between completing the catalogue of his family's collection (1869) and undertaking a catalogue of Francesco Caputi's vases (published in 1877) Giovanni Jatta allowed himself to be altogether converted from it by Heydemann — for concreteness in the study of funerary vase-painting a great setback, since Heydemann's agnosticism all but renounced concern with the chief reality, the art's having to address itself (of course beforehand) to real and particular bereavement.

The "problem of enormous difficulty" is posed us by all the archaeological aggravations which, sending dates now up, now down, can be hung, have to be hung, on the great double crux of the passage in Herodotus' ii.81 about avoidance of woolen cloth in worship and burial (only). Double, because there is first a textual question: is Herodotus simply saying (as in the attractive "short reading" of MSS A B C) that the Egyptians in their limited taboo agree with an Orphic and Pythagorean one (ὀμολογέουσι δὲ ταῦτα τοῖσι Ὀρφικοῖσι καὶ Πυθαγορείοισι), or is he slipping in a correction, asserting Egyptian agreement with Greek practices called, only called, Orphic and Bacchic, being essentially Egyptian and Pythagorean (ὀμολογέουσι δὲ ταῦτα τοῖσι Ὀρφικοῖσι καλεομένοισι καὶ Βακχικοῖσι, ἐοῦσι δὲ Αἰγυπτίοισι καὶ Πυθαγορείοισι; so the unattractive yet vulgate text, adapted in modern editions from the "long reading" of MSS R S V)? Besides that there are some questions of interpretation. Do I have to defend my own impression that (for lack of a second article) the "ands" of the Greek are like hyphens, with the effect Orphico-Pythagorean, Orphic-Bacchic, Egyptio-Pythagorean? I trust not, but in either case, and no matter whether long or short reading be preferred, "Pythagorean" has to be the last word of this first statement of the passage, putting on Linforth (*Arts of Orpheus*, pp. 45-46) the burden of contending that this is no embarrassment to its second statement, οὐδὲ γὰρ τούτων τῶν ὀργίων μετέχοντα ὅσιόν ἐστι ἐν εἰρινέοισι εἵμασι θαφθῆναι. Is there not quite a reinforcement of his argument (that "there is after all no objection to attributing *orgia* to Pythagoreans") in our having been able (p. 102) to produce a Pythagorean, Archytas, witnessing to his own attendance at (and studious attention to) *teletai*? Impending difficulties should forbid too much enjoyment of some certainly pretty embellishments of this matter. But one is a conspiracy of sources to defeat an objection not unreasonable at just this turn, "yes, but *telete* is one Greek word, and *orgia* another; does not your Professor Linforth himself say (p. 45) that the second word 'may mean anything done in the name of religion?' " No side-issue, least of all a verbal question, should distract us from that which is the main one here, simply this, whether the Dismemberment *telete*, rite and indispensable book, existed in time to inject its symbolism of balls and mirrors and so forth into a phase of vase-painting roughly datable by its reflections of campaigns of Alexander the Great; unquestionably it affected the Campana plaques of Cicero's time, accounting for paradoxical mirrors there. Nevertheless, it is interesting and not unimportant that, first, both those Greek words are applied to the Dismemberment rite or book, Pausanias saying *orgia* (in the ascription to Onomacritus, viii.37.5) and Clement of Alexandria saying *telete* (Kern's *Fr*. 34); next, that in a critical (incredulous) listing of the works of Orpheus used by the lexicographer Suidas in the eleventh century A.D., the plural number in the titles of both the two works taken away from Orpheus to be given to Onomacritus, *Teletai, Chresmoi,* should be momentous. For one thing, should not the plural of *Chresmoi* incline us to trust the plural of *Teletai*? Knowing (from Herodotus, vii.6) not a little about Onomacritus as collector (χρησμολόγος) and tidy compiler (διαθέτης) of prophecies, we can have little difficulty in supposing him a collector of effective rites (τελεταί), and should be ready to grant that if Onomacritus really did write the story and authorize the ritual of the *telete* which imitated the Titans' dismemberment of Dionysos, he not improbably did the like for a rather elaborate rite (involving a pillar) in worship of the same god which seems to be recognized in the forty-seventh *Orphic Hymn* (third century A.D.) and to be at the point of an allusion in the *Antiope* of Euripides (*Fr*. 203; of 410 B.C. as T. B. L. Webster and B. Snell date it in the latter's *Scenes of Greek Drama*, p. 71, n. 1), and quite certainly can be traced back through Attic vase-painting into the lifetime of Onomacritus, chresmologer to Peisistratids; on the vases the "Dionysos about the Pillar" becomes a dummy of the god (minimum, a mask), but (as seems not to matter) the *Hymn* περικιονίου and Euripides' *Antiope* imply no more than coils of Dionysos' ivy. Here we approach trouble that beggars metaphor, for it is impossible to stop short of the question "and did Onomacritus in that book of *Teletai* include one for the cult of Dionysos recognized in the forty-sixth *Orphic Hymn* Λικνίτου, worship of the Baby cradled in the shoe-shaped Winnowing Basket (*liknon*), nursling of the nymphs?" Having begun with a textual problem (how much did Herodotus' pen really write about an Orphico-Pythagorean practice?), we incurred an archaeological one of the first order of difficulty when it was not possible to avoid the endlessly debated vases showing pillar-idols of Dionysos, in pictures which have been taken to be allergories of the *Choes* ceremony on the second day of the Athenian *Anthesteria* (though their detail so directly contradicts almost all we know of that affair), or of the Vat Opening (*Pithoigia*) of its first day (though there is no written evidence of an idol improvised for this), or to commemorate a banished and forgotten phase (with "wild women") in the history of the *Lenaia* festival, or to be play of Attic imagination about doings of Boeotian neighbors.

Further Considerations on the Date of the "Derangement"

BUT NOW with the plural of Onomacritus' title forcing some consideration of Dionysiac rites concerned with a *liknon,* these represented on works of art which for the most part are much later than those Attic vases, Roman things, there takes place a fusing of the textual question (what did Herodotus write in ii.81?) with what for short, too short, I must call the problem of the villa Item (what does it mean when, in a Pompeian wall-painting, a North African mosaic, the design of a cameo, a terracotta relief in the very series ["Campana"] which contains a sure reflection of the Dismemberment *telete,* Dionysiac persons use a *liknon* to discomfort a female who more often than not has wings?). This comes about because these monuments, some of which perhaps belong to Cicero's lifetime, give one of that writer's more slipshod passages most interesting bearing on a textual subquestion: if the attractive short reading in Herodotus ii 81 is sound (so that Herodotus is only saying that the Egyptian taboo on wool is like a certain Orphic-Pythagorean taboo) when and how was it corruptly expanded, to make "Herodotus" write more and a correction of that more: "they agree in this with Orphic-Bacchic religion so-called (really Egyptio-Pythagorean)"? Cicero in a count of Dionysuses (*De Natura Deorum* iii.58) mentions Orphic worship of one of the five. Surprisingly, this is not the first on his list, though that is the Dionysos, *Iove et Proserpina natus,* corresponding to the son of Zeus and Persephone who was victim of the Titans according to Diodorus' nearly contemporary citation of "Orpheus in the *Teletai*" (v.75.4). Instead, Cicero's Orphic Dionysos is the fourth, who is really the Theban one; Cicero wrote *quartum Iove et Luna, cui sacra Orphica putantur confici,* but thanks to a passage of Lydus' *De Mensibus* (iv.51, words written in the fifth century A.D. but drawing on the same source) we can correct the moon-struck blemish; this is the son of Semele, Cicero's ear having heard his servant's Σεμέλης as Σελήνης. As presumptive evidence of later interpolation of the Orphic corpus, all this — even the appearance of disagreement between Cicero and Diodorus — should be welcome not only to those who with Linforth regard the long and vulgate reading in Herodotus ii.81 as corrupt and Pausanias' ascription of the Dismemberment *telete* to an early author, Onomacritus, as mistaken. It should also please the thorough Patronian, unwilling to believe that the Dismemberment *telete* (whether "neat" or diluted somehow with Eleusinian ideas and symbolism) had time and opportunity to work so powerfully on the Tarentine potters and their Apulian customers as to frighten both out of a comfortable and perfectly natural eschatology of completion in love; an eschatology actually so demonstrably accepted by the potters of an almost immediately previous phase of this ware as rather to spoil the beauty of what we must nevertheless admire as the prettiest exhibit on the other side.

I mean the scarcely contestable fact, relevant to the question of time and opportunity but also to the matter of antecedent tradition, that doubtless before the middle of the fourth century B.C. the Pythagorean who was Tarentum's greatest man revealed his acquaintance, an eyes-and-ears acquaintance, with a *telete* — this fact in all the beauty of its setting of inseparable considerations. One of these is that what two of Archytas' senses so intently studied was the behavior of the very thing, *rhombos* rumble-wheel, which Orphic worship (Onomacritan for Pausanias) and the Eleusinian mysteries had in common; another, that anyone resolutely determined to paste the (Herodotean) label "Orphico-Pythagorean" on a phase of Italiote vase-painting could perhaps make it stick, at least loosely and briefly, if he chose the group of vases which Trendall in his *LCS* (p. 62) has named Intermediate; calling it so for more than one reason but mainly because of a special character in its matter and style that is between early Lucanian (Heraclean) and early Apulian (early Tarentine), and so trailing quite a string of historical questions if it implies Heraclean artists taking refuge in Tarentum from Lucanian conquest of their city. Questions that involve two of the persons in the little line just reviewed, but here is not the place to debate whether it was Tarentum's loss of Archytas (by retirement if not by death) that let the Lucanians into Heraclea, still less what it was that (later) Alexander the Molossian did with Heraclea (spitefully if not quite treacherously take it from Tarentum, or recover it from Lucanians?). What here matters in this Intermediate Group is a certain combination of three factors. The first is that a particular sign of wide occurrence in a variety of uses (modern as well as ancient), the pentagram of interlaced triangles, is in one connection and one only — with health and wholesomeness — a Pythagorean symbol, and the only place (so far as I know) where it has that connection in Greek art is on a lekythos of this group, Turin 4427; there it is scrawled on the palaestric block occupied by an Eros cast (by his switch) in the role of gymnastic trainer, and in fact he seems to be blessing a rather tired athlete's eugenic marriage *LCS*, p. 64, 218; my pl. 6a and b). So much for "Pythagorean." Much more might be found for "Orphic" if the once fashionable idea, that Dionysiac initiation should mean Orphism, could now be confidently applied to the eleven vases of this group (nos. 309, 377 and nine between) in describing which Trendall found he had to write not "Dionysos" (as for only three, nos. 374, 392, 393, two of these being eccentrically "rustic" pieces) but just "youth with thyrsus." A reasonable shrinking from "Orphism," as a word not really safe to use, need not prevent us from recognizing that, not less reasonably and in quite safely proper terms, *Orphic* inspiration could be in some measure claimed for these pictures of initiates, if we could have confidence in Pausanias' assertion that the work entitled comprehensively *Teletai* and bearing the name of the bard, Orpheus, whom Aristophanes in line 1032 of his *Frogs* at the Lenaia of 405 B.C. hailed as inventor of *teletai,* was really written in the sixth century by Onomacritus.

Let it stand at "could" (not "should") "be claimed"; moreover, let no one suppose that any word just written betrays our clinging to an error now almost eradicated from scholarship, that "initiation" is quite good enough for the whole meaning of τελετή. But in any debating of the issue just now before us (whether the eschatology revealed in the god-spliced and station-ary, or daimon-conducted and scampering, love-affairs of mortals on pots of the Hoppin-Lecce group lasted to the main ware's end, uneroded by the anxieties of teletic religion), the negative side must not be cheated of full development of the argument which the by-ware, Trendall's Intermediates, offers in an essentially chronological sub-question. Those aforesaid anxieties, "holy terror's" attack on wealth about which Plato has so much to say in a work of *circa* 375 B.C., can it be that all that does not show itself in art until the red-figured vase-painting of Tarentum's attack on the purses of bereaved Apulians had been for several centuries dead, buried and forgotten? Not, that is, until the time of the Campana plaques (which, as no one since Miss Simon's detection of the telltale mirrors dares dispute, reflect the Dismem-berment *telete*) and of certain allied works of Roman art, things for which it is convenient to borrow Cicero as provisional dating-peg? Convenient, and no liberty, since words of his about *sacra Orphica* that are *still* of Dionysos have some relevance, and should be especially interesting to us, who with our eyes on red-figured vases of a time only a little less than three centuries before the date of Cicero's death can see Orpheus detached from Dionysos and (apart from Kore's share of him in some Nekyia?) in Aphrodite's possession.

I agree that a certain subdivision recognized by Trendall (mainly works of his Hamburg Painter, pp. 72-73) within this Heracleo-Tarentine (or "Lucano-Apulian") by-ware might be deployed, at least, to support the following contention: "No: if you cannot see in the smaller vases of the Intermediate Group a simply teletic Orphism establishing itself already (perhaps even before the main line's Hoppin Painter took his sentimental turn), this taking place in the *thyrsigeri* and *thyrsigerae* of the lesser pieces, then look to the few big ones, and not without first noting that for the Group's creator (in his nos. 357, 362, your preparation for his no. 371) the company of a satyr is not indispensable for recognition of 'maenads' in girls that hold a thyrsos. Tell me, you who have been making so nuptially much of a second phiale nested in the first one, how any trace of *amore* intersexually *elisiaco* is to be made out in the 'three's no company' composition of his pl. 34, 3 (no. 371), where the maenad is guaranteed 'greeter only' by the stacked phialai — *four for a symposium* — carried by the second youth. To make this matter of sexual segregation even, what is 'bridal' about the gathering in Trendall's pl. 34, 1, where one of those thyrsos-girls of the place's staff looks on as three women, *mystai* safely beatified and quite content with that, welcome one more such to the strong sunshine of Elysium. That is no 'nuptial' parasol, whatever you may be prepared to make of the one in your fig. 6, and of others."

There is at any rate cause enough for curiosity about the contents and influence of the work which in the canon of the long-and-widely circulating poems "of Orpheus" was entitled *Teletai,* whether this book came of the historical Onomacritus' well-attested opportunities for research and all-too-inventively Orphic compilation in the service of Hipparchos at Athens before 514 B.C. or more anonymously of an interest much less seriously religious, antiquarian, in the Hellenistic age; in that second case, to be connected on the one hand with the fact that the first allusions to the myth of the Titans' dismemberment of Dionysos plainer than the ambiguous mutterings about thunder and lightning on the Corigliano tablets are made by writers of the next, the third, century B.C., Callimachus and Euphorion, and on the other hand with something that chimes with Cicero's *sacra Orphica* for his fourth Dionysos, namely a development of Roman art which cannot have begun much before the middle of the first century B.C., adapting the ritual of Greek *teletai* of Dionysos, one of them certainly the Dismemberment rite, to the themes of household decoration. However, in the present region of "enormous" problems my study cannot afford more curiosity than is practical for its two responsibilities, getting Patroni's ruling idea its respectfully critical due, getting to the point or measure of due concreteness in regard to the most interesting phase of the vase-painting to which he imputed a certain eschatology, "nuptial" for short. Thus I must beg to be excused discussion of Adolf Krüger's contention, against Kern but with Kern's encouragement, that the *Teletai* attributed to Onomacritus by Pausanias and by both these scholars contained a *telete* for Eleusinian Demeter (besides its Dionysiac matter). It is partly that Krüger failed, in the space he had, to make his point (*Quaestiones Orphicae* [diss. Halle 1934] pp. 57-60), as I must judge.

Content of the Orphic Texts: Nature of "Orphism"

BUT IN confining ourselves to a question, not shirkable, "what altogether, was the Dionysiac matter of that Orphic book with a plural title?," let us be prepared to find that from Krüger's own standpoint, insisting on the importance of a certain interlock, this particular failure mattered very little. From *our* own (with its opportunities of exploring the interest of that Orphic-Eleusinian interpenetration on several vases, one or two more than just the "hellscapes" in which Orpheus stands at Persephone's right hand), it is lucky that being thrown back from Krüger on Kern involves nothing more frustrating than an invitation to play the simplest possible, least exacting, game of "hunt the thimble"; if there was a *telete* for the Marriage of Persephone in the Orphic scriptures, but not in the (Dionysiac) compilation named *Teletai*, where in the range of these scriptures would there have been room for it? In the four Orphic poems about Hades and Persephone there would have been plenty of room, if Kern was not mistaken in distinguishing so many (*Fr.* p. 116). That is no doubt the right answer but it is not the bright one, which with "come on, make it 'hunt the timbrel' " would lead delightfully but prematurely to what A. Winkler and A. Krüger have combined (as we may say, in spite of the great interval of time) to make the most excitingly curious single object in all our subject-matter, the *tympanon* about the happiest, most mutually amorous, representation of Persephone and her husband, as serenaded by Orpheus on Naples H. 3222 (fig. 11); Euripides, before them, had provided for our finding the thing very interesting, by disclosing in a lyric passage (*Helen* 1347-1352) how it might be given a connection with the couple's happiness, as symbol of Demeter's acceptance of their marriage won by Aphrodite's drumming; Krüger improved the fit of Orpheus' intimate part in the picture when (*Quaestiones* 68f) he developed hints of Malten and Maas that Euripides might have based that chorus of his *Helen* on an Orphic scripture; in between, Winkler had mined the matter with suspense and excitement, by venturing to judge the timbrel a modern restoration; if someone at Naples could be roused to sponge it, there would soon be nothing there, if not (for the sentimentalist) worse than that — a revelation of suspended wheels, for Persephone fixed reminder of the rough abduction ("Die Darstellungen der Unterwelt auf unteritalischen Vasen," in *Breslauer Philologische Abhandlungen* 3:5 [1888] p. 19).

If only to clear the way for some at least sufficiently methodical consideration of the Dionysiac bundle of *teletai* in the scripture which (as I grant) must have influenced the Campana plaques and some other Roman works of not very serious art, and could have influenced not only Italiote vase-painting of the fourth century B.C. but also Attic of the fifth and late sixth if Onomacritus was the bundler, I had better give plainer assurance that no slighting of the aforesaid interlock is intended. For plainest, let me say that (because it indispensably belongs to a certain future effort of concreteness, for catching a painter's "I-to-them" relation) there must be discussion, before my study closes, of one of the boldest claims that can be made for Orpheus — that his (and not Adonis's) is the head looking down on an Eleusinian subject not untouched by Orphic literature, Triptolemos' departure, from its fantastic place in the floral ornament of a volute krater in the Vatican (W 4, Trendall, *VIE*, pl. 51: a charming vase anyhow, but rather better than that if in some severely guarded sense we may hold that a certain Orphic whole has been addressed to a certain kind of bereavement). With that said, it should be enough, here, to add that we should be ready to find, between some Orphic writing and some Eleusinian matter, a more genuine relation than George E. Mylonas seemed willing to allow when he wrote: "the Orphics were not averse to adding to their own myths and practices . . . in the hope of attracting more people to their sect. Thus they incorporated in their traditions the myth of the abduction of Persephone by Plouton, although it was incompatible with their basic doctrine of Zagreus, the son of Zeus and Persephone" (*Eleusis and the Eleusinian Mysteries,* p. 228). It is not out of mere respect for Mylonas' primacy in Eleusinian studies that I name and quote him. If Patroni's "critical due" is to be rendered as due enquiry for ordeal-making counter-eschatology and due severity in urging it (till this breaks?), there should be use for the light streaming from the passage cited upon an evidently still current idea of Orphic religion which I could not wish to ignore, one that sees it as the *affair* of a sect, a sect which (most pertinently for us!) is even proselytizing, rather than as the *fact* of a great accumulation of interested writing. If the last is not an effective phrase, let me say that I mean a pile, on the whole having in its stuff no essential shape or consistency, of works in hexameter verse written by persons who for their various purposes needed to borrow Orpheus's authority — more than the dozen writers for whom, beginning with Pythagoras, we have names, thanks to what has percolated into Clement of Alexandria's *Stromateis* or Suidas' lexicon from the researches of Epigenes or an even earlier prober (it is Ion of Chios, contemporary of Kimon and Perikles, who names Pythagoras). If "concreteness" is now of pressing importance and a gush of names can begin to make it, Kern's pages (63-64) collecting onomastic *testimonia* from Clement and Suidas are not unimportant. But it would be a grave oversight if one did not perceive the typical importance of a person without human name or real existence, a fictitious character figuring in a stage-joke that (for lack of a little more logic in the spleen of it) does not quite come off, the satyr who (to excuse cowardice) produces a deuterocanonical scrap "of Orpheus" at line 646 of Euripides' *Cyclops.*

I should feel that pressure for concreteness had become exactingly intense were I required to arrange a figured set-piece, all but a *tableau vivant,* of typical contributors to Orphic writing. But if the demand were made, there would be a use for that satyr; beside Zopyros with Brontinos and perhaps Kerkops (for Pythagorean seriousness) and Nikias of Elea with or without Onomacritus (for ceremonial) should there not be posed some anonym (more impressive than a street-corner *orpheotelestes*) to represent the great department of apocryphal, merely improvised, humbug scribbled or performed in the name of Orpheus? It should be no disqualification that Euripides' satyr never got to the point of asking a fee for, still less to that of reciting, his "spell of Orpheus just perfect" for safely remote control of the task of blinding Cyclops. Anyhow, there is a question – if not a string of questions – to which he belongs: looking over the shoulder of some scholar found addressing himself earnestly and comprehensively to mastering the *variety* of the so-called Orphic tablets, including the new Pharsalus tablet's outright contradiction ("don't drink right," *ArchEph* [1950-51] 99, against "don't drink left," Kern *Fr.* 32 a, of its counterpart (otherwise) from Petelia, that satyr from Euripides' *Cyclops* would be quite in place, especially if capable of timely interruption. Any train of thought about the batch of funerary tablets must of course begin with the question, are the ten scraps of inscribed goldleaf really Orphic, in the sense (the only proper one) that in spite of differences of content more noteworthy than any mere corruptions, the verses on them were attributed, by all historically concerned, to Orpheus? "Of course! As it was with my own good thing, *they had better be*!" With that heard and heeded (as derisive chortle), the train aforesaid should be saved some trouble. That is, such vain questions as the following: "out of what poem, respectively, in the canon of Orphic writings did the ten scraps of verse come?." Or, "there having been in the Orphic corpus – how opportunely! – a *Descent into Hades* which the probers reassigned to Prodikos of Samos (Clement) or Herodikos of Perinthos (Suidas), should we not exert ourselves to sort the tablets out, in order of their possible place in the text of this 'Descending Soul's Guide and Prompter' (if it was that)? Before the Corigliano group should come the five pieces of the Petelia family (what to say at the start, or very near it, to get the memory-restoring drink from the proper brook, Kern *Fr.* 32 a and b I, II, III with the Pharsalos text as just referred to); from the Corigliano group eject Kern's *Fr.* 32 f, a misfit even metrically, but should we not recognize the Rome tablet 32 g as akin to the texts local to Corigliano-Thurii (what at the journey's end the soul purified by expiation should say to Persephone and some other gods, including Eubouleus, father of Orphically all-available Mise, Kern's *Fr.* 32 c, d, e)?"

There is no harm in knowing that such questions have been asked; but what we are seeking in this region of the golden tablets is footing firm enough for progress to and beyond the topic, ordeal-making for the nuptial eschatology of completion assumed by Patroni, of Orphic teletai of Dionysos. That mainly means lucid enough tabulation of the assumptions (about the *lamellae aureae*) upon which I must proceed. But, well before that, may I accept that satyr's help in cutting the first foothold? The special usefulness of Euripides' satyr, the good he can do in our own affair, comes of his improvisation being so vividly and compendiously an example of something with which we have to cope on the vases, Orphic "inflation"; it is very much our business to gauge how far this really goes, as far as "holy terror" or short of it, and if this satyr is in fact proffering a scale, had we not better take it (if this may be done without offensive mixture of metaphors)? There can be a degree of this inflation not even ordeal-making for Patroni's theories. We cannot deny its happening in some measure to late Apulian red-figure, having there found Orpheus, formerly of no account except as pitiable, performing as Aphrodite's indispensable coadjutor (much more than satellite) in her takeover of the ware's eschatography (fig. 13; cf. pl. 12). But only because her takeover (from Dionysos) would have had no authority without him? That is an idea which the cowardly satyr of the *Cyclops* rather encourages, and not just because without Orpheus' authority his claim for his "really first-rate" spell would have been void; is there not some reason for accepting the author of the *Cyclops* as author of the *Rhesus,* where (943f) a point is made (by the Muse reproaching Athena) of Athens' even owing the Eleusinian Mysteries to Orpheus? If I have not misunderstood and exaggerated the purism of George Mylonas, this should count (from his point of view) as the extreme of Orphic usurpation; but as Linforth has shown (*Arts of Orpheus,* 262-267) the thought "Orphic? It had better be!" was one that spread widely, and when on Tarentine vases for Apulian burials Orpheus makes his appearance as Aphrodite's minister of bathing (the earliest occurrence being that in which Aphrodite's presence is most certain, on the "H.A." krater, pl. 12), the Patronian cannot be debarred from likening this to the certificates of foundation by Orpheus or a disciple of Orpheus taken out for several Attic observances besides the Eleusinian Mysteries, also for the mysteries of Hekate in Aegina, for cults of Demeter and Kore at Sparta, for the religion of Phrygia, and even for the cult that should least of all have needed a foreigner's guarantee, the worship of Dionysos at his own birthplace, Thebes (this last, however, a strangely special case: see Linforth's comments, *Arts of Orpheus,* 210-212, on Diodorus i.23).

Nuptial Ablution or
Moral Cleansing by Teletic Rite?
The "(Re)union Hypothesis" Again

BUT IT IS not long before objections and measurable difficulty begin to beset the plea, reasonable in itself, that since it is so evidently blessed by Aphrodite, the goddess of marriage, the bathing for which Orpheus makes music in the series of vase-paintings that begins with one on the still rather old-fashioned "H.A." krater in the Group of the Lycurgus Painter can scarcely be less cosmetic and nuptial than the ablutions at which Dionysos was present (pl. 8b for Lecce 620 by the Hoppin Painter) or represented (*CVA* Italy 4 IV D r, pl. 3, 1, for Lecce 629 by the Hearst Painter; not less important than 620 where Dionysos appears in person, for the deputizing satyr's partner in the nuptial preparations of this girl is Hermes Chthonios, guaranteeing death and eschatogamy). The consideration useful and propulsive for us is not the rather doubtful suggestion of momentous difference in some of these musical bathing-parties being (if I may use broadest North-American) so contrastingly stag-parties. It is rather that some of the funerary tablets, precisely those which field archaeology can associate (if not more than tenuously, through the Corigliano Eros) with Aphrodite's encroachments and the "Great Derangement" of Apulian red-figure, combine with some few symbols of the "deranged" phase to inject a second puff of Orphic inflation, and now it is at the expense of Aphrodite. "Don't make everything turn on *Ana Aprodita*; she is there for the wool-clipping rich Apulians, who wanted her in and now could not do without her, the great goddess of their own eschatology (have you not noticed that the cutters and painters of Messapian inscriptions are like some Rhodians and North Africans in not rating Persephone worth a name separate from her mother's?). If you like, see this musical bathing as mystic preparation for translation to a future life in which the *Ana Aprodita* of Haas' section 1 (*Messapische Studien,* pp. 27-33) is more majestic, or has more to give, than the *Damatira* in section 6 of his theology (pp. 43-50); there is perhaps even Greek warrant for the idea that Aphrodite has paradise (her ἄλσος ἱμερόεν) and Persephone only its dank approaches (according to a possible interpretation of a scrap of verse cited in a strange Gnostic tract, Kern *Fr.* 352). *But mystic cleansing* here must be (as in all the cults with which Orpheus' name was ever connected) *moral cleansing.*" I cannot regard this as sophistry, and it is only too easy to feed such thoughts from the material which we have begun to consider. What are the Corigliano tablets, most of them, but certificates of "moral cleansing"? True, like all the other mortuary tablets save an exception at present negligible (the Roman one), these were made by Greeks for Greeks and not, like the vases, by Greeks for incompletely Hellenized neighbors, Peucetians and Daunians still set in some ways and tastes of their own. But what makes our present transition, via the various tablets to the Orphic compilation *Teletai,* rather a trial, an awkward pass, for the Patronian is a certain aggravation of difficulty that is the work of vases only just recently published, these seeming to confirm a suspicion for which there were grounds already, that some of the tablets were not without bearing on the symbolism of the late vases, and that what gave them this relation was their both making allusion to a remissive rite, the Dismemberment *telete,* prescribed in that very book. At all events, anyone set on maintaining that the eschatology expressed in the latest vase-painting for Apulian burials is only a cannier version, more theologically tactful (as regards the customers' *Aprodita*) and more circumspect and scholarly (as regards Orpheus), of that implied by the Hoppin Painter and the Hearst Painter in their pictures of surely nuptial ablution on vases in Lecce had better prepare to cope with the situation created for him now that Mrs. Erika Kunze-Götte's publication of the slim oinochoe Stuttgart KAS 161 (*CVA* Germany 26, pl. 52, figs. 1, 3, 4) has been followed by Hellmut Sichtermann's publication of the squat olpe Jatta 1618 (*Griechische Vasen in Unteritalien aus der Sammlung Jatta in Ruvo,* pls. 136-137). The first effect of some details of these vases is as of a STOP-DON'T-TOUCH sign, inviting the Patronian to stay happily in the patch of nuptial eschatography which in a certain stretch of the ware's middle period he has succeeded in finding, but warning him not to go on to lay foolish hands on the new symbolism which (it is contended) marks the beginning of something different, or on anything, anywhere, neutral or recalcitrant; the things for catching or bouncing in the picture on the Jatta olpe, an unmarried girl's playthings, are (he is asked to note) of no more concern for him than the ball and mirror at Stuttgart, straightest salvation-stuff out of the Dismemberment *telete.*

As conjoined obstacles or nuisances, the two pitchers, the thin and the thick of their matter, make an odd-looking pair, especially as there is quite an interval of time and style between them; the Stuttgart vase must belong to almost the latest phase of Tarentine red-figure, the gaudy-yet-dusky ware which used to be assigned to Canusium, while the olpe in Ruvo has been put by Trendall (cited by Sichtermann, p. 53) in the group of his Iliupersis Painter, who in the "ornate" line cannot be very far from abeam of the Hoppin Painter in the parallel "plain" line (cf. Cambitoglou and Trendall, *APS,* p. 47, in relation to what comes on their p. 55). But in the present connection – with *teletai* of Dionysos – the later piece demands to be considered first, because of a most arresting likeness to art's most certain reflection of the Dismemberment *telete,* common to two types of Campana plaques, in both of which a satyr wearing a pelt and holding a mirror joins in orgiastic dancing (Erika Simon, *Hommages à Albert Grenier* 3, pl. 283, fig. 1 and pl. 284, fig. 3). One may be allowed to doubt some of the allusions to this particular *telete* which Miss Simon is inclined to make out in various types of these Roman plaques; she might well have left fig. 7 of her pl. 286 to the *telete* of Dionysos Liknites (exultation after Iris' discomfiture?), instead of seeing the satyr and nymph as "acting" the Tearing by dancing away from each other, so as almost to tug the baby's basket-cradle apart. But I must accept as absolutely certain her contention (p. 1422) "der bisher unerklärte Typ des Spiegeltänzers ist eine orphische Prägung" and my only objection to what she says next ("der Spiegel hat seinen festen Platz in Mythos von Zagreus") is one coming of the feeling that I may myself have made too free with the name Zagreus for Dionysos as trapped with a mirror, ball and other bait by the Titans; there was Callimachus' authority for it (*EtymM* 406, 46), but (as Linforth has remarked, *Arts,* p. 311) the Orphic scriptures had no use for the word, so far as can be traced. Now, the impression which in *CVA* Germany 26, pl. 52 (my pl. 17) the Stuttgart picture makes when reinforced with the pelt-clad campana satyrs brandishing a single mirror need not be quite so stunning as, for us now, Mrs. Kunze-Götte's interpretation of its detail would make it. According to her reading of this, the pelt-clad young man bounding *away* from the queenly woman or goddess holds two mirrors, in his right hand a stemmed one such as those satyrs have, in his left hand a (simply round) folding mirror. If this were so, it would be the strange excess that, together with the lad's direction (off and away from any beauty to be mirrored), would tell what on the plaques is told just by the satyrs' indifference, for all their mirrors, to the nymphs who are their partners in absorbedly orgiastic dancing: these implements are not cosmetic in purpose. On the contrary, with the queenly person on the Stuttgart vase seen as hostile Hera, they might well be her double provision ("take all I have of both sorts, and welcome!") for the Titans' trap. This would be pleasant emphasis of Hera's spite, and quite in the spirit of the myth (where the baiting of the trap for an infant and unpredictable prey was properly lavish), but are we not recalled to its letter? For surely the round thing in the departing youth's left hand is a ball; ball, and not the *rhombos* of the same story — the strings belong to a cradling carrier, of which one can see two more loops, not to a rumble-wheel, which would be less solid, with the strings passing visibly through it. This is not my first reference to the Stuttgart pitcher KAS 160, and some features of the scene on it need no reemphasis, two that invite Dionysiac interpretation (kantharos on invisible ledge, and the youth's pelt) and one that is more specifically a temptation to Orphistic reverie, the unhooded ovoid thing speckled like, but too big as well as too pre-Columbian really to mean, a turkey's egg.

The Patronian need not be struck dumb by all this. But the rejoinder available, "a ball (see Ovid, *Metam.* x.262) as well as a mirror (see Lecce Painter, here pl. 8a) can, on either side of a grave, be useful in courting," might be made to seem rather lame by an Orphist coached to make the most of a vase of some specific value (or at least attraction) for an attempt to erode the other side's firmest ground (that is, the incontestably nuptial eschatography of the Hearst, Hoppin, and Lecce Painters, which we have studied, and the symbolism of pictures of incontestably erotic myth, which so far we have barely reconnoitred, though evidently [fig. 15] one of a series of Aphrodites who have been marked for keeping in view belongs to a legend which we have Horace's explicit leave [*Carm.* iii.27.73] to reckon nuptial, Europa's bull-ride). This "erosive" vase is of course the olpe which I have already contrasted with the slim-necked oinochoe in Stuttgart, at Ruvo in the Jatta collection and even more recently published (H. Sichtermann, *Gr.V. in Unteritalien aus der Sammlung Jatta in Ruvo,* numbered 3-4 in *Bilderhefte des Deutschen Archäologischen Instituts Rom.* [1966] pls. 136-137, no. 78 there; not described in G. Jatta's *Catalogo*). Like that of other choice vases which Sichtermann and his photographer H. Koppermann have exhibited in this work, this olpe's decoration invites prolonged study from the phaseological point of view; indeed, I find the Italiote part of their book quite daunting, in the message it has for the elderly novice, that the threads of development in the best Tarentine red-figure, namely what was done for the richest Apulians, are more than he can hope quite to master. Nevertheless, for taking our bearings, not only in relation to the three "*un*deranged" vase-painters just mentioned but also in regard to the formidable topics (variety in the golden tablets, variety of *teletai*) momentously besetting the chronology of "holy terror," it should be a great help that this olpe's picture (of nuptial preparations, as Sichtermann saw) has been classed by Trendall as a late work of the Iliupersis Painter, and the same connoisseur has put near to this painter in style the volute krater which was no. 1094 in G. Jatta's catalogue of his family's collection and is now K 36 (pp. 33f, pls. 52-54) in Sichtermann's book.[1] Because (with hellish front and paradisal back) the volute krater 1094 or K 36 stands in a very interesting relation to the much later piece which is already our classic of the theme "reunion," the volute krater Munich 3297 with hellscape, it can add a good deal to a point already made (when we noted that in Middle-"Apulian" red-figure's tamer scenery, as mapped by Cambitoglou and Trendall in their *Plain Style,* the neighborhood of the Hoppin and Lecce Painters adjoins that, more impressive, of the Iliupersis Painter whose turn will come in their *Ornate Style*). In order that the Ruvo olpe (only near the Iliupersis Painter) should not be lost to sight in the attention which the Ruvo krater decorated by him must have, I had better not delay to point out where and in what connection its special interest lies. Like almost all pitchers, this olpe is single-pictured, but the scene, on such a squat vessel quite extensive, had to be divided between the plates, and most of what matters in it for our own questions is on the second, pl. 137, where what is taking place between the woman stooping (to lay a basin of water on a more or less cubical block) and the woman seated (holding a lekythos of perfume tilted on her right knee, as if about to scent the water) is bound to remind us at once of what kept the bride-groom and chthonic Dionysos waiting on the Hoppin Painter's bell-krater Lecce 620, where the peculiarity of its Dionysiac splicing (pl. 8b) was not the god's actively personal part (matchable in pl. 8a for a follower's work on Lecce 623) but the bride's being still at work on her hair, washing (and scenting?) it at a basin placed on a block, not at a normal laver. Not quite so soon, but as soon as one's eyes have moved on from the Jatta olpe's scent-flask to the quartered ball bounced by the girl far right, yet another vase-painting comes to mind from Lecce, by the Hearst Painter on the calyx-krater no. 629 (*CVA* Italy 4 IV D r, pl. 2, 3 and pl. 3, 1), where Dionysos is not seen but his deputy, a satyr, is assisting Hermes of the Dead to take care of a girl who has just used a laver. It was helpful that the god there was so plainly H. Chthonios, busy with what the girl needs for the rest of her last journey, cloak and shoes; but the telling thing for us just now, in relation to the Ruvo olpe, is

---

[1] Smith's references to the Iliupersis Painter, here and elsewhere, have been modified, to remove a misunderstanding to which Sir A. D. Trendall kindly draws my attention. [J.K.A.]

the combination of gifts which the satyr for his part has for her, a flask of scent (alabastron) and a round object which, judging mainly by size, I have taken for a ball; Romanelli in his text for the *CVA* saw it as a fruit. If I was then right, it was then already time for accustoming ourselves to the idea that *pilae pictae* are not just for wooing, though that is all we see of their purpose in Ovid's text: time (unless it was an eschatological, eschatogamic, mistake to basket the Hearst Painter with the Hoppin and Lecce Painters) to recognize the ball for catching or bouncing as a nuptial symbol, whether more or less prettily patterned like Ovid's and the two certain ones on the Jatta olpe (Sichtermann's pl. 137), or plain (like the probable third there, suspended to left of the bounced ball, or the thing in the right hand of the Hearst Painter's exuberantly helpful satyr; put a magnifying glass to pl. 2, 3 or pl. 3, 1 in *CVA* Italy 4 IV D r).

Anything that the Hearst Painter enters he rather enlivens, for he is an unwittingly amusing clown. But liveliness is no acceptable substitute for knowing what one is about, and it requires an almost grim effort of circumspectly purposeful concentration to take advantage of what Sichtermann offers if, fresh from those Lecce vases, we turn to his examples of the not very distant school of the Iliupersis Painter, that artist's *own* krater (pls. 18a, b) with its interestingly *partial* anticipation of the Munich Nekyia (pl. 1b) — partial because, first, sinners (Theseus and his friend) are punished, but without an Eleusinian judge to condemn them, and, next, a family is reunited in the (Dionysiac) bliss of another life, but with no hint that they owe this to Orpheus — and also the olpe decorated by the Iliupersis Painter, with its interesting emphasis, in a scene of nuptial preparations, on balls to toss or bounce. In a sense, this too is pre-Orphic — no one is going to foist on Sichtermann's pl. 137 the interpretation "girl being prepared for initiation as ball-furnishing Titaness in the *telete* of the Trapping and Rending," whereas "young Titan, or lad taking the part of one" is the most obviously plausible reading of the Stuttgart oinochoe (that is not to say the right one, for a scholar who has learnt what I called "the Rocavecchia lesson" will not confidently read any very bizarre pitcher without sight of its krater, not available for the Stuttgart oinochoe). Because the best we can do for Patroni's ideas is to show them surviving the worst that can be urged against them, it is evidently to our purpose to hear out that worst, inviting the utmost in enterprisingly thorough ridicule of the nuptial eschatology, and since Sichtermann's most timely disclosure of the relevance of Trendall's Iliupersis Painter it is plainer than ever that we can expect a setting of bounds, a "before" and an "after," in any Orphistic response, the latter scornful enough, but the other patronizingly concessive. If I have not sufficiently insisted on the cosily Dionysiac conservatism that even an Orphist harper on "holy terror" would have to acknowledge in the combination of pictures on this artist's volute krater 1094 in the Jatta collection, let me take this last chance to figure what Sichtermann and Hartwig Koppermann present, the arrest of Theseus and Peirithoos in my pl. 18a after their pl. 52, and from their pl. 54 in my pl. 18b the scene of the family's reunion, husband, wife, little son. I should overreach myself if I made a theological and eschatographic milestone of the contemptible showing made (above the hellscape, pl. 18a) by the bird which at a later stage of the same ware will belong to the supplanter of Dionysos and partner of Orpheus, Aphrodite (cf. pl. 16a, for a vase at San Simeon). But I can safely emphasize, re-emphasize (for it is a matter of both sides of the krater), the connection with the Lecce match-makings, at least those on which we are shown all three parties, Elysian bridegroom, Elysian bride, and Dionysos (pl. 8a and b). Meanwhile, no doubt, the Jatta olpe by the Iliupersis Painter (the pitcher with all those balls on it) is beginning (only beginning!) to justify the word "erosive" which I ventured for it, by its already suggesting: "how can you possibly know that Lecce 629, *CVA* Italy 4 IV D r, pl. 2, 3, is not to be interpreted according to K. Kerenyi's half-nuptial or "scortean" eschatology, in which Dionysos' part is enjoyment of a *droit de seigneur, ius aliquot noctium,* in his infernal realm reasonable enough? For that or the way to it — why not? — reckon most of the things seen on this side of the Hearst Painter's calyx-krater, the bath, the scented hair-oil, the cloak, the shoes; *not the ball,* though she will need it soon enough, when the Polyparthenos shall tire of this woman." But turn from the Jatta olpe to the Jatta krater. Taken with the two sure splicings on earlyish bell-kraters in Lecce, and with the reunion scene in Munich of pl. 1b (sure, however much the presence of Orpheus as bard and of Eleusinian Triptolemos as judge may complicate it) and various vase-paintings moreover (e.g., figs. 4 and 11) which now raise about the most notable of all infernal couples, Hades and Persephone, the questions "united for ever (as the Corigliano tablets assume), or periodically reunited?", does not the reverse of the Jatta krater (pl. 18b) complete the justification (uncouthness redeemed?) of my phrase "(re)union hypothesis" as compendious expression for Patroni's assumptions? On the obverse (pl. 18a) there is more to take in than the dose of irony, weaker than that which the Munich Nekyia administered but strong enough, in Persephone's ready provision of light for the secure arrest of two inseparables who had come to break up her contented union with Hades. For it is important not to overlook what is provided for Hades' comfort on that ledge under the tree, the panther's pelt which reminds us of a convention of late Campanian eschatography (more steadily Dionysiac than Apulian red-figure, and full of pelt-sitting persons), but of course much more interesting in a nearer connection, namely with the pains taken on the vase's reverse to express unmistakably the theme "reunion of a mortal family in a (simply) Dionysiac paradise," providing thyrsos to mark the pourer of refreshment as a nymph, but shield and doffed pilos to fool-proof the man refreshed and therewith his son and wife; not even the most slovenly eyes could report "Dionysos with Ariadne and thiasos." What the idea of a Dionysiac paradise rests on, what gives Dionysos the right, or rather fitness, to keep one and staff it with his satyrs and nymphs for the benefit of deserving mortals, that is indeed a fundamental matter. Perhaps desperately so, beyond penetration. But what must now follow will not ignore the question.

Of the problems now besetting the path of our acknowledged duty to Patroni, and requiring such a mixture of circumspection with our concentration, one that is beginning to make itself felt (for the impending topic of *teletai* with and without a capital letter) could be put in the words "what attention — if any at all — should be given to the theology of the Corigliano tablets, those which perhaps refer to the Dismemberment *telete* being addressed to Persephone, Eukles (surely Hades?) and Eubouleus, who is invoked also in the papyrus that seems to allude to that *telete* (Kern *Fr.* 31, 18) and whom the Orphic scriptures (in what we have of them) regularly — if not quite always — identify with Dionysos (Kern *Fr.* 237, 3-6; *Orphic Hymns* 30, 6 [cf. 29, 8], 52, 4, also 72, 3-4 if the meaning there is that Tyche was born of Eubouleus' bloody rending); in 42, 1-2 Eubouleus is the father of Dionysos Thesmophoros but that is a special case, extravagantly so, the irrational case of ambisexual, all-available, Mise's parentage, and (unless the near-assonance is objectionably near-droll) we might anyhow reckon it a near miss, not further off the mark of strictest usage than is Eubouleus as name of a full brother of Dionysos in Cicero's *De Nature Deorum* iii.21.53. Full brother not, of course, as son of Semele: son of Zeus and Persephone like the Eubouleus identified with D. in the only *Orphic Hymn,* no. 30, which is for Dionysos simply (without epithet), and also (of course) like Dionysos of the Dismemberment myth and rite (Diodorus, v.75.4). There Diodorus is citing a scripture much more impressive and much more in the line of our present concern than any of those Pergamene hymns of a much later time, "Orpheus in the *Teletai.*" It was that reference (to a work on which Pausanias was to hang the great name Onomacritus, and therewith a momentously early date) which turned the path of simple duty to Patroni's deserts, their escorted promenade of arduous verification, into a grand defile of problems — only a few, but there with all their vegetation, rock-growths that are (some of them) among the choicest curiosities of scholarship, in the literature of the Pillar Idol or that of the religious paintings and reliefs in Roman dwellings. To go digressing up and into this would be the rankest dereliction of duty, which just at present is the obligation to make sure of getting from Trendall's Iliupersis Painter not less than the best of what his school offers for the method — a reciprocal ordeal — chosen for verification of Patroni's eschatological premises. But I am not proposing to proceed in blinkers. I do not have to claim, I can take for granted, that part of the interest and importance of Patroni's ideas is manifest in the test appropriate to them, applied now to find out whether they are of stuff to survive (with counter-attrition!) objections developed from Orphistic ideas still interesting and once fashionable. But before we return to the Iliupersis Painter and his quite preciously simple foil to that other reunion, on the Munich krater, for its consummation requiring (if we must take the vase's back with its front) threefold or fourfold cooperation — of Nike, deputies of Dionysos, Triptolemos and other judges, perhaps also of Orpheus — let me claim that it is part of Patroni's deserts that his ideas should at any rate be seen to have a good address, in the same region of practical scholarship as the great problems of teletic archaeology. At all events, escort-duty to the former requires at least incidental awareness of the latter, posed respectively by the Attic vases, partly of Onomacritus' time, which seem to demand to be related to the pillared *Perikionios*, as the *Orphic Hymn* no. 47 calls him, and by a famous room of a Pompeian villa, with wall-paintings of what is certainly a *telete*, as certainly of Dionysos, almost as surely in the aspect which the forty-sixth *Hymn* calls *Liknites*: it is in regard to the participants that controversy begins. As so posed, separate problems, but in a setting which, as we shall see presently, suggests connections.

Return to the Iliupersis Painter is resumption of escort-duty, that is, of ordeal-making, and for that unshirkable work the olpe by the Iliupersis Painter (Sichtermann's pls. 136-137) should be not less helpful than his associate's own volute-krater in the same collection, my illustrations of which (pl. 18a and b, after Sichtermann's pls. 52 and 54) lent themselves to the contention: "see, in rebound from this concentrated little hellscape and its pendant the unceremonius reunion by grace of Dionysos, what a difference conviction of sin had made by the time of the Munich krater, on which promotion to the like bliss required both Eleusinian and Orphic authority, to say nothing of obscure doings, involving sluicing with a pan before (?) an award of grapes, implied for Dionysos' own department by the 'happy ending' celebrated in the back neck-strip (figs. 1b and 7)." Whereas the particular and specific mischief of the krater Jatta 1094 by an associate of the Iliupersis Painter is to start the train of thought which ends in fear that the classic eschatography of reunion on Munich 3297 implies corruption, by the *agyrtai* and their peddled religion of expiable guilt, of the original eschatology of (re)union, simply and naturally Dionysiac, innocently optimistic, which the Jatta krater itself illustrates, on the other hand the Iliupersis Painter's own olpe (without the Jatta number, but K 78 in Sichtermann's book and published in his pls. 136-137) might be made a vessel of scorn for such appeals to significantly late mythography as are about to be made by my figs. 4 and 11, though the vase itself of course belongs to the time of simple optimism. How so — all the more interestingly because the erosive or corrosive effect depends in some measure on a gamble like Winkler's forecast of wheels to emerge discouragingly from modern over-painting — we need to see as soon as possible. But, for a thread of still present concern with mortuary plates and the neighboring topic of *teletai* we had better not quit the other man's vase without a last look at its obverse, for the two details, panther's skin and scepter, which are quite telling about Hades, saying "Dionysiac yes, but not Dionysos."

Relationship of
Dionysos, Hades and Persephone

I NEED NOT disclose just here the whole configuration of facts which makes this information important, for that would demand untimely discussion of a late pelike at the Hearst State Monument (pl. 16) on which a companion of Persephone has all the attributes of Dionysos Melpomenos *except* a pelt to sit on. The point most necessary to make, in preparation for the briefest summary tolerable of working assumptions about the whole set of scrawls on gold foil, is as follows. As represented by an associate of the Iliupersis Painter on the Jatta krater, the husband of Persephone is like her Eukles of the Corigliano tablets linked in firm association with Dionysos (Eubouleus), but makes an even neater fit with the words of the invocation of Plouton in the eighteenth *Orphic Hymn*, Ζεῦ χθόνιε, σκηπτοῦχε. Here, as in the later phase of Tarentine vase-painting less incontestably dominated by an optimistic eschatology of completion, Hades' principal attribute is a scepter indistinguishable from that of Zeus, eagle-tipped (not owl-tipped, Sichtermann noted, correcting Jatta); this lasts, but the pelt disappears. To write so is of course to invite the challenge: "are you aware what you are already proffering us, spiked on that point of yours – something very like admission that the Dionysos of the ware's middle period, your '(re)uniter' employed or implied by the Iliupersis Painter, the Hoppin Painter, the Lecce Painter, before the derangement which you more or less acknowledge and seem to be connecting with the Lycurgus Painter's interest in Aphrodite, commercially so well-timed, is after all (all your evasions of Orphism!) Dionysos of the Dismemberment *telete,* son of Zeus and Persephone?"

This seems to require two statements in provisional rejoinder: first, cheerful agreement that the first clear sign of a change that opens the foreground of eschatography to Aphrodite and Orpheus but does leave Dionysos the background occurs in work of the school of the Lycurgus Painter; I have not the slightest doubt that this is just where any careful student of the "H.A." krater's shape and plan (pl. 11a and b) and of its floral ornament, drapery, head-types and superficial anatomy (pls. 12 and 13) would place the man or woman who decorated it. Next, let us have registration of what – being just a fact – cannot be embarrassing, namely

that, in the theology of the *Orphic Hymns,* a god with the name of the third
deity of the Corigliano trinity, Eubouleus, and sufficiently identifiable with
Dionysos, is son of its Persephone (29.8) by the god Plouton (29.3) who
corresponds to Eukles in the tablets' trinity and is in his own hymn (18.3)
addressed as "sceptered Zeus of Underground" before his own name is
uttered (in the next line), yet in Persephone's piece (29.7) is clearly enough
distinguished from another Zeus, her father. It should not be forgotten that,
while those tablets are contemporary with late Tarentine red-figure, probably the *Orphic Hymns* form a work of the third century A.D. But there can
be nothing fatuous, there may even be useful practice, in filing facts of
W. Quandt's careful text of them, with no longer (since the vivid lesson of
Mise's relevance) any squeamishness about their time and place, if also with
no deeper respect for them than fits the likelihood that, in a center formerly
so extremely bookish (and still so pious) as Pergamum, their writer was not
cut off from all that was then extant of the canon of Orphic scriptures.
Whether in fact there be in that long Pergamene litany any trace of quite
early and Onomacritan *teletai* is certainly an impending question. For
present business with two vases of the Jatta collection let us take what is
propulsive in the theological parallel just noted between a certain group of
mortuary tablets and a certain few of the *Orphic Hymns.* From the prospectively disconcerting krater we may pass to the similarly disconcerting olpe,
unless I have underexploited our opportunity to observe a corollary probably important, though only a by-product of the mutual ordeal of two
hypotheses, the Patronian's "still nuptial," the terrorist's "now (at last)
cathartic." What we have just seen, with some merely eye-opening help from
documents five or six centuries later, is that the threefold (Persephone,
Hades, Dionysos) theology of the krater by the Iliupersis Painter's associate
(pl. 18a and b) is the threefold theology (Persephone, Eukles, Eubouleus) of
the main group of Corigliano tablets with the sin and the strain left out. I do
not mean that there is not sin, damnable sin, on the obverse of the krater,
where we see the wife of Hades lending her good if sputtering light to a
police-woman's trussing and knotting in the arrest of a criminal not without
significance for the joint effect of the vase's back and front, having intended
to destroy the most illustrious union in a world of eschatogamy. My point,
which may seem important presently, when it is the turn of the Roman
monuments which lend interest to the peculiar theology of Dionysos which
was so nearly Cicero's, is perhaps better made as two. (1) As with its perhaps
sin-hinting accretions (two more or less teletic figures, Triptolemos and
Orpheus, and a vessel of purification) the Munich Nekyia only emphasizes,
there is no compelling reason to think that in this other scene of eschatic
reunion at the back of the Jatta krater the three lucky mortals are justified
sinners, only now together again because deputies of Dionysos (like the
present nymph, or a satyr) have collected from each a certificate of expiation (like the tablets addressed at Corigliano to the very trinity — partly

visible on the vase, the third member very plainly implied — of the Jatta krater). (2) Nevertheless, I cannot find, even in the duty of proper severity to the silliest or most crudely tendentious modern writing about a Zeus-begotten Zagreus, any reason to resist what considerations just reviewed suggest, the idea that the Dionysos implied, as agent of reunion, by the Jatta krater, and quite manifestly seen match-making on kraters in Lecce, is the son of Persephone and of a father very easily regarded (since in fact thus depicted, and even thus named) as *a* Zeus. It is very much our practical business to make the best of this, altogether: not just in the sense of accepting without distress the fact on which Cicero's source insisted, that Greek literature and art had elaborated a richly inconsistent mythology of Dionysos; if it is really true that there is neither acumen nor even energy in archaeological research without "the art of the bounce-off" let us be quite positively grateful for the cushion of contrast provided for the rebound to Dionysos Liknites; he should be another mother's son, Semele's, the fourth Dionysos of the author cited by Lydus (*De Mensibus* iv.51) and by Cicero in *De Natura Deorum* iii.58 (cf. Kern *Test.* 94), Cicero mishearing the Greek read to him, but not failing to catch the information that this fourth in the list had an Orphic *telete,* the only one which the list mentions (Lydus: ᾧ τὰ Ὀρφέως μυστήρια ἐτελέτο; Cicero: *cui sacra Orphica putantur confici*). I have no doubt that this, for the son of Semele, is the *telete* depicted in elaborate detail on the walls of a room of the Villa of the Mysteries at Pompeii, and more summarily represented in other works of Roman art, including a certain type of Campana plaque (another type in the series *alludes,* as we already well know, to the Dismemberment *telete* for the son of Persephone; "represents" would say more than I am sure of). My reasons for that confidence I must certainly disclose, but in a better place and not where they would be an interruption, separating the testimony of the Iliupersis Painter's associate's krater from the complementary witness, perhaps more gravely ordeal-making, of his own olpe in the same collection (Sichtermann's pls. 136-137).

Aphrodite or "Telete" in Chattel-Symbolism; Archytas and His *Platage*

PROSPECTIVELY DISCONCERTING krater; "similarly disconcerting" olpe, but "complementary." If the phrases, serving their purpose, left haze behind, let me try to fan it away. The scene of reunion on the krater was so clearly and simply an illustration of the eschatology of its period that it lent itself only too well to the "yes, but only for a period" of what is left of the partly demolished case against Patroni, since (from the Munich Nekyia) a *later* scene of reunion could be produced in the context of which were features that a determined antagonist of Patroni's ideas could construe almost as a placard: "NO BLISS WITHOUT MORAL PURGATION," with even Dionysos' signature to be added (after a quick turn of the pot) to those of Orpheus and Triptolemos. Similarly, on the Iliupersis Painter's olpe, in spite of the mischief that this vase too can help a later piece (fig. 13) to make, the picture was not intrinsically in conflict with the (re)union eschatology in its original, quite un-terrorized, formulation; for an earthly marriage, the detail of which happened to recall preparations for an un-earthly, ultramundane, affair on a calyx-krater by the Hearst Painter in Lecce, and ceremonies for what was even more plainly an eschatic marriage, with the personal blessing of Dionysos, on another vase there, a bell krater by the Hoppin Painter (pl. 8a). Still similarly, the olpe's threat to Patroni's ideas could not be seen without some peering into the distance, at the detail (so virginal!) of that late mythography, but (once apprehended) the prospective trouble might seem more formidable, more directly and concretely threatening the nuptial eschatology's claim to the things most seriously in dispute, the objects that constitute the chattel-symbolism on which the latest phase of Tarentine ("Apulian") vase-painting relies for a certain complex effect — complex because it is a matter partly of characterization, partly of narrative point, partly of decoration, many of these symbols (balls and timbrel in that now threatening affair of Europa, fig. 15, but also "sistra," lavers, alabastra, rumble-wheel whirligigs, pastries large and small) being good excuses for the ware's chief means of its climaxing gaudiness, white or yellow paint. No doubt, if we were to commission some modern draughtsmen to do us an allegory, the most adroitly economical one possible of what is mainly the issue in the present stretch of this study of ours, he would only need to draw a sufficient heap of such things between just two figures, Aphrodite and Telete, contending (with rival rakes?) for the whole pile. If he should make a difficulty of the point that (the manner of late Apulian red-figure being what it is) Aphrodite and any personification of teletic religion would look exactly alike if all characterizing symbols had to lie in that target of their rakes, an allowance of not more than two subsidiary figures, warranted quite perfectly correct company, should make his meaning unmistakably clear: to identify one of the principals, add a winged Eros of late Apulian type (not one of those "he might be Death" louts of early Italiote red-figure; as significant companion for the other, insert Orpheus in Thracian dress and actually harping, for the not quite improper objection that in late Apulian red-figure Orpheus belongs to Aphrodite would have to be silenced with a quotation from Pausanias ix.30.4 (Kern *Test.* 142), Ὀρφεῖ δὲ τῷ Θρᾳκι πεποίηται μὲν παρεστῶσα αυτω Τελετή, sufficient for the purpose. It is certainly interesting that in a haunt of the Muses, on Mount Helicon, the woman with Orpheus in a sculptural group was seen as Telete, not as a Muse, by Pausanias, though the harping there was to a congregation only of animals, not (as on the vase of my pl. 12) to men intent on a rite – to say nothing of a matter which we have been inclined to find, provisionally, momentous for some problems, Pausanias' having denied (one book back, viii.37.5) that Orpheus wrote the book *Teletai,* by his statement assigning it to Onomacritus. Anyhow, our present business is with things of certain kinds that would be represented in that imagined heap so literally in question: for is it heap of symbols merely nuptial, or heap of things handled (as some such objects surely were) in a *telete* and capable of being tallies of eternal salvation for anyone who – as a vase-painting could easily show – had had to do with this or that one of them?

But naturally, for most of those very things there were also quite neutral uses and associations, and just in this lies the present power of the preoccupied women on the Jatta olpe, in combination with the excited women of a much later vase, as they are shown in my fig. 16 for part of the "Europa" amphora H. 3218 in Naples, to create serious embarrassment for the Patronian rake, as it reaches out to pull to the nuptial side two symbols very common on late Tarentine vases, each in the form of a thing known to have been used in *teletai,* respectively Orphic and Eleusinian, namely ball and timbrel. I had better improve my weakly vague word "serious," but without the false suspense of "fatal?," for I mean to offer my fig. 15 (from the Berlin amphora Furtw. 3241) as specific relief of the difficulty now developing. Yet I cannot at present be sure that it will be so accepted (taken, I mean, as Aphrodite's provision of a new plaything for the heroine's new life, instead of being read as something for marine fun and games at the more acrobatic end of Europa's escort for a tedious journey). At all events is it not a rebuff, after suggestions that nuptial mythography, especially in pictures of the affair for which Horace wrote the summary "*uxor invicti Iovis esse nescis*," was decisively on Patroni's side, for me now to be met by the girls of a Europa vase (Naples H. 3218, fig. 16), the women, mostly unmarried, of the Jatta olpe, and two young persons from the Palatine Anthology, the girl Timareta (vi.280, Gow and Page, no. 45) and the apparently Tarentine boy Philokles (vi.309, Gow and Page, no. 41) united to warn us that those very things proposed for registration as nuptial symbols, ball and timbrel, may be, can be, jointly or separately symbols of virginity, immaturity? Philokles has further trouble to make, threatening to involve a third thing, the difficult ladder-like feature which spreads from Tarentine to Campanian and Sicilian vase-painting. But we have nearly enough for the present. The anonymous epigram for Timareta, dedicating her ball and her timbrels to Artemis before her marriage, goes not unsymmetrically with what Leonidas of Tarentum wrote for Philokles, no longer a little boy and now dedicating to Hermes his ball and his *platage,* a submusical toy comparable with Timareta's set of *tympana* (since the verb corresponding to the noun *platage* can mean "to make a timbrel's noise," *AP* vi.218). In the *telete*-recalling, all but Orphic, rest of what Philokles discarded, playbones and rumble-wheel, there are rich reserves of interest — as likewise in certain local associations of the *platage* (might one not call it the national toy — if it was indeed more toy than just fidget-absorber — on the strength of the variety which Archytas conde-scended to invent, the great Pythagorean of Tarentum whose keen interest in the rumble-wheels of *teletai* began to seem important just now, though it was a pity that there was nothing to tell which *rhombos*, the Eleusinian or the Orphic, he had studied?). But just for the present moment it is more striking that with only a trifling chiasmus of difference (a single tympanon, a set of balls) the playthings which Europa will *leave behind* (fig. 16) when the Zeus-bull goes off with her correspond to the playthings which Timareta discards before marriage.

The Jatta olpe (Sichtermann, pls. 136-137) would be an anticlimax were it not, very suggestively as we shall presently see, something of a booby-trap for the eager Patronian, though if the set of balls there should tempt him to unmaintainable distinctions, that may be the beginning of his discovery of some resources. Meanwhile, at any rate there is nothing in the olpe's picture of a mother's preparations for a daughter's marriage quite so insidious as I can guess certain features to be in yet another version of Zeus' wooing of Europa, on a Vatican vase (amphora X7, Trendall *VIE* 2, pl. 54c). It will not be to our disadvantage with the Jatta olpe if I ask attention first for a curiously foolish detail (foolish because a patch of modern overdaub, curious because perhaps wager-worthy) of the Vatican picture, below the right foot of seated Zeus. The more or less ladder-like effect of horizontal markings in this light area cannot be quite accidental, yet it makes no sense as part of the landscape. It would begin to take on meaning — in its context of *maidens,* disconcerting to a Patronian unless he knew where to look for counter-encouragement — if a few sweeps of a rag soaked in alcohol uncovered one or more examples of the baffling cross-barred symbol which perhaps some scholars, our youngest, may live to see securely identified with Archytas' *platage*; in the meantime, *sistro apulo,* as some pioneers in the last century called it, is perhaps the least inept makeshift (the blob-streaked "ladder" at least looks like a *sistrum,* whereas uneven bars [perhaps], and beating [certainly], would be needed to justify "xylophone," the fashionable term till [only very recently] Trendall found fault with it, *LCS* 1, p. 454). At all events, I can scarcely hope for a fitter occasion of conceding that the *sistro apulo,* whether the blobs on its bars mean bells or mere beads to shake or rattle, or little metal tongues to play "pring-prang-prong" with, or just provision for the silent fidgeting of a restless child or a bored woman, must in its countless occurrences be given precisely the same standing as the ball symbol in the ordeal of mutual attrition between the nuptial hypothesis and its teletic alternative. Either both are nuptial symbols, according to some principle (of far fetched irony?) which the Patronian theory of eternal life has yet to establish, or (as the Orphist can now so comfortably argue, knowing that a Tarentine child Philokles discarded a *platage* and a rumble-wheel as well as ball and playbones) they are convertible toys; just toys, in some pictures of myth, but sometimes (in more frankly funerary themes) seen — by our Orphist's eyes — to change into symbols of a dead person's acceptable purity. Which of course (it can be contended) any plaything may in the proper setting become if (like rumble-wheel and ball and toy mirror) its sort is one of those prescribed for the most supremely apt of purity-conferring affairs; that is, the Dismemberment *telete* of expiation, specific purge of mankind's original sin, as some men, more or less "local" men, conceived that to be: namely the Titan-derived guilt of infanticide-deicide-cannibalism which the Corigliano tablets (according to one not unreasonable sorting-out of their confused references to a punitive thunderbolt) do show to have been on the conscience of a valley of southeastern Magna Graecia in the second half of the fourth century B.C. Timbrels (in spite of the aspect, as playthings, just now illustrated by those of two girls, Timareta in her dedication and a companion of Europa in my fig. 16) have to be hung on another (if not quite irrelevant) hook of symbolism, Eleusinian and propitiatory rather than cathartic (even if Krüger should be proved right in his guess that Onomacritus' *Teletai* was the Orphic poem which taught Euripides what a *tympanon* [*Helen* 1347] once did for the peace and contentment of Hades and Persephone). But the *platage,* though Clement of Alexandria and Arnobius do not in their inventories of god-bait encourage us to think that it was prescribed for the Dismemberment of Dionysos son of Persephone by the author of *Teletai* (whether this was Onomacritus, warranted early enough by several centuries to have affected both vases and tablets, or another writer), would nevertheless quite logically (indeed almost as naturally as the explicitly prescribed bait) have had at Tarentum a place in the apparatus of this particular *telete,* if in the second half of the fourth century B.C. it was indeed done there. This, as to the *platage* toy or fidget-absorber, I grant to be valid reasoning in view of the *platagai* of two Tarentines, first the *telete*-going, all but Orphico-Pythagorean sage and magistrate Archytas who, some few years before or after 360 B.C. condescended to invent one, and then his compatriot Leonidas who (whether his epigram for Philokles is a record or only fancy) has one for mention in the list of four toys dedicated by this graduate from infancy, another article being a rumble-wheel such as Archytas studied at *teletai,* and the rest (save the *platage*) being not less explicitly named than this *rhombos* in the apparatus of the trap and the corresponding *telete* (with *AP* vi.309 compare not only Kern's *Fr.* 34 for Clement and Arnobius but also *Fr.* 31, though only two of Philokles' sorts, playbones and whirligig, happen to be mentioned in this teletic papyrus from Gurob). It is no doubt high time that we were back at the Jatta olpe of Sichtermann's pls. 136-137, which for the Patronian, once warned against over-interpretation, can be a quite profitable point of rebound. But first it must be made altogether clear what it is that I have just insisted on conceding.

This is not that the laddery sistrum-like thing *must* be identified with the *platage* of Archytas, though I cannot think of any likelier solution of the puzzle, none certainly that better agrees with the facts of occurrence for the more than fifty examples of the feature which every experienced student of Italiote vases must have seen (especially, this fits the symbol's distribution, the thing being most at home in late Tarentine vase-painting, but not inconspicuous — as Trendall found worth stressing, *LCS* 1 454 — in the art which this most influenced, Campanian red-figure of the school of the CA Painter; yet also it fits the clear signs of esteem and demand, among adult women, for the thing itself, these of course not at variance with what is conveyed by the intentional paradox of Ἀρχύτου πλαταγή as a proverbial phrase, that in the submusical device of the then leading physicist of music there was something transcending its childish kind). But rather, what I desire to acknowledge with all necessary emphasis is that (without any Christian Father's "yes, the thing is mentioned") it should be the privilege of the Orphistic critic of Patroni's persistent optimism *to help himself to* the ladder-like symbol. And this for special and preferred use, along with the very best, the most impressively teletic-seeming articles, ball and rumble-wheel, of the miscellaneous exhibits of the argument which claimed reinforcement just now from, of all things, the setting of a scene of eschatic reunion, the new setting in the Munich hellscape (pl. 1b) of the old theme made so comfortable (pl. 18b) by the associate of the Iliupersis Painter, not under the latter artist's compulsion (?) to allude to Orphic sin-scouring and Eleusinian Judgment. As I have just allowed myself a parenthesis, the briefest possible, of dissent, I am obliged to add that the ladder-like symbol is indeed present on the Munich krater, though (like the vessels for scouring, the two sluicing pans) it is not seen without turning the pot round (pl. 1a), and where it hangs (between the two *ELEP*-hinting young people) is not the best place for an allusion to the Dismemberment *telete* of expiation (we must not forget our good grounds, p. 24, in the vow made by Aeschylus' Electra and in the provisions of Theran Epikteta's will, for conjecture that the gatherings at heroa are sometimes wedding parties, and in regard to that particular heroon this guess is not unlikely). But at any rate I should be the last to press an argument *ex (librorum) silentio* against anyone maintaining (in Orphistic derision of eschatogamy) that the *sistro apulo* had as much title as ball and mirror and whirligig to be read on funerary vases as symbol of salvation earned through that *telete,* given (as must be) that late Apulian vase-painting is really Tarentine, done where Archytas lived and ruled, and within a generation of his death. And the first to recognize a considerable asset for the Orphist in this thing, should the claim be really maintainable, for if *teletai*-frequenting Archytas goes with that acquisition this (on his own testimony, Diels-Kranz⁶, 1, p. 435, lines 2-5) is someone who in the shades could be presented by the Aristophanes of *Frogs* 1032 to Herodotus as "more or less, one of the Orphico-Pythagoreans of your ii.81."

On the Jatta olpe, of which I have let myself write as if it were somehow a trap, yet somehow a source of tactical advantage, for the Patronian, there is a figure, shown in the first (136) of Sichtermann's two plates for the vase, who so far has had very much less of our attention than the three other women (pl. 137) of the same scene of nuptial preparations, scenting of water for bridal ablutions. Who among the four is the bride is not really made quite clear; the Patronian might (inadvisedly?) be inclined to pick the rightmost, bouncing the best (least shabby, least worn) of three visible balls. But coming from consideration of the *sistro apulo,* let us not miss our opportunity of the following most profitable collation: *of* the figure till now ignored, standing on the extreme left between a suspended phiale and a column Ionic though baseless, and holding in her left hand an open trinket-box, like the one (also open) which is *part* of the means used to denote an important Aphrodite (fig. 14, next to Poseidon, on the left of this illustration), *with* one of the three Aphrodites whom I indicated (p. 97) as especially encouraging and course-marking for anyone undertaking dogged perserverance in fairness, fairness short of partisan favor, to Patroni's assumptions. I would not say that, in this practical regard, we must rate her the best of the three, for certainly, at the present turn with the nuptial symbolism of the ball impugned, we cannot afford to forget either what hangs under the phiale of the Aphrodite who (at San Simeon, pl. 16a) interested us by her likeness to the Lycurgus Painter's idea of this goddess as outfitter of brides in a place where she was Pan's neighbor, or what Aphrodite has in fig. 15 (Berlin F. 3241) for Europa, to make good the loss of a ball presumably from fig. 16 (Naples H. 3218). But the Aphrodite of my fig. 14 (Naples H. 3256) has some special merits, above all that she is quibble-proof. She also is datable (after November of 333 B.C., for the battle of Issus is taking place below her), and (as must be more important) her principal attribute (since she has it to *hold*) is not the open trinket-box already mentioned but, of all things, a ladder-like *sistro apulo,* something quite uncosmetic and not less an object of contention, as symbol in dispute between rival eschatologies respectively nuptial and "terrorist," than is the quartered ball for bouncing and catching — perhaps, too, involved with ball and tympanon in the coy refinements of Europa mythographies, though at present there can only be mere suspicion of its lurking, mole-like, under a repainted feature which I have already described, on the Vatican amphora X7. But the special value of the Aphrodite of my fig. 14 is that even more strikingly and decisively than another also holding a *sistro apulo* also in a context of fellow-deities, placed (that other one) above Hermes and opposite Apollo on the volute krater in Bari published by M. Gervasio in *Iapigia* 3 for 1932 on the third unnumbered plate between p. 480 and p. 481, she is unmistakable and unquestionable; on her, in her Olympian company, no one will waste the guess to which the San Simeon goddess is doubtless exposed (since it fell, from Walters, on the comparable Aphrodite of the Lycurgus Painter), "just another nymph."

"Nuptial" Interpretation of "Chattel-Symbolism" Defended and Expanded

I THINK WE are very near a climax of provisional triumph for the nuptial eschatology of Patroni's hypothesis; "provisional" is my allowance for what, in the last ditch of resistance to it, an Orphist might prefer to make of the figure holding trinket-box and ball in the infernal bathing-place of the London amphora F 332 (pl. 5), in whom Walters saw and we too should see an Aphrodite, though a glib alternative is only too easily improvised: "justified sinner (see the ball of her participation in the Dismemberment *telete*!) passed by Persephone and Eukles (E. of the tablets!) through their antechamber of purgation (see all those things for washing!) with no fuss at all; she has not even to close — much less 'park' — her parasol. Nor is Eubouleus of the tablets unrepresented. In the 'basement' (pl. 5a) and on the vase's reverse (pl. 5b) can you not see his epicene and winged daughter-son, Mise-Iakchos? Is it not almost like the tomb at Messapian Rugge (Haas, p. 49) where Mise's name is inscribed near a torch-sign which in fact (though Haas does not expressly say so) is cross-headed like Persephone's there in London?" In any event (and it may be one of conjuring up an Orpheus, fig. 13, drawn by the hand that drew that "justified sinner"), there is all the more reason now to discourage the Patronian, with a good measure of proof so nearly achieved, from a game of false objectivity with the balls, fresh and less fresh, of the Jatta olpe for the sake of appending a corollary only a little less rashly glib to the observation which soundly (and with much profit, presently) relates the cosmetic function of the leftmost figure of the olpe (with trinket-box already open for a bride's preparations) to the cosmetic *facet* (denoted in fig. 14 for the pantheon above Issus by such a box similarly ready) of that aspect of Aphrodite in which she is a worship-worthy goddess, important to human piety, as the power that not only ripens the nubility of women but *provides* for its fulfillment in all the decorum and good-will of solemnized marriage. Rational foresight being part of that good-will, not all that Aphrodite undertakes to provide is strictly cosmetic, in the sense of beauty and finery for the wedding — as Gervasio's Bari krater helps to illustrate, for there the second attribute of the Aphrodite who resembles the Naples one in identifying herself *partly* by characteristic *sistro apulo* happens to be a fan, persistent symbol-in-chief of matron's status as we already know and well appreciate, the thing being (in the form we most often see) such a nice combination of dignity and common usefulness. Of course what has hardest pressed the defender of Patroni's assumption of an all but Swedenborgian *amore elisiaco* to explain the behavior and chattels of the people of the latest funerary vase-painting has been the slur (now almost removed?) that having set out to patronize an idea much too cosily sentimental from the first, more so at all events than another sincere champion of Patroni (Carlo Albizzati) could altogether stomach, he has taken quite the most *inept* of all means to support and promote it. Oh, the doubly-dark blindness (it could be protested) of constructing a system of symbols of nuptial maturity out of things belonging essentially to immaturity, and from that, just that, deriving their uniquely rich interest for the history of religion; for in the main they were the apparatus of what was done to a baby in the rite of most modern relevance (through its assumption of original sin) in a corruption of religion all the more outstanding for its denunciation by Plato in his weightiest work, that infection (a prick-purse eschatology of terror) for which South-Eastern Italy was surely ripe by the time of the Issus vase; had it not been *condoned* there by the region's sagest man, Plato's friend Archytas, for we have his own admission, using a word (τελεταῖς) that recalls Plato's sour pun on "death insurance," of having frequented its rimbo-rumbo? If I have been cryptic, or excessive, in reckoning the Jatta olpe's ball-play (and ball-reserve) to be a booby-trap set specifically for rash reaction to the sting of "perversely inept," there had better be amends and explanation. That slur is such, that if it is false it can only have come of its caster's unpreparedness for irony, irony in more than one or two quirks, something like a system or structure of it. At any rate, of the matter's two practical points one is the fitness of not entirely forgetting that in judging Apulian red-figure at all capable of irony we are going quite beyond what the aforesaid champion of Patroni, Carlo Albizzati, would have allowed; the other, very much more important, is surely that our retort (if we have now frankly taken sides and wish to make one) must have some stuff and bracing in it. More than I can find in the perhaps not really mistaken admonition to read momentous differences between the three similar playthings on the Jatta olpe, even with the promising ring of concreteness in the consideration proper for introducing it, as follows.

"Even without the lost remainder of the grave-set, we know that the subject of the olpe's picture is not 'For a Wedding' but 'For Her Wedding'; cannot we be sure that the bride (the dead) is not undesignated? The Iliupersis Painter did not have, centuries before the Aldobrandini Marriage (with its own pedestal-perched basin and its temperature-testing matron) got onto coffee-tables, the advantage that a modern exhibitor of the olpe might count on — that anyone equipped for taking even the slightest interest in its picture would be forearmed against mistaking for the bride the woman (mother, of course) responsible for scenting the bowl of water (see Sichtermann's evidence that it was warm!) now being set on the block. But is the fact that also there are centuries between the designing of the Jatta olpe and Ovid's dipping a pen to write 'balls with ornament painted on them', *pilae pictae,* in a list of things good for a suitor's success (Metamorphoses x.1.262) any bar to our concluding that the bride is the girl bouncing the now most engaging and bounce-worthy of the room's three balls, the one with the fullest, freshest, pattern? You are not asked to recall (though Kerényi made it so interesting) the Heraclean bell-krater, Naples H. 2872 and now no. 305 on p. 61 of Trendall's *LCS*, with an inscription 'They have let me have the Ball' put to explain a scene where a hulking Eros (for Kerényi as good as Death) is dropping or bouncing a ball between a woman whose mirror, tainia, and demeanor mark her nubile, all but *nupta,* and another woman more self-possessed who should be her mother (if she is not rather the appropriate goddess, Aphrodite). You are only asked to give weight to two truths you already know, of which the more important is not the first, that the smartest, prettiest, thickest paint wears off, but the second, namely that for one leading the life of a Greek or Hellenized woman there could be nothing more acceptable, on any occasion of gifts, than the best means of averting boredom and of keeping health, something to play ball with."

One need not be a specialist, acquainted with all the Greek and Italic evidence of euphoric ball-playing (extending, as we even know already, to the afterlife), to grasp that some of this is true — even embarrassingly so, in a certain rebound. Our sufficiently understanding why a ball should be attribute of Aphrodite in my figs. 14 and 15 and pl. 16a, only brings home how far we are from knowing why the *sistro apulo,* elsewhere equally her attribute, should have been no less indispensable to a woman's welfare; so generally requisite that now (in the light of the Sicilian frontispiece and many Campanian illustrations of the second volume of Trendall's *LCS*) it can be seen that the old *apulo* of this useful makeshift is not really a very good fit. Perhaps one does need some special experience (of a certain effect in vase-painting of Greek restlessness and common indolence) to seize the practical fallacy which makes bad argument out of acute observation in that appeal to the Jatta olpe (on behalf — let this be very clear — of a view that would allow an *ironically* nuptial value to the ball symbol, rejecting all connection with the apparatus of a *telete,* quite contemptuously: "obsession with holy terror is your proper state, if you have not mind enough to comprehend (a) how a renewable necessary of life can belong to two phases of it successive yet markedly distinct, (b) what an opportunity there was in such an overlap for Greek wit's chief propensity, to irony." But as matters practically stand, it is rather the Greek vase-painter's propensity to variation, of which (struggling with the difficulties of all the connoisseurship, stilometry, "what's whosing" requisite today) so many students have had impressive, even disconcerting, experience, that would determine the reception, now, of an argument ("freshest, so accepted suitor's acceptable present") which relied on a count of marks on the three balls of Sichtermann's pl. 137: most on the ball which a girl is bouncing (so denoting it as all but matronly), fewer or none on the altogether maidenly two obsolete on the wall, which the bride will leave hanging there when she goes to her husband's house (unless, like Timareta, she lets some little shrine of Artemis or the Peucetian equivalent have the old playthings).

Here is where the sign that is hardest to read, the blob-streaked "ladder," must come to the aid of one of the easiest to make out, the quartered ball. For validity (with us) as nuptial symbol, the ball is not quite dependent on cross-corroboration, since we have seen it, almost often enough, as attribute of Aphrodite, and do not need refreshing in the elementary facts of that department, first that of her attributes some (her Erotes and her birds) are live and some are lifeless, and next that the latter belong to her giving and not to her getting, with the partial exception of her fragrant censer; this is for her worship, but thereby it is also among the chief amenities of a wedding. Nevertheless, understanding of both symbols, ball and *sistro apulo* as the other used to be called, has much to gain from a little more consideration of their interplay in the rather arch irony of Tarentine vase-paintings of the Rape of Europa. This will require some preparation.

A moment ago, it was opportune to recall Timareta and her ball, a still rather compromising thing from our present (frankly Patronian) standpoint, because nothing could be less nuptial than a possession so merely girlish and virginal, made over to a virgin goddess before its possessor's wedding. Similarly compromising, as I have already shown myself ready to admit, was the *platage* made over to Hermes, together with other childish things, ball and playbones, by the growing boy Philokles — unless I was wrong in the notion which gave this matter relevance, my presuming him and his *platage* to be Tarentine, as Tarentine as the author of the epigram, Leonidas. If I was not mistaken in that, it was not unmethodical to suppose that this toy of his was no common *platage* but the sound-maker *cum* fidget-absorber *de luxe* which a great pioneer of the science of sound, Tarentine Archytas, conde-scended to invent. If I may assume that this physicist's problem was at least a little like the one he had in another such condescension (how to make a toy bird that would really fly, or at least really glide), may I not begin to connect the Tarentine *platage* with countless Tarentine and a good few Campanian and Sicilian vase-paintings which show the ladder-like object (a thing for sound, it is generally agreed)? I mean that if what Archytas undertook was an improvement in a certain traditional plaything, namely how to make a rattle, or rattle-substitute, that was really musical, we need not disbelieve the vases when these seem to tell us that his superrattle, or better-than-rattle, gained quite a vogue, "caught on," with mature women, and (if I may use a wince-worthy phrase for its necessary precision) espe-cially with married gentlewomen. For we must not take less than full advantage of the evidence which establishes the thing which I must still call *sistro apulo* as one of Aphrodite's uncosmetic attributes, in the same cate-gory as her ball and fan, one distinguishable from that which takes her trinket-box and mirror. Perhaps "compartment" would have been adroiter than "category," for we must not forget the big chest, provider's stock-box, which is Aphrodite's most inclusive attribute: it may be that the Cleveland Aphrodite with her name explicit in an adscript, pl. 19, is an even better reminder of this than the one characterized by her company and also by several attributes, live as well as lifeless, on a San Simeon vase (pl. 16a). But the San Simeon Aphrodite, like the also Pan-neighbored one ready for Hippodameia's marriage gave us practice in relating this goddess to significant companions, which now can have application to two Aphrodites characterized by *sistro apulo*.

Musical Symbols; Apollo and Aphrodite

IT MAY BE only accident that Aphrodite with this and a fan is balanced by Apollo with his characteristically "grand" lyre on the Bari amphora no. 873 (pl. 23). But I am encouraged to see design there by observing that on the Issus vase (fig. 14) Apollo's grounded lyre (and held bay sapling) balances her *sistro apulo* held (and trinket-box grounded) not much less exactly, at opposite ends of the row of deities, with only a slight permutation (in relation to the neighboring figure with shafted weapon) which puts Apollo last at his end, but Aphrodite only last but one at hers – not unreasonably, for there the absolutely last figure is a visitor from another element, Poseidon. Almost absurdly much is made in Tarentine vase-painting of proper musical education in reckoning a free man's ripeness for marriage, and I am inclined to think that we shall not be mistaken if we allow ourselves to see a certain scale in this social matter, Apollo's grand music ("grand" as we speak of a "grand piano") and two lower grades, "gentlemanly" and "ladylike" as I must presently explain. There would perhaps be obtuseness (to a local factor) in resorting too smugly to the generalization, probably true, that on Italiote vases a woman with a regular instrument (harp of any form whatever, or pipes) can only be seen as a trained slave or barely respectable hireling (if she is not more than a mortal woman, a Muse, or – as satyr's nymph – rather less), the musical education proper for a well-born girl expecting marriage being none at all. It is true, I judge, that the wares to which the ladder-like symbol must natively belong, "Apulian" red-figure and "Gnathia," were made at Tarentum. It is, I must think, not unlikely that the *sistro apulo,* which from the contexts of its occurrence is certainly at the very least submusical, will turn out to have been the *platage* of Tarentine Archytas, and thus (as the invention of such a man, μάλιστα τῶν Πυθαγορείων ᾽επιμεληθεὶς μουσικῆς by Ptolemy's impressive rating,

Harm. i.13.31) something rather above that minimum, in a rudimentary degree a musical instrument. I must not indeed imagine that the shape *qualis scalae,* guarantees a scale of notes, and have to acknowledge that it is very far from sure how (from metal tabs on the rungs, plucked?) the sounds were produced. It is only clear to me, after discussion with my friend Professor Ghisi of Pisa, distinguished musicologist, that the wildly aberrant, tabless but pick-played, specimen in a ludicrously provincial vase-painting (on Naples H. 3382, from Capua) scarcely deserves the authority Heydemann let it have (*AdI* 41 [1869] pp. 309-320, pl. P; cf. pl. Q; not in Trendall's *LCS,* but that need not mean that this barrel-flask's quite lavish illustration of instruments in actual play, including a rectangular gong, is altogether modern fraud). At all events, one of several threads to keep in hand through all this is the need of not entirely missing whatever signal the Issus vase in Naples and Gervasio's Bari krater have to give in their both balancing Apollo's lyre with Aphro-dite's *sistro apulo.* But in straining to catch something of the idea with which both vase-painters are playing in this linking yet opposition of Apollo and Aphrodite — both belonging to Tarentine music, but at its opposite ex-tremes, with him expert in its grandest instrument, her a trifler with (if not the mere dispenser of) its pettiest — we must beware of promoting Apollo (whom the dialectic inscriptions of tombs do not even recognize) to any really direct importance for the funerary religion of South-Eastern Italy, like that which we must acknowledge for Dionysos, Aphrodite, Eros, Hermes. I see the practical aspects of the matter as no more than these two: first (and of no very immediate urgency just in itself), that to serve the warning notice "don't take Apollo for a chthonic god" by no means implies "and don't you dare to imagine that he could ever have anything to do with Aphrodite even in her terrestrial work of getting living mortals married." On the contrary, as the frontispiece of the second volume of Trendall's *LCS* has only just recently emphasized, by its furnishing a wonderful "new" Sicilian wedding to complicate an old Campanian problem, there is an area here, round about Apollo's ceremonial relation to Aphrodite, for special curiosity and vigilance.

For us at this moment, a *sistro apulo* suspended to the right of the bride on the bowl of the Sicilian pyxis, actually contrastable with the great triangular harp of the male musician (Apollo?) who on the vase's lid faces a female figure (Aphrodite?) there conning a scroll, makes Trendall's frontis-piece rather more relevant than the much better known bell-krater of the Campanian Ready Painter (Naples H. 608, *LCS* pl. 202, 1) on which "Apollo and pet, or bridegroom (as sometimes in Apulian work) ready to strum at his own wedding?" takes the place of the puzzle which that artist's addiction to censers and to importunate waterbirds perched on laps or in lavers (*LCS* p. 515) poses more often, "Aphrodite, or bride who, besides getting cus-tomary gifts of this goddess, has been able to borrow her swan?" My second and more important point, much easier to make with the help of what

Trendall has furnished us, is that this mutually musical involvement of Apollo with Aphrodite on Tarentine vases in Naples and Bari has quite practical repayment to make for any attention given it; for what could be more so than elementary practice in coping with the innuendoes of the *sistro apulo,* not less important in mythography than the ironies of the ball and more difficult? More difficult, at any rate, since the Jatta olpe gave us at least some inkling of how a *pila picta* might well be a symbol of double meaning according to its condition, fresh or worn, however disconcerting it then may have been, in peering ahead to a much later picture (Europa and other maidens in fig. 16), to find it used so categorically, together with a timbrel just as in Timareta's dedication, as symbol of *virginity.*

The first use I propose to make of the *sistro apulo* hanging up to our right of the woman with bride's *stephane* on the Sicilian pyxis in Basel (*LCS* 2, frontispiece) is to accept the encouragement, which (in the light of the pairings-off in Naples and Bari) I can now see it offers to cancel the cowardly question-marks after my namings of Apollo and Aphrodite in my incomplete description of the secondary picture on the lid – deficient especially in its not having mentioned and stressed the stock-box with dove perched on it, denoting Aphrodite no less surely than the stock-box with perched swan (not without some intrusion of "the ironies of the ball") on the San Simeon pelike of my pl. 16a. The dove in its place up there on the lid of this skyphoid pyxis does more than complete the characterization of Aphrodite begun by the box. It alerts us to the presence of two more of Aphrodite's belongings in the big picture below; her other bird, and her son. It is probably important that we should not altogether slight a third winged element of the bigger composition, for between the two live ones, Eros above and the swan below, there is a carved sphinx as support for the arm-rest of the bride's chair, this not simply ornamental if the monster is to have its usual significance, funerary. But since our business is chiefly with the *sistro apulo,* as something of Aphrodite's department, part of her stock for equipping brides, it is more interesting that also down here, where this *sistro,* the thing that may be the *platage* of Archytas, is hanging on the wall against which the bride's chair is placed, Aphrodite is present, with still something more to give out, a spray for the bridegroom to wear (I am sure no one any longer takes the man of the vase's bigger picture for a second musician, on the strength of the white streak which surely is not a pipe but the very familiar "swagger stick" of late red-figure's best-born westerners). The force of her likeness, in peplos and headdress, to the sure Aphrodite on the lid is quite irresistible, given (as we are at this level) Aphrodite's son and Aphrodite's waterbird; quite enough for the recognition without any appeal to a feature which would in any case make it difficult to see the figure on the extreme left of the larger picture as a living bride's mortal mother, namely the deadly sphinx in the design of the bride's chair.

"Elysian Love" Distinguished from the "Bridal of Death" through Musical Symbols

BUT THE LETHAL symbol is noteworthy and welcome, because it helps to make the skyphoid pyxis in Basel quite a weapon against quite a nuisance, the "bride of death" metaphor. Here, if anywhere, is the Dead as Bride; but in the blond young person rather nervously chinning his gentlemanly stick who can see Death? How timely it is that this Sicilian illustration of *amore elisiaco* is so simply concrete will be appreciated by all who have read, with the promptness it deserved, Kyle M. Phillips' most interesting commentary on the marvellously rich illustration he has just provided of the mythography for Andromeda's exposure (*AJA* 72 [1968] pls. 1-20, pp. 1-23: especially pertinent, the passages touching, even indirectly, on the nuptial symbolism of the Tarentine vase-paintings thereof and certain amazing survivals of it, p. 19 but also pp. 9, 10, 12). The author, in sometimes letting himself write of Andromeda as the bride of death, was indeed slipping – but only into such metaphorical language as not only Greek poets but also *mutando mutato,* religious Christians have used, the latter so almost recklessly that the emptiness of the impulsively rhetorical metaphor, altogether (whether Sophocles let it pass in *Antigone* 816, to be bitterly cancelled at the line 917, or as Charles I of England happened to use it in his last hours) should be plain enough. No doubt there is an even more ponderable matter in the fate, in Patroni's own thinking, of "un concetto eufemistico che considera la morte quale un matrimonio con Hades" (*Ceramica* p. 160); did not Patroni arrive at his apprehension of a frankly nuptial eschatology by way of gradual conviction of that euphemism's unimportance? Unimportant, but evidently still a nuisance: worst when a subjective obstacle to a modern's penetration of deeper levels, but having been to some extent really current it can still make real haze. I do not mean to condone one or two blunders, made I cannot remember where but in the name of Grammar, this taken in vain ("well, 'soul', you know, is feminine in Greek": not in the present connection useful knowledge, as is quickest grasped from the variation of gender in what is said by or for the dead on the tablets buried with them, at Petelia, Eleutherna, Corigliano and elsewhere, Kern *Fr.* pp. 104-108). I had in mind the circumstances which make it welcome that the illustration which we have just had of *sistro apulo* in an affair of simplest eschatogamy, dead "lady" routinely unveiled for such a regular "gentleman," was from a Sicilian vase, the exceptional one published in the frontispiece of Trendall's volume of plates for *LCS*; the ware as a whole (pls. 225-256) is so simply womanish in the subjects and tone of its figured decoration that — especially in view of the warriors with whom a related, at any rate *sistro*-borrowing, Aphrodite-honoring, phase of Campanian red-figure still teems (*LCS* pls. 176-177) — one is tempted to wonder "and what did the dead *men* get in Sicily in the last forty years of the fourth century B.C., after Timoleon made it possible for funerary vase-painting to flourish again, in this Lentini-Manfria Group and so forth?"

That would be the merest mooning, reverie just distracting, if it led to forgetting that it was the ladder-like thing, in a nuptial subject related somehow to an adjoining picture which grouped musical Apollo with bride-equipping Aphrodite, this *sistro apulo* turned *siciliano,* that gave the Basel pyxis of a Sicilian class roughly contemporary with the Tarentine Issus vase its relevance to some of our own problems in the symbolism of work done at Tarentum on pottery intended not for use or even burial there, funerary ware for Italic neighbors. Relevance to the general problem of all this chattel-symbolism: things teletic, are they, belonging to earthly rites procuring infernal bliss through expiation of sin? Or rather things eschatogamic, through their association with earthly marriage fit to express certain hopes of ideally natural companionship, hopes of its renewal, or hopes of the fittest compensation for missed maturity? But relevance also to a particular question about the most subtly *engaging* (better word than "difficult"?) of these things, perhaps nearly ripe for recognition as the *platage* of a Tarentine authority on musical intervals (fit then, though nominally mere toy, for women as well as for children? fit at least for "ladies," debarred even from the rather unsubstantial, quite unprofessional, lyre of "gentlemen"?). I do not mean, as yet, the question "how, on the whole, does this thing look in the strongest light, the light of the mythographies, to which it was by no means exposed in a bit of mere guesswork about its possible presence under a smear of redaubing in a Vatican 'Rape of Europa'?" That matter I recognize to be much more important than any parting suggestion I can ask leave to make meanwhile in regard to one of the data we have been given (and must use?) about the *sistro apulo.* Given thrice, if I am not mistaken in judging that the Sicilian pyxis in Basel presented us with what was after all only a third "helping," rather more subtly flavored, of the contrast which the gods-deploying painter of the Issus piece in Naples and the gods-stacking painter of a *naiskos* composition in Bari both found to their taste, interesting, piquant even: the difference — so extreme as to make us suspect hinting of a mean? — between the great instrument which denotes Apollo as supreme master of the highest kind of music and the humbly musical thing (at best some pring-prang-prong cousin of the jew's-harp?) which can denote Aphrodite because, like jewel-box and fan and bright new *pila picta,* it is one of several things she has for brides.

Here the worst blunder I could make would be to fail to perceive that there are interests to respect. The one that is anonymous, that of the die-hard Orphist, is perhaps less respectable than another, "sociological," of which Dr. Moses I. Finley has helped to make me aware. But the first should have his opportunity to file, in protest, a different reading of the musical theme which, on the lid of the Sicilian pyxis, should have some relation to a detail, subordinate but more or less musical, of the nuptial theme on the bowl below, namely, the familiarly ladder-like thing which was one of Aphrodite's attributes on the aforesaid Tarentine vases in Naples and Bari, but is here her gift to this already crowned and now unveiled bride. Orphistic objection can hardly fail to fasten on the shape of Apollo's instrument, big enough but triangular (so why not harp of Orpheus, as in fig. 13 and pl. 12?) and the conspicuous length of the scroll on Aphrodite's lap (what but a great Orphic scripture, if the harper with her is Orpheus?). Yet the minstrel is not dressed as Thracian Orpheus should be, and to the nuptial occasion below, on the bowl of the pyxis, the shape of the harp on the bowl's lid might seem proper enough, if there is nothing wrong in judging the matter by a pair of likewise "two-storied" weddings that are however Tarentine, with the professional musicians women (*CVA* Denmark 6, pl. 261, 1a; Italy 32 IV D, pl. 12, 1; this opportunity to remark also a bridegroom's unprofessional contribution to the music of his own wedding should not be missed; see in the same Italian fascicle, for Turin IV D, pl. 14, 1). Now that there has been resort, on the opposite side, to a corpus of vases not Tarentine, Trendall's *LCS*, it is only fair that the case for interpreting late Tarentine vases by "holy terror" (resourcefully Orphic or just cringingly Eleusinian) should be encouraged to exploit, to better purpose, such advantages as it can borrow from two or three other pieces in that book.

Nothing could be more "cringingly Eleusinian" than a certain submission of mystery-mockers to purification by blood and squeal (as on no. 102 of Trendall's Sicilian series, pp. 602f, pl. 236, 1, if the subject is Melampus with the Proetids). But we must not forget our business with symbols, especially tests impending for the *sistro* sign. That vase-painting, though remarkably monumental and occurring on a Sicilian vase of the same Lentini-Manfria Group as the Basel pyxis, is really of much less importance than some others, Campanian, for our practical problems of sign-reading. On our way to one more interesting still, later in the same phase of the same ware, the picture on a hydria in Newark (New Jersey) (pl. 20) should meanwhile repay consideration, Trendall's no. 19 of his fourth division of Campanian red-figure, a piece which he publishes in pl. 176, 1 and assigns to Beazley's CA Painter (for Trendall an almost surely Cuman Greek). As on the Sicilian vase of Trendall's frontispiece, here on this Campanian one is the thing which we have been calling "Apulian sistrum": better preserved than the Sicilian example and catching the eye at once, suspended in the shrine-like building (*naiskos,* rather than *heroon* for a mortal?) where a female figure stands with a mirror which seems to be not for her own use, so stiffly is it held out, almost as if for the benefit of the woman standing outside to our left, in significant asymmetry sexually with the soldier to our right. Significant, that is, if I am right in judging that the central figure was meant for Aphrodite, triply so denoted, by a gesture (*proffering* that mirror), and two attributes, *sistro apulo* and censer. I would not press this too obstinately (against the only alternative, that she is the dead in her *heroon,* represented as ready bride), but must certainly emphasize the Apulian (that is, Tarentine) precedent (and because she, this companion example, is comparatively early, belonging to work related in style to the decoration of the "H.A." krater of my pls. 11 and 12, on the Tarentine side I would rather cite the enshrined Aphrodite who is put to match enshrined Herakles on the Antigone amphora in Ruvo, Sichtermann, pl. 114, then adduce the swan-burdened goddesses in comparable settings on late "Apulian" pieces in Sèvres, London and Potenza).

At any rate, what makes the Newark hydria so opportune is that, without strain on a certain thread which we must keep intact (attention to the *sistro apulo*) it can mark for us the beginning of a stretch of Campanian vase-painting to which we must submit to be introduced, at just the present turn. That is necessary mainly because in this phase the Campanian artists are so increasingly subject to Tarentine influence that our by now obsessive concern with "Apulian" symbolism requires some noticing of even Western ways. In fact, it is towards the end of that stretch, Trendall's Part IV of Campanian red-figure, that there is something which (when we are ready for his no. 720, pl. 208, 6, republished in my pl. 21) will demand very cool and candid inspection, for a hardpressed Orphist might perhaps hail it as crowning mercy, at next to his last gasp all but proof of his case: disappointing only in its imposing a further concession to the (re)union eschatology, allowed longer survival, but only at the price of coming to purse-pricking terms with teletic religion. Not far back, I allowed myself the word "interest," in a sense scarcely permissible without reference to persons. A colleague, indeed, is one of my reasons for being grateful for that Newark peg for the *sistro apulo* (where it can stay in sight above competing topics of its system of symbolism); if my own idea of it is not mistaken, and the thing accordingly is one of the most curious of all symptoms of women's social disadvantage, then it is not of much less concern to the Finley standpoint (as I beg his leave to call this interest) than a matter already adduced for it, eschatography as adapted for "inferiors," and another which I must not ignore, the same as altered for children. But if moreover "Orphist in some difficulty" — in difficulty, specifically, about Aphrodite's appropriation of symbols which should be Telete's — is a convenient and allowable personification of intelligently obstinate criticism of Patroni's ideas in their application to Tarentine provision for Apulian burials, this has an interest, which fairness must certainly recognize, in "Apulianizing," quasi-Tarentine, transformations of the funerary vase-painting further west, in Sicily and Campania.

(Re)union and Purgation Reconsidered; Orphic Tablets; Ambiguity of Symbols

CAMPANIA ESPECIALLY if actually this would allow a stretching, even slight, of the calipers, for longer gauging of erosive change. I must hope that I have not quite failed to show that chronology enters into all intelligent objection to imputing a nuptial, an all but Swedenborgian, eschatology to Italiote artists decorating grave-sets for the funerary trade in the fourth century B.C. At its least intelligent and interesting, such opposition would be withdrawal — in impulsively vehement shrinking from "such mush!" — into a region not very favorable for chronological or any reckoning, pastures of reverie about a proselytizing sect leading an "Orphic life" much more systematically ascetic than Plato's Ὀρφικὸς βίος (only a diet, I judge, Orpheus' own, supporting life without taking it?) of *Laws* vi.782C. Such meditations would not be unfree to speculate about the childish things and expiatory doings of the Dismemberment *telete,* matters which Miss Simon has made quite unshirkable in any thinking required of today's brains about grave-goods of Italy's fourth century B.C., ever since she disclosed undeniable traces of this rite in less serious products (household decorations) of a less serious century of that era, Rome's first. But are they not in their natural range (as long as tethered to Herodotus's ii.81 and the topic of sectarian peculiarity in clothing) more likely to develop an obsession with drapery, in search of Orphico-Bacchic discardings of repugnant wool, to match what is indeed quite verifiable, the all but complete eclipse of meat-eating in late Italiote red-figure? This last is a curious fact, but perhaps only so in view (too distant for significance?) of the collop-dangling tables of archaic Attic vase-painting, and though I should be the last to deny the relevance of wool (the very stuff of the Apulo-Tarentine symbiosis in prosperity!) I should be slow also to make a footnote for that passage of Herodotus out of a fact also verifiable (and the Newark hydria's neighbor in Trendall's *LCS* gives at least illustration, pl. 176, 2), namely that a matter in which the women of a certain phase of Campanian vase-painting are more Bacchic than their Apulo-Tarentine peers, their improvizing upholstery with fawnskins, goes often with something to which the women of "Apulian" red-figure are remarkably disinclined, half-nakedness. On the other hand, the most rational criticism of Patroni's ideas is essentially measured and measuring, perhaps most so in the respect which allows me to say that chronology is its cutting-edge.

As in this: "yes, that eschatology which it saves breath to call 'nuptial' did establish itself in Tarentine vase-painting for the wool-folk of the Apulian uplands (a prudish lot, men and women, as you will find out if you are really interested in how they wished Tarentine artists to dress them). *But time was on the side of something else.* Something the reverse of sectarian and private, as revealed to us in the weightiest evidences of the most potent influence of that immensely mixed thing, Orphic religion, namely the sneers of Euripides, the protests of Plato, the grim frankness of Poseidonios (if his is the clear mind behind a half-clouded passage of Strabo, x.3.23, which seems to begin by meaning that Dionysiac *oreibasia* is related to ordinary human business with exploitable mountains much as our Sierra Club — with only a little stretching — is historically connectable to the prospecting and lumbering and so forth of California pioneers, and which [certainly] ends by distinguishing Orphic lore from Dionysiac according to its parallel relation to another line of commercial exploitation, religious imposture in its several varieties). At any rate, can there be doubt that Plato, the least bitter but the most explicit of these witnesses, attests as general, catholic with a properly small *c*, a certain religious situation — consciences everywhere sick and dreading damnation and everywhere resourceful quacks, scripture-primed and thus eagerly ready with acceptable medicine, warranted by Orpheus yet mercifully delicious to take? Or that this was unlikely to be preservative of the simple optimism which (since there is trace of it in Plato's own writing, *Phaedo* 68 A) may perhaps be all we need to explain the otherworldly matches made by Dionysos or deputy during a certain phase of the 'plain style' of Tarentine vase-painting, or to account for what now (in a partly Campanian calibration) we most need to recall and keep in mind, the nymph-attended (thus simply Dionysiac) reunion of a widower with wife and son on a volute krater decorated by a follower of a more or less contemporary master of the 'ornate style,' the Iliupersis Painter (pl. 18b)? Surely, then, anyone who cannot bear to think that this general condition and the treatment it so readily got affected the old faith in an Elysium of companionship supervised by Dionysos (so appropriately, if the manager was Dionysos-Eubouleus, son of Hades-Eukles and Persephone!), may expect to have much to explain away. Not only in Tarentine work, in a late phase of which an intrusion of Orpheus which is not the trite one is so challengingly conspicuous, but also in what this borrows (so suggestively for the undertaking to be 'concrete') from the language of chattel-symbolism which Tarentine red-figure begins to use at about the time of Aphrodite's encroachment, in league with Orpheus, upon Dionysos' dispensary of bliss-in-(re)union. Argue, if you like, that this symbolism restores primacy — and Orpheus — to Dionysos, because some of its signs, two of the most frequent, ball and mirror, and one other, the rumbling whirligig, can be matched outright in the apparatus (bait!) of a *telete* of Dionysos attributed to Orpheus, while two more (of some special interest, certainly, if late Campanian ware is to be ransacked) can be seen fit, on reflection, to belong to this rite: the bunch of grapes or raisins (in what other form could Dionysos be torn and eaten by mock-Titans?) and the *sistro apulo* (if the thing, though interestingly capable of travel, began at Tarentum, what else can it be on the vases of its place of origin but the *platage* of Tarentine Archytas, and how could that, the national, anyhow supremely babe-engaging, toy be left out of the insidious apparatus of a *telete* of baby-snatching which Archytas himself, if we may judge by his interest in whirligigs' rumbles at *teletai,* probably attended? But if you reason so, you have made over this symbolism to another thing capable, as the Corigliano tablets witness, of travel, the religion of holy terror."

Well, let the Vienna bell-krater 182 do its Campanian worst, at the place where this evidently seeks to put it, as the low, late, extreme (pl. 21) of a development of which the other markers are two securely Tarentine vases; for mean, the Munich "Nekyia" krater 3297 in the relevant parts of its surface, the reunion of a widower with wife and young son at the administrative center of Hades' Realm of the Dead (pl. 1a) and what I have ventured to call the "Happy Ending," for is not that what is personified by Nike with her two prizes, wreath and bunch of grapes or raisins, for awarding to a certain young or rejuvenated man sequestered in Dionysiac company in another and smaller picture on the opposite side of the vase (fig. 1b)? The high, early, extreme of the comparison is naturally that other reunion of widower, wife and son at the back of the volute-krater numbered 1094 in the Jatta collection (pl. 18b, after H. Sichtermann's pl. 54). The proposed comparison requires, for fulness of its proper effect, a fourth piece more or less contemporary with the Jatta krater, the Tarentine bell-krater Lecce 623 attributed by Cambitoglou and Trendall to their Lecce Painter; on the obverse of this (pl. 8a) is the picture in which we have already recognized (pp. 68, 127) one of Dionysos' matchmakings, finding curious then what I may hope to find useful now, its requiring so much more exertion of the two males concerned than the comparable wedding with the same god's blessing on the bell-krater attributed by the same scholars to their Hoppin Painter, Lecce 620 (pl. 8b). The Lecce Painter is a less accomplished artist than his senior (and teacher?) the Hoppin Painter. But it is not to be explained as an accident of incompetence that this dead girl, still perched where (by Hermes Chthonios?) deposited, seems — if I may use the right words without apology — only half alive; this is part of an intended effect, of which other parts are in the bridegroom's having to teach her use of the mirror and in her need of Dionysos' encouraging, in fact enlivening, pat or grasp.

At all events, the still half-dazed girl of Lecce 623 is good for sharpening eyes — to very keen interest in what the still all but frozen man of Vienna 182 has for his family (mirror and bunch of grapes) in a picture which Trendall (*LCS* 1, p. 529, no. 720) assigns to his Rio Painter (pl. 21). This attribution I must take as meaning: Campanian, yes, but by an inheritor of the "Apulianizing" strain of Tarentine influence already effective in work of the CA Painter (just now cited for his needing to show Aphrodite's *sistro apulo*) but much more manifest in the styles of some of his associates or successors, especially the men or women collected in ch. xvii of *LCS* as an "Apulianizing Group," from one of whom, the Boston Ready Painter, Trendall's connoisseurship finds the style of the Rio Painter descended, at one remove (that is, through the Nicholson Painter); see *LCS* 1, pp. 495, 501, 522, 529. What matters practically is that, having business with the assertion that "time was on the side of" forces not favorable to the comfortably simple ideas expressed in the Lecce unions and the Ruvo (Jatta) reunion, we cannot expect to do much better than with this Apulianizing Rio Painter, if what we are seeking is someone late enough to represent, or rather to be tested for, the extreme of mischief in a development which we are asked to recognize and to measure thoroughly, having been set the Jatta reunion as its zero and the Munich reunion as its midway point.

The terms of this invitation or challenge require us, of course, to make the effort to see the Munich volute krater 3297 (or at least what is shown of it in my fig. 1b and pl. 2b) as this would be apprehended by a mind strongly (excessively?) impressed by two considerations: on the one hand Plato's implying, for even the first quarter of the fourth century B.C., no small spread of teletic religion, on the other hand its own quite direct perception of a great increase of something – religious sophistication, not just artistic elaboration of shared themes? – in the Munich krater's presentation of two subjects which the Jatta krater had already combined, *Their Majesties' Justice* and *Family Reunion* (pl. 18a and b). To set up the Munich krater as exhibiting only the mean of a development leading to the Vienna krater's reunion (pl. 21, with this third widower strangely laden, strangely unconscious) should imply a concession somewhere, but certainly it would mean diagnosis of a specifically teletic difference (sin-conscious now, but rite-trusting, rite-enjoying) in the religion of the Munich krater. In this interpretation, no doubt the Dionysiac strip would get most emphasis, though it could be thought that there was more obtrusion of *teletai* (by a particular reference but also in general) in the big hellscape below which is the setting of the Munich widower's reunion with his wife and little boy. While the packing of the Judiciary (in Triptolemos' being supplanter of Minos) should recall Pausanias and his noting (x.31.11) of Polygnotos' hellish stress on the supremely awful sanctity of "the Eleusinian *telete*," should not the presence of Orpheus at Persephone's right hand remind us, first, of Aristophanes and Euripides and their combining (*Frogs* 1032, *Rhesus* 944-945) to attribute so much to Orpheus' revelation, both *teletai* altogether and the Eleusinian mysteries in particular, and next of Plato's precision of insistence on *teletai*, as both the effective and the attractive part of this infectious religion of expiation (*Republic* ii.364 E to 365 A, 366 A to B)? But would not the adroitest point-marshalling make much more of the Dionysiac strip on the Munich krater? In the first place, because in "Happy Ending's" bunch of grapes there is something for tactical combination with another, that held by the all but frozen widower at the Vienna "extreme of mischief," pl. 21; next, because of what radiates at Munich from a combination within the little picture (fig. 1b), where the principal's thyrsos says "initiate of a *telete* of Dionysos" and the washpan hoisted by the satyr adds "and thereby pure." Here, it might be thought by anyone really concerned to make out a change in the rules — a change since the Jatta widower was admitted to reunion in armor, light but nevertheless profane, pilos and shield — is something of quite far effect, going out to touch even the Corigliano tablets with relevance.

The argument would, I suppose, be this. "Don't you see? The difference between the first and the second reunion in the present stretch of three is like the difference between the religion of the Petelia-Pharsalos-Eleutherna tablets (Kern *Fr.* 32, a and b, Berdelis, *ArchEph* [1950-1951] 99) and the religion of most of the Corigliano scrawls (Kern *Fr.* 32 c-e). In the Petelia group of inscriptions, all that the dead needs is just what the widower on the Iliupersis Painter's krater (pl. 18b) is seen getting, if this is the right drink of water from one of two brooks, administered by one of the 'wardens' (φύλακες) authorized to give it (here the most natural person, a nymph, with the most proper badge of authority, a thyrsos). The two results of the drink which the Petelia tablet guarantees for it, refreshment and recovery of memory, fit well enough the needs of the present warrior, only just relieved of helmet shield and big cloak, and still in a state which lets him turn his back on his wife; they have of course no bearing at all on the Happy Family of the Munich krater. There (pl. 1a) the widower's only burden is the lightest of possible cloaks, a chlamys, and the three are intimately reunited already, in such contrast to the happy group on the first vase, where the wife is out of her husband's sight, the unrecognized son has stepped back and is keeping his distance, and the husband's only thought — since he has eyes only for the nymph and her pouring — might seem to be 'I am parched with thirst,' as is said in all five tablets of the Petelia class (all but the Pharasalos tablet adding 'mortally!'). On the other hand, the message common to all three of the Corigliano tablets cited, addressed chiefly and quite directly to Persephone, is an assertion of kinship and of purity, purity in a special and judicial sense, purgation by settling for wrong done. It is not quite enough to note how all the various points of this *shared* content, including the dead's claim to be divine after all, with blessed kinship recovered through purgation acceptable to the proper Court of Justice, can be matched on the Munich krater. That the Munich reunion (pl. 1a) contrives to have what only Kern's tablet Corigliano *e* includes ('the crown is mine already') is something to add to the impression which the principal picture's composition manages to give by a certain balance — by putting the almost swaggering husband so near Persephone, separated only by the figure of Orpheus (for us subjectively, almost personification of the Corigliano hexameters!), part of an arrangement which on the whole is eloquent ('see, they are unchallenged') for the husband's group, the Happy Family and Orpheus being so evidently in deliberate counterpoise with Triptolemos and his fellow-judges, who are put significantly close to Persephone's *husband* (it should be not less significant that right above is Penal Justice, with drawn sword; that this picture has vertical ramifications of meaning has had notice enough already, p. 43-44)."

This is the best, or nearly the best, that a "terrorist" could make of the Munich Nekyia as mean of a scale of family reunions designed to exhibit in funerary vase-painting an encroachment — of the fears and precautions of teletic religion — answering to the difference between the Petelia-Pharsalos memorandum for a journey and the Corigliano passports. Part of the aptness of the proposed extreme, Campanian, the Rio Painter's picture (pl. 21) of a reunion in which the bandoliered widower carries what might have been thought presents for wife and son respectively (if only he had begun to present them!) is that it comes curtly. If the mirror and the bunch of grapes are not reunion presents ("you are still beautiful, my dear, and grapes for children are to be all the rage in later monuments") must they not cut all discussion short? What can we then make of them if not what Miss Simon made of mirrors and grapes in the reliefs of the Roman plaques, ritual things of the Dismemberment *telete*?

If that is what they are, then we should see them as passports, tokens of justification comparable with the Corigliano tablets, but telling more explicitly what the written allusions to thunder and lightning in the tablets at most only hint, if what the scrawls really mean is that the dead as mock-Titan has undergone mock-blasting in a *telete*, and is thereby pure and saved. At any rate, in that view of the mirror and bunch of grapes they are the symbols which have ensured this man's passage, in a state rather like surgical anesthesia, to a place rather like a hospital's recovery room, where his wife and son have found him. Her right hand is already administering the touch which will revive him — compare a similar detail of the same painter's krater in Rio de Janeiro (Trendall, *LCS* pl. 209, 1). Then the symbols will be flung to the ground, but his arms about her.

It is really much more urgent that I should not (through maladroitness) conceal how I judge the teletic interpretation of the Rio Painter's Vienna reunion (pl. 21) than that words should be found to say how it has gone with Patroni's *amore elisiaco* in the ordeal of mutual attrition contrived for it. Quite evidently, that is now over, Patroni's hypothesis having victoriously survived what was pitted against it, another which grudged his ideas validity beyond a brief phase of the middle period of Tarentine vase-painting, contending "no, the hopes expressed in the (re)union eschatology had to die, for time was on the side of something else, not less powerful than in Plato's diagnosis of it, natural human venality's trading on human anxieties natural in such a self-conscious century, selling delightful superstitions that were (as Plato stressed) so much better than just specifically relieving, being so much fun."

If I may suppose my own impression of the Vienna reunion to be not very much less interesting than what is rather like a post mortem for a cock-fight (though not pointless for our concerns, if it drives home that the weakness of the counter-hypothesis was precisely in the incautious "had to *die*"), may I say that in spite of the victory just conceded I cannot regard as merely irresponsible the interpretation of that vase-painting which has just been aired, interesting enough once we grasp that it made a choice? Choice of response in a certain dilemma of evidence, between signs hazily looming that grapes should be allowed to share the nuptial symbolism so well established, at least in Italiote vase-painting, for mirrors, and reasons, which may seem to be more concrete, for letting grapes share the teletic symbolism which, as I have repeatedly admitted, Miss Simon has proved mirrors to have in certain Roman terra-cottas, two types of Campana plaques where, in the hands of orgiastic satyrs who are with women but ignore them, they can only be explained as required for miming the Dismemberment *telete.*

More concrete, these reasons, in the sense that Miss Simon has been able to adduce something palpable, one more sort of Campana relief, on which again satyrs are behaving strangely, and this close to a vine of grapes which is growing out of an image of Dionysos (*Hommages à Albert Grenier* 3, pl. 285, fig. 5). But with strangeness of a wrong sort, clashing cymbals (surely respectful?) into it; should we not rather look to an author contemporary with those plaques, Diodorus in his iii.62.7-8, for the evidence that is really pertinent to teletic grapes? For there I must recognize something fit to supersede the merely a priori consideration "what better mock-Dionysos for mock-Titans to pick apart and eat?" First Diodorus explains the fable of dismemberment as an allegory of wine-making, and then he notes that the Orphic text (and dramatic practice) of *teletai* are in accordance with this (σύμφωνα τούτοις). However, with the evidence looming (through a certain haze, but quite massively) of nuptial grapes, there is a dilemma to recognize and to make somehow propulsive, in the direction that was promised when I acknowledged that vindication of Patroni's *amore elisiaco,* if attainable, should not leave the neighborhood too untidy; there should be some provision, in a clearing, of orderly benching for any residue of pretty questions, if no more or better accommodation than should be needed for making their attractions visible and approachable.

One such is already with us. For if we are already taking as proved the proposition that an eschatology of reunion continued to express itself in late Tarentine vase-painting for Apulian burials, and even in decadently sub-Tarentine work by such outsiders as the Campanian Rio Painter, and also are taking as now fairly presumable (till very definitely challenged) that this implies persistence of the original *range* of hopes, including nuptial completion of the unmarried, may we hold that this means persistence of the old optimism in all its *simplicity*? Or have we to acknowledge that in their respective languages, that of late Tarentine eschatography at its most sensitive and most enterprising, and the patois (if not rather "pigeon") of a Campanian prolongation, the Munich and Vienna reunions have just said "no" to this, but with both adding "there was still all the old bliss for those who had bought it and whose next-of-kin could furnish eschatographic receipts"? I should judge this a benchable question, still open and quite attractive, knowing however that there is a phrase to amend or at least explain before I dare take this problem to its place. To the very hinge of this question belongs the bunch of grapes carried by the Vienna widower, in a sense not true of the grapes (however interesting) which Nike or Happy Ending has for, or has just collected from, the hero of the Munich krater (if the principal of the intermediate picture, fig. 1b, is this vase's widower in an intermediate state, before achieving the reunion with wife and child shown in pl. 1a). My indication that there was evidence, nonetheless massive for the theological haze it happened to loom through, of a nuptial symbolism of grapes, referred to a fact of late Tarentine red-figure fit to cause some hesitation before our concluding that the bunch carried by the husband on the Rio Painter's krater in Vienna was, at some traffic-control, taken with the mirror which also he still holds as a sign meaning "pass this widower, all sins are forgiven, for reunion with his wife and little boy; he was mirror-Titan in a Dismemberment *telete,* and in that role tore off, chewed and swallowed, his proper bit of grape-bunch Dionysos." This cautionary matter is the repeated association of grapes with that ware's effeminate Eros.

Eros Transformed;
"Nuptial" Chattel-Symbolism Re-justified

Now THAT EFFEMINACY, because it is a suddenly occurring transvestism (putting him in a bonnet, with jewelry to match) makes difficulty, not lessened by involving the temptation to connect him, through an inscription in a Messapian tomb rather near Tarentum, with the haziest figure of Orphic theology, hermaphrodite Mise. However, because there is no writing on the vases to match the inscription at Rudiae-Rugge, it is fair to give Mise no better status in our problem than that of provisional chimera (on present showing, monstrously impossible), especially as the transformation of Eros can be not unconcretely explained as assimilation to his mother, which (as we have seen) the best customers of Tarentum had grounds for desiring and power of enforcing. But at any rate, if I emphasize that the important association which it illustrates is frequent, there should be a good enough example of the grape-laden Eros of late Tarentine vase-painting in the one carrying both mirror and grapes in the interior picture of the Braunschweig cup no. 314, *CVA* Germany 4, pl. 41, 3. And for special cogency in regard to the mirror and the bunch on the Vienna bell krater of my pl. 21, which is not Tarentine, only a Campanian pot decorated by a follower of a certain adapter of Tarentine conventions, may I refer to a Campanian vase-painting which has been for me a monument of eschatogamy — as striking as anything Tarentine at Lecce — ever since I was allowed to study it at Nostell Priory some six years ago? It gets its deserts in Trendall's *LCS* pl. 185, where figs. 1-3 for this oinochoe, no. 51 of Lord St. Oswald's collection, in the text of Trendall's book no. 297 on p. 481, assigned to his LNO (Lausanne-Nostell) Painter, let one see all round the picture of an otherworldly wedding, at which Dionysos is present, if not with the eagerly intimate cordiality he shows in his Lecce "splicings," my pl. 8a and b. Seated, here he takes a less active part, but one for which he has dressed (bandoliered like the bride-groom) and which gives him a certain say, as he turns (with instruction, or gracious acknowledgement?) to the woman far right, who holds what on the Tarentine "H.A." krater (important if there is aetiology in pl. 12) is divided between Eros and Aphrodite, wreath and dish of little pastries (wedding cakes, if the aetiological point of the obverse of the "H.A." krater is aimed at what the best authority, Orpheus, lays down for a bridegroom's prepara-tions). It will save beating about the bush if I may say that this, for my reading of the picture, is the bride, though the mirror and bunch of grapes carried by the other woman facing the bride-groom to our left of Dionysos make her very much more important to any question there may be about the scene of reunion on the bell-krater in Vienna. "*Telete* tokens? Nonsense: mirror and bunch of grapes belong to what happens at a wedding, and any eye trained to read compositions must infer (from where I stand, how I hold my mirror up to the young man) that there was a point at which the bridegroom was given them to hold." Whether we take this as the Nostell woman's expression of her own importance (amounting to a claim to be recognized as nuptial Aphrodite?), or as comment on what the Vienna widower is still stiffly holding, it is something we can use — as a warning not to be too eager to take in a teletic sense even the symbols to which mysteries of purification or propitiation can make some claim, such as we must let the Dismemberment *telete* register for mirror, ball, and whirligig, and might let it file for grapes and *sistro apulo,* as well as for symbols in the form of things essentially cleansing, laver, hydria, washpan. Useful, too, as reminder of a resource, not so far profitable in any decisive way, but not exhausted (especially in regard to the *sistro apulo*), that some of these symbols can be pursued into a domain of Aphrodite, nuptial myth. If I must make up for a shortcut ignoring beatable bushes, I need to say that my sorting-out of those women in the Nostell eschatogamy (*LCS* pl. 185, 2-3) complies with a pretty clear (inexorable?) indication given by the divine neighbors of a girl, posi-tively obtruding her cakes, on another vase of the same Campanian group, the neck-amphora Naples 127950, *LCS* pl. 188, 2-3, assigned by Trendall to Beazley's Painter of New York GR 1000, to whose style the style of the

LNO Painter of the Nostell vase stands close, as Trendall notes (*LCS* 1, p. 479), while his place in the pedigree of late Campanian red-figure could be said to be that of "grandfather" to the Rio Painter, whose Vienna reunion caused me to adduce the Nostell wedding (*LCS* 1, pp. 522, 529). I saw and noted the Naples vase in the course of the same journey which let me remark the Nostell piece, but until Trendall published them only two plates apart I had failed to see how the obverse picture of the Naples neck-amphora (*LCS* pl. 188, 2) and the single picture of the Nostell oinochoe (*LCS* pl. 185, 1-3) explained each other.

The Naples composition is much the stranger, and so gets more from this exchange than does the Nostell grouping. No great harm would have resulted from wrong choices for the Nostell women, that is, had I been misled into taking the deferential figure with wreath and dish of cakes for a mere bridesmaid and into supposing that the woman more impressively dressed (with an almost chasuble-like mantle to dignify her) and posed so self-assertingly (as if coaching the bridegroom in something to be done) represented the eschatic bride. In the connection most important hardly any harm at all, for it would still have followed that the mirror and the grapes were nuptial things, even with the holder reduced from goddess to bride, and the application of this to the Vienna reunion would have been not more than a little lamed (a little, of course, because with her "here's where you hold these things, young man" the Nostell goddess has a part in explaining how widowers consigned to wives can have mirrors and grapes to hold without being justified sinners). On the other hand, our discerning who is really the bride on the Nostell pitcher (the deferentially stooping girl, with right foot on a little rock and both hands laden, wreath in the right, dish of cakes in the left) is almost a condition of our having patience to make out the setting of a figure all but exactly like her in pose and attributes on the Naples neck-amphora 127950 (*LCS* pl. 188, 2) decorated in the same Campanian workshop by an associate, the Painter of New York GR 1000.

It is only when we have understood the Lausanne-Nostell Painter's picture in terms of eschatogamy, a dead girl applying to Dionysos for a mate, the young man who (thanks to the cooperation of a goddess) is almost ready for her, that we are quite out of danger of supposing that from an earlier phase of Campanian red-figure (the phase capable of imagining Europa embarrassed by coast-guards or another slightly later, capable of putting young males and a very un-Cerberan dog to hang about the place of the Danaids' punishment, *LCS* pls. 100, 1, 171, 1) the LNO Painter's colleague had inherited a devil of reckless parody, now tempting him to make fun of a standard pattern of Tarentine vase-painting for Apulians, one we know so well from volute kraters and some amphoras, with the dead person in his or her monument, flanked by other figures commonly (but not always) representing survivors. It is perfectly true that in the work of this artist, Painter of New York GR 1000, a vein of clowning has been detected and even studied (*AJA* 66

[1962] 323-331), and it could be thought that not only here, in a certain "stop! stop!" effect of importunity between the girl (thrusting her dish of cakes out of her monument) and Dionysos (turning abruptly to notice her), but also in the same man's variations on the theme of eschatogamy on vases of the same double grave (tomb 185, Cumae), he had let himself indulge it (see Trendall, *LCS* pl. 187, 3-4, encounters of a girl, inseparable from her cake-dish and mirror of nubility, searchfully roaming in a region of unattached men where — if I may take a liberty with a single letter — *sunt apud infernos tot milia formosorum*).

The curiosities of this truly reunion grave "a due letti" (Gabrici, *MonLinc* 22, 644-647) are more than we have time for. But it is Campanian, full of vases of an earlier phase of the particular school of Campanian vase-painting to which the Rio Painter's Vienna reunion belongs, and these raise quite a chorus of warning against rashly preferring for the things he so stiffly holds in my pl. 21, mirror and grapes, a teletic reading ("sinner redeemed for whatever is to follow") to an eschatogamic one ("widower consigned to wife and child"). Moreover, some of these vases should be propulsive — for unfinished business with the *sistro apulo* as well as towards the "benching" of attractive questions "in a clearing," for which work there must be some preparation. Especially, such as may help to make what if promised in "clearing" come off properly as work instead of palaver, not failing to do some usefully inclusive limiting as well as making for wider views. But at present anything good for that is not to be hoped for except as by-product of a rather narrow reconcentration of attention: namely on what, for our understanding of the Vienna widower's symbols, the womanish mirror and the grapes, may come out of a resemblance partly noted already, between two pictures by forerunners of the Rio Painter, associates in a Campanian shop of commercial eschatography. The first composition, on the Nostell oinochoe, we remember as the LNO Painter's eschatic wedding of two mortals, by grace of a god familiarly chthonic (whether we have been calling him Dionysos or Eubouleus) in partnership with a goddess still nameless for us (*LCS* pl. 185, 1-3), though we are almost ready to call her Aphrodite. The other was on the front of a vase (pl. 188, 2) that is indeed from a reunited couple's grave, the Naples neck-amphora decorated by the Painter of New York GR 1000, with what we have already begun to construe as a dead woman's bid for the attention and services of the very same team of chthonic deities, if I may write so before she herself has quite noticed (behind her), the presence of the team's female member, *holding as before a bunch of grapes,* but not the mirror she had at Nostell (instead, wreath). Our concentration cannot, I know, excuse me from a paltry stoop of tidying ("policing" in the North American sense) to remove a false clue which has been mere litter since a gust of mere irony blew it in, the idea, vitiated by anachronism, that on the Vienna krater of the Rio Painter the reunited widower will perhaps have a division to make, for the beautiful wife a brilliant scratchless new mirror, for the boy's boyish appetite a bunch of the sweetest juiciest grapes. It should be no distraction, it may even help more than the effort to make out what late Italiote symbolism was systematically meaning in its combinations and permutations of such bunches with many more things than the at least complementary cookies of the Nostell and Naples mate-seekers, if stooping to get rid of that bit of litter should cause recollection of a phaseology of grapes which scholarship has had to recognize. It is only in art of or closely derived from the archaic age that their associations are purely and simply Dionysiac. At the other, Hellenistic, extreme they can be without symbolic meaning, even on tombs – just a dainty for children (and their pets!). But in between, in Italiote vase-painting of the fourth century B.C., hints are given, obscure and certainly inviting research, of a connection with marriage. It would be a pity to muddle any consideration of this with a preconception: "fertility stuff, surely" would be not less rash than "surely somehow Dionysiac." Without making prematurely much of the "phiale, pilled" of the student's card-file by giving the cake-dish of so many eschatogamic vase-paintings the importance of the pastry shared in "splicing by spelt," *confarreatio* the most august rite possible for a Roman wedding, one must not be too disdainful of the possibility that for Italiote marriage the import of the bunch of grapes or raisins may be both flatly unsymbolic and quite secondary, snack complementary to the starchier morsels.

But I cannot propose more attention to the phases of that matter than seems necessary for taking proper leave of the Rio Painter's krater in Vienna, pl. 21. Quitting it, I mean, with a sufficient impression of its symbolism (which must not fail to take in the white feature – curiously like a panther's pelt? – sketched on the widower's thighs, as well as the surer things, grapes, mirror, bandolier), and in the right direction. That is, taking the way that leads back to perfectly Greek and fully metropolitan Tarentum; this and not Cumae (Trendall's home for his Rio Painter) or any other Campanian place of pottery must be center, theologically and otherwise, of the clearing (act or fact) required for any problem-park. No doubt the sketchy white on the Campanian krater in Vienna, especially the ghostly hint as of some big cat's head on the man's left knee, is a scarcely negligible part of what has given me already one pretty question for benching there to attract some fitter enquirer (namely whether, even with Patroni's eschatogamy vindicated, there may not be trace of "holy terror" and its teletic mummery in at least the latest vase-painting of Tarentum; if the Rio Painter meant a Dionysiac panther's pelt by this smear of paint, that would make this Campanian widower almost a match for the very late Tarentine man whose pelt and mirror, reinforced by a possibly teletic ball, reminded us so disturbingly, of Miss Simon's certainly Titan-miming satyrs). And for our tentative word "clearing" has there not been some gain of meaning already, in the possibility or rather the probability that we shall have to recognize Aphrodite in

Dionysos' partner in eschatic match-making on two Campanian vases just scrutinized, the Nostell pitcher and the Naples neck-amphora? There is some promise of more room and wider view in the likelihood that we shall not be able to distinguish the goddess whose bunch of grapes there complements the bride's dish of cakes from the mother of the effeminate Eros, effeminate in a transvestite way, who quite often has grapes to dangle on late Tarentine vases made for Apulians whose chief goddess of the dead was *Ana Aprodita* and for whose taste Tarentine vase-painting had to make Aphrodite's son, from the neck up, only too like his important mother. One of the most vivid lessons of Trendall's new book is in its exhibiting how, in two of three wares subject to the influence of late Tarentine vase-painting Eros at last, if only at last, acquires a woman's bonnet, catching an infection of transvestism *at its second jump* — for (as we know so well) Tarentum's own Eros only got his necklace, earrings and woman's headdress in a "Great Derangement" — on the whole a certainly obscure event, but least so in this small part of it, the assimilation to his mother being more distressing than unaccountable, as we have just recalled.

It would be burying a topic which, though subordinate, I need to keep well in view if I let any other aspect or connection of Tarentum's revamped Eros suddenly cause entire disregard of the reason that has reintroduced him, his role as purveyor of grapes, casually dangled, or flown with, or (in one curious example, on a kantharos numbered F 440 in Walter's *Catalogue,* 4, for the British Museum), raining their juice for him when he puts a krater under their vine. But it would be a pity to miss the cue, timely for the clearing that is to make for more orderly and attractive dumping of problems, which Trendall's *LCS* signals as it shows how little difficulty Tarentum's now corrupt Eros — corrupted to please Apulian neighbors — had finally in making himself acceptable at a great distance, not only to the unsure taste of more or less de-Hellenized Campania (pls. 191-193) but even to the Greeks of a patriotically Hellenic revival in Sicily (pl. 238, 7, pl. 243, 3, 5, 6, pl. 245, 1 and so on). It heightens the interest of this that in the part of this book which so richly illustrates a rustic imitation of Tarentine red-figure more slavishly faithful than any phase of Sicilian vase-painting, namely pls. 72-77 for the Lucanian Primato Painter and his followers, only one of the many Erotes (pl. 75, 3) is bonneted, and that imperfectly; but for knowledge of two surer epicenes elsewhere in the Primato Painter's work (*CVA* Germany 8, pl. 78 for the Karlsruhe nestoris B7), one would have attributed the strange effect to incomplete removal of modern repainting.

Does this suggest, as giving quite sufficient room and basis for what is now proposed, nothing more than the proper combination of available knowledge and alerted curiosity in regard to three aspects (or relations) of late Tarentine red-figure as a funerary ware, its genetic factors of international compromise naturally first, next the reach of its influence, naturally last the limits of, the barriers to, its influence? But for there being in that "proper" such a weakly question-begging word, this (so far as it goes) is no bad beginning of a response to the prod of certain ironical data of a debauched type's circulation. It fails in respect to what, in a phrase which I can hope will seem less affected presently, I must call our cosmetic duty to the pretty questions benchable. But it supplies a sense, certainly required, of their setting's being a field of radial influence, with its effective center in the exceptional prosperity of Taras-Tarentum, this remaining "perfectly Greek" with a justice of meaning which the fate of Kyme, of Poseidonia, and even of Herakleia can help us to appreciate, but only so exceptionally thriving and influential because of an exceptional accommodation — in commerce amounting to ideal symbiosis — with neighbors to the north who were not Greek but (apart from a few obstinate scruples and prejudices) quite showed that they regretted it. That is all very well as a little essay in perspective, a certain effort of spatial comprehension, taking in the flocks on the downs, the looms and the dye-works and the docks at Tarentum, also the wool-hatted rich of the sheep-downs, not so Greek-struck, myth-struck, stage-struck as to be shy of dictating preferences. And not leaving out the docks' merchant-ships, some of them laden for a westward voyage, with the best woolens of the middle Mediterranean filling most of their cargo-space. Yet leaving room enough for certain ironically momentous goods, destined to infect not only Oscanized Cumae but even fastidious Syracuse with the only positively stupid and offensive preference of Tarentum's Apulian customers, an Eros unnecessarily, almost accidentally, transvestite?

But for the purpose of the planned problem-park — if its purpose is to make Italiote studies much more engaging and absorbing through making a few promising opportunities a little more convenient — that is not much of an advance beyond the gain already made, long ago as "long" goes in such a study as this, when it was seen that confident defense of Patroni's insights in regard to the occasion and meaning of late "Apulian" vase-painting required correction of his delusion about the place of it; very tender correction, because in his placing it away from purely Greek Tarentum in the Apulian uplands there was accidental but just respect of a truth which is more and more verifiable in this art's distribution as the charting of it proceeds, namely that as to the special taste and demand fostering the ware's most earnestly elaborate products, the sense that things so very truly monumental were quite worth payment of the bill presented for their size and their myths and their heroizing architecture to the cashbox or to the barn of a surviving kinsman, this only existed there, not at Tarentum. Irony, anyhow, though it has just shown itself capable of heightening interestingly the strangeness of something which was otherwise just odious, an unnatural type of Eros, should surely rank much below *suspense,* if now we are inexorably posed the question "and what, for the values of archaeology which is always 'proceeding,' constitutes prettiness in a problem?"

May I at least take the risk of answering so, not unaware of what my estimate invites? Petulant imputation of being master of a sort of suspense, the wrong sort, is almost worth provoking, at just this point of an affair which still has to do with unsettled claims, of certain persons, Dionysos, Aphrodite, Orpheus, to appropriate or perhaps to divide certain things of the very stuff and essence of Late Tarentine red-figure, common things in the sense conveniently implied by our speaking of chattel-symbols, a category in which no one would think of including Dionysos' thyrsos or his nebris, or any part of Orpheus' exotic dress, but from which no one should think of excluding some things of Aphrodite's department which are rather stock than "stock-attributes" — mirror and other cosmetic things, also fan, ball, *sistro apulo*; add *rhombos* (*rota volubilis,* whirligig), though as essentially childish this rather rare symbol might count as more truly one of her son's belongings than anything he more commonly has, in the goods he routinely delivers for his mother's care of brides. I cannot pretend that the otherwise convenient word "chattel" really fits one article of the system in question, the symbolic bunch of grapes. But this thing must go with those others. Making then, another entry in the list of claims unsettled? I do not propose to incur the complaint "unsettled, yes, and now shirkingly to be shelved, because — on some floor of your jungle cleared for the taxi-dancing of your betters, scholars at any rate both more nimble and more resolute — certain attractive problems are to be 'benched'."

Orpheus, Aphrodite and Persephone in the "Great Derangement"

IF THIS DEMAND for settlement is one which (now, after some clearing of the general perspective and before an unpretentious setting of questions) can be paid in mere views, I can be prompt and definite. Dionysos has *not, in right of his Dismemberment telete,* any claim on any of the things just mentioned, which all, even the grapes, are symbols of Aphrodite, and her right to them is through their association with marriage, in one or other of its aspects. This "shelves" nothing quite absolutely, not even original sin. But it can cut down to not very much what needs to be said if I am now to keep an undertaking not to shirk a statement of working assumptions about the Corigliano inscriptions.

Orphic, they say? "They had better be," the only right answer to that, should not by now be cryptic. A more practical question: for anyone settled in the assumption that the vase-paintings yield no implication of original sin cancelled by *telete* what interest can there be in the Corigliano texts, which confess sin, perhaps inherited sin, and can without wild speculation be thought to connote redemption by means of a certain *telete,* in which the fate of deicidal ancestors was mimed? In two respects they remain usefully pertinent. First, in regard to their theology, for our admitting Aphrodite's claim to the symbols of Apulo-Tarentine eschatography does not mean that we must pretend to blind ourselves to her manifest partnership with Dionysos, which in the present operation of clearing and view-opening is being disclosed even elsewhere, in fact in Western red-figure generally, on Sicilian as well as on Campanian grave-sets; the two lekanides of the Cefalù Painter from tomb 313 Lipari wonderfully enrich the impression we had already begun to get from vases of the Cuman tomb for man and wife, no. 185, as they could be reinterpreted in the light of Lord St. Oswald's oinochoe (Trendall, *LCS* pl. 249, 1-3 and 4-6; for the Campanian pieces, see *ibid.* pl. 188, 2 and also pl. 189, 6 in conjunction with pl. 185, 1-3). Of all aspects of Dionysos the fittest for this partnership, in which D. furnishes the dead with abode and servants but (after a short while) leaves the proper sexual sorting to Aphrodite, is surely Eubouleus of the Corigliano inscriptions, if these can be read as designating Dionysos infernal "crownprince." Next, in a secondary but not too remote connection with Orpheus, our own unignorable Orpheus of the musical bathings on late Tarentine vases (figs. 5 and 13); the tablets and the whole Corigliano site in the aspects that date it and give it, altogether, some resemblance to the mounded cemetery of cremated Macedonians at Derveni, can be allowed relevance to those vase-paintings, even if it is plain that the ablutions pictured are not for Corigliano's kind of purity, but belong somehow to Aphrodite's department of sorting and matching and spouse-retrieving, and must have something to do with *her* standard of presentability, requirements mutual for unitable couples (Hades and Persephone not excluded, as pl. 5 so wonderfully illustrates) individual for reunitable widows and widowers.

For the present let us treat as if they were distinct topics for separate benching two aspects of this bard and "culture-hero" of right and decent religion, Orpheus as Aphrodite's charmingly persuasive gospeler of nuptial bathing, and Orpheus as minstrel at the right hand of Persephone, as in figs. 11 and 17. About the latter Orpheus scholarship's question is of course "can the Eurydice legend spare him?" There would be here a problem to bench for that Orpheus, were this already the place to ask and develop my own "why not?". But the other matter, the simple challenge presented to the erudite hypothesis of "holy terror" by Aphrodite's Orpheus of cosmetic bathing, has already found a setting, in the topic of regional respect for the authority of Orpheus. I must not labor beyond usefulness the metaphor of "clearing" settings and approaches. But, for the present affair, I am sure it is worth saying that the work is not quite done when we have made out on the map the streak of such respect, *quite variously exampled* (but contemporary?), that runs from Petelia-Strongoli, some fifty miles due east of the last success of Alexander the Molossian against Lucanians or Bruttians (capture of Cosentia) and some thirty miles southeast of the supposed site of his final defeat at Bruttian Pandosia, through Thurii-Corigliano, the place (according to Justin) of his burial, to Tarentum, forking then to Pharsalos in Thessaly (where the Petelia tablet was matched) and Derveni in Thrace, where the cemetery has cremation-mounds like Corigliano's but is much more surely military and is dated by coins of Alexander the Molossian's close relatives, Philip II and Alexander the Great, respectively husband and son of that sister of the Molossian whose merely orgiastic addiction to Orphic religion did not in the least prepare scholars for the site's great surprise, the Derveni papyrus, dry but treasured commentary on a cosmogony attributed to Orpheus.

All that is interesting, but gets some of its interest from the streak's stopping (on the west) where it does, so near the place of the Molossian's disaster, with no extension over to Sicily or up to Campania. I cannot feel that I am showing excessive respect for Trendall's authority in now owning that if the name of Orpheus had occurred in the index of *LCS* I should have thought less benchworthy now the idea which got no more than an airing in my pp. 87f, namely that Orpheus' sudden importance in late Tarentine work done for Apulian bereavements is one of various symptoms of the region's penetration by northerners, namely Macedonians and Epirotes, men who though soldiers not unnaturally possessed what the Tarentine vase-painters of an earlier time had sufficiently shown they lacked, reverence for Orpheus. It is at least interesting that two innovations of the latest vase-painters of Tarentum were so unequally fit to travel, its new effeminate Eros and its new respected Orpheus, one and not the other penetrating the funerary art of regions which this lesser Alexander failed to reach. It is of course just as well that the former should now come to mind, for his incidental usefulness in another connection; without him, I could not claim that there was precision in the five words *cum* question mark subjoined to the "streak" of respect for Orpheus, "quite variously exampled (but contemporary?)." Proof that the Corigliano tablets are of about the same time as the Tarentine vases which make much of Orpheus (datable by their relation to Tarentine vase-paintings of the battle of Issus) and also the mounded cemetery at Derveni (dated by coins of Alexander the Great and his father) depends on the effeminacy of an Eros on a plate found in one of the Corigliano mounds. My "variously" and my question-mark make allowance for the tablets from Petelia and Pharsalos, in eschatology so radically different from the Corigliano texts and less datable, but — if only by their hexameters — making the same claim (or pretense) to be Orphic, and in their very difference from the other tablets hinting kinship with the (re)union eschatography of the Orpheus-requiring, Orpheus-magnifying vases.

However, it was for an affair of vivider perspective in the business of truer setting for two or three presentable questions that we needed to couple Tarentum's journeying transvestite and Tarentum's new Orpheus, so stay-at-home. For such help as they may be to the beginning of my next chapter, in making distance, making some horizon, for what is to be in view there, may I now refer (or repeat reference) to some Sicilian or Campanian vases recently published in Trendall's *LCS*? If anywhere in Sicilian vase-painting there be temptation to descry Orpheus, Orpheus in his Tarentine role of Aphrodite's coadjutor in blessing marriage, this is surely on the lid of the skyphoid pyxis in Basel photographed for the frontispiece of Trendall's second volume. I need not repeat the reasons that sufficed for reading this figure, in spite of his outlandish *trigon*, as Apollo, but must not overlook the rich commentary furnished for this pyxis (so typically nuptial) by two lekanides (not less so!) of Trendall's Cefalu Painter, Lipari 749B and 749A (*LCS* pl. 249; my pl. 22). Rather than keep another vain pretender, the figure in Oriental dress on the Campanian bail-amphora Vienna 235 of Trendall's VPH Painter (*LCS* pl. 114, 8), for ludicrous anticlimax, let us get him in the meantime out of our way. "Him," *pace* Trendall, who sees an Amazon here, may be right, and that gives this exotically capped, kilted and trousered person, with however no sign of female breasts or of jewelry, his pretensions to the part of Orpheus. As there also is no sign of music — neither an instrument nor what might have made up for its omission, musicianly robes more flowing than that mere kilt — we cannot take the claim seriously. It is not quite impossible that this is a butt-Orpheus, one more Campanian joke, for Trendall has already (*LCS* p. 280) convicted this artist, his VPH Painter, of caricature. But if that is what we should make of any manhood imputable to this certainly strange figure (strangest in its pose, almost a star-gazer's, and more than the routine *doryphoros* at the pot's back can explain), it is not of much service in the present matter of veneration for Orpheus and sense of the need of his authority at various turns of practical religion.

Aphrodite in Sicily and Campania Throws Light on Apulian Orpheus

ANYHOW, THANKS TO Trendall's illustration of the coy facetiousness which infects this artist's heads of girls (protomes of fig. 10, fig. 11, and especially fig. 12, of *LCS* pl. 114), there is an easy path for us to leave his Vienna puzzle by way of a consideration involving Aphrodite and leading conveniently to the Sicilian Cefalu Painter's pair of nuptial lekanides from a single Lipari tomb, important for a most useful concentration of deities (my pl. 22a-f). Useful in the first place because we have use for evidence, somewhat plainer than the Basel pyxis afforded, that the transvestite Eros invented by Tarentum to please Apulians, did at length reach, and not displease, Siceliote Greeks (*LCS* pl. 249, 3), a welcome which is perhaps more interestingly horizon-making than Campania's acceptance of the Ivy-Leaf Painter's version, more odiously faithful, of the same type (*LCS* pls. 191-193). I must presently try to make good what I claimed for the figures on the two lekanides out of tomb 313 Lipari, nine including Aphrodite's two regular birds and Artemis' dog, as able to suggest a little more meaning for the already important eight (as, with the two corresponding birds, they may be counted) on the parts of the Sicilian pyxis in Basel used to make the frontispiece of *LCS* vol. 2. But, having made much, at one stage, of Tarentine protomes (as symptoms of accommodation to a neighboring cult of Aphrodite), we must not in the meantime lose sight of the faintly ridiculous sample of the Campanian VPH Painter's "just a pretty head" vases in the lower tier of pl. 114 in the same volume, figs. 10-12. The first two illustrate Trendall's observation (p. 280) that the style of this Vienna-Philadelphia-Hamm Painter "makes some of his characters look like Pooh-Bah, as if they had been born sneering." The third face, not at all unamiable, but Trendall's judicious choice for illustration of the VPH Painter's lapse (p. 280) into mere caricature, if taken together with a skyphos in T's Cassandra Circle in the same phase of Campanian red-figure (a piece meant to be more than faintly laughable in the surprise intended, "I'll bet you were not quite expecting the little dear to turn grinning hag at the mug's back"), *LCS* pl. 117, 2-3, might seem now to raise a partly retrospective question of method, if it can indeed seem that such deliberately ridiculous drawings challenge my own conclusion that the heads on small Apulo-Tarentine vases mean Aphrodite, Tarentum's due mass-provision of Apulia's *Ana Aphrodita* and that their most freakish quirks of design betray nothing archly subtle, only a slickly clever hand's bored haste. I would stand by that inference, one of the topics I propose to bench. But certainly we need acquaintance, immediately, with the Aphrodite of the serial story told on the lids of the two Sicilian lekanides from Lipari decorated by the Cefalù Painter, beginning on Trandall's no. 326 (Lipari 749A, my pl. 22a-c) and continuing onto no. 325 (749B, my pl. 22d-f). We need her especially because, though only at the rim of our clearing, in Sicilian work done under Apulo-Tarentine influence (as the transvestite Eros of pl. 22f guarantees), here is a sure Aphrodite uncommonly crisply defined, in relation to other gods present or implied, her own Eros but also Dionysos and Apollo, even Artemis, and also in relation to the dead person of the tomb (no. 313 of a Lipari excavation).

It should be already obvious that *amore elisiaco,* eschatogamy, is involved, but I may need to lay some stress on the connection of this *kind* of vessel with marriage; we can hardly say that it is less nuptial than even the nuptial lebes, *lebes gamikos,* since a miniature lekanis is sometimes part of that (*LCS* pl. 171, 4; pl. 209, 3). What the two lids have to tell begins (my pl. 22a) with a reassuring figure (assuring us that we did well in not admitting Orpheus to the lid of the Basel skyphos of *LCS* 2, frontispiece). This is Apollo, denoted unmistakably by the omphalos (under his lyre) and the presence next to him of his sister, not less unmistakable with her hound, boots and torch. Part 1 ends (my pl. 22b and c) with the neatest configuration of the whole affair: a satyr in gala array (bandoliers, "thigh-garter"), with a timbrel in his left hand, reaches with the other for Artemis' torch, while (a little nearer Artemis, and causing her to put her right arm restrainingly round the hound's neck) one of Aphrodite's two birds, the dove, is seen alighting. The phiale in Apollo's right hand now takes on meaning; with a libation as well as with music, he is prepared to celebrate what his maiden sister is about to allow, someone's passage from virginity to a marriage to be brought about by Aphrodite with Dionysos' blessing in a region belonging to him — at any rate, staffed by him, if I may use that word without incurring scorn for merely facetious economy of double allusion, to the satyr who wants Artemis' torch for a girl's wedding and to the thyrsos of Aphrodite, who is so preciously unmistakable in the picture's continuation on the lid of the companion lekanis, Lipari 749B from the same tomb, 1-3 (my pl. 22d-f).

The symbolism of this second picture is so exploitable for our purposes as to offer dangerous temptation to digression, or rather retrogression, premature return (via the box and birds and deities of the likewise Sicilian pyxis in Basel) to the things of Aphrodite at the centre of our clearing, in truly Apulo-Tarentine eschatography. But let me continue at this sequel's beginning, pl. 22d, not without due attention to the extreme neatness of connection. The prelude ended on a chord announcing "a marriage impends"; the notes of it being no fewer than three, the satyr's need of a torch such as his master held at one of the Lecce weddings (pl. 8b), the arrival of one (the more mobile) of the two birds belonging to his master's coadjutor Aphrodite, his own fourfold gala girdings (four of them if I now include the bracelet with the thigh-garter and the two bandoliers, all quite properly of second-class material, wool not precious metal). Passing from the right of this composition to the left of the other, we are not surprised that its first figure (pl. 22d and e) represents the bride, stripped for her nuptial bath at the laver which stands between her and the seated figure of Aphrodite, but wearing bandolier and thigh-garter of apparently the same precious material as that of her bracelet (beady, however). Then follows a certainly very pretty play of symbols — quite pretty enough without our supposing that the bride's mirror of nubility acquires a little supplement of significance from its tip's touching the stem of the laver which she must use before the affair, beginning with this bath, that will entitle her to the mark of matronly status, a fan, which (on the other side of that laver) Aphrodite already has for her. Telling clarity of symbolism was not, as we know, the forte of the painter of the Basel pyxis, but he did not fail to find use for both of Aphrodite's pets, perching the dove on top of her stock-box for brides (where this appears on the lid of the pyxis, near the goddess), and making the water-bird preen itself near the footstool of the actual bride on the bowl of the Basel vessel. Having made more intelligent use (as harbinger) of Aphrodite's dove, the Cefalù Painter now is also subtler than his predecessor in what he does with her water-bird, promoting it (according to its capacities in the more goose-like nature here imparted) to be an actor in its scene, which the Basel bird, mere abstracted preener, is not, though — owing, as we do, Aphrodite's *sistro* or *platage* for adult women great arrears of attention — we should be glad of a balance in the composition which causes the bird on the floor to send our eyes up to the ghost of a *platage* on the wall.

If I am not mistaken in judging the tale as told on the two Lipari lids to be one of the most suggestive documents in all eschatography, giving out light that reaches beyond Sicilian puzzles to fall on Campanian and Apulian ones, it is not beneath notice that into the position and demeanor of this bathroom goose or swan (under the laver, straining its neck past the stem of it almost to the point of threatening the girl who is about to use the thing) the Cefalù Painter has been able to put a hint of defensive resentment. For any serious student of tides of influence there is at least half-an-hour's good exercise in a collation of the water-birds, Sicilian, with which we have just made acquaintance, and others, Campanian in a not less "Apulianizing" phase of their ware, of the Boston Ready Painter (e.g., as in pls. 201-204 of Trendall's *LCS*); perhaps more and better than mere exercise, if there be no mistake in the thought likely to result, that now at last there is a glimmer of meaning in two Campanian enigmas, *figures encumbered with waterfowl as with lap-dogs,* on Naples H. 808 and Naples RC 78 respectively (*LCS* pl. 202, 1, pl. 203, 3): the first Apollo, guest of chthonic Dionysos to judge by the upholstery of his seat, himself merely host and not master of the creature (goose? swan? crane?) perched on the skirt of his robes, where this bird announces that the present god is ready with music for a dead girl's transfer from his own sister's care to that of the bird's mistress, who appears on the second vase. And there, with her recovered pet on her lap and a thyrsos in her left hand and an otherworldly pile of rocks to sit on, this creation of the Ready Painter is not much less fully characterized as chthonic Aphrodite, concessionaire of Dionysos, than is the corresponding figure (pl. 22d and e) on the lekanis Lipari 749B — though it is certainly time that we noticed what the Cefalù Painter adds to close the tale told on the two lids, an Eros with good Sicilian black in the near wing (cf. *LCS* pl. 226, 2, 4, 8; pl. 227, 2, 5; pl. 229, 1, 2; pl. 232, 3), but distinguished from those eight by his wearing a woman's coif, which he would never have acquired without the operation of two factors, influence of the transvestite Eros of late Tarentine vase-painting, also of course of its antecedent, Apulian pressure on Tarentum to make the funerary type of Eros more reassuringly like his mother (if there is not a third to be fitted in between those two, peevish exaggeration in Tarentum's response: "You'll know the sweet now, with *her* head stuck on *him!*"). But as certainly it is time for me to take care that the Campanian Ready Painter's quite peculiar contribution to the means of proper appreciation of the Cefalù Painter's adroitness in symbolism is not overlooked in any surge of gratitude for unexpectedly centripetal bearings of importance from two so peripheral, far-Western, lekanides. Without the Ready Painter's pictures of Aphrodite's water-bird making itself so much at home *within* the basin of the nuptial laver (as not only on the two Ros oinochoai, *LCS* pl. 204, 1-4, but also on the Paris one, Louvre ED 607 *El cer* 4, pl. 30), it might have seemed affectation to read "oh dear, no trespassing, I hope" into the taut behavior of the Sicilian bird *under* its "own" laver.

If we are still working at "clearing," ambience-making, not quite yet at "benching," two aspects of the eminently eschatogamic serial told by the Cefalù Painter on the two matching lekanides bought by a girl's survivor(s) for a burial on Lipari are now of quite practical interest. The more important, no doubt, is the contrast with certain Tarentine vase-paintings which this presents, in spite of the sure sign of Apulo-Tarentine influence just remarked in the bonnet of the Lipari Eros (pl. 22f). The impressive and delightful play of symbolism (pl. 22a-c) which the Cefalù Painter allows himself, in making Apollo's presence and present function, as well as virgin Artemis' connivance at a maiden's wedding to someone of another Dionysiac world, so unmistakable, offers us something curiously opposite to affairs of Orpheus on pl. 12 (cf. fig. 13); the Sicilian Painter is showing us Apollo about to harp a girl out of his own sister's state, virginity, into marriage by way of a bath at Aphrodite's stemmed laver, with Dionysiac touches (the satyr's "lend us your torch," Aphrodite's official badge a thyrsos) to show that neither the marriage nor even the bath are to be of this, our, world. On the Tarentine vases there is not much doubt that Orpheus's harping is similarly *conducive* — by way of a stemmed laver into marriage, for on the "H.A." krater (pl. 12) as well as on the Jatta oinochoe Aphrodite is in charge, and on the Bari amphora no. 873 (pl. 23) she is at least represented, by her censer (to say nothing of a possible, indeed probable, thyrsosed Aphrodite in the other-worldly scene on the reverse. But except on the squat lekythos no. 1047 of Bibliothèque Nationale in Paris, it is plain that the persons for whom Orpheus is thus playing are men, and there is no sign of unearthly eschatogamy in the context; on the contrary, for at least the "H.A." krater and the Bari amphora, the right long word would seem to be aetiography, the depicting of some beginning in the ways of *our* world, with Orpheus' authority as sanction, and no grandeur of jargon can prevent its being (for us) sub-ludicrous if (as must be) the subject is a certain lesson of Orpheus, the great ordainer, to primitive man (in general, or Illyrian ancestors of the Apulians?), that even males must take a bath before marriage. Benchable questions should of course come of the contrast which the clearing of a westward vista has just exposed; does it mean that the far west, which could stomach Tarentum's transvestite Eros, is here found to be rejecting something? What? the authority of Orpheus? Or only the need of it for a decency so elementary? For any better presentation those questions may be worth there can be no room at present. But a practical corollary of the Lipari lekanides, announced jejunely as a second "aspect" of their "eminently eschatogamic serial" but not yet developed, had better be used now for what makes it practical, its being a means to a vivider and more exploitable sense of the victory won for Patroni's hypothesis, won for that idea of his, *amore elisiaco,* which the ugly coinage "eschatogamy" was minted to serve.

Funerary Purpose of
Apulian Red-Figured Vases
Re-examined

THAT HYPOTHESIS DOES not need any more defending, but one who has been enabled to see the truth of it will do well to provide himself, for saving of time and temper, with a certain apparatus of retorts, handily concrete, sufficiently comprehensive. Apart from one merely "Apulian-izing" bell-krater in Vienna, it was through as well as of Apulo-Tarentine material that the (re)union eschatology verified itself. But what is now observable is a certain convergence, from quite a distance but not beyond the influence of late Tarentine vase-painting, of effective corroboration, and for the purpose just named should it not be available?

At any rate, there should be stimulus in parrying the following. "Yes, of course those two lekanides in that Lipari tomb are nuptial things. So was the Attic *lebes gamikos,* model of a heater for the nuptial bath, in a house, just a dwelling house, at Olynthos. The lids of those two Sicilian dishes for the best tid-bits of a wedding, more appetizing than the pastries and the fruit, seem to have pleased you, and certainly they are much more charming and interesting in their decoration than that other long-treasured wedding present as three plates (71-73) of David M. Robinson's *Olynthus* xiii exhibit its hackneyed pictures. How is it, then, that you cannot imagine the lekanides so pleasing a real bride that she kept them for the rest of her lifetime and (thanks to a good son or widower) longer?"

This should be taken as a most timely invitation to put the evidence (figures, symbols, scenery) in some more handily practical concentration. In the first place, it requires not a little experience, more than such an objector is likely to have had, to be properly impressed by the Dionysiac touches or features to which I have appealed already, one in what befalls Artemis' torch for night-prowling, requisitioned so impudently by a dove-heralded satyr, another in Aphrodite's badge of authority for bath-house duties, a thyrsos recalling the satyr beyond all question eschatogamic (greeter, calmer, out-fitter) in the "stop that girl!" episode of a hydria from the Degrassi grave which in the meantime Trendall has assigned to his Lucanian Policoro

Painter (*LCS* pl. 25, 2). No doubt, insistence on those details would be quite likely to prompt, in counter-objection, reference to the Dionysos who heads the procession of divine guests largely Olympian to a marriage that is by no means infernal, on the François vase, or even (turning the tables) to my pl. 8b; "do you really know, by any analogy definitely in mind, that the Dionysos holding a torch for the impending marriage of those young persons, on a wine-vessel too, the bell-krater Lecce 620 by the Hoppin Painter, is not just cosily allegorical, telling us only that it was really the wine-bowl of a certain marriage-feast, information which P. Romanelli's "da Rugge" on p. 8 of *CVA* Italy 6 supplements by telling that when one of the spouses died it was buried with her or him?" We are well aware that this at least is answerable, by appeal to the action, scenery, and artistic pedigree of a very closely related picture, pl. 8a, on the bell-krater Lecce 623, in which Dionysos assists at a nuptial "coming-to" which is surely not earthly in any but a chthonic sense. But while the Lecce Painter's no. 623 is specific protection against missing the point of his predecessor's no. 620, what can such vases do to discourage an interpretation of the Lipari sequence which would exploit its *difference* from them, its not showing a human lover for the girl and Dionysos to unite them, and this to revive a theory which it would be stupid as well as ungracious to deem already quite dead, Kerényi's; did he not grant to Dionysos *ius aliquot noctium* and to every fit woman, after death, some brief enjoyment of his love?

Perhaps my own interpretation of what the two lids altogether tell almost deserved to be molested from this direction, by its oversight; nothing was done in it, neither exegesis nor even mention, for the second timbrel, that which Eros holds on Lipari 749B at the very end of the sequence (pl. 22f), in a situation certainly complex. It has engaged him with Aphrodite, turned to face his obtrusion of the thing he has in his left hand ("timbrel time, mother?" "not quite yet, dear"), but reaches beyond her; so artistically elaborate is the balance of his relation to the girl far left, in a scheme that makes ingenious use of this bathroom's two aids to undressing for an integration of her crouch with his rise, that thus we are made to ask, did the Cefalù Painter mean anything by a certain effect of this, a counterpoise of her mirror of nubility, low and slanted down, with his more decidely nuptial timbrel, high and slanted up as it is shown to Aphrodite? Made to *ask*: I must hope that no one will find affectation in my judging that asking is enough, for a certain obligation to Kerényi and some opportunities that should reward our acknowledging it.

Quite apart from the good example, acknowledged already, of Kerényi's "oh, get threads!," it must be ever remembered that this scholar's hypothesis of a *droit de seigneur* for Dionysos, involving timbrels because requiring preliminary *dances* of the women, is in certain respects a good thing, a doubly good thing, though no fully absorbed specialist could conceivably share it; commendable in the first place, for marking an acceptance of Patroni's good insights that goes beyond even loyal Albizzati's (if that amounted only to "amore funebre, si, elisiaco, no"), and next because, in spite of a mention of Ariadne (too incidental to be compromising?) it allows without a qualm that for late Italiote eschatography Dionysos is scarcely less strictly a personage of the underworld than is Eubouleus of the Corigliano inscriptions. Right as it is that scholars should nurse a special reserve of energy for putting down abuse of the Corigliano tablets, there cannot be too much acquiescence in the presumption that in Italiote and Sicilian red-figure any mere mortal served by Dionysos or by one of his underlings, male or female, satyr or nymph, is dead already.

There are corollaries of this: *quae quibus anteferam?* First, if that is where respect for Kerényi's memory should put it, there would have been no difference between his and our reading of the sequence on the Lipari lids 749A-B, as it begins in my pl. 22a and ends in my pl. 22f, except in regard to the concluding timbrel, not the satyr's one on the first lid but that which Eros is pressing on an Aphrodite more than commonly Dionysiac – having a thyrsos. From the position Kerényi held and of which we must get at least empathy, the view is that this maiden has to bathe before Aphrodite will pass her for all that this second timbrel so pregnantly implies, noisy dance for Dionysos and the caresses rewarding it; for us too, even where we stand after what I might call our Lecce lesson, the meaning is that this girl, never married in her earthly life, is promised Dionysiac fulfilment in this new one. The Cefalù Painter, in things of Aphrodite's department, dead wool and live bird, put on or put with the satyr, as also in the thyrsos of the satyr's master here made badge of Aphrodite's present authority, has not failed to stress Dionysos' part in this affair of no fewer than five divinities (including two to mark the preliminary and virginal aspect of the girl's need which is mere *lack*). But what impends is surely not less than real fulfilment of the whole need in due union with another beatified mortal, such as (with Dionysos in person to bless it, or a satyr or Eros to lead it merrily off in a good start to the rhythm of the girl's own timbrel!), was rather richly illustrated in a series of Tarentine vases of the school of the Hoppin and Lecce Painters.

Further Aspects of the "(Re)union Hypothesis"; Role of the Gods; Aphrodite Adorns "Elysian Brides"

No doubt these illustrations might be trotted out once too often, with some loss of force if they began to seem like a stage army; as already acknowledged, it would be well if the present almost menial operation of making room and light for others' feats or at least enjoyment could, in its attack on brambles and obscuring boughs, clear some ground for reinforcement of the achieved proof of Patroni's theories. Reinforcement by concentration, in some "corner for the captious," where the unconvinced or the merely dazed could find, separately stalled but as a neighborhood ever-poweringly cogent for the (re)union hypothesis and its Bacchic paradise, (a) the Dionysos who marries dead couples unassisted, (b) the Dionysos who does so with the assistance of Aphrodite, (c) Aphrodite doing so with little or no sign of Dionysos' help, (d) the satyr whose service proves a couple dead, (e) satyr(s) proving a numerous company dead, (f) nymphs who alone or with satyrs serve the dead. That is work for a footnote, if such recapitulation is not to be obstructive — of (among other considerations) the topic of an apparent shortcoming of the (re)union eschatology, not at all obvious as long as we are only concerned with Tarentine vases, but curious if scarcely troublesome when, on a wider view, it is discovered that other Western wares do not show any such shrinking from male symposia, parties at which the fare is wine with fruit and pastry and the entertainment music or *kottabos*-shooting. From these (bating one or two exceptions perhaps to be allowed) wives are notably absent. Women of another sort may indeed be present, and this (if we may really reckon these pictures of couched men — not always young — to be no less funerary than most other Italiote or Siceliote vase-paintings) only increases the interest of the difference, the contrast with the Apulo-Tarentine near-vacuum as well as with the strictly connubial dignity and privacy of the "Totenmahlreliefs" or their Lilybaean equivalent in paint. For these sculptures (or corresponding pictures) are according to mankind's best hope, best, I mean, in Plato's scale as we know it from the "*locus classicus* of eschatic reunion," *Phaedo* 68 A. He is aware of a meaner one, Orphic as Plutarch happens to reemphasize in his own reference (*Cimon-Lucullus* 1) to *Republic* ii.363 C. hope of never-ending conviviality, μέθη αἰώνιος as Plato's Greek rather more bluntly says.

Campanian red-figure, unlike Tarentine as we have noted, has no place for Orpheus. But it is especially there that we seem to be given illustration of the provision, "so much more fast-young-mannish" (νεανικώτερα) "than Homer's or Hesiod's," made by Mousaios and his son (Plutarch says "the school of Orpheus") for rewarding the pure and just (Trendall, *LCS* pls. 104, 3; 121, 1; 153, 5; 178, 1 and 2; 186, 1 and 2, 4; 187, 3 and 5; 205, 5). Very rarely (and then most interestingly) we can in work not Tarentine let ourselves begin to suppose that we are being shown a widow (just dead) about to retrieve a husband from feasting.

For a famous Lucanian example (very nearly ridiculous), see Trendall's *VIE* pl. 1, d, *LCS* p. 53, no. 268, by the Palermo Painter whose "giver of good fast service," the satyr Onnaseuas, has already interested us in a connection with eschatogamy. There should be another, Campanian and less striking, but perhaps more important because it does indeed come from the *tomb of a man and a woman* and is gravemate of other curious things, on a bell-krater with which we already have some acquaintance, *LCS* pl. 187, 3, by the Painter of New York GR 1000. Partly because *via* the Lipari lekanides we have come (if I am not mistaken) within only a short distance of a really momentous climax in the importance of chthonic Aphrodite, the theological linkings afforded by this grave, T. 185 Cumae, are not unexciting. They follow from an observation already made, namely that the questing woman on this bell-krater (very different from the girls, ripe for dismissal by the widow, on the Lucanian piece in the Vatican, this person's mirror marking her as neither waitress nor entertainer of the company) can without any wild flight of fancy be *identified,* thanks to the dish she has in her other hand as she invades a symposium, with the heroine of the neck-amphora Naples 127950 *from the same grave*: that is, with the woman who is there stooping out of her own monument to catch the attention of the leading deity of two who are passing in Indian file (*LCS* pl. 188, 2, attributed to the same painter). There is actually more for development of this than just now we learnt from an oinochoe also "Cuman" but not in Naples and not from this tomb. In regard to the Naples neck-amphora from a double burial that oinochoe, in Lord St. Oswald's collection at Nostell Priory, was helpful because really striking likenesses in the symbolism of its ample and richly detailed scene of eschatogamy showing chthonic Dionysos (with bandolier and thyrsos) taking part with chthonic Aphrodite (who has mirror and bunch of grapes) in the marriage of a girl (recalling the Naples woman by her similar stoop, similar dish of rather large balls of pastry), to a man surely no less dead, made it easy and nearly safe (even without presuming *re*union at Nostell) to guess the prayer said by the dead woman leaning out of her monument on Naples 127950 to importune the passing pair (god with thyrsos and bandolier, goddess with wreath and *bunch of grapes*): "please, one or both of you, help me to find my dead husband."

But we have not yet attended to the evidence which would allow an economical expansion of that, if I may claim economy without seeming to intend drollery in thus taking some advantage of the funerary meaning of ἥρως. Anyhow, emendation to "help me to find my hero husband" would show better recognition not only of the conspicuous palm-branch held by the symposiast *turning to notice* the intrusive (or better, arriving) woman on the same painter's bell-krater from the same double grave Cuma T. 185 (*LCS* pl. 187, 3), but also of the painted soldier duly corresponding to the solid remains of a spear in the man's share of this grave's goods (Gabrici, *MonLinc* 22, 644 and 645), as he appears on the skyphos (Naples 127979) of Trendall's pl. 189, 6 in *LCS,* one more vase of this double burial which the Painter of New York GR 1000 can claim, *ibid.* p. 490, no. 367. If it already seems that recognition of Aphrodite is likely to dispute with recognition of "holy terror" the chief place in our problem-pound, then it is important to observe how inexorable on this skyphos is the consequence of the assumption we have been making in the interpretations approved with so little debate for the tomb's "help me to find him" neck-amphora (*LCS* pl. 188, 2), its bell-krater of frustration mid-way ("how cold it is, boys, and as talismans my mirror and dishful are not working"), pl. 187, 4, and the other, pl. 187, 3, with final success on it ("they do work, for there he is and he sees me"). To anyone for whom this is all proof that the woman of T. 185 survived her hero, it must seem that the person who has charge of him on the skyphos aforesaid (*LCS* pl. 189, 6) can only be a Dionysiac Aphrodite; in a contracted way, suitable to the cramped space available, sufficiently characterized. This greeter and guide is a little more warmly dressed than the presumed Aphrodite of the neck-amphora in the same tomb; otherwise, in pl. 189, 6 it is as if Dionysos' partner in pl. 188, 2 had (before dismissing him) dropped her wreath and grabbed his thyrsos, without letting go the bunch of grapes which (like the Aphrodite at the Nostell eschatogamy) she dangles from her left hand. At any rate, to an "Aphrodite?" question this guide of the hero in armor certainly belongs, in a higher degree of likelihood ("yes, probably") than the central woman of the obverse pictures of two more vases from this tomb for burial of a soldier and a woman, although what both these women principals hold, one in a heroon or naiskos flanked by two more women (Trendall, *LCS* 1, p. 502, no. 430), the other in the open between two companions of her own sex (*ibid.* p. 502, no. 430; cf. *MonLinc* 22, 644, for both vases, the hydria and the amphora) is very well known to us already as an attribute of Aphrodite. Whatever here, on Campanian vases in a tomb of a man and wife in Oscanized Cumae, it may mean for local theology, the mere occurrence of this runged thing is interesting; here, as in Sicily, symptom of Tarentum's influential lead in eschatography, and this doubly if that ladder-like *sistro apulo* should be recognized for Archytan, one of the two supertoys which a Tarentine sage condescended to invent: now, to match the bird seen to fly, a *platage* heard to give out notes, a ladderfull. There is no doubt of Aphrodite herself having it to hold on two Apulo-Tarentine vases, respectively the one partly republished in my fig. 14, the part that shows the battle of Issus taking place under a pantheon of gods that is more than Olympian, and the Bari krater which in its own way belongs also to history, having been employed to illustrate an aspect of Fascism between p. 480 and p. 481 of *Iapigia* 3 for 1932, but is more important for a heroon or naiskos exceptionally flanked by gods. For any merest spider's thread of relevance (perhaps exploitable in due course?) that may happen to run in the direction of that pair of Tarentine vases, it should not go quite unregarded that the two pieces on which the thing is shown in the grave-set of tomb 185 Cumae are not works of the person who, so far, has been dogging us in our way through it, the Painter of New York GR 1000. We can trust Trendall's discrimination in reserving them for attribution to another Campanian, Beazley's APZ Painter, who gets the lettering of his compactly telling label from his franker imitation of the Apulo-Tarentine manner, a bit less slavish, however, being short of *ad nauseam,* than the Apulianizing of Trendall's Ivy Leaf Painter, who makes such a pet of Tarentum's new Eros and whose own and different way of setting us practical problems in the recognition of a Dionysiac Aphrodite can be surveyed in pls. 191 and 192 of *LCS*. In a practical connection with the "ladders" on two vases of the APZ Painter in T. 185 at Cumae this sampling of the Ivy Leaf Painter's vagueness may presently be worth inspection, even though the *sistro apulo* is not there (or anywhere?) one of the latter's symbols.

There is perhaps not very much need for drill in spying sure Aphrodites, not less sure than the two Tarentine goddesses just cited, the "over Issus" Aphrodite and the "Fascist" Aphrodite, guaranteed by a sufficiently numerous and dense company of other gods. But before there can be any claim of competence for public service as impounders of pretty questions must there not be some showing of a sense of worthwhile, attractive, probability? Perhaps only to be shown by proof of having had, and having understood, a sense of uncertainty, and in the present clearing for such centripetal light as centrifugal influence may strike out even the Campanian Ivy Leaf Painter should be good for something. True, his assimilation of the central, Apulo-Tarentine, matter and manner has been excessive, if what we especially hope to utilize in the rimward vases, Apulianizing pottery of Campania and Sicily, is some such blend of likeness and difference as makes the sequence of pictures on the Cefalù Painter's Sicilian lekanides from T. 313 Lipari so profitably suggestive (pl. 22). Here of course is a Dionysiac Aphrodite of exemplary certainty, and there is surely use for such touchstones — immediate use if sharpening or graduating a sense of certainty is any part of our present business with more or less questionable matters. Without regard as yet to more ambiguous persons handling a *sistro apulo* or something else of Aphrodite's department in works of two sedulous apes of the Apulo-Tarentine manner, the APZ and Ivy Leaf Painters, we should count it advantage, not a set-back, if Dionysiac Aphrodites we made out in pictures by two other Campanians a little less Apulianizing can only take next-to-highest-rank, as very highly probable, when rejudged according to this perfect criterion, this Lipari Aphrodite whom no half-Oscanized Cuman but a brightly imaginative Siceliote Greek has so completely characterized, on matched nuptial vessels in an antithesis which musters the functions and symbols of other gods, in fact opposite gods, to reinforce Aphrodite's own in denoting her. If there be use for a scale, and this sure (and with her thyrsos, surely Dionysiac) Aphrodite is already proffering one, the sooner we are able to take and apply it the better.

But as one of the criteria of a presently benchable question she will be none the worse for now being turned, only briefly, in a direction very urgently in need of any centripetal light beamable from peripheral marvels — pointed, that is, at the Dionysiac company at the back of the Tarentine amphora, no. 873 in Bari, from an Apulian grave at Canusium (pl. 23). Does an Aphrodite lurk there? On the obverse of this vase, at any rate in the (upper) picture corresponding, she is not present, though in this entirely male grouping we can see things of her department, a censer, a pedestaled laver such as the Cefalù Painter's Aphrodite had charge of, and in hand for use at that laver, as instrument of sprinkling or splashing or sluicing, in an affair for which Aphrodite's associate Orpheus is making music, a shell of the very sort — conch-like for some kind of sea-snail — that is seen lying under a pedestaled laver in the Tarentine vase-painting most citable for Orpheus' association with Aphrodite, on the "H.A." volute krater, pl. 12.

Indeed, it can now be observed, in the light of our peripheral illuminant, that the principal picture on the "H.A." krater offers a parallel, none the less arresting for being almost laughable, to the Cefalù Painter's sequence on the two lekanides of Lipari T. 313; there Apollo had, with the acquiescence of his maiden sister, harped a mortal maiden to a nuptial bath evidently not of this world; Aphrodite was naturally in charge of it, but her thyrsos put it in or at the verge of paradise. On the Milan "H.A." krater an Aphrodite surely nuptial but as surely not subterranean has a dish of cakes, and Eros has a wreath, ready for the result of Orpheus' undertaking to charm (musically) a living Thracian or Illyrian, stuffily overdressed by any Greek norm, into stripping (like his compatriot on the Bari amphora) for a bath to be given him by one of his campanions out of the laver which we can see, this by means of the conch-like shell, not yet in hand but quite ready, which we can also see, under the laver. And for light on the Bari-Milan matter at the very center of my clearing, on Tarentine vases bought for Apulian burials in the pastoral uplands at Canusium (their "capital," if it really clipped their best wool?) and Rubi respectively, we have not yet used up the resources of that area's far rim.

I do not mean that I must beg leave for endlessly repeated reemphasis of an observed fact, that what on the "H.A." krater, in a Tarentine vase-painting, is ready for a marriage, which (however exotic or prehistoric) is surely terrestrial, corresponds all but exactly to what is held by the LNO Painter's Campanian bride presenting herself on the Nostell pitcher to Dionysos and his partner in readiness for a marriage which is not of this world: that is, only with this difference from what is divided between Aphrodite and Eros on the Tarentine krater, that the Campanian girl's held wreath is fully closed and her pastries are of dough rolled neatly spherical (instead of being pinched up to a point); compare *LCS* pl. 185, 3 with my pl. 12. That may be worth some stressing, but there is a clue fresher and more exploitable (for bride-hunting on the Bari amphora from Canusium, in the object at the very end of the preliminaries for another eschatic marriage as shown successively on the Cefalù Painter's Sicilian lids for the set of lekanides for tomb 313 Lipari, namely the timbrel which a transvestite, all but Apulo-Tarentine, Eros holds up to an Aphrodite who has fan and thyrsos, as if the time for this tambourine had already come (pl. 22). In any glance just had at the reverse of the Bari amphora (pl. 23b), curious, perhaps already arresting, things were seen; becoming doubtless exciting, if a glance at the obverse of Bari 873 (taking in both levels) begets a question directly concerned with the very problem proposed as most urgent for impounding in the next chapter? At all events, is there enough dignity for a chthonic, Dionysiac, Aphrodite in the thyrsos-holding figure seated at the extreme left of the reverse's shoulder panel, separated by the figure of a satyr from a couple who seem ready for eschatogamy, if the woman with thyrsos and timbrel (of a bride bathed and ready?) is about to be claimed by the youth with thyrsos and bunch of grapes, next to a satyr who helps to volunteer a symmetrical reminiscence of the Lipari sequence; if the figure most to the left in this panel of Bari 873 urges us to remember that on Lipari 749B *LCS* (pl. 22e), a sure Aphrodite held a thyrsos as well as her more regular fan, this satyr far right invites us to see a nuptial occasion in the light of what he has in his left hand; should it not remind us of the torch requisitioned by a satyr on Lipari 749A (pl. 22b and c) for the sequel's sequel, the marriage which is to follow the ablutions supervised by Aphrodite on 749B?

"Enough dignity?" is none the worse for being not quite fresh (for those are the right words for the scruple, which was more felt than expressed, in regard to the Campanian Aphrodites, dangling grapes, that were reckoned only "very highly probable"). But it is only half, or less than half, of the present question, not to be completed without our including the figure to the right of the monument in the continuous frieze low on the obverse of Bari 893 (pl. 23a). Should we (instead? also?) recognize the Aphrodite whom we are quite expecting to find, whom at any rate it would be useful to find, in the female figure seated on a big bag which reminds us of one of the best attested, best understood attributes of Aphrodite, her store-box for outfitting brides, and actually holding in her left hand a characteristic of the same order of certainty as that wardrobe-chest? It is such a fan, matron-making, as we saw held in the hand free for it by two quite certain Aphrodites, the Sicilian one who also held a thyrsos (on the Lipari lid which has just suggested a meaning – "marks ready bride" – for the timbrel high at the back of this Bari amphora), and the Tarentine one whose other hand had a ladder-like *sistro apulo*. And that sure Aphrodite, though Tarentine (with double significance if that runged thing was Archytas' all but musical toy), might well cause our attention to rebound now to Sicily again. For on the krater of her occurrence (in Bari, like the present likewise Tarentine amphora, pl. 23) she with her sound-maker seems to be, or can be suspected of being, in a more or less musical balance, instrument for instrument, with the god at her level, Apollo and his lyre; thus rather as on the Sicilian skyphoid pyxis which makes Trendall's frontispiece for the second volume of *LCS,* though there the enigmatic ladder of sounds (*notes,* if Archytas invented it?) has slipped down to where the bride is, in the main picture, and up there on the lid this Sicilian Aphrodite (perfectly certain, triply guaranteed, by wardrobe, by the bird on it, by the business below) is intent on the text of Apollo's epithalamium.

If my present purpose would be to get due precedence and display for the problem of which "Aphrodite?" is the concisest statement, then nothing is more needed than the utmost goading of curiosity; accordingly, it does not come amiss that in the frieze of the Tarentine amphora Bari 873 the figure claiming recognition, though not unsuitably cushioned and most suitably equipped, is seated where — apart from the contingency once compendiously tagged *ELEP* — one would scarcely expect to meet this goddess, even in her chthonic aspect, if the monument nearby marks a cemetery and tells us to take most of the persons rather feverishly busy there for survivors. But we must be careful, with as much practical caution as practical curiosity. Perhaps there might be debate whether the single rather skimpy tainia, dark but scarcely black, is funereal enough to denote shaft of a tombstone; for the present it is surely much more interesting that at all events Aphrodite's Eros (pl. 23) is present, holding two noteworthy things. One is a broad and dappled "gala tainia" such as dangles from the flower-garnished phiale of the figure that perhaps represents his mother; the other is a wreath ("horned") of just the sort that figures so curiously in the surroundings of perhaps the most remarkable of all the persons who set us the question "Aphrodite?." For that wreath and that woman or goddess, see respectively the left and the right of my fig. 17, reproducing a drawing of the Nekyia on a Tarentine krater in Karlsruhe. Luckily we are not unprepared for the consideration which gives it peculiar importance among hellscapes, having made acquaintance with Tarentine vase-paintings which seem to exhibit Aphrodite as superintendent of a place of purification in a well-watered part of the Garden of the Hesperides (figs. 7 and 8, pl. 15), but we should not fail now to take note of the pelike, also Tarentine, in Catania, well published (the bathroom and hydria complementary to the picture of the Garden not omitted) by G. Libertini in *Museo Biscari* pl. 90, 768. The Catania vase reinforces two features which are arresting, respectively, in those other Apulo-Tarentine pictures of a woman's limbo of purification in the Garden of the Hesperides. I mean, not only the provision of vessels for drawing water in the Lycurgus Painter's Garden on the Jatta krater in Ruvo, those hydrias which (whether handled or sat on) make some of the inmates (including Aphrodite herself) look deceptively like Danaids (my fig. 7, Sichtermann's pl. 121); surely also, the wardrobe which in the other Garden at the back of the Archemoros krater in Naples almost commands us to recognize its sitter as Aphrodite (fig. 8).

Indeed, as converse or complement of the Naples Garden, the Catania pelike is quite extensively remarkable. But perhaps, before we address ourselves to what, altogether, is there, I need to knock in the nail which will be mischievously loose, endangering coherence, until I have said more exactly (than so far) where I find a possible Aphrodite in the Karlsruhe Nekyia, fig. 17. Is she not where — in all possible senses — there is most suspense, in the group at the right of the picture waiting, with at least some little anxiety (perhaps confined to the person midmost, getting sympathy from the person hindmost), for the effect of Orpheus on King Hades? We ourselves must wait — for a denser configuration of evidence? — before we dare say that the person foremost (wearing a wreath of wheat) is a symmetrically mystic, Eleusinian, counterpart of Orpheus opposite, namely Triptolemos, whom indeed we are quite used to seeing (so wreathed) opposite Orpheus in hellscapes (pl. 1a, fig. 11), but in the role of judge, not of advocate, which must be his part here if he is Triptolemos at all. If the hydria of the "sympathetic" figure (surely not murderous Danaid!) in the middle of this group marks her as one who has passed through Aphrodite's place of purification in the Garden of the Hesperides, or (an alternative which we must allow) as one who is seeking admission to it, then her sympathizer, whose hand on her recalls Dionysos' pat for the dazed girl about to be consigned to her eschatic mate in my pl. 8b can only be Aphrodite.

Punishment of the Danaids; the Nuptial Bath Refused

I REGARD IT as quite beyond dispute that the woman with a waterpot in this group is no Danaid ("ready bride seated on or very near hydria" being a commonplace of late Tarentine red-figure, *CVA* Belgium 2 IV D b, pl. 7, 1 a-b; France 3, pl. 26, 1; Germany 13, pl. 42, 4-5). But it is just as important that I should concede the presence of a Danaid in the Karlsruhe Nekyia; not the woman with the waterpot who should be so safe with Orpheus charming for her while Persephone's mother's pet and new Directress of Eschatogamy show their support of her, but rather the woman with the other hydria, friendless low right. It is no secret that there is some evidence in Italiote sculpture and vase-painting (earlier than the earliest allusion, *Axiochus* 371 E) that the myth which did away with the Danaids' impunity was a Tarentine innovation. It will be part of my due benching of the "Aphrodite?" problem to suggest that the new and severe myth was corollary of a new use for a wet spot, not quite at, but not far from, the Snake's Tree in the Garden of the Hesperides. I must shortly find a place, my only place, for any more raking-in of matters outlying, from the rim of the clearing which is to serve quite another purpose presently. So I must suppose that this is my last chance of taking advantage of what I may fairly call a parallel to a parallel, for both *the* new myth about the Danaids (that after all they had to suffer punishment, a wet one) and *a* new use for the Garden of the Hesperides, in some measure the use noticeable on Apulo-Tarentine vases from the time of the Lycurgus Painter onward, reached Campanian red-figure. I must hope that my italics for words so small will not be charged with affected splitting of a hair.

Of course the new myth reached Campania; did not Beazley's Danaid Painter there make a joke of it, inspectable by any visitor to London (*CVA Great Britain* 2 IV E a, pl. 8, 15; Trendall, *LCS* pl. 171, 1)? So did the notion of the Garden of the Hesperides as a place for at least the *reception* of mortal women. Now, the vase which proves at least this (*LCS* pl. 147, 1, assigned by Trendall to his Whiteface Painter, a *predecessor* of the Campanian Danaid Painter in the same Capuan group, p. 381, no. 139, cf. p. 429, no. 486) does in fact suggest more, that they came there to be bathed. For it happens to be a three-handled waterpot, a hydria, like the vehicle of the Danaid Painter's very Campanian joke, like the vessel carried by the "no Danaid" (bathward bound, or come from bathing?) reassured by the person whom in the Karlsruhe Nekyia (Tarentine) I would gladly take for Aphrodite (fig. 17), and of course like that of the real Danaid lower and lonelier in the same picture and those of several no less sure on two Tarentine volute-kraters in Leningrad with which we are already acquainted (figs. 4 and 12, pls. 3a and 4a). It is a pity that (as long as we are at all concerned with things peripheral and Campanian) I must paradoxically treat those Leningrad Danaids as if they were of merely tangential bearing. Of course it is really on their account that certain fourth century vase-paintings of the Garden of the Hesperides are so interesting, because they give fuel for the start, course and arrival of the train of thought which ends in taking the true full measure ("and we thought it was for baths!") of the Danaids' frustration on the Apulo-Tarentine volute-kraters St. 424 and St. 426, in the vase-paintings which are such a transformingly rich supplement of the jejune version of their punishment by water in a relief from a tomb at Tarentum (Klumbach, *TGrK*, Beilage A). No doubt we cannot hope to be excused from probing the Campanian parody (*LCS* pl. 171, 1), which puts in a curious substitute for the irony which it drains out. But our really pressing need is of Trendall's leave, which I cannot believe he would refuse, to retitle ("Welcome to our Garden!") the picture on the hydria of his Campanian Whiteface Painter, *LCS* 1, p. 381, no. 139. For does "Three Hesperides by serpent-guarded tree' take enough notice of the embrace which the figure on the right is getting from the figure in the middle? Unless this can mean "welcome *back*, sister, our snake has missed you," should it not remind us of arm work only a little short of embracing, the pat or pressure of reassurance (fig. 17) received by the not-Danaid with hydria in the Karlsruhe Nekyia? And if of that, surely also, first, of the women with hydrias who on the Tarentine Lycurgus Painter's picture of the Garden (fig. 7) are *neither* Danaids nor Hesperids; next, of where and for what those women have to go with their waterpots, as shown in the provision for the Garden's transient visitors that is distributed between the two sides of the Catania pelike (*Museo Biscari* pl. 90, 768): on one, bathroom (laver, big hydria there) in use by women, with Eros to suggest the purpose of it all; then, with a turn, Eros again, meadow, snake's tree, three boxes or baskets for a bride and her women to ransack; luckily, one of them is a wardrobe chest, to remind us of another near which lay the thing functionally correlative to that laver and hydria, namely sluicing scoop, as we saw it in the picture of the same Garden at the back of the Archemoros krater (fig. 8, pl. 15). With such washpans we have had much and shall have more to do, for quite evidently a vase deeply involved in our master-question "Aphrodite?," the Tarentine amphora Bari 873 (pl. 23), should be *locus classicus* for at least its aetiology (if the youth's pan below is there advertising itself as "modern" for the primitive shell above); all that matters for any concern we are beginning to have with the Danaids parodied in Campanian clowning is that such vessels, for sluicing oneself out of a high laver, one in each party of Tarentine? Danaids, the damnable (as they seem) of fig. 4, the damned (as they certainly are) of fig. 12, happen to yield the clinching proof that *the eternal punishment of the Danaids is an affair of bathing gone everlastingly wrong.*

Here let us make the best of a discovery which we cannot evade, that there is a silly thing, that Campanian parody, at the heart of a serious (if ironical) matter important to us. If it seems silly, that perhaps is just our resentment of its teasing; this "Danaids at penal task, some males, and the dog of one of them" is so very far from the sort of good *clear* fun provided in the also Campanian Parrish Painter's "Europa and Steed pass the Customs, with honors" (*LCS* pl. 100, 1). What, indeed, can the Danaid Painter's dark joke do for the right curiosities about the eternal punishment of the once immune Danaids? One right just here, right tactically, for impending business, should be this, whether Aphrodite had anything to do with it. First, surely, among questions of broader interest will be: is this an Italiote novelty? Tarentine, then, or does the Campanian joke lessen that likelihood? Is there any tug of conflict between implications of two Tarentine data, one (verifiable in Klumbach's *TGrK,* p. 10, no. 42, Beil. A) That their punishment occurs in Tarentine sculpture, strictly local art which should be unaffected by Apulian (upland) taste in eschatology, another the fact that in Tarentum's funerary vase-painting, dependent on that taste, even more is made of this subject? Much more, as with the Karlsruhe Nekyia in mind (fig. 17) one may say in any case, even should a doubt suggest itself about one of those Tarentine vases, Leningrad St. 424 from Ruvo (fig. 4): in spite of the features that make it just natural to assume that the chief scene of St. 426 (fig. 12) is its sequel, how sure can we really be that the five women with waterpots on St. 424 are the Danaids whom we must recognize in the corresponding five on St. 426?

The correspondence itself can be reckoned fivefold, altogether: (1) the number of persons, (2) the hydria for each, (3) between the five women one sluicing pan, (4) between them one mirror, with (5) in fact a transformation, wreaths (two visible) into "headsavers," rings on which to balance waterpots (four visible, one in use, one held, two worn slipped on like extra bracelets, the fifth invisible only because the pertinent pot is in the way). But then a difference, starting a train of thougt quite disturbing, discloses itself in there being no open trinket-box on St. 426 among its quite sure Danaids (fig. 12). That into which one of the five women on St. 424 is peering (fig. 4) brings much more to mind than memory of the women similarly peering, ready bride by her dress and many other signs, in the Catania picture of the Garden of the Hesperides (Libertini, *Museo Biscari*, pl. 90, 768 left). Making us of course recall the Garden's bathroom, with laver, great hydria, and women using the place, at the back of the Catania pelike (*ibid.* pl. 90, 768 right). But also many other women none the worse and more damnable for their having hydrias, the most interesting perhaps — even more interesting than the five or four (one Aphrodite?) in the Lycurgus Painter's Garden (fig. 7) — being the one in the "huddle" (with Aprodite and Triptolemos?) in the Karlsruhe Nekyia (fig. 17). For did she not establish a precendent? In regard to this upper of two women with waterposts in the Karsruhe hellscape we made a choice by which we are still abiding: not she but the other, low right, was a Danaid. Why not now give the five women on Leningrad St. 424 the benefit of this, as blessed souls, batched so for Hermes' convenience, fresh from Aphrodite's bathing place in the Garden of the Hesperides? Very cheerfully give it, in the good cause of Patroni's eschatogamic insights, which have had sufficient demonstration but can never have too much, and here now is more, in what the trinket-box, absent from the hellscape St. 426 (fig. 12), does to reinforce the mirror of St. 424 (fig. 4) in proving what for any ministrations of nuptial Aphrodite hardly needed proof, that any bathing had by the five women of St. 424 was *cosmetic*?

And give up (for some half-felt scruple of method, is it?) our enjoyment of the most powerfully interesting *pair* of mythographies in Italiote vase-painting?

This, I have to grant, is what the obverse pictures on the bowls of Leningrad St. 424 and 426 can very well claim to be, if what makes them a pair is rather more than their both being pictures of Danaids, history (must we then not suppose?) having troubled to deliver them together in one single package indescribably "gift-wrapped." Indescribably, if I can only begin description by saying that the outer envelope is whatever glamour should invest firsts, even of the second class, "practical" firsts such as these: apart from two or three figures inconspicuous in contemporary Nekyia of the same ware, the earliest criminal Danaids, provisionally (earliest, till proof of that for the Taranto relief — not likely — or the Campanian parody — not logical?). Anyhow, as is more important, if we have to take figs. 4 and 12 as such a parcel, the inner wrap in which they come paired is irony, and the words for its quality are "resourcefully extreme." But, as we know already, the two pictures, though doubtless painted in the same shop, are not works of the same hand, and there is no record of their vases belonging to the same burial. Indeed, though I should be sorry to have to think the painter of St. 424 incapable of conceiving, and of pleasure in representing, damnable persons boisterously demanding their due, I must acknowledge a good reason for treating the bowl's whole obverse (including the groups of recognizable deities top right and top left) as practically ambiguous. This in my being sure that I do not really know what finally the man with the say, head of the bereaved Peucetian family at Ryps-Rubi, must have said, whether "brief fool's-paradise of Danaids, trust Aphrodite to see it does not last" or "dear little girl, see her there with those already sure of their fulfilment — how otherwise than sure, with such a rally of encouraging gods, two on the left for celibacy quitted, three on the right for the nuptial bath and what follows it!" I cannot acknowledge that there is any priggish scruple of hair-splitting "method" to blush for in that confession. But it is not unmethodical to get on with any present job, and if the dilemma just implied about Leningrad St. 424 (fig. 4) already seems convertible to "how does Aphrodite come into that picture, for or against those confident women?" this is propulsive, towards grappling with the Campanian parody of the doom of the Danaids. For the question that is hopeful there (especially since Trendall's provision of a context, *LCS* pl. 171, 2 and 3-4, for the Campanian Danaid Painter's Danaids hydria, pl. 171, 1) is surely "does Aphrodite lurk in this absurd affair?" Promising, at any rate, for present impatience with peripheral considerations, least negligible however when their outlying material is conducive to getting benched in her right place as cardinal problem of late Tarentine red-figure, central problem altogether of the last phases of Western vase-painting, Siceliote and Italiote, and so at last finishing this chapter.

Symbols of Marriage and Courtship; Europa; Further Light on the Danaids

ON THAT CONTEXT-MAKING, plate 171, of Trendall's *LCS* let the "absurd affair" (in fig. 1 there) have the benefit, first, of what (besides the style of Beazley's Danaid Painter) is common to all three of the vases which T's instinct for suggestive arrangement has included there, namely a wreath of blobby flowers, ready for proffering. Ready for proffering *to a nubile woman:* this can be added for fig. 4, the "courtship in earnest" side of the nuptial lebes F207 in the British Museum (the experienced, knowing how to take pets, especially childish cruelty to them, will have read the other side, fig. 3, as "child, a *man* has sent this apple; time you learned to use a mirror"). It can be added also for fig. 2, chief of several pictures on the neck-amphora F194 of the same museum, without much risk objection. Indeed, I cannot imagine any at all being made to an explanation of the whole scene by words put into the mouth of its agile Eros. "Mother, time for me to scramble off the basin of this laver up that rock to hand this wreath and this fruit to the muffled girl who is looking out of the window up there. She should be able to see for herself that the local all-but-Kallirhoe has arrived on the local all-but-Ilissos, man-faced bull as on the local coins, with the water for her nuptial bath; I will tell her what (since I have to turn my head to talk to you) she probably cannot see from up there to our right, that you have (in a pitcher!) the scent, and also the mirror, which she will need." This provokes a question or two (especially, why — in view of the skyphoid pyxis Moscow 510, Sicilian Adrano Group, *LCS* pl. 5-6, not to mention the Aldobrandini Marriage — this bride, with her bath still to take, should be *prematurely* muffled). But not a protest that in "bridegroom," which "bride" implies, I am cheating, begging the question. Such a complaint I do risk if I suggest, as I must, that the wreath held by the youth seated among Danaids in the "absurd affair," almost exactly like the wreath which Aphrodite's Eros has for the visible bride-heroine of the at least bizarre — bizarrely Atticizing — affair just under it in Trendall's fig. 2, is also for a bride, his own, invisible but not far off, for the Danaids and their business with water imply her.

Nothing being much better for truth than petulant objection to it, it is perhaps just as well that there is difficulty on the Danaid Painter's Danaids hydria, just enough to make it, now, exasperation point for anyone — must there not be someone? — bored with eschatogamy, the idea, too warmly and sweetly cosy, the jargon, bad and threatening worse, commanding, as it does, tenfold analogy in the *-gams* of botany, there being at least eight more than the *crypto-* and the *phanero-* which everybody knows. To a certain virtuosity of point-seeing, likely to be good for extreme, fully profitable, provacation of this stimulating dislike, a rather better Campanian joke, *LCS* pl. 100, 1, should be not unfavorable. It is a picture by an earlier artist, Beazley's Parrish Painter, burlesquing the myth of Europa's abduction by Zeus in the guise of a bull, and wit-sharpening for our present purpose because, as the Danaid Painter's joke must do, it makes fun of implications of the given myth valid enough but necessarily ignored in serious renderings, and also because on the Europa krater, as on the Danaids hydria even more strikingly, *an enjoyer of the joke* is provided, a lounger free to take in its incongruity. A wreath or two and a hat enter into both jests, no doubt too disparately for notice in collation of the two pictures. But for both scenes one might write the title "On the Way Through." What the Parrish Painter seizes is that the Bull-Zeus cannot cruise indefinitely with Europa on his back, that for the god's purpose they must land somewhere, that long before landing he and his passenger (she especially) will have been sighted by coastguards, part of Τῶν ταχθέντων περιπολεῖν τὴν χώραν but surely presumable anyhow without invoking Xen-*Vect* 4.52. Such — armed, on their feet already, amiably, admiringly coping — are two of the Parrish Painter's three men, but the third is a lounging civilian, whose long white cane is like that chinned by the nervous bridegroom in the frontispiece (Sicilian) to the second volume *LCS,* and another carried by the suitor on our Danaid Painter's nuptial lebes (*ibid* pl 171, 4), also yet another belonging to the "difficult" person on the Danaids hydria (*LCS* pl. 171, 1) — difficult not in his perfectly functional role of an irony's required relisher, but in belongings that do not seem to fit his circumstances, notably this long white stick, for if only he had a kerykeion instead we could have explained the traveler's hat, traveler's cloak, everything but the dog and the woolen bracelets, as right for a Hermes (Chthonios) specifically right for the situation. But this difficulty need not infect the jest itself if, like Europa's passing the Customs with honors (wispy wreaths, two if one looks carefully), it is an "irony of the way through," as I may suggest without in the least meaning that this was the monorail of Campanian humor.

If I am not quite mistaken, what the Danaid Painter has seized is a fact that we can ourselves by now concede, that the punishment of the Danaids, *as the West invented* it, was a disappointment *in limine,* a progress-balking failure. This is the essential and novel thing, as of course the frustrating leak is not, that being only an aggravation, ingeniously ironical, since the disappointment was of a bath, the cosmetic bath implied by the Karlsruhe Nekyia (fig. 17) as well as by what we see in Tarentine pictures of a certain intermediate limbo, Aphrodite's part of the Garden of the Hesperides (figs. 7 and 8; Libertini, *Museo Biscari* pl. 90, 768). Not that the leak, *though so stalely far from novel,* since derived from an Eleusinian sanction which was depicted on Attic black-figured vases long Polygnotos put it into his "Nekyia" at Delphi, is uninteresting. It may even be that warning is needed of a certain booby-trap, upsetting (for any victim of it) to the place of jar-leaks in the historical order of things, lurking in Plato's giving tham a connection with "parable-making of some bright fellow, *doubtless Sicilian or Italian*" (*Gorgias* 493 A). If so, it is to be had in Ivan Linforth's "Soul and Sieve." (*Univ. Calif. Publ. Cl. Philol.* xii, no. 17 [1944] 297-298, nn. 6-10). Linforth is well aware, nn. 7-8, of the Attic vases, one of them surely and perhaps both datable back to the sixth century B.C., which seem to illustrate the infernal punishment for scorners of Attic (not "Sicilian or Italian") mysteries, put to pour into leaky vats; but I am glad of this opportunity to add that the impression given by the drawing which his n. 7 cites — that the kilted pourers on the Munich amphora might be white-fleshed, so female, so Danaids — is not true. From a point of view (in avoidance of "teletic" mirage) occupied through much of the present study it is more important that in the Italiote innovation doing away with the Danaids' impunity we could quite reasonably register a Western rebuff to inconveniently Panhellenic pretensions, only too well promoted by Polygnotos (not to mention Sophocles), of Eleusinian mysticism.

I cannot treat myself to any far ramble away from a contention which I have to make clearer, that in the particular curiosity before us, where an invention of Italiote moralizing is subjected in its turn to Italiote clowning, the wreath held by the situation's temporary victim, the youth dazed among

Danaids, undergoing their punishment at the threshold of his own new life (*LCS* pl. 171, 1), implies a woman to receive it, and prepared to receive it by agencies explicit in the same painter's picture of a dead woman's summons, by means of such a wreath, to her nuptial bath (*LCS* pl. 171, 2). "Dead" is not rash; what matters in this regard is not so much that here (for once) the bridal muffling of the face at the window looks like shrouding, thanks to a ghastly effect in the Danaid Painter's tone-play in just this part of his neck-amphora London F194; the telling thing, even more inexorably signifi- cant than the lethal sphinx making "third bird" with Aphrodite's two in the Sicilian eschatogamy of the frontispiece to *LCS* 2, is the deadly siren on the neck of this side of F194, Trendall, *SIVP* pl. 13 (b), *LCS* p. 430, no. 495, *CVA* Great Britain 2 IV Ea, pl. 10, 5). But the question "rebuff?" is not unimportant, becoming a little formidable as it expands into "rebuff, after all, of what?" Is it a rejection of moral jurisdiction, with some spice of malice, as follows? "The Far West cannot recognize as mortal sin failure to seek initiation in far Eleusis; we should be glad to assign our damnation (and the specific penalty, everlasting frustration by leak) to the most urgently fit persons, namely those more or less Argive women whose absolution from the guilt of husband-murder, though rendered by a panel of gods, Zeus, Athena, Hermes, is such a difficulty, such a scandal, for our (re)union eschatology." That is a solution repellently blemished by what a writer on *The Art of the Soluble*, Sir Peter Medawar, has crisply condemned as "cheek" (p. 142), and I cannot see that the task of usefully leaching the levity out of it is made really any easier by the exhibit before us, a Campanian joke about the Danaids, or even by what is suspected of the Western theatre's license in parody, though Deinolochian liberties taken with Aeschylus' trilogy are not inconceivable. Its best recommendation is its alternative. This would be an adaptation, disowning crassest corollaries (especially the one driven to take the waterpot of an Athenian bachelor's monument in the fourth century B.C. as a sensible damnation present, at once and forever useful) of an idea not new, aired without disfavor in Dieterich's *Nekyia*, p. 70, n. 1. The ugly assumption it will be seen still to require could doubtless be mitigated, if that were still desired, by harping on the idea of a Western rebuff to other Greeks, making this now consist in expurgation of an unnatural tradition. But at best this alternative is a theory partly dependent on wire-drawn word-play, if the following is not unfair to it. "With only a pull, τέλος γάμου ('the fulfilment that is marriage') becomes γάμος τελετή ('solemnized marri- age a mystic affair'); those who die unmarried are thus scorners of a mystery, and should incur the standard punishment, perhaps had, historically, been thought to incur it; even without reference to pots on tombstones of celibate persons in fourth-century Athens, there is an argument for this in the verifiably youthful agility of several of ther persons, male and female, rushing to pour into a vat, and in the childishly short stature of another male who is actually pouring, on an Attic black-figured lekythos of the turn of the sixth to the fifth century (as dated by Miss Haspels, *ABFL* p. 66), which demonstrably reached the West (Palermo 996, from Monte Saraceno near Ravanusa east of Agrigento: *AZ* 28 for 1871, pl. 31, *ABFL* pl. 19, 5). For the West this was as demonstrably too much, a wall-painting at Roman Ostia (G. Calza, *NS* [1928] p. 156, fig. 17) neatly supplementing the evidence of Apulo-Tarentine and Campanian vases, for this like the picture on the Palermo lekythos is of Ocnus and the Ass and their nearest neighbors in Hades, and again the neighbors are persons who carry vessels to be emptied into a vat which also is part of the composition. But the seven brisk young persons, four male and three female, have turned into a glum group of three women, and it has a label, [D]ANA[ID]ES." The second theory of substitute damnation, Danaids suffering in place of persons whose fault was failure to reach maturity (not Eleusis!) must seem so ill-founded — in so far as it rests on quibbling philology involving an idea too unnatural perhaps even to be matter of expurgation — that it is only fair to let it make the best possible of its archaeological case, and perhaps that would not be made without my pointing out that a certain loophole of evasion is blocked. If not here, somewhere, sooner or later in a study not disdainful of Patroni's ideas, there was bound to be critical utterance, marginal at least, of what I must recognize to be rather more than a half-truth. "Oh well, it is a law of nature that left to itself human art (which indeed would be nowhere without nubility) prefers its subjects young." But this cannot be invoked on behalf of the more interesting of the two theories, as I am bound to think it, being inclined to judge (and even to be half-hopeful of showing) that the theme of Western resistance to at least certain options of Eleusinian tradition is capable of quite useful development. Hypothetically, we might regard the Attic lekythos dug up near Ravanusa in Southern Sicily as good propaganda (in the line of "holy terror," trip-shirkers' δεινά) for Attic mysteries. But for specific counter-objection to the "inhuman," unwed-damning, interpretation of it, one could not rely on the corollary, "why not, then, disdainers of Eleusis, naturally of both sexes and as naturally, automatically young?" — given a bearded, balding Ocnus as chief figure of the picture in question.

All this amounts to very respectful treatment of the late Campanian parody of what I take to be a natively Tarentine theme. My adverb is not meant to rule out the influence of Apulian sentiment, nor should it suggest that the Campanian piece (which Trendall would date between 335-315 B.C., p. 427) is much later than the Tarentine vases (of a phase roughly datable by its reflections of Alexander the Great's victory at Issus in 333 B.C.) which in what they show or hint make only irony, not fun, of the girls' *compound* frustration: *of* cosmetic bath and consequent mate, *in* diversion of part of their means of bathing to an affair hoped merely intermediate, but really an endless disappointment, "filling a breached vat" having had at least a century's currency as proverbially impossible task, for so Xenophon, *Oec.* vii. 40, warrants; anyhow, as now imposed and endured, the extreme in painful waste, of time, of steps, of vain submission to a dreadful rhythm of strain fatigue (part of the Campanian hydria's respectable importance is that more than any other monument of the Danaids' sufferings this joke makes their submission interesting: *policed,* were they? or did some manically intense hope — of a husband after all — sustain them?). To this aspect of the new legend it makes no difference that one of its Tarentine illustrations, on Leningrad St. 424 (fig. 4), is ambiguous, essentially so, ambiguous in its very conception it I am not mistaken in reckoning this the supreme example of banausic hedging, leaving the bereaved woolhat, coming on the piece in its place in the long shed at Ryps-Rubi, his choice between "Newly dead Danaids at height of fatuous trust, fatuous lust" and "Completion's soon to be: here is the beginning of what the Danaids were cheated of." Though it would be hard to overestimate the interest of the Campanian version — above all, in its own special connection with a matter which we have just been finding practical, the outlying, not Apulo-Tarentine, evidence of an Aphrodite of eschatogamy — I have to recognize uncertainties there too, of a less tidy sort. Even when we have noted that the Campanian red-figure troubled to show better, its best, jest visibly relished, and have added that even the Danaids of one of the Leningrad kraters (St. 426, fig. 12) must have had mortal spectators (before the man and the woman high left began to think of a game of Elysian catch to be played with her quartered ball), the left of the Campanian picture of the Danaids remains a little difficult. Only ironically, by someone bored to fury with the new word and the old, Patronian, idea, could a mere dilemma be propounded for this, as compactly in the following. "Policeman, perhaps, not unsuitably uniformed (hat imitates chief's, cf. St. 426 in Fig. 12), furnished with not inappropriate means of discipline (pl. 21b having given him a rod for their backs, police-dog, doubtless Cerberus-sired, for their heels and ankles)? Or only mere eschatogam, on brief leave of absence from 'un *menage* dell'altro mondo' (Albizzati's words, his p. 166), to exercise their eschato-puppy while his companion, his 'completer', bounces her eschato-ball in their eschato-courtyard, or relaxes indoors submusically (pring-prang-prong) with her eschato-*platage?*"

Chattel-Symbolism Re-examined:
Nuptial or Funerary?
Laodameia in London

I F, AS WAS, rather heavily said, petulant objection is always good for the truth, what's the good of this? Well, first, there could be little harm in the most artificial tantrum reminding us of that page of *Saggi di esegesi sperimentale sulle pitture funerarie dei vasi italo-greci* on which Carlo Albizzati did the loyal thing, loyally clear presentation, by his mentor's idea of eschatogamy, which thing was yet the beginning (to be judged fatally flawed) of loyally delicate shelving of it. It is necessary (not less necessary than decent recognition of Albizzati's aloofness from the wilder speculations about the Danaids, p. 209, n. 1, cf. n. 2) to let several lines of his p. 166 speak for themselves, save for aid from some more italics. "Donne, giovanotti, satiri, Eroti, sono tutti sovraccarichi *dei medesimi oggetti che conosciamo dalle pitture di culto funerario.* Se questi fidanzati preparano gli arnesi del *menage,* il solo rapporto amoroso supponibile con in mano tanta grazia di Dio, e un *menage* dell'altro mondo. Ecco il giovane che presente alla ragazza una patera funebre" (sluicing pan) "mentre esse ha in mano una corona da morti." There is of course really a question here "who has the matter upside-down — Albizzati with his washpans and horned wreaths *per se* mortuary, or the Neo-Patronian contending that the chattel-symbolism of the vases is originally and inherently nuptial?

A question quite pretty. That last word would be fit to shudder at, if it were meant airily, archly; I mean it dully, as technical jargon, indispensably convenient once it is explained what is packed within the little hold-all. Let my explanation be that I recognize two values especially as qualifying a question for benching in a park of attractions, the higher of the two being, as it were, a property of the problem's lap and arms, its power of holding one in delightful suspense, so that then most of life is actually impatience for the next number of *Notizie degli Scavi di Antichità.* If the problem about the Orphic god Mise is not quite such a question this is because, as we have conceded, it must be allowed some sleep, with Mise at rest as mere chimera for the time being. But whether on part of a vase or on part of a tomb, one or two more inscriptions, even incomplete like Hass's B.1. 45 from Rugge, would suffice to rekindle excitement.

The question between Albizzati and us could never be of that higher order, but surely it is not poor in the value next highest to such suspense, engaging irony. If anything should be called the launching pad, or diving board, or pit-head, of this study, it is something in which Albizzati too had a stake, the vase-painting on Leningrad St. 420 from which Albizzati's fig. 155 (p. 209) and my fig. 2 are taken. For such points as I am now concerned to make, first against but then for him, it is perhaps very lucky that Albizzati's showing is opposite his fig. 54 on p. 208, which but for a topic still present and urgent, Danaids in Italiote vase-painting, would not be so interesting as I now find it, though the picture reproduced, from a Tarentine bell-krater in the Vatican, has nothing directly to do with them. It shows us a goddess with torch and criss-crossed box or basket followed by Pan, who has two things to hold, his usual reed-stem and a horned wreath, Albizzati's "corona de morti." His pace is less hurried than hers. But they belong to the same affair: love affair perhaps, but not his, I must think, after considering his arms and hands, soberly employed. Rather, her turned head, taken in regard to his measured striding, seems to say "come along, or we shall be late!" Late for what? Wedding? Funeral? Or both, the "both" that is eschatogamy? We are so used by now to the association of Pan with Aphrodite, and it is just Pan's reed that encourages us to suspect that the link with Aphrodite is not inscrutable – whether the plant is shown in a stemmy form as here and as Pan has it in Aphrodite's company on the San Simeon pelike, pl. 16a, or has been cut up to make a syrinx, as for Pan grouped with Aphrodite and Eros above questionable Danaids in fig. 2. Between the goddess of the nuptial bath (aspect of Aphrodite which is at the very heart of the question, "Danaids or not?," just there) and the god of places pastoral but (somewhere) reedy, the connection must be that Pan's responsibility to human affairs (he would not be a Greek god of her second class without one) is for the availability of water. It is ironical, but if irony is engaging all the better, that on the Tarentine Lycurgus Painter's calyx krater, Br. Mus. F271, at the most explicitly detailed wedding attended by Pan, the marriage of Hippodameia and Pelops, where not only the nuptial laver but the source of its water is shown and the god's importance to the affair is acknowledged by the artist's putting him on Aphrodite's right to balance Eros on her left, the foliage which he there holds, with gala ribbon streaming from it, corresponding to Eros' horned wreath, is not a reed (Margot Schmidt, *Dareiosmaler* pl. 3). Berries and all, it is a branch or sapling of very nearly the same sort as one shouldered by a guest at another wedding, the misbehaving centaur next "Laodameia" on another Tarentine calyx-krater Br. Mus. F272 (Trendall, *SIVP*, pl. A after p. 16) (pl. 24). It is nearly time that Albizzati was allowed his revenge, in the counter-ironies which can be developed (sufficiently for my purpose of simply benching attractively a work-inviting question) from the ostensibly sinister, lethal, occasion *in Tauris* of many things on the page opposite in his fig. 55, my fig. 2: things (and persons too?) which in their repeated occurrence we have been reckoning decidedly festive and nuptial on the whole.

But that turn will be a breaking-off, from paradoxes multiplying rather too fast and disconcertingly in the train of thoughts which a sure Pan and a probable Aphrodite in his fig. 54 set off. In that particular line, before we leave it, the supreme irony has to be, for the present, in the vicissitudes, a certain manipulation (dare I say?), of the horned wreath, Albizzati's "crown for the dead," as it goes from the right hand of the Pan of his fig. 54, whose companion may have been meant for Aphrodite, to right hand of the Eros who balances Pan as companion of an Aphrodite *not* doubtful, who indeed would (from her wardrobe symbol) have been read as specifically nuptial even were it not evident that there she was presiding at the marriage of Hippodameia (Margot Schmidt, pl. 3; Oliver, fig. 2 on p. 27). *A* Hippodameia, bride of Pelops, for we know another, the bride of Peirithoos, and this gives us something to do. There is a practical consideration — perhaps especially for anyone who would like to substitute an addled Hermes for the "eschatogam with puppy" on the Danaid Painter's hydria, but also for us in our coming attention to Albizzati's stake in Tauric details of my fig. 2, above all its quasi-Aphrodite — in the need of accounting *usefully* for the paradox that on a vase just referred to for a matter of foliage, Br. Mus. F272 (pl. 24), between her young husband defending her and the centaur molesting her the name written up for her is another's, Laodameia's.

Trendall has not publicly derided, but has privately told me his doubt of, the traditional explanation of the second (upper) picture on the same side of this calyx-krater (Trendall, *SIVP,* pl. A after p. 16, p. 21), Phaedra's love--sickness. We shall not lose sight of the "almost Hermes" of the Danaid hydria and shall be on our way to confrontation with the "almost Aphrodite" prepared to make a picnicking Taurian holiday of the butchery impending for Orestes and Pylades (fig. 2), if we let Trendall's doubt (suggested by the figure like a *paidagogos* among the women of a Love-visited lady too sad for bed) now prompt some questions. Recalling the "real" Laodameia, proverbial for continuing love of a young husband untimely lost, we may well ask whether the present love-sickness should not be hers rather than Phaedra's, for was not Phaedra proverbial for love adulterously, incestuously, unfaithful to a good husband? Why not Laodameia now, on a vase where we can read her name, undeniably though awkwardly present — *over* the heroine (who should be Hippodameia) of the lower picture, *under* a surely subordinate figure of the upper one?

My own concern with the vase of pl. 24 has mainly to do with bespeaking some corner, some dell, of our reserve of engaging problems for things not quite right, things gone interestingly wrong. It may, alas, be that the actual trouble on Br. Mus. F272 is not (at least in isolation) even interesting, if it can be very simply diagnosed in the observation that the painter, having used the space below Laodameia's feet to write Peirithoos' name above *his* head wrote, labeled her as soon as he could, after what his eye judged to be a becoming interval at the same level; was it, then, just an accident, with unlucky consequences running to beyond Roscher's *Lexikon,* that Protesilaos' widow's name found itself above the anonymous head of Peirithoos' bride? If the only objection to this is "how unengagingly simple!," that too is all that the succinctest explanation (a prefixed "ex-") of the *paidagogos* need fear; for he will be the hero's oldest, closest, servant, bringer (to the matronly lady on the extreme right) of evidently bad news: "dear lady, as I have just told your daughter-in-law, she is the Trojan war's first widow." Perhaps, then, the Laodameis of London F272 is disappointing as a paradox, no mistake after all. But the question "does Italiote vase-painting make mistakes?" is not a frivolous one, because (in any particular reference) there is involved "how Greek is it?," at least, and sometimes other issues: several, perhaps, in the case of an "accident" to Apulo-Tarentine vase-painting of a slightly later phase than the Laodameia's bad news belongs to, for there we have to reckon with the strains of what has become colossally "big business."

Purifacatory and Other Symbols Reconsidered; Some Misfits

ALREADY, SURELY, THAT phase has been reached on the volute krater in Leningrad, St. 420, the principal picture on which (fig. 2) has already interested us as an illustration of Euripides' *Iphigenia Taurica,* one really knowledgeable, so that we could recognize in the thing at her feet the tool of the heroine's lustral calling. In the same scene it made excellent sense too in other connections, actually visible or beyond question implied. Materially, in a correlation with other vessels shown, those *lavers* on which depended its function of scooping and splashing water, water fetched for those lavers in that at present empty *hydria.* Ideally, in various involvements with the plot of a play turning on *several* purifications by water, really sinister or happily feigned — so that it stood for the mortal danger to which Orestes and Pylades were exposed, yet promised their rescure from it, as well as the event for which Nike (if not Iris), Athena, Artemis and Hermes were seen to have gathered, Attica's capture of a statue and its cult. Discovering what such things meant in late Apulian vase-painting (especially, our learning that they were not for pious waste of wine but for spilling of water, spilling that was more or less useful, even here) was momentous for our initiation into the symbolism of late Apulian red-figure, though at that beginning, in such spinsterish company (Iris or Nike, Athena, Iphigenia, Artemis), there could be little hint of nuptial application, and one impression now, resulting at last from all we have had to see of fig. 2, might well be a certain sense of embarrassment.

Slight perhaps, but too complex for easy stifling: something is seen to be (accidentally) silly, the mirror of Nike or Iris, pointless for her business with Athena, something else perhaps promises to be a nuisance, the parasol of the Taurian lady. Whether she be Iphigenia's water-fetcher, with things variously mortuary in that basket, or hostess of the nearest Taurian men in a holiday picnic which one of them is inviting a tame deer of the sanctuary to share, does she not threaten to impair, to dilute confusingly, the equipment of Italiote studies for a task of high "priority," *detecting* Aphrodite? It may be (especially if what that discipline most needs is to teach itself concern with the *services* of this goddess) that Aphrodite's selfish sunshade does not quite deserve the rank which, thanks to a bit of the frieze of the Parthenon that is in Paris, it has among her attributes. But of the figures with interesting, if not quite incontestable, claims for recognition as Aphrodite three of the most important do have it. They are: (1) the person (already denoted Aphrodite by the wardrobe chest she sits on?) in an absorbingly curious context in the long frieze of the "Medea" amphora, Naples H. 3221, which has some relevance (as I shall have to show) to two matters of present business, the problem of the London "Phaedra" and the problem (less nearly disposed of?) in the setting of the London Danaids: see Margot Schmidt's *Dareiosmaler,* pl. 17 (cf. pl. 16) or Anna Rocco's pl. 88 (cf. pl. 87) in *Arch-Class* 5 (1953) (I cannot make out the Dionysiac elements noted in her text, p. 181; is it not rather as if some young men, ready for their companions in the new life, had been admitted into Aphrodite's cosmetic limbo to claim them?). (2) Much the most important, the person recognized as Aphrodite by Walters (and by myself as in a cosmetic situation, double bathroom where after all that dust and all those tears Hades and Persephone have been made fit for each other), Br. Mus. F332 in my pl. 5a and b. (3) The goddess in what should be the same bathing place (but with only one laver, by which she sits, as near as possible to it) on Leningrad St. 498, in a scene painted by the very hand which decorated London F332; suspended above her, a quartered ball like that hanging from the corresponding figure's open trinket box on the London amphora, where too the person with parasol sits rightly close to a pedestaled laver (fig. 6). As I read the subject it is this: in the presence of nuptial Aphrodite (with censer and quartered ball, familiar symbols, reinforcing the meaning of her laver), and of another person, either goddess (if she is Persephone, for whom however I cannot judge the matronly fan — without torch — quite sufficient), or mortal and now dead Eurydice (for whom any fan, even as simple as this one, would do to say "that minstrel is my widower"), here in either case is Hades making terms with Orpheus. Given the composition (especially what is visible in it behind Hades), I should suppose these to be: "We have eschatogamy here, as you can see; *re*marry, you two, and *both* stay."

In present circumstances I have to rate this picture less important than its London counterpart by the same hand, for the latter deserves special welcome as specific corrective of a particular false clue threatening (from the lethal work of Iphigenia's vessel, fig. 2), actual mischief in the very direction of Albizzati's bias. How lucky it is that of the similar three-handled pan lying under one of the lavers in the London bathing place it cannot be said "oh no, not nuptial; that's just for death." Besides doing so indispensably much to shade the symbolism of sluicing-pans from false light, the London bathroom (it is high time we noticed room-making walls in both pictures) does not depend on agile speculation for any part of its interest. What my fig. 6 shows, from Leningrad St. 498, would be even untimely, if the speculative interest (very great!) of the situation and company of its unquestionable

Aphrodite should conduce to neglect of something of real importance as a sympton — symptom of an obsession — in what is shared with that Aphrodite by a mere "Aphroditoid" sun-shaded and vessel-beset accidentally on the Iphigenia krater in Leningrad, St. 420, fig. 2. In this "-oid" have we a person benchable with the strayed (and in straying tumbled) Laodameia of London F272 and a false or addled Hermes from London F210?

Benchable, if thus — in their company — bench-worthy. There would be arrogance, such as no seniority could justify, no senility excuse, in fussing forward with a blueprint, excessively detailed, of the great thronged pleasure ground which, no doubt, study of the Western red-figures could become. But there is no harm in hoping that this field will never lack a pound for the collection of *collectively interesting* strays. I dare not press the analogy with whatever law or custom may prescribe for the impounding of unlucky children at county fair grounds, for the strays of the phrase just italicized would be for accumulation — or rather congregation — not for claiming. Congregation for useful correlation's sake: thus on the one hand modern mistakes, if suggestive companions for any of the rest, should be free to enter (with that Laodameia in, can the false Phaedra be kept out?) and on the other hand "bench" and its overworked family gain promotion to another, severer, category of words, having almost technical fitness for a situation in which the practical value, for scholarship, of such hospitality depends on the scholar's accepting the responsibility of every every host (at all save "perpendicular" parties) for promoting, physically *arranging,* conversation.

If in such words there be any threat of whimsy's embowering, all too precisely over-arching, whatever exedra or parlor must be provided for effective concentration of ancient errors and accidents in fit modern company, fit to make them eloquent, then there should be some metaphor-pruning advantage in our picking, for next thing to go in there, something that will have to go on all fours and settle down on its flank, the Danaid Painter's man-headed bull from the neck-amphora Br. Mus. F194 (*LCS* pl. 171, 2, *SIVP* pl. 13, b), as interpreted in an opinion respectfully rejected by Trendall (*LCS* p. 429) "Dionysos bringing Semele back from Hades." Perhaps no other modern malapropos is more interestingly fit to be shut in with those ancient ones, the Taurian lady who has appropriated three of the attributes or circumstances of Aphrodite (fig. 2), with Laodameia announced in Hippodameia's place (pl. 24), with the white-caned gentleman walking his dog, whose hat, cloak and infernal situation make us long for some way of revealing him to be Hermes, and with one more person out of fig. 2, the winged one, whose presence and position, if she be Nike, also her kerykeion, are easily understood ("take it from Zeus that all is ending well, especially for *your* city, Athens"), but not so easily her mirror. More than attendance of that false Dionysos is required if modern scholarship is to be tellingly represented in the parliament of misfits; much would be lost — especially for some Roman questions which I have promised not to shirk — if we could not include the winged female of my fig. 18, who looks (in function as well as form) so much like NIKA but whose name on this Apulo-Tarentine fragment has been read as that of DIKA, though she, as punitive justice, is so differently denoted in other hellscapes (*AZ* [1884] pl. 19, cf. pl. 18). However, some justification of my high rating of *him* as thus *misunderstood,* chimera quite precious in its exemplary defiance of concretely rational method, is the first thing now required. Dionysos' becoming (save his face!) a bull to retrieve his mother Semele from the Underworld is a modern distillation from conflation of two rites, one Theban, the other Argive, not integral theme of a legend. There would be quite uncommon contempt for fact and situation (including the artefact next on Trendall's pl. 171, the so significantly Atticizing *lebes gamikos* decorated by the same artist, Br. Mus. F207) if I affected to condone such a mistaking of the man-faced guadruped on the Danaid Painter's neck-amphora Br. Mus. F194, *LCS* pl. 171, 2 — really a stream god, represented according to an eminently verifiable convention of the region of Naples, which can be studied on the coinage of the very place, Nola, where the piece was found, and here most interestingly adapted to an Attic tradition of nuptial bathing, which slighted the stream Ilissos in favor of a spring very near it, Kallirhoe. But in a good cause, namely making the enjoyable best of even the meanest Italiote vases, there can be no harm in letting the mistake serve as sauce for the certainly insipid little neighbor of *LCS* pl. 171, 2, the Danaid Painter's nuptial lebes published in pl. 171, 3 and 4. It is notorious that this ware, Campanian red-figure, is less closely connected than some others (Tarentine red-figure and its Lucanian derivatives) with the Attic tradition of vase-shapes. But, by exception, the Campanian *lebes gamikos* is not only Attic in origin, it originates (as all know) in an Attic prescription for nuptial bathing according to the custom just mentioned, and where Trendall has shrewdly put the present example it is specific extinguisher of objection (which might otherwise have been clamorous?) to "quasi-Kallirhoe on quasi-Ilissos."

But I must not let this only too engrossing monster, False Dionysos or Mock Ilissos, cause any shift of emphasis, which should properly fall mainly on the signs of funerary vase-painting's obsession with Aphrodite and the symbolism of her department, which is one, we must ever remember, of service, cosmetic service in the main and most directly (though not altogether, as all the *platagai* we have seen and even Laodameia's ball can remind us). Even in his temporary disguise as usefully shocking example, the present quadruped is not likely to be upsetting in that way, for we shall not soon forget that the London vase to which he belongs introduced us to an important new Aphrodite, a sure one, going about her water-requiring business with Love's assistance. Besides, it was a symbol belonging to that affair of getting a dead girl punctually to her eschatogamic bath, a wreath of a certain kind, that was our clue to what the *same* artist mainly meant in his largely absurd (though somehow still fitly funerary) adaptation of the Tarentine subject, the Danaids' punishment by water frustratingly diverted from its cosmetic destination. That not-quite-Hermes just now taken from the Danaid Painter's Danaids hydria for collation with other persons or things more or less off their mark was what remained (whether as waste or otherwise) after what that wreath, in an effect to which two others contributed, brought about, namely our seeing (and being disagreeably pricked by?) the point of the Danaid Painter's joke. Here was a youth consigned to an eschatic bride, but *for lack of guidance* stranded in a situation of mutual ineligibility, all the more ironic for indication that the proper girl was not far away, since (as especially the Karlsruhe Nekyia, fig. 17, demonstrates?) the Danaids' fate is to fail *where,* "where" in a strict and simple sense, others succeed. That indeed Hermes is the personification of infernal guidance, that in one Tarentine picture (on Leningrad St. 424, fig. 4) it is not impossible to regard him as having just given it to some of those aforesaid others (five drawers of water from that same preliminary place, but exempt from diversion of the eschatogamic water drawn!), are reflections bound to supervene — and to lead to discovery of a quite interesting supplement to, or near-match for, the Danaid Painter's man with hat, cloak, white stick, and dog facing him. This is in the upper and easy part of a vase-painting otherwise enigmatic, rightly attributed by Margot Schmidt to the Painter of the Munich Nekyia (*Dareiosmaler* p. 58, pl. 23), person with hat, cloak and *dog facing him, playing with him,* but there is no slim white stick; instead, the figure with the dog has the kerykeion of Hermes.

As to the enigma below him, in a practically separate picture, involving a herm, man with lyre and Cerberus leased to him, two other men (one a paidagogos?) and a patiently seated woman, the best we can do is to take it as concretely as possible, declining the once fashionable speculations about Samothracian mysteries, accepting Miss Schmidt's valid assurance that this is a work of the Painter of the Munich Nekyia (pl. 1a), which disputes with the "Reassembled Family" in Ruvo (pl. 18b) right to rank as most impressive monument of the reunion eschatology. We have immediate use for her attribution's corollary, that perhaps this "Way to a Woman Waiting, past Herm and Cerberus harmless on Orpheus's (?) leash" is only an enigma because there is an even greater admixture of private eschatography with myth than in the Munich krater's "Widower's roundabout Way to Wife and Son" (fig. 1b). That was excellent "attitude drill," and in the rest of our confrontation with bizarre works of the Campanian Danaid Painter we shall doubtless be the better for it (if the false Dionysos in the pavilion of misfits be nursing a rejoinder certainly invited: "as Delphic-Lernaean Semele-fetcher conflated from 293 C and 299 B of Plutarch's *Greek Questions* am I *any less* concretely objective for Vesuvian Campania than you wildly Atticizing quasi-Ilissos ridden by quasi-Kallirhoe?"). But just now it should be more interesting that the unquestionable Hermes dog-caressing but kerykeion-holding, higher up on the British Museum's calyx-krater F270 (*Dareiosmaler* pl. 23; *AZ* [1844] pl. 14), has company not at all enigmatic, in fact most profitably familiar. For there the three persons, taken with the one bird and the female person's significant baggage, pretty well match the likewise fivefold combination which we found important on a San Simeon pelike (pl. 16), conveniently Tarentine like this calyx-krater (not to touch, just jet, on features of the San Simeon vase better than convenient in their promise of giving the false Phaedra of my pl. 24 something neatly definite to say in decisive farewell).

Partial Explanation of Misfits, with Help of "Cosmetic" Aphrodite

ANYHOW, ON THE London krater F270, to our left of the dog and the sure Hermes, *Pan* is seen, with again something ready to remind us of his responsibility to Aphrodite for the water of her nuptially cosmetic work. But his rush-stem, which was intact at San Simeon, has been chopped up for a syrinx as on Leningrad St. 424, fig. 4 where (above women, whether Danaids or not, concerned with water) he was grouped with figures, *Eros and Aphrodite,* corresponding to the rest of the *present companions* of Hermes on London F270. On F270, as on the San Simeon pelike, Aphrodite has with her one of her two birds, the same one, the waterfowl, swan or goose. Also as there, on the London Krater Aphrodite has something to mark her as outfitter of brides, but it is a great bag (plain in *AZ* [1844] pl. 14), not the wardrobe chest of that pelike and many other vases. Aphrodite's present boon *for us,* a second one — for having already made us see the point of the Danaid Painter's jest on his hydria ("absurdly in need of being found, extricated from among those impossible girls, and guided to the right one for that speical wreath's proposal of eschatogamy"), she can now show that it was not the sting of something reckless and heartless, as humanly bad as the worst in facetious sympathy attempted in the "contemporary card" department of a North American drugstore — we had better take and use at once. For her reassurance ("but guidance is *assured,* for that *is* Hermes, who is no stranger to what Pan and I do for eschatogamy, whose dog moreover is for just such findings") cannot come better than thus abortingly, at the beginning of a feeling, akin perhaps to Albizzati's resigned acceptance of a reign of nonsense but worth experiencing if checked soon enough, that there is a drowning of reason in Western red-figure's obsession with the cosmetic Aphrodite of eschatogamy.

Obsession it is, and the extreme measure of it needs to be taken, not less than can be gauged from its symptom on Iphigenia's side (fig. 2) of Leningrad St. 420, their severity not less deeply interesting for our knowing that this vase bears work by the hand that painted rejects of that eschatogamic Aphrodite, Danaids, on St. 426 (fig. 12, pl. 4). Nevertheless, it is real relief ("not as mindless as you thought, and at worst significant") that Aphrodite has to give in regard to all the anomalies or chimeras just impounded: not only that "Hermes after all," but those others, the combination of a Phaedra inapposite with a Laodameia displaced, the shiftless (?) shiftings from types of Aphrodite or Danaid in the Tauric scene, that picture's adapting a nuptially cosmetic vessel to Iphigenia's deadly splashings, its worse than unresourceful borrowing for Athena there of Aphrodite's *own* Nike, equipped with mirror as if for the latter's success in competition with the farmer at the Judgement of Paris, the defiant displacement (Attic if not Delphic-Argive) of a monster belonging to heraldic art of Naples and the rest of Vesuvian Campania, the false Dike with wings stolen from Orpheus' Success in unlocking Hades' door, good practice for her stealing the wings of Hera's sinister Iris at the Villa Item (cf. M. P. Nilsson, *Dionysiac Mysteries of the Hellenistic and Roman Age,* pp. 124-125, n. 25).

"At worst, significant." Least comment is needed by what the obsession with Aphrodite itself explains. Quite the worst of those more or less faulty things impounded is the one *folly* there that is altogether a genuine antique, the wrong Success (Aphrodite's) fetched to congratulate Athena *in Tauris,* the proffered mirror precious as crowningly significant blunder of overreaching in what is otherwise (fig. 2) a *tour de force* of making-do, an intelligent illustration of the *Iphigenia Taurica* done with the resources of eschatogamic vase-painting. This at the back of the same krater (pl. 2) resumes its proper scope, with a great heightening of irony all round in the reverse's resulting crop of paradoxes, extreme yet in terms of eschatogamy resolvable, no longer "sex-insulting" if mirror, fan and timbrel are for transmission (already visible!) to the dead man's natural mate.

Among signs of Aphrodite's very great importance it is fair to reckon the repeated, versatile, helpfulness of particular examples. What I now invoke for help in getting rid of the false Phaedra and reinstating the deposed, fallen, Laodameia, namely Aphrodite's side of a San Simeon pelike (pl. 16a), has been of use to us already in quite a variety of confrontations. To hail it now as our little masterkey would be only fulsome, no worse. I should be doing worse if, as a soberly retrenching improvement in that very line of grateful metaphor, I proposed "keyhole" — of first insight, that is, into a certain hydronomic cooperation of Pan with nuptial Aphrodite exhibited (as a rule less penetrably than at San Simeon?) in quite a stretch of Apulo-Tarentine red-figure, from the time of the Lycurgus Painter's composing his "Marriage of Pelops" to or beyond the date of the "Young man's infernal quest for a patient woman" by the painter of a less obscure classic of reunion eschatography, the Munich Nekyia (pl. 1). For the San Simeon pelike has been, we may say, of some really general use: in more problems of Tarentine vase-painting than that one, and even beyond the limits of its own ware's art (to mention no other foreign and Farther-Western things, was it not quite indispensable for arrival, by way of the box and birds of two Aphrodites, at the full meaning of the Sicilian eschatogamy, two-storeyed, which is the frontispiece of vol. 2 of Trendall's *LCS*?). We have of course to be circumspect in reaching for the present matter's handle, namely the connection between San Simeon 5696 (pl. 16a) and London F272 (pl. 24) furnished by a sufficiently engaging correspondence.

This is that two of the things hanging on the wall of the False Phaedra's bedroom, namely a quatered ball and a gabled box of comparatively choice material (bone, if not ivory, with figured carving), answer to two of the three things carried by Aphrodite as she stands on the obverse of the pelike. The third thing she handles there is like what the woman of the united couple on the reverse (pl. 16b) holds out to her man, a phiale, a link that does nothing to discourage us from reading the overse picture on the pelike as *preface* to their union, a prenuptial conference of the three gods most concerned with the preliminaries of marriage, depicted with plain allusion to the nuptial bath. This, of course, is the indication given in Pan's presence and participation (the wreath he holds should count for at least as much as the festive Taurian's in fig. 2) and in its being the "wetter" of Aphrodite's two birds that *now* is perched on her wardrobe for brides. It might risk ironical applause and cries of "how far can you fetch?" to claim significant contrast in its being the other, not the waterfowl but the dove, that perches on a corresponding wardrobe *during* the wedding depicted on the Sicilian vase just referred to, where the epithalamium for it has already begun, intently followed by Aphrodite, its scroll on her own lap, *LCS* 2, frontispiece. The point of chief interest, valid without any looking away to Sicilian or Campanian vases, is that according to Apulo-Tarentine practice the pairing of those two things, ball and gabled box with handle, conspicuous on the wall of the bedroom in pl. 24 should mean rather that the person there so disinclined for her lonely bed is a young wife like Laodameia than that she is a matron of Phaedra's standing. But it is timely for our present hope of enthroning Aphrodite in not much less than her full importance for Apulo-Tarentine eschatography that we should remain well aware of that art's dependencies, now that we find ourselves led to a fresh (or refreshed!) consideration, a renewed concern with symbolism as an *affair,* having business to do, meaning to deliver.

The Dowry-Box and Related Symbols; Marriage of the Living at Ancestral Tombs?

THAT TOPIC IS not unlikely to require, from those concerned with it, a special effort to be not less businesslike. My own beginning of making it had better concern itself with the more difficult of the two symbols on the wall of Laodameia's bedroom, which as I read them deliver a message which I cannot believe was in the painter's mind, even at the back of it, yet of practical import to countless Londoners and visitors to London: "If anyone tells you, even on an official label, even in a booklet, that that girl too sad to go to bed is Phaedra, do not believe him; you can trust the name written, a little out of place, on the vase." Thanks to several other vase-paintings besides the pelike's obverse picture (more than one, fig. 15, in which a ball is Aphrodite's own concubinage-present to Europa, and a second, pl. 5 in which — if interpreted according to a theme of the Locrian reliefs — a ball should be one of her wedding-presents to Persephone), we know why just one of the two symbols, the ball alone, would have sufficed for saying that. But I have to confess that without prompting from the San Simeon pelike, on which a prenuptial Aphrodite has both, I should not myself have been sure that Laodameia's gabled box joined in saying it, and I am reminded by a significantly rash entry in a notebook of recent travel that I was once uncertain of the degree of emphasis in the box's share, greatest if ball is for bride but box for bridegroom. I should not dare to quote that mere jotting, of doubtless jarring informality, if this did not seem to be in the cause of better method, the best, the severest possible, with good crews of good computers doing for our Aphrodite not less than all they can do.

"Kybosh on dowry-box idea, on any idea of its being exclusive *from* the woman's side." Let me say at once that I now reject, as unmethodically premature, especially in its blindness to the matter for which we coined compendious *ELEP,* this marginal postscript of a note I once made of an Apulian amphora exhibited on a table in the hall of fourth century red-figure at the Musée du Louvre in Paris. I have no number recorded; if that is discreditable, it should be some extenuation that the note has only three words for a stale mythography ("Death of Priam?") but many more for the really interesting picture below it. "Woman running to right with fan and deep cylindrical box; heroon in which youth is seated on mantle, shaft of spear in left; youth running with pedimented box and normal-leaved sapling."

What was "the dowry-box idea"? It has been observed that the gabled box was something which Eros might bring for a bride (the box in his left, wife-dignifying fan in his right, on Br. Mus. F424, H. Hoffmann, *Tarentine Rhyta,* pl. 13, 4), and there was no question — apart from any mere quibble Andromeda's might suggest — that it belonged to marriage; in this regard the picture of a wedding on the Apulian squat lekythos F399 in the British Museum (*Élcér* 2 pl. 23A) is especially citable. Not just because there, as in the bedroom from which we have just ejected Phaedra as much too mature, too far past her own marriage for the pair of freshly nuptial things displayed, gabled box and quartered ball, we now see, on the wall behind bride and bridegroom, those very things suspended, with something now eroded and no longer certain between them. Now, though it does not do to be insensitive to punctuation, I cannot really believe it important that the head of a woman stooping to set down a nuptial kalathos at the gabled box from the other things nearer the bride and more certainly belonging to her, whether the feature more abraded than the ball should be mirror (as in London I guessed), or fan (as Bineteau drew it for *Élcér* 2 pl. 23A). Much more interesting is a consideration suggested, inevitably, by this picture, where among the things of the wedding three receptacles are shown *open,* kalathos (inevitably), trinket box (as often), deep cylindrical basket (as very rarely). Curious it certainly is that there disclosure stops, the gabled box remains shut, having evidently nothing to contribute to the bride's personal finery. But how naturally so — if its content is for her husband, the dowry she brings him, and there is much that seems to make good enough sense of this guess.

Unlike the trinket boxes, this houselike one is something about which women show no prying curiosity (contrast fig. 7, right). They by no means lack opportunity to handle the thing. But when they have it, what they seem to mean by it, especially if there is a mirror of nubility in the other hand, is an assurance in reverse of a famously candid milkmaid's warning, its drift being: "By no means, sir; my face (however faultless) is not my fortune." Since evidently we are approaching a crisis of method, turning somehow on *ELEP,* weddings at heroa and patterns of attendance there, I could not complain if at this very point I were challenged to a test of sense of context, and then it would seem rather urgent to show what difference it makes when a woman with a box of this quite peculiar sort holds also a mirror. My exhibit would begin negatively, mirrorless, with Lecce 805, skyphoid pyxis yet not Sicilian, an Apulo-Tarentine piece found at Ruvo (*CVA* It. 6, pl. 53, 2). A good starting point for three reasons besides the nuptial associations of any skyphoid pyxis: (1) interrelations are plain: the woman who among these three has the gabled box, yet (like the rest) lacks mirror, is *not* the bride — who of course is in the middle, and has, at this actual moment of all the instructions and preparations, no need of self-inspection (these are now far advanced, we may note, having trained ourselves, pp. 88, 181, to read timing in alabastra like the one which the girl's second attendant proffers);

(2) once again, here is interesting *symmetry* of gabled box and quartered ball (the bride's second woman having a ball to give her); (3) it is most timely that Lecce 805 can be provocative. That is, of petulant objection at its most welcome; vehement but extinguishable soon and propulsively, as follows: "I congratulate you on having picked a g.b. which no one could dream of interpreting (seen among all those women) as bridegroom's present to bride. But in your elation at happening on a void somehow advantageous, not the box's, but its holder's exceptionally yet conveniently (!) having nor mirror of nubility, you forgot to look at Romanelli's text, missing its revelation that she does have something besides the box, namely a cross-headed torch infernally like Persephone's. In wishing the gabled thing to be Persephone's favorite's dowry-box, what are you wishing into it? Infernal money, drawn from, presently to return to, the Bank of Eschatogamy, President Eukles Plouton, Executive Vice-President Aphrodite alias (alibi?) *Ana Aprodita,* in place of Eubouleus Dionysos (retired)?"

This is not altogether a nuisance, even in its delaying attention to a cryingly ready bride, about to proceed with mirror held in her right hand, gabled box in her left hand, on an Apulian rhyton in the Kestner Museum in Hanover (no. 820, Hoffmann, *Tarentine Rhyta* pl. 43, 1 and 2), or to another, perhaps less ready, but my own favorite in this category, on an askos in the British Museum (pl. 7, Apulian, numbered 1928. 1-17.68, not in Walters' *Catalogue*), respectfully showing her mirror and box to Eros, who can now tender her a ball and garnished phiale. In the first place, let us be glad that it was flung at us so soon after our providing, and getting some tenants for, a place of useful congregation for ancient anomalies and fit modern company. Because the material of eschatography is drawn, naturally, from two worlds, slips of confusion between them can be expected; much the most apposite allusion just now would be to an Apulian volute krater in Sir John Soane's Museum in London, especially to the part of it republished by S. Reinach in Millin-Reinach, 2, pl. 25 (my fig. 5). There, above an Amazonomachy, are shown Athena, Apollo, Artemis, *all seated;* then, *standing,* Herakles; suspended, two bucrania and symbols which puzzled Reinach ("mirror or patera, little temple") more than they should now baffle us (conventional sluicing pan of eschatogamy and gabled box, both with reference to the marriage of Herakles to Hebe, part of his apotheosis). This is quite an object-lesson in the *operation* of chattel-symbolism, and its "you see why they sit and he stands" follows nicely upon a gabled box's part in another message, the Laodameia krater's "poor thing, and they were only just married." But a lesson also in its drawbacks, if these gabled objects, quite certainly nuptial symbols in any case, had precisely the allusion to marriage which I am inclined to see in them. In judging that the one on the Laodameia krater of pl. 24 means "Protesilaos' dowry, unspent, unstored, just handed to him," nothing worse is imputed to the artist than venial anachronism, of which he may have been quite conscious and even relishing.

But the same symbol, as transposed from one world at Phylake to another in Herakles' Olympus, becomes then inpoundable anomaly, absent-minded, silly, I must indeed grant – unless either (a) such boxes were not for the purpose I divine, or (b) the symbol in question, on the krater in Sir John Soane's Museum, is wholly (not just partly, as I could well suppose) modern restoration. From this there is a bycrop of practical points: none more useful than that which painfully impresses, reimpresses, the truth's acute need of technicians, in two complementary sorts. For one, the men with wonderful new computers, to help us to cope with the extraordinary (in view of the factor of irony, one might say the monstrous) variety of a funerary art expressive through symbol, coded situations as well as coded things. The other, men and women with the precious old patience and dexterity – "old" in a generation of experience in restoring extant truth (with all its gaps!) to Attic vase-painting – to rid eschatography of falsehood acquired in the time of highest esteem for late Tarentine red-figure (the corruption is probably less than the shcolars' worst fears; but [just for example] who today would risk a full commentary on the apparently paradisal back (fig. 11) of the Naples "Nekyia" krater, H. 3222.

With that now said, it should be feasible to take better advantage of the Apulo-Tarentine amphora in the Musée du Louvre in Paris adduced (p. 197) because of a certain practical need for redress, for I had to confess having underrated (or worse, having cheated of half-discerned importance) a strikingly exceptional occurrence – in a *man*'s hands – of the gabled box. My own mistake was one that would never have been made had there been full preparation, administered by fully exercised technicians, of the novice standing *νήπιος* before that amphora, and presuming in his inexperience that anything brought to a dead person's heroon must be the bringer's offering to the dead. Even already, with very much less than complete information carefully and resourcefully sifted, I have had to recognize that evidence not without special bearing on what Apulian Horace called *Lacedaemonium Tarentum,* namely in Epikteta's provision for weddings at the heroa of her family in not less Laconian Thera, discloses two other possibilities: what any survivor has at any heroon may (conceivably) be gift *received* (as wedding present), or gift held ready *for* another *survivor* (bride or bridegroom).

Present attention to the sequence of three figures on the Paris amphora, one of them a man holding a gabled box, is part of quite an operation, to which that nubile male is useful as an exploitable exception: of cardinal importance, I think, but only in the sense that he is the hinge of a turn of work required of us by the women and Erotes, some of them seen already, now penned in the question's waiting room. In that strip of the Paris vase, interpretation had best grope from left to right: here is a woman whose deep cylindrical basket and fan might be thought addressed, in a certain sense, to the youth in the heroon. Perhaps it would be a relief to think otherwise, but we are well acquainted (pp. 24ff.) with dead men who have been given fans to transmit to dead women, and so far, here in our left-to-right drift on the Paris amphora, have met nothing compelling us to decide "no, that's not eschatogamy stuff consigned to the young or rejuvenated man's eschatic mate." Passing on, beyond on, beyond the man in his heroon to the man with a gabled box, can we keep this open mind? Certainly there will be a very strong temptation to beg the question, thus: "Now I see, this is one of those cemetery weddings with incidental ancestor-worship, 'as Electra vowed, as Epikteta willed'. In the middle, ancestor: on either side, spouse, each with the especially spouse-making thing, she on the one hand with the fan which is quite pointedly so (in sharp contrast to the mirror of a merely nubile girl, symbolism on which the reverse's 'maidens at grave' happens to insist), he on the other with the dowry (who shall say that this is not husband-making, at least where husbands unmade by divorce have to return it?)." If the first re-emerger from the question's now unlocked waiting room should be the Eros of Br. Mus. F424 as already familiar through pl. 13, 4 of Herbert Hoffmann's *Tarentine Rhyta,* with fan in one hand, gabled box in the other, the neat coincidence might be so overpoweringly felt as to suggest this extension of that thought. "Indeed it must be so, just so, for a rightly bi-worldly but (for once) wrongly eschatogamic reading of the three persons on the Paris strip, heroized man, living woman, living man, would be altogether defeated by the third's gabled box; even if one could think of dead man's getting boxed money from (or rather, with) *dead* girl herself *unknown* to the former's surviving kin, could he imagine one of those kinsmen (none of *hers*!) to be the source of it?"

Erotes of this question are welcome. But we need its women to mend a flaw in that argument, which no repair, perhaps, could make conclusive, as long as its subject is a box never opened, yet which need not depend on a shock of showy coincidence. A flaw, or at least a great need of bracing, cannot but be felt if after perceiving how much the interpretation as dowry boxes depends, after all, on a special view of a single example (once thought unfavorable!), we come to recognize not only that an objector would be quite right if he claimed that our case depends, as from a single hook, on the Paris man's being recipient, getter not giver, of the gabled box which he holds, but also that the objection would be at least unanswerable if, in development it went no further than "a pity (is it not?) that we cannot unroof the little house."

However, in the very nature of the question most immediate, the Paris picture's own "what does *all* this mean?," there is a prod to push such a challenger from that to this: "since we cannot unroof the box, there can be no better insight than the least irresponsible guess, namely this impressively double one: that the living man's offering at the dead man's heroon contains *material* (*a*) in keeping with the markedly peculiar design of this sort of box, including the regular decoration (with human figures) as well as the house-like shape; (b) complementary to the woman's offering (deep cylindrical basket or box, and a fan) on the other side of the dead man's heroon." This is not unmethodical, and I have to remember that, in my attempt to explain away incongruous, "sex-insulting," transactions at the back of the Iphigenia krater in Leningrad (pp. 26, 195), I have furnished means of a now unwelcome expansion of (b), thus: "complementary, that is, to the woman's gift of two eminently fit presents for *transmission* to the dead and heroized man's eschatic bride, fan and basket of finery." But I believe this to be a mischievous development, obstructive of things worth doing – of more than the rescue of London school-children from the misinformation of conscientious docents expounding that magnet-piece, Br. Mus. F272, to boys or girls red-bussed from classes in the *Hippolytos* or *Phèdre.* To show that it is not for nothing that in shape, color, and carving the gabled boxes are fit to remind us of pedimented and sculptured treasuries at Delphi will require our reassembling enough of the regular carriers, women, including the mirrorless mock-Persephone, against (or rather, for useful correlation with) the exceptional man – exceptional because painters of weddings do not often undertake a composition of the excessively strict symmetry enforced by the Paris amphora's grudging of room, allowing just enough space for the artist to be lucid, if he practiced great economy: "no, notwithstanding what is at the back of St. 420 (pl. 2), these are not survivors expressing goods to eschatogams, this is *ELEP,* marriage at a heroon, as foolproof as I could make it, for you might not have understood that the woman's fan was hers to keep if I had not shown the man in physical possession of *his* spouse-maker, the dowry."

Some threads would be lost if the women, all with the significant box, some with the mirror of nubility which so enhances its significance, were balked of prompt enough reentry, which they must have, but subject to our not committing the criminal unfairness of making punctuality an excuse for suppressing the opposition's right to risk its own guess about what is treasured or housed in this primarily houselike thing (for only superficial qualities or features, color and figured carving, put us in mind of treasuries, treasuries almost too exceptionally grand, it might be thought, for reckless comparison with things small and common, namely, national repositories at a great international sanctuary). To have a rival guess made should at any rate give leverage for any work to be done with the boxes of these women. I cannot think these things and their concomitants unimportant, for some interest in them will surely be required in what may well prove (for posterity if 'not sooner!) to be one of the most attractive avenues of Italiote studies, that which the more elaborate pelikai of Apulo-Tarentine red-figure, as gradually they are published, are already beginning to constitute. It is a promising hypothesis (as in *CVA* It. 32 IV D, p. 9 F. Gino Lo Porto has already hinted) that many of these are "biworldly," eschatogamic only on the reverse, the plainer side, with the obverse reserved for aspects or implications of earthly marriage. Even the San Simeon pelike of my pl. 16a and b could be included, though so much less "grand" than such pieces as Torino 4129 or 4149 (*CVA* It. 32 IV D, pls. 12-13), and a brief glance back at it is scarcely untimely, while two considerations are still fresh, namely that dowries belong to the world of mints and banks (so that there Aphrodite with her gabled box should be the arranger, with Pan's hydronomic help, of ordinary weddings) but also that we have slips of inattention to reckon with (can we trust our painters to keep the gabled box *out* of eschatogamies?).

Alternative Explanations?
"Aphrodite's Code"

BUT IF THE oppositions should exercise another right, to remain coyly agnostic ("for box ever closed what but mind kept wide open?"), speculation must take off. With a few precautions (especially against reawaking the Mise chimera with perhaps strange consequences to this very neighborhood, such as Laodameia's having to let her husband's untouched money and her own preciously health-maintaining plaything become pilferings of Phaedra, "false" no longer, from Orphic gear of Hippolytus, ball-man and dolls'-house-man in the Dismemberment *telete* as an interpretation of Theseus' taunt in lines 952-954 of Euripides' play which was once not unfashionable would perhaps have let us see him), there can be no harm or discredit in speculative search for an alternative to the guess that such boxes hold dowries. I hope I have not left the need of one obscure. Even Aphrodite being means to an end, other knowledge, the highest importance imaginable for her gabled container of inscrutable things would be practical value — as a criterion — for verification of a suspected boundary of worlds in a certain department of Apulo-Tarentine vase-painting, the promising one to which just now I alluded. But there can be no such use of it, even the most tentative, if the guess aforesaid is not a good one, that is, evidently much better than the next best.

Let this flight of search be allowed its least arbitrary launching, namely from the "roof" of the thing least different, the rather houselike but vaulted (not gabled) box in a Roman wall-painting, at Ostia, of Dionysos (LIBER PATER being initiated into his own religion (*NS* [1928,] 158, fig. 19, G. Calza). Above it is written MYSTERIA. How much it matters that no handle shows is scarcely discussible in regard to a painting partly faded, and there is nothing very momentous in a reflection which this might meanwhile prompt, that the handles which the gabled boxes regularly have are more essential to a thing belonging (in its physical passing) to the *transaction* of marriage than they could be to anything more incidental, less contractual. Should not, then, this be the cue delivered by the Ostia box, that for the other and ridged sort the extension of choice offered (to anyone set against my own guess) is "things religious, sacred enough for reverent seclusion, or things childish, more naively so than ball or *sistro apulo* (*platage*): unlike them, childish enough for shy concealment by the bride"?

In either choice (both having to reckon with the houselike container) this should mean figurines, household gods in the one alternative, dolls in the other — mere dolls, not bait for a baby god in a *telete,* so long as we may continue averse from an Orphistic interpretation of the chattel-symbolism of our vases, one desperately involved in a teletic eschatology of terror which (in spite of Plato's allusions to such a thing) is no longer presumable for any concern of ours. No longer, that is, if my text-fed idea of it died (at p. 155 or thereabout) of weary attrition against the harder facts of ceramic material confirming Patroni's notions: hardest, no doubt, the Apulian Campanian vases with pictures of families reunited. Surely no one preferring the first of the three insights which have proposed themselves for this inscrutable matter, dowry, wife's θεοὶ κατοικίδιοι, obsolescent dolls, need be required to argue in defense of his choice. But even the third was not — as a possibility conceived — quite a waste of thought, since thinking it was bound to remind us that two of the most prominent symbols of the (re)union eschatology of completion as Neopatronians can discern it, namely the ball and the "ladder of noises," *sistrum* or *platage,* are not much above the level of toys, and that the quite evident data of *their* matter, more plainly but not less strangely than the dolls-divining fancy, are entangled in an obsolescence-persistence paradox. For both ball and "ladder" are on the one hand quite decidedly, quite surely, nuptial symbols, having established themselves in the most transparently intelligible category of intimate attributes of nuptial (bride-equipping) Aphrodite, together with the wardrobe chest (or big bag) she may be given to sit on, and things she may be given to hold, trinket box, gabled box, matron-making fan. Yet on the other hand the ball belongs decidely, definitely, one might risk saying characteristically, to the recreation of unmarried girls, as we know so very well, from Homer's Nausikaa (*Od.* vi. 100.115f), the Palatine Anthology's Timareta (vi. 280), and the coevals of Europa on an Apulian vase (fig. 16). "Oh well, all whom you name were near marriage, very notably nubile, and nubility, not only marriage with its proper accompaniments, comes from Aphrodite." Besides disregarding the little *arrhephoroi,* from seven to eleven years of age, on the Acropolis of Athens so considerately lodged at a ball-court (*EtM s.v* ἀρρηφορεῖν, Ps. Plutarch, *X Oratorum Vitae* 839 C), that is a quibble logically. But it is not untrue, as my pl. 19 quite strikingly emphasizes (the warranted Aphrodite so obligingly comprehensive at Cleveland, guaranteed by adscript naming her, and an object-lesson in her having nuptial wardrobe chest to sit on, mirror of mere nubility to hold), and the observation will deserve the kindest word we have in our gift, "propulsive," if there is any rebound from it that can clear and shorten the way to our getting Aphrodite near enough to her practically right place in Italiote studies.

As "practically right" means "where it will be easy, or at any rate much less hard than now, for others to recognize her and interest themselves in her evidently great importance to the chief field of Italiote art, its funerary vase-painting," there is at least a start of this in our beginning now to gain appreciation of the mainly obstructive thing in the present and last coil of the way. May it not be this perhaps, that though much of Aphrodite's symbolism, our means of *beginning* to know her as she figures in Italiote eschatography, is clear enough, three of the most intimate symbols, three which she may even handle, have (for our eyes seeking to read them) intrinsic faults? The last is a word perhaps too mild for what is defeating in one of them, the gabled box, opaque and impenetrable. The other two, ball and the ladder-like thing, are less essentially frustrating, because their perversely polar ambiguity (belonging to marriage, belonging to before marriage) could in one myth of Apulo-Tarentine vase-painting, Europa's, be invested with obvious meaning enjoyable then and now too, our own relish of it being nonetheless real (and creditable!) for being partly subjective. By this I mean that the irony which the vase-painters themselves intended has meanwhile been improved by an all but Apulo-Tarentine person (native of A., lover of T.), unable however to see *their* vases buried in his own Aufidus valley, Horace, in the last three stanzas of the twenty-seventh piece in the third book of his *Odes.*

Our preoccupation with symbols ambiguous or worse being part of a preoccupation with Aphrodite, the most necessary part of our training for not overlooking her presence, our interest in this passage should have a reach of at least six lines back from the one of delightfully bad Latin (73, bad with assumed Hellenism, *uxor invicti Iovis esse nescis*) in which Horace said what the vase-painters at Tarentum told by means of more or less "casual" balls or *sistra-platagai*: "you are wife — yes, *wife* — of Zeus without knowing it." Horace's relevance to the sly vase-paintings would be less real and less practically suggestive (of quantity's specific remedy for present troubles of uncertain quality?) if in line 73 he were not mouthpiece of the sly Venus *perfidum ridens* in line 67 and if he had not noted (in that line and the following) that she had her son with her. At any rate, is there not an immensely profitable rebound to be had from Horace's *et remisso filius arcu*? Especially if contrived in a certain direction, back to a group, made up of those two deities with nuptial Pan added, on the pelike of my pl. 16a, where Aphrodite is "foolproofed" by a rich concentration of symbolism. Indeed, by a distinctly double dose of it: part of this offered in the mere grouping of persons (prompting "just a ready bride with her outfit of dowry, wardrobe and ball? no, with Pan and Eros both there, probably not"), part in an irresistibly sufficient denoting of Aphrodite by attributes, the water-bird being (since I have already counted Eros) the finally overpowering one. As surely it is unless I am wrong in judging that we should be rather slow to suppose, without clearer evidence than the very loose conjunction of *platage* and waterfowl on the marvelous Sicilian pyxis which gave Trendall is frontispiece for the second volume of *LCS,* that Aphrodite had *spare* geese or swans for general distribution, routine inclusion in her outfits for her clients. At all events, it seems to be practically desirable that investigators should become quite fully aware of the *perfidum ridens* in the symbolism of Apulian vases, and not fail then to absorb the remedial lesson of the San Simeon pelike's obverse that, especially in an age of IBM cards and computers, there is great value, if not perfect safety, in number.

I do not mean that scholarship's proper attitude to a uniquely equivocal system of signs requires any particular scholar who has accepted Italiote red-figure's invitation to itself, made in due form as "enjoy yourself here, but for heaven's sake *thoroughly*," to suspend his pleasures (all but that touted one of suspense itself) until an internationally adequate crew of mere spotters and statistical sifters signals "ready, sir!," this corps having reduced to some provisionally conspectual order all extant combinations and permutations of Aphrodite's code — including (as not merely *ELEP* requires) all the who-has-what of groups at heroa and gravestones. Certainly, the stipulation's emphasized word includes "methodically" and, altogether, the phrase looks forward to great computations, the completest cross-analysis possible. But mainly that sharp and adjuring tone must have meant *"not childishly"* (as those do who reserve enjoyment — and this great and perhaps crowing — for reacquaintance with myths of their fifth form reading). If meaning that much, then this also, its nearly unutterable but not unpractical implication, *"still less, inhumanly"* (as many in fact do take up the subject, their interest in the vase-paintings having so little to do with the hopes which so many of the pictures express). Anyhow, the propulsive consideration is that the actual ambiguity or worse of particular symbols present need not deter a scholar from enjoying himself in the most modest of exercises in number, that of putting two and two together to make (as was made on, and indeed from, the Hearst Monument pelike) light as well as coherence. But only provided that the little operation is the very opposite of what North Americans call "puttering" and others "pottering"; it must be done with an important direction *set*, to serve ultimate thoroughness, and if the putter has already committed himself to some guess about an inscrutable symbol he must show himself decently considerate of his spotters by disclosing in advance any already conceivable combination that, by occurring, would refute the guess. The gabled box lends itself rather well to illustration of this.

For no symbol is less self-explaining, and few of the good intentions in the *agenda* of Italiote scholarship are more praiseworthy than one which this quite impenetrable thing can perhaps begin to promote, namely better interpretation of storeyed (tiered) designs for late Apulian vases, especially less inept dealing with the "basements" (continuous friezes) of amphoras of Panathenaic shape. That is not the only good direction in which this singular clue, *caecum caeca regens vestigia,* offers service; thanks to certain amazing revelations (*AJA* 72 [1968] pl. 17, figs. 53 and 55) of Kyle M. Phillips' thoroughness in investigating the mythography of Andromeda it can be seen that a derivative (or, more exactly, collateral descendant) survives into the Christian Middle Ages and beyond as part of an *integration* of symbols not unrelated to the eschatogamic code of late Apulo-Tarentine vases. It is excitingly curious that in the margin of a twelfth-century drawing of Andromeda a symbol like our Greek sluicer can be made out (Phillips' *trulla,* his p. 19 and pl. 17, fig. 53) — significantly like, because it appears *between* symbols corresponding to that washpan's correlatives, on the one hand pedestaled laver requiring for its effective use just such a thing as this scoop, on the other hand a vessel for first filling the basin used in such scoop-and-splash bathing. Presently (in applying the control already volunteered, a watch set for the very combinations settled to be *worst* for my guess of dowry-box), we shall need to investigate a feature of this same manuscript's opposite margin which can certainly be related (through the corresponding element in a fifteenth-century variant of the composition, Philipps' fig. 55) to the box with polyhedric lid that is so curiously placed in an Attic vase-painting much more than a thousand years earlier, namely the small container which on the vase is put almost as far as possible from its Andromeda's two wardrobes, and in fact right at the feet of Perseus, as if to say "this however is for you." Meanwhile it is already high time for the promised reentry of women with boxes less like pyramidal or polyhedric pavilions, more like normally gabled buildings.

This had best begin with one whose occurrence where she is good for our practice in making out wholes, namely in the continuous frieze of the "Medea" amphora Naples H. 3221, enhances another claim to precedence, her being exceptionally good for our practice in detecting Aphrodite. Heyde-mann in his catalogue (p. 507) had no name for this figure, shown in my pl. 25d as dangling a gabled box from her left hand and with the other controlling the flutterings of a string-tethered bird. Because of recent en-counters — with the San Simeon Aphrodite, quintuply warranted even quite apart from her gabled box, with the Lipari Aphrodite in a partly similar context (near a laver, moreover attended by an Eros whose work for her requires a timbrel) — it is scarcely possible to withhold from this person the name which we see written out for the Aphrodite wardrobe-benched at Cleveland (pl. 19). But it might seem that a person on the opposite side of this Naples amphora H. 3221, in the same continuous frieze, has quite as much right to be given it, being already in possession of Aphrodite's parasol and also of a seat on Aphrodite's wardrobe for supplying brides (pl. 25b).

Moreover, above her there flies a bird, free now yet all but exactly like the one tethered to the suspected Aphrodite on the other side of this amphora — though it is fair to note that its flight (with a message of favor, that being the meaning of its ribbon) seems to have started at some distance back. Close behind the person with all those marks of Aphrodite, almost touching her back, there is yet another of this goddess's intimate attributes, the ladder-like submusical instrument which we have twice seen in Aphrodite's own hand as distinctive for her (cf. fig. 14) in groupings of gods. But here it is held by a woman (if not a goddess, our goddess, after all) whose forward stoop (towards the person on the big chest, with a parasol to hold) and backward glance (at a woman seated on a salvaged and reerected capital, and holding a great flower with three blooms "hose-in-hose") give her some importance, to the composition at least. Guardedly — guarding especially against undue influence of her timbrel's promise of infectiously cheerful noise — one may say that aesthetically she contributes almost as much life as cohesion to her group of four persons. Four, since certainly we must include the figure that is pictorially its occasion; the young man with a wreath for someone in his left hand and raising the other (in a gesture more respectful than his stance?) as he addresses himself to the leading woman in the adjoining file of three, the one who is in firm possession of two exceptionally well-attested attributes of Aphrodite (though without the support it has from the Apulo-Tarentine vases of my figs. 6 and 13 I should not have let the Parthenon frieze's august warranty of the parasol count for as much as the inscribing of Aphrodite's name — at Cleveland, pl. 19 — is worth in the other regard, her right to sit on wardrobes). But Aphrodite's appropriation of those things — even the "selfish" parasol — and of many others too, mirrors, fans, alabastra of perfume, *sistra-platagai,* balls, various further sorts of container (box, basket or bag), is something altogether secondary, symbolic reflection of her dispensing them. We have had almost too much already of the *perfidum ridentis,* but it will save time, and perhaps really conduce to tidiness, if we may take this part of the present frieze as another of her sly ambiguities. If human life were longer, my own impression that the sitting person with the parasol, not the stooper with the *platage,* is indeed Aphrodite (and that the man is saying "ma'am, I have come for her" not "dear, come with me") might have been worth passing for verification to the searchers and sifters of a computing staff, with these then put to exhaustive scrutiny not only of the postures of suitors as distinguishable from other sorts of respectful applicant but also of any fine shades of system there may be in Apulian prudery (its squeamishness being doubtless a matter — in the very long run — for practical enquiry, as I may admit without any confidence that there is decisive importance in a certain exposure here — of most of one breast of this Aphrodite or Aphroditoid (if I am not mistaken in seeing at the edge of her chiton even as much as that very slight sag towards the frank semi-nudity contrastingly normal in some schools of Campanian and Sicilian red-figure). As it is, let us accept the ambiguity, grateful for there being something we can do with it, even towards answering the quite engaging question, "and where are they, these four persons?" For is it not an enrichment (with increase of interest, not of doubt or difficulty) of the ambiguity remarked in the Garden of the Hesperides at the back of the "Archemoros" krater (fig. 8).

There too the exciting certainty was that Aphrodite was present, it being better than interesting thus to find that Olympian establishment away from home in what North Americans might call a "concession" at that place. But on the "Archemoros" vase *which* was she of two neighbors? The person sitting on a wardrobe chest? Or the person standing up next to her, exchanging glances, extending (if not quite proffering) the most wife-making nuptial symbols, a fan, holding in the other hand an alabastron, symbol of nuptial *preparation* nicely complementary to two which the figure on the chest has, sluicing pan at her feet (for bath taken?) mirror in her left hand (for finishing touches, like the mirror in the like hand of the Hearst Painter's woman in Lecce, who demonstrably — *CVA* It. 4 IV D r, pl. 3, 1 — has just taken a bath and is being proffered an alabastron of scent? The cream of the Medea amphora's enrichment of this is of course the young or rejuvenated man (pl. 25a) who more than makes up for the low ceiling's exclusion of the apple tree and its snake. His arrival is verification of the guess which all three tree-displaying Gardens of Apulian Hesperides encouraged, namely that what Aphrodite had to do with that wet place was in fact her endless affair of eschatogamy, of finding male companions for the dead of her own sex — after due provision of the bath with which the (re)union eschatology is obsessed and perhaps of most of the other requisites of an earthly bride.

"Dowries, then, included in that 'most', with no 'perhaps'? Is it for that that you are saving up the other Aphrodite who is on the far side of the vase (pl. 25d) but in the same corridor of its decoration, dangling a typical box of your gabled sort, whom you have not quite ignored but so far have treated as if, paired there with her equally inactive son not to mention her firmly captive bird, she were just 'Aphrodite in Abstract', having nothing to do with the men, women and Erotes in the rest of this continuous frieze?"

Well, this unambiguous Aphrodite is not unimportant; in the first place, it is interesting, and perhaps might be worth someone's probing, that even an invitation to a brawl cannot help assuming her indisputable. And next, far from condemning her to the isolation as a feature properly studied with blinkers on the student's face, let us acknowledge that she and her whole horizontal context, together with countless comparable streaks in late Apulian red-figure, belong to what in the *archeologia aggionata* (of computing hardware and smocked collecting "software" to feed it) will be almost a subdiscipline, the as yet unborn art of reading amphora friezes. To this my figs. 19-21 from pl. A of Gerhard's *Apulische Vasenbilder* might be reckoned distantly antenatal salute, no better; the merest casual sample, in passing, of the variety which altogether — not just in respect to a particular part of the designs — makes the late Apulian amphoras so attractively difficult, really integrative mastery of the various elements of their funerary significance being evidently worth all that the newest resources of scholarship can do for it, resources that students in my own generation do not command. All that just how we can hope to get from this sampling, the three Berlin amphoras F 3241 (figs. 15 and 19), 3242 (fig. 20), and 3244 (fig. 21) is their help onward — *to* much better controls of my interpretation of the gabled box than the Aphrodite who has one (pl. 25d) in the frieze of the "Medea" amphora H. 3221 in Naples, *with*, at the same time, certain impressions. One of them should be this, that the notion in question, of dowry box being more likely than portable shrine or dolls' house in the given connection with marriage, had a rather narrow, if indeed quite complete, escape from the stultification threatened by its occurring in the hand of an Aphrodite so nearly other-worldy, only half a turn away from another Aphrodite conducting an eschatogamy in the Garden of the Hesperides, a rite and a region which had nothing to do with money and banking (the escape's logic having been that "a miss was as good as a mile"; the box which a distinct Aphrodite-in-general, unemployed moreover, could well retain was withheld from the eschatogamic group of my pl. 18b). But much more practically important would be this other: reassurance that so far as we can see (farthest, to the revels of a generation able to exploit sure knowledge of the whole idiom of Apulo-Tarentine eschatography, but for the most practical purpose not so far, to my own opportunity of making more accessible and more inviting some chief figures, especially Aphrodite, Dionysos, and Aphrodite's Orpheus), we could not be better employed than as now indeed, in the present remedial attention to the two most defiantly difficult, anyhow, of that idiom's neglected symbols. *Two*, for the ladder-like sign is once more in sight, occurring (twice) on one amphora (F 3244, fig. 21) of the Berlin sampling, as well as (once) in the eschatogamic group (pl. 25) of the "Medea" amphora in Naples, where it appears together with (another figure's) hose-in-hose flower which — however monstrously strange — needs so much less explaining, since we have already seen it held, fig. 18, by a comparable woman, companion of a similar box-sitter in the same place, Garden of the Hesperides. I cannot think that there is much need here of transcribing Pindar's strange allusion, *Ol.* ii. 73-75, to official encouragement of an interest in the wild flowers of paradise; but we may well regret that we cannot ask him how he would relate ingemination ("hose-in-hose" flowering) to small and pliant chains of blossom favored in the "policy" of officious Rhadamanthys (a notably self-assertive member of the staff of Hades even in Apulian vase-painting: see pl. 1a).

The "Dowry-Box": Reconsiderations

"REMEDIAL" ATTENTION? Has it really been so? At any rate, it is time for two improvements of procedure, if what we are doing is to be done as by servants of servants, mere prompters and prodders of agents of a wide sweep of foraging necessary before the master's machines can be even fed, nourishingly at least.

For one thing already promised them, this doubtless more important than the need to remedy a certain oversight of which I am concious in regard to the "ladder" symbol, where is the definite specification of a killer-context for the gabled box, perhaps no more than barely imaginable now, which however would relieve those foragers of any further heed of my idea of it, should any of them ever stumble upon the prespecified combination? Here it is, quite sufficiently, I think: deadly to my interpretation as dowry casket would be any configuration of vase-painting in which a suitor *proffered* this thing to the woman of his suit, there being two considerations as to what makes "proffering"; how does the man hold himself, what (if anything) does his other hand hold? Even one of those "foot-up stoopers" (as seminar slang has them) would not pass muster as thus lethal if he *tendered* a wreath or fan or other suitable gift in one hand, and in the other merely *dangled* the box — all, indeed, that he could be expected to do with it in any picture of the actual exchange, if the box's content was dowry, his to keep. Having had some hint already (while, very recently, recruiting for a pavilion of useful anomalies) that there is a practical difference really immense between mistakes starkly irrational and so difficult to make that no argument may coolly presume them made, and mistakes just careless or thoughtless, we should be slow, I think, to make stultification, ruinous contradiction, out of other-worldly occurrence ("oh, silly of me, I just forgot that money does not circulate there" being infinitely more imputable to an Italiote vase-painter than "dear me, did I make the man act 'no, dear, thank you, and see that it gets back to your father?' ") But the matter of incongruous occurrence cannot be just burked. For this sort of box enters into the mythography of Herakles' Olympian marriage, more often than I have noted already (fig. 5), and this will presently need closer attention, for already it revives a question we know to be important, how far can the most sophisticated Italiote vase-painting bear to go in *metaphor*?

It would of course be a question of fully cardinal importance, if metaphor, of which Patroni once was tempted to make too much, could be turned against the observations registered in Patroni's final insights, to this contempuous effect, "what a gratuitous mare's nest that cosy eschatogamy was! All that dowry stuff, in *kind* (ἔδνα) as packed in those rectangular chests and boxes or in round baskets, in *cash* (προίξ) as chinking in those little dangled, swaying, toy-treasuries, it only meant that she ('soul' being feminine!) went grandly, as death's very bride." That there is honor in coming grandly dowered is a Greek enough idea, as all know from its getting rather vividly picturesque development in Euripides' *Andromache* (lines 2, 146-153, 872-873). On the other hand, as we, at least, have had an opportunity to find out, the notion that the personification Death or even the substantial gods Hades and Dionysos practiced infernal polygamy is one with which the Greek mind found it hard even to play, taking much more naturally to the idea of the infernal powers' making matches or blessing reunions.

No doubt it would be discreditable, a slovenly failure of energy, if having just found space (figs. 19-21) for the Berlin amphoras, I found no application for the striking illustration of this on one of the, F. 3241, fig. 19 (cf. fig. 15): above mere "-omachy" liveliness, on (A), Europa escorted, Aphrodite concerned to see that one of the escorting nymphs gets (for transmission) the least "grand" of Europa's ἔδνα, the ball; on (B), man and woman whom Dionysos has just united (or reunited) and their recent escorts. But it is more important that I should face the consequences of my own admission that the gabled box (as for the dowry) suspended for the Olympian marriage and apotheosis of Herakles painted on a lekythos in Sir John Soane's Museum was not less absent-minded, silly even, than some anomalies I had had occasion to collect, the muddle on the Laodameia krater resulting from careless placing of an inscription, the obscurity that resulted on a Campanian vase from the painter's addiction to white canes, this cheating Hermes of his kerykeion, the infelicities on St. 420 in Leningrad that came partly of an obsession with Aphrodite, partly of a practice in drawing Danaids. The consequences to be faced are that, having now to cope with yet another instance of a dowry box for Herakles, on an Apulian olpe in Sevres (*CVA* France 13, pl. 40, 17, 26-28), I am challenged to sustain that comparison, and I may as well say at once that between addiction and obsession is where I would put the cause of both examples, in London and in Sèvres, of the anomaly now in question, the money-box, doing its symbolic duty as neatly as on the Laodameia calyx-krater and more effectively, the present allusion, to Herakles' marrying immortal Youth, Hebe, being quite foolproof (as the other, to the widowing of L. so soon after marriage, was not); yet nevertheless looking (to those captious enough) a little silly, hanging there *when* there was not, and *where* there never would be, any circulation of money. Whichever it may seem nearer, addiction or obsession, the inveterate habit of resorting to a distinct shape of box to mark the separable part, not for herself, of what a bride brought to marriage, required time for forming. To this it is perhaps not quite irrelevant that late-among-late in Apulian red-figure would seem right enough reckoning for the "dusky" Sèvres olpe in question, which shows a gabled box of the usual-unusual material suspended almost fussily close to Herakles, to whom his constant patron and present sponsor Athena turns ("yes, take it, it does not matter that you have one on your head already") as he reaches for the wreath tendered by Happy Ending (Nike) flying in with what we know as the nuptial phiale in her other hand. But the really important point is made by the Attic vases of earlier date which establish this thing, gabled box with cord or strap for handle, as an international commonplace of weddings: e.g., Leningrad St. 1791 (decorated by Beazley's Eleusinian Painter), *CR* Atlas 1860 pl. 1, 3 or FR pl. 68; cf. 1809 of the same collection, Stephani, *VSKE* 2 pp. 345f. It happens that the Attic vase-painting which by spacing and placing makes cunningly most of the distinction between the bride's *hedna* for herself and her *proix* for her husband — even more than on St. 1791 the Eleusinian Painter does by extricating the dowry box from all the fuss and congestion and hanging it up on the wall not far from the bridegroom's head — does in fact allow the container a different form in different materials: wood (I must suppose) for the whole of it, and the lid going up to a sharp point (not to a sharp edge). That, at any rate, is how I must see it in the drawing of Berlin 3237 made for Bethe and in the photograph made for Phillips (*AJA* 72 [1968,] pl. 6, fig. 17 [*sic*], pl. 7, fig. 16; cf. the almost miraculous agreement of rendering in the fifteenth-century MS adduced by Phillips, *ibid* pl. 17, fig. 55). This, with *proix* by Perseus' right foot and as low as possible in the picture, widely separated from the two great chests of *hedna* respectively right and left of Andromeda's head, is the most telling indication known to me of any part of the vicissitudes of Andromeda's dowry: before Cassiopeia's disparagement of Poseidon's Nereids, *intended* for the suitor *originally* successful (whether this was Phineus or Agenor), after Ammon's double-dealing oracle, *exposed* with her by Cepheus, after the rescue from the monster, *claimed* with her by Perseus. But that is not to say that I can mark any distinction of function between this exceptionally rendered and especially happy example and the normally gabled box of normal ivory of the Apulo-Tarentine routine (more cluttered than clever!) for the "marriage after all" symbolism of this mythography (*AJA* 72 pl. 10, fig. 24; pl. 11, fig. 29; pl. 13, fig. 39). Anyhow, it is past usage, investing it with conventional meaning ("husband's share, you know what"), that gives the impenetrable object, as it occurs on the Sèvres olpe, its compelling voice, decisive before scruples have time to make themselves felt: "no, this is not Herakles resting between two Labors, congratulated by Athena as Serial Success brings him, for the most recent feat, her customary token; this is the *end* of it all, with promotion to Olympus, marriage to Hebe the Prime of Life in person, and her assurance of his being for ever and ever undiminished Herakles."

Here is efficiency: as a working symbol, the gabled box on the Sèvres olpe is simply perfect, and except in a certain interesting connection any supervening scruples (of the "what a metaphor I have been made to swallow!" sort) should be of no account. But until it can be comfortably assumed that

Patroni's ideas, his eschatogamic insights, are quite invulnerable, it will remain important to appreciate the difference between such exposure to sound metaphor, effective because perfectly genuine even if more than a little like Medea's fantasia on the theme *dos* in the twelfth letter of Ovid's *Heroides,* 119-124, and on the other hand the difficult effort required of our minds by the invitation to metaphor (idealization) made by the third section of Albizzati's *Saggio di esegesi sperimentale sulle pitture funerarie dei vasi italo-greci,* pp. 164-187. This in its place there, as "figurazioni del culto funebre idealizzato" with two pairs of Elysian lovers (as they are for us) constrained to give it immediate illustration in figs. 15 and 16, following the second section on "rappresentanze realistiche del culto funerario" with illustration not less businesslike (groups at gravestones or heroa) has to be recognized, in spite of Albizzati's loyally filial relation to Patroni, as a determined attack on what, at all this length, I have been defending, though giving it such ugly jargon, eschatogamy, to wear.

A New Approach: The Heroa of the Vases—Do They Represent Real Monuments?

I SUPPOSE I may reckon it lucky than an opportunity of briefest possible, least interrupting, counterattack has arisen quite naturally in the course of what has been, for some lines past, and will be, for some more hereafter, rather like a janitor's evening tour of light-switches – end-of-chapter service in plodding elucidation of eschatogamy's darker symbols. Among these, let us not forget is that one of more abnormality than is easily kept in mind, in spite of the miraculously mediaeval nudge given by the normal *trulla* marginal for Phillips' Andromeda: I mean the sluicer with too many handles, two more than a sluicer in fact had, the purpose of the excess being to make this symbol of purity more strikingly comprehensive by thus arbitrarily giving it the bowl of the second thing, foot-basin, required for an effective bath at a stemmed laver of the sort seen next the one-handled *trulla* scoop on the mediaeval MS (*AJA* [1968] pl. 17, fig. 53) and next Persephone's three-handled washpan in my pl. 5. At this our present stage, when the enemy for assault is endlessness, perhaps not even duty to Patroni would justify a seemingly belated counterattack on Albizzati were there not a sufficiently seizable connection between actual conventions fatally ignored in Albizzati's assumptions of "reality" (the liberty taken in certain excesses of or round about conventional heroa in late Tarentine vase-painting (which

I hope to explain as unreal) and the convention that did in fact concoct the washpan symbol out of two distinct things. This quite expressive sign for purity is not of the same order of difficulty as the gabled box, impenetrable, and the "ladder," so altogether dubious (how worked, why valued). But I think it does deserve to be kept in sight, together with them, during the last steps of our way to what remains to be done for (rather than with) Aphrodite, her Orpheus, and Dionysos, because (if I am not mistaken) this unreal but intelligible thing is the only symbol of the whole code which has any insurance to offer against our being taken in by what well merits its capitals if I need not hesitate to call it the ware's Great Cheat, Apulo-Tarentine red-figure's concealing (for entirely natural reasons of its own convenience) the extent to which the development of funerary luxury both at Tarentum and in Apulia was a *subterranean affair.*

This involves questions very concretely practical, some perhaps almost immediately so; thus, not only what we are to make of all the tons of *carparo* sculpture and architectural detail, not really very much like the heroa of the vase-paintings on the whole, that is recorded in Hans Klumbach's *Tarentiner Grabkunst,* but also whether we may not claim for Aphrodite (as shrines) some of vase-painting's supposed heroa of mortal women (for example, at the back of the Antigone amphora of the Jatta collection in Ruvo, J. 423, Sichtermann, pl. 114). Or again, whether we should not claim for Dionysos (as lovers belonging to his paradise) the couple (thyrsigerous) whom Albizzati would have reckoned realistic survivors at a realistic monument, on the amphora Villa Giulia 15609 (*CVA* Italy 1 IV D r, pl. 4, 1). However, the "Cheat" and any not unprofitable, because propulsive, questions it may pose had better remain at the proper place for considering it, which is not far ahead, and any steps which Albizzati's metamorphical evasion still requires us to take can only lead there, I must think. But meanwhile it would be a pity not to take advantage of an incidental benefit volunteered by two of the Berlin vases (figs. 19 and 20), in our sampling of amphoras. I do not especially mean, though I may as well acknowledge, the personal qualm of conscience urging immediate completion of a duty, easy but so far only half done, to the *ambiguity* of the "ladder" symbol which occurs twice in the long frieze of one of them, F. 3244, fig. 21. I adduce this pair of vases because already, just after our promotion of the washpan symbol to a place among rewardingly "difficult" ones, it is so instructive that these amphoras do *not* cheat, not at any rate after the fashion in which the pan symbol, unreally two-in-one, may be said to do so.

With that unreality it is at least comparable that so many late Apulo-Tarentine vases, volute kraters and also some amphoras of less "stratified" design than those of my sample, subject the dead to a two-on-one load that is unverified, and quite unlikely, especially at Tarentum and any place following its custom of burying its dead within an area limited by fortifications: a certain particular overload of monuments, on the vase's obverse elaborate heroon with "portrait," on the reverse the shaft and basis of a substantial stele. But on the exceptional vases just referred to there is no such duplication; what we find is monument shafted (F. 3242, fig. 20), *or* naiscoid (F. 3244, fig. 21), and the naiscoid one is of a very simple type (without portrait) that is even verifiable (F. Lenormant, *Gazette archéologique* 7 [1881-1882] p. 173, for Tarentum; cf. R. Pagenstecher, *Un-teritalische Grabdenkmäler,* pls. 1 and 17 d, and P. C. Sestieri, *NS* [1940] p. 118, fig. 56, for Metapontum).

Our having now to glance at Albizzati's "idealizations" (for such interest as they retain in their meanwhile straitened circumstances) should remind us that in regard to a paradox aggravating the difficulty of another symbol, the "ladder," we badly need a better exhibit than we have already in the clearest and altogether best showing (*his,* p. 216, fig. 59) of certain mere hints of the thing, important only for *where* they happen, barred (runged?) features in a repainted part of *maiden* Europa's background on the Vatican amphora X7 (cf. Trendall, *VIE* pl. 54 c). That can be so soon provided that it better be had now, even before my doing my duty of explaining "straitened." The paradox in question is of course almost exactly like that in which the ball symbol is entangled, the ball as a plaything belonging to girlhood, from very young (as was the age of the *arrephoroi* boarded in the Akropolis ball-court at Athens) to nubile (as Europa and her companions were), yet as a symbol capable of marking the beginning of married life and so of becoming the personal badge-attribute of the goddess who provides for that, Aphrodite. If I am allowed reference to the unpublished reverse of an Apulian amphora in Bari, Museo Archeologico no. 872,[1] the ladder-like thing (which I have taken to be a submusical instrument, quite possibly Archytas' *platage,* "thrupper" *de luxe*) can have nearly equal documentation. Only nearly equal, even with the thing demonstrably on a par with the ball as attribute of Aphrodite, because on this side of the parallel I cannot produce a document in writing for girls' *platagai,* equivalent to Timareta's certificate (*AP* vi 280) of having had a "darling" ball (and, let us also note, dolls and dresses for them) until just before marriage. While the match for Aphrodite's providing Europe's new and nuptial ball (Berlin F. 3241, figs. 15 and 19) is the scene on the Vatican calyx-krater AA1 in which Aphrodite *sends Eros down* with Europa's nuptial "ladder" (Trendall, *VIE* pl. 52 d), the picture of Europa on Bari 872 is rather better than a match for that other on Naples H 3218 (fig. 16) which indicates that Europa's Bull-Zeus interrupted bull-play. For Bari 872 shows "ladder" lying on the girls' playground, and ball too.

May I take for granted, and as now requiring only brief reminder, my contention that as a specific purge for eschatogamy Albizzati's recourse to metaphor, his theory of idealization, was of no effect, because Patroni's Elysian lovers failed A. in a matter of posture, failed, that is, to be quite

---

[1] Obverse in R. Paribeni, *Immagini di vasi apuli,* pl. 18. [A.D.T.]

invariable in their general rule of occurring as a sitter with stander. When both were found sitting (or, more often, scampering off together) this was not good for the notion which Albizzati had developed from the typical pair given him on the pelike of his fig. 15 (*Saggio di esegesi* p. 165), namely that such groupings of man and woman face-to-face *idealized away* a "real" monument, leaving the survivor standing before the dead, the latter now equally lifelike, though still in the posture he or she would have had in the memorial portrait, *sitting* (Albizzati's fig. 4). "Straitened circumstances" was, I must hope, not too affected a phrase for the situation which has by no means reinfused any merit into past objections to Patroni's ideas, but is of some practical, work-making, interest to us; funerary archaeology's situation since some general loss of faith in the "real" which Albizzati's idealizations took for granted.

In any consideration of this a North American cannot be to submissively conscious of his handicaps, especially if one of them is very long absence (not just great distance) from Taranto. Yet he cannot be too resolutely particular and specific, and to the point — realism above ground — claimed by Albizzati in the flanking "offerenti" of *Saggio di esegesi* fig. 4 a sufficiently direct answer can be found in the *place*, defiantly subterranean, reported by the late R. Bartoccini (*NS* [1936] pp. 177-178) for another seated youth (not too unlike Albizzati's, if one thinks away the latter's visitors), shown in B's fig. 91, p. 179. Unearthed at Taranto, this "giovanile sorridente figura maschile seduta..." was indeed something to exclaim about, with a "here, at least!" Here, at any rate, was a *type* that Bartoccini could hail as "analogo a quello delle decorazioni vascolari coeve." But, being painted on the vertical stone sealing the underground entrance to a chamber-tomb, it did only too little, perhaps less and worse than nothing, towards beginning to fill up the void which forced Pagenstecher to be so far-fetching (from the Greek mainland) in analogies (his were sculptural, pls. 10-11) for the figures which late Italiote vase-painting puts (so much more visitably) above ground in pillared and pedimented heroa, structures to which the framings of figured monuments from several regions of the Greek world have at least some likeness. It is fair to concede loss of a real enough pediment (and presence of pilasters!) to D. Zancani's "stele funeraria tarantina" published in *BdA* 20 (1926-27) p. 17, fig. 1. Not too unreasonably this youth with something for a snake was compared by him with youths who have something for a dog in the heroon of an Apulian vase and the framed panel of a Thespian stele respectively (his figs 5 and 6; the stele is one of those adduced by Pagenstecher; Zancani's fig. 7 matches his youth's suspended helmet on an Apulian amphora, the style of which — propulsively for us? — reminds me in some measure of my Holstein-Berge Painter, with whose gabled boxes and other symbols we shall have to make better acquaintance). But the very thing which proves that the Tarentine snake-feeder's monument must have had a pediment and may have had (like most heroa of the vases) conspicuous akroteria, namely the fragmentary stele from Aegina of pl. 110, fig. 2 in Le Bas and Reinach's *Monuments figurés*, in forcing us now to notice the Tarentine stele's "window" and the horse outside it and to take a second look at the snake also compels us to recognize that almost everything there, everything but the helmet's pattern, belongs to a definite system of funerary art alien to Apulia. Accepted by the makers of Tarentine terra-cottas as well as in the widely diffused "Totenmahlreliefs," it was neverthe-less rejected by Apulo-Tarentine vase-painting with evidently conscious aver-sion. The *"inside* horses" (freely admitted to the heroa of Apulian vases, not descried through a window) and one apparently welcome snake on a Lucanian nestoris of a ware derived from Apulian red-figure (Trendall, *LCS* p. 176, no. 1042) only serve to emphasise this; not distressingly of course, for we surely have no right to make grievous paradox of a result of a condition well enough understood already, the symbiosis of wool-clipping-pot-buying Apulia with wool-working-and-shipping, pot-making-and-painting Tarentum. *Ana Aprodita* and her transvestite minions stand ready to remind us of the former's enforceable right to some corrections in what it took — for its presumably dear dead — from the latter.

Certainly, we should remember that it is possible that the boy servant now in Berlin, in function recalling some children of Apulian vase-painting but in his ethnic ugliness so out of taste with it, namely Klumbach's no. 155 (Beil. C), did indeed stand above, not down below in, the Loiucco hypogaeum at Taranto, L. Viola having made out traces of a superstructure (*NS* [1881], 529). No doubt it is less likely that a relief from the same property, Klumbach's no. 68 (Beil. A), at 12.5 by 18.5 cms. markedly out of scale with the heroa represented on Apulian vases, stood above ground. But L. Bernabo Brea could write of the woman's suspended things, mirror and fan of feathers, "appartengono al mondo apulo e trovano infiniti confronti nei vasi dipinti" (p. 219 of his "Rilievi tarentini in pietra tenera", *RivIstArch* 1 [1952]), and had he wished an eschatogamic point could have made it, *nubilis immo nupta*. Again, as a frieze the *carparo* relief in Munich with a glimpse of the Underworld (including Danaids), Klumbach's no. 42 (Beil. A), should be from a chamber tomb; however good it is for me to get the indirect reminder of unfinished duty to the gabled dowry-boxes of vase-painting (which may have friezes of lively figures) this has no bearing on its heroa (which do not have them); For I cannot think I have leave to force one *from* the sure Danaids of the relief *through* the allowable, strangely optional Danaids of Leningrad St. 424 (fig. 4), *to* the extravagantly unreal heroon of that vase's reverse, seeming to stand in the farthest of beyonds, where its privileged inmates, anyhow, come to life and wife (pl. 3b). Yet P. Wolters in publishing the Munich fragment (length 55.5 cms; height 25) in *AntDenk* 3 (pp. 35-36, pl. 35) reported traces of weathering and deduced that "der Fries unter einem Naiskos wie eine Predelle angebracht war"; we must hope that there will be someday a visitor from the *carparo* region of Italy to check this inference on the spot, the thing's present spot. Work of rain, above ground or of even longer seepage below? For some degree of *physical* resemblance to the tenanted heroa of Apulian vase-painting, my own choice from among Klumbach's material would be his no. 66 in Beil. B, unprovenienced, for the "frozen" frontality of the two girls standing in its niche does not altogether destroy resemblance to heroa in which libation is shown or implied. But would not Klumbach's own interpretation ("trespassing" *survivors'* offering) entirely do so?

At any rate, unless at my own great distance from the region I am badly underinformed, our duty to what is left of its funerary sculpture and architecture can only be the untender one of a definitely conscious effort to understand the shift of curiosity away from them, effect of course of the funerary vases, which neither give, nor show any need of, cross-verification, and might be said to mock the wish for it. Not that this quite implies that scholarship, taking to heart the systematic scale, mere hole onward to hypogaeum second-class and first-class, disclosed by Viola (*NS* [1881] 524-532 [414-422]), must for any seriously practical issue regard the funerary art and architecture of Tarentum and Apulia as an elderly European must now expect to find his remembered railroads of the City of New York, gone underground altogether. Scholarship will never make a small matter of Hannibal's capture of most of the city of Tarentum (Polybius viii. 28), and this was effected in an operation depending on fire signals between a heroon outside the walls and something like one within, a building probably roomy (for temporary concealment of a formidable band of conspirators) and certainly tall (for the passage of signals over the city's walls), belonging to the tomb of one Pythonikos. Exceptionally so, however? Well, "outstandingly" is part of the given fact. Add, in any case, the remains (found in 1843, boldly restored in 1855; now destroyed?) of an elaborate structure surmounting part of the underground cemetery on Vito Lagrasta's property at Canusium-Canosa (E. Gerhard, *AZ* 15 [1857] pl. 104; V. Macchioro, *Apulia* 2 [1911,] 159-163, pl. 4, fig. 4; cf. pl. 3, fig. 3). In the old drawings (Wredford's?) which M. republished it is not up there but down below, along the sunken alley in the entrances to the cemetery's chamber-tombs, that one can make out some likeness to the heroa of vase-painting. Nevertheless, we may reckon the records thus preserved for *tempietti funerari* already lost by the South-East of Italy as sufficiently balancing solid remains extant in the South-West, including Sicily (for the mainland, at Paestum, P. C. Sestieri, *NS* [1948] pp. 155-165, 172-183, figs. 2-6 and 13-22; for Sicily, at Agrigentum, P. Marconi, *Agrigento* pp. 122-126, figs. 76-80). But at most the count for Calabria and Apulia (three or four structures doubtless *more* elaborate than is really relevant to the heroa which on Apulo-Tarentine vases can be reckoned naiscoid, shrine-like, because of a pediment and a couple of engaged [?] columns), cannot affect the only datum of field archaeology which at present is really pertinent, its having indeed confirmed regional use of pedimented monuments, but only in a form so exceptionally plain by the general standard for Greece that verification killed faith in the "tenanted" heroa of those vases, which were already questionable on other grounds, spatial and even geological.

Any resolute marshalling of the Asia Minor examples of shrines for the dead would make for endlessness and in fact would be pointless here, especially as the funerary shortage disconcertingly striking in South-East Italy is really not of buildings but of portraits. I mean by portraits such sculptures and pictures as in fact, from almost every region of the Hellenic-Hellenistic world, do (given their usual framing) invite comparison with the pavilioned dead of Apulo-Tarentine vases; yet blankly unlike either is the plain type of naiscoid grave marker which Lenormant (*GazArch* 7 172f) reported as *normal* for Tarentum, not without corroboration, as we know; for quite apart from specimens extant from Lucania or represented on Lucanian pottery even Apulian vase-painting reverts to the simple type when cramped for room (fig. 21). But for a certain all-inclusive excess, relevant to a particular aspect of Apulo-Tarentine unrealism, is not the famously pavilion-like tomb at Pisidian Termessos (Heberdey and Wilberg, *ÖJh* 3 190ff, figs. 64ff, Durm, fig. 480) quite citable? So we may allow, especially on the way to a fully conscious break with the assumption of *realistic* subordination — of mere vase-paintings necessarily faithful dependence on its "betters" in scale and solidity — which perhaps was less Pagenstecher's than some senior's, one of the academic taskmasters of his *Unteritalische Grabdenkmäler* (if not after all the *locus classicus* of this attitude should be p. 112 of an earlier work, M. Collignon's *Les statues funéraires dan l'art grec*, where it was suggested that figures in heroa of the vases could be of value for retrieval of wonderful lost things, even things Athenian).

The Termessian monument's interesting excess — interesting for our own concern with *unlikely* overloading of the dead, big and ornate heroa on Apulian vases stultifying (or stultified by) massive stelai at the back of the same pots — is not of course in its gable-over-gable, the pedimented shelter of a pedimented sarcophagus, but rather in the way which this particular dead person gets, without overloading, a third thing, a "token" stele of about the same *proportions* in its own setting as some of those "massively" superfluous ones, this carved in low relief on a pediment of the shelter.

There are more tricks of real stone, quite as pertinently bad for simple faith in the realism of Tarentine paint "rendering" monuments, in material that is also from Asia Minor but has figures and so more likeness to vase-painting; I mean the funerary reliefs more or less delusively bristling with *interior* stelai, as in figs. 3, 5 and 8 of E. Pfuhl's "Das Beiwerk auf den ostgriechischen Grabreliefs" (*JdI* 20 [1905] pp. 51, 52, 54). Some of their relevance (as eye-sharpening foils, in any case, to Italiote vases with excess of monuments; for even better than that, if they can help to give an eye for really computer-inviting variety in our own material) is in a certain difference. While these reliefs also imply an overload, comparable to that of many

Apulian volute-kraters even in the particular terms of it, *portrait* in naiscoid framing (main and entirely manifest essence of a monument of this East Greek sort) but also *shaft* (dubious detail of the background), the comparison works out chiastically, in instructively criss-cross contrast with the vases, on which shaft is not the doubtful term.

For the Apulo-Tarentine heroa enshrining portraits, structures which stand free above ground, freely visitable, there is not yet (as we have begun to see) sufficient confirmation; nor can we have much hope of any to come, given what is already known of the burrowing habit of funerary luxury in *carparo* regions of the southeast of Italy. But the need even there of exterior markers of some kind is something that does not require proof, and practical archaeology though barren of heroa has in fact turned up the shafted sort; I need not refer to Viola's merely Roman finds at Tarentum — see rather (for the same place) B. Neutsch's fig. 29 in *AA* [1956] 236. On neither side in this matter, on the one hand that of the East Greek slabs really naiscoid, really enshrining portraits, but adding unlikely hints of shafts which the burial "lost" (never had!), on the other that of the Apulo-Tarentine pictures showing on one and the same visits to monuments respectively likely (shafted) and unlikely (tenanted heroa), can the excess be quite purposeless, and with regard to most of the vases of this sort and to a whole category of the East Greek reliefs, those for women, it is not very often that we may judge the purpose to be decorative symmetry or pattern-building *ob horrorem vacui*. What is of timeliest interest in the women's reliefs is their contriving to make mere props, or rather eminences, for more or less telling symbols, by means of shafts which in the men's reliefs do suggest merely glimpse of a second tombstone.

Symbols of Marriage on Women's Graves: Their Relationship to the Vases

THE SYMBOLISM THUS exalted is not quite that of the vases, but the codes overlap. Thus if I had not thought that I could safely take for granted the symbolic meaning of fans of all shapes and meterials, to denote wife and mistress of a household, then — along with women off Etruscan sarcophagi, off Roman walls, as well as from within the things really and solidly like the presumably unreal heroa, the little niched monuments from Lilybaeum sheltering pictures — no doubt matrons (or their servants) in these East Greek reliefs would have been adducible. As may be seen now in Pfuhl's fig. 5 and fig. 6; of these two, fig. 5 (where a little servant has the fan) gives the better illustration of shafts like tombstones multiplied to show off household goods (cf. fig. 8); in fig. 6 the broader support looks less sepulchral, but the combination it gives room for, flat box with feet (for trinkets?), fan, kalathos, if now connubial equivalent of one which we have been regarding as nuptial, should be propulsive. As I must promptly try to make it. But no doubt some others are worth a glance: fig. 7 for its bearing on a distinction now practically in question, nuptial ("here's a bride") or connubial ("here's a wife") with which another question is involved there and in other stone reliefs (as in the Lilybaeum pictures also) — whose are the children shown? Or rather, whose offspring? Of the principals? Or are they — however surprisingly little sometimes — their servants? We have been, and still are, so much concerned with aspects prospectively nuptial (not only of burial, in eschatogamy to follow it, but also of burial places, which in what *ELEP* of the living compendiously stands for are also for marrying) that now recognition of the difference, and examples of the connubial alternative, retrospective to life on earth in the household groups of Pfuhl's figs. 7 and 8, are good to have, and not just for the tidiness of symmetry. Even within eschatogamy there is a line to be drawn according to whether it completes an immature person, or renews connubial life. Acquaintance with some versions retrospective, here as in the "Totenmahlreliefs," is indispensable to properly circumspect (and thus effectively eye-sharpening) comparison of the heroa of Italiote vase-painting with solidly real things most suggestively like them, having the deep niches and figured painting which the stones from Tarentum or Metapontum actually lack, as well as an obtrusive symbolism which corresponds in part with that reckoned nuptial (by me) in funerary vase-painting. I mean the wonderful little monuments from Lilybaeum-Marsala which — apart from an inopportunely athletic slip in the submusical department of their symbolism, jumper's weights reported instead of dancer's clappers — were so well published by E. Gabrici in *MonLinc* 33 (1930) cols, 1-112, pls. 1-7 (figs. 5-9 in cols. 51-58 for some of the children, all but invisibly lurking on interior surfaces forward). These structures though so small (most of them being less than a meter in height), are true heroa — none truer, for as a rule one of the two convivial persons, reclining man and seated woman, one and never both, is *named* and hailed as "good hero" or "good heroine."

No doubt our most practical interest in these memorials of persons Punic by descent (worshipers, still, of Tanit) but already Hellenized, even Romanized, concerns the invariable subject's very nearly invariable fringe, a string of things of which most repeat familiar elements of the eschatogamic symbolism of late Apulian red-figure; certainly four of them, mirror, fan, spinner's work-basket (kalathos), timbrel; perhaps dowry-box (only sometimes: see Gabrici's pl. 3, 1, with the keyhole conspicuous, also pl. 3, 2); whether the threefold accessories of energetic dancing, clappers and cymbals besides tambourine, make up for absence of ball as well as of ladder-like *platage* is a question beyond me, but we may let them remind us of Trimalchio's wife, and her readily available accomplishment (Petronius 70.10), not merely of surer Semites, such as Herod's niece and step-daughter.

My "eschatogamic" has of course burnt a bridge, implying that I cannot make out, in the setting of our own problems, any way of return to a teletic, Orphistic, mystic mumbo-jumboish explanation on the vases of their mirrors, fans, kalathoi and other baskets or boxes: torches, timbrels, also the other sort of submusical instrument in the form of a tabbed ladder, yet another in the rhombos rumble-wheel: pretty (and wholesomely exhilarating) balls for catching or bouncing: bump-cakes and other pastries, bunches of grapes: stemmed lavers and the correlative vessels of their use for full bathing, other vessels for serving food or drink, especially the handleless phiale and the kantharos with peculiar, antennae-like, handles. In a provisional conclusion, exposed now for testing by others with all the newest rigor, it is my position that there is nothing in all this, even the cross-headed torches, that does not belong to one or another of the aspects of marriage, the preparations for it, the conventional celebrations of it, the well-being or married life, its wealth, health, and dignity, as estimated according to very shrewdly simple values, making almost as much of provision for the wife's health and good spirits as of that for the husband's capital expenses. It is confessed, in that demand for the most resourcefully modern testing, that this position has discomforts and that they require advertising.

But the first for mention is only a verbal trouble, the insufficiency (not merely the botched-up novelty and ugliness) of the word "eschatogamic" as applied to the chattel-symbolism of Apulo-Tarentine vase-painting, which, because of a value less traceable on the other funerary wares of the West but conspicuous, as we know, in a Theran document culturally linked to the former, is sometimes not pure eschatography. It is not enough to say, it would be rather off the mark to say, that this is only because the ruling optimism of the art first named, something certainly very like the bachelor Swedenborg's hopeful insistence on a *ius amandi coniugem in caelo*, is diluted or complicated by flattery of the hope of posterity, respectful posterity, whose worship of their ancestor the vase-painter is now getting room to show, at least in Apulo-Tarentine shops, increasingly productive of more massive vases, volute kraters and "panathenaic" amphoras. One of the holds to seize here, as well as one of the questions for resourceful control as aforesaid, has to do with an exceptional custom of close burial, *near* if not *at* home, within city walls, known for Tarentum if not yet fully confirmed for the communities it Hellenized. That was not just a matter of its being less trouble (requiring a shorter walk) than at, say, Cumae, to renew a garland or a fillet; did it not encourage sharing with the dead the *rejoicings* of the living? It is not surprising that so many Tarentine vases, so few Campanian ones, show at tombs or heroa what Theran Epikteta desired and secured for the place of her own family's monuments, festive weddings of descendants.

My hammer for this point of great practical importance, especially at the present transition, last chance of help in coping with the worst difficulties of ambiguous symbolism, would be a Campanian picture purely eschatographic, insistently eschatogamic and most circumstantially so, being on one of several vases from the tomb of a man and a woman in the great cemetery of Cumae, pieces decorated quite accordingly, with pleasant revelation of the widow's hope of tracing and rejoining her husband. I mean the obverse of the amphora Naples 127950 (Trendall, *LCS* pl. 188, 2), where (as already mentioned, p. 170) the effect is the very opposite of the impression given by some Apulo-Tarentine vase-paintings, those which show the dead person's getting perfunctory worship from preoccupied lovers. Here the persons flanking (or rather, passing) the dead widow's heroon are neither mourners nor lovers: they are the very powers of eschatogamy, Dionysos and Aphrodite, to whom intently (all but out of her niche in her yearning for reunion) this mortal is appealing. The picture is effective foil, at any rate, for practical use in one of the theological questions presently benchable, problems for the sake of which all the present scrutiny of symbols has to be so searchingly minute, this namely, whether in the work of some Tarentine artists, notably my Holstein-Berge Painter, considerations of earthly love (or of love in general, doubly comforting to reunited couples renewed in their posterity) cause an eviction of mortals from heroa, Aphrodite (or her consort Ares-Mars) usurping their place.

Mortal of Goddess in the Shrines of Apulian Vases?

DOUBTLESS THERE IS very great force in the counter-objection which presses two points home against that imagined substitution, the following. First, that this idea comes shatteringly to grief in its collision with my Holstein-Berge Painter's enshrined *men*: the warrior on his Berkeley krater, for example (pl. 26a), being (arguably) not Aphrodite's consort but just hero-ized mortal in the proper martial setting for an *adult* male, that cuirass (in this view) doing for his phase of life what in the heroa of some other vases a petted animal does symbolically for boyhood; second, that apart from three or four "live attributes" — dove, waterbird, presence Eros, presence of Pan — the marks of Aphrodite are more deceptive than this guess allows for, chattels belonging to, or rather borrowed from, one or the other or both departments of her provision for women, their ripeness and their marriage. I should be the first to acknowledge that our having seen, in some sure context of myth or mere theography, Aphrodite holding a mirror, Aphrodite in possession of a fan, or ball, or "ladder of sounds," or deep cylindrical basket, or open trinket box, or seated on a wardrobe-chest or near a correspondingly big and comprehensive bag, is not enough for perfectly confident recognition of this goddess in an isolated figure provided with some or even all of these things. That a *combination* of her other, *live*, sort of attributes can be altogether irresistible, even enjoyably so, we know, from the attention we had to give to a decidedly peripheral pair of things, not Apulo-Tarentine, the lekanis lids from tomb 313 Lipari (pl. 22) on which the Sicilian Cefalù Painter had depicted a girl's passage from the protection of the gods of celibacy, Artemis and her brother, to the ministrations of a person with a thyrsos who was however no mere nymph or "maenad," being mistress of Aphrodite's whole team, her "dry" bird (dove), her "wet" bird (swan or goose), and Eros, whose timbrel (the second one in the whole continuous sequence developed on the two lids and *final* in a certain chain of symbolism) may prove quite suggestive presently, in connection with obscure subjects of a Tarentine artist, my Holstein-Berge Painter. But in the meantime those Sicilian lids (pl. 22) combine with the two sides of a Lucanian nestoris (*LCS* p. 170, no. 958) to suggest patience, patience at the very least, with an idea which from the Patronian's Elysian point of view is not attractive, namely that at a certain point in the development of Apulo-Tarentine red-figure, an Aphrodite no longer particularly chthonic takes over, to the point even of turning ancestors out of their heroa, in which sometimes she installs herself, sometimes Ares, whose credentials as *de facto* consort (being Homeric and moreover reinforced by the best archaic art, on the François vase) might be thought better than any available for Dionysos in the fifty-fifth Orphic Hymn which (at line 7) describes Aphrodite as his august partner (assessor, throne-sharer, πάρεδρος).

Treated tenderly, developed from the association of Ares with Aphrodite on the Primato Painter's Lucanian nestoris Karlsruhe B7 (well republished by G. Hafner in *CVA* Germany 8, pls. 78-79), with the Cefalù Painter's Sicilian lids left as more or less adjustable features of the matter's background, this idea can be protected from ridicule and even lent some importance, in its bearing on the weakest side of Patroni's theories. The side, that is, which invites reminder that of the myriads (perhaps) of Apulian vases extant in collections and presumed to be grave-goods not more than a few hundreds, at most, came with records of their finding, that accordingly the vast majority of those extant pieces, all but some exceptionally big ones, *show* no tombs, and in the gay manner and more or less Erotic matter of their decoration might seem fitter to be wedding presents (cherishable to the last) rather than grave-goods; that even after Miss Scarfi's extremely thorough work at Monte Sannace, exposing (as we have seen) some sophistry in this line of objection, it can still be said that the contention "it's all funerary, and the love *chiefly* eschatogamic" has never been subjected to the test of counter-exploration, purposefully extensive excavation of *inhabited* sites in upland Apulia.

Nor is it quite impossible to exploit the Sicilian lids on this captious side of the question, though in themselves so surely documents of a chthonic partnership between Aphrodite and Dionysos. The argument would begin with an observation true enough in both its points: "you are concerned with late Apulian red-figure, and the Lucanian nestoris at Karlsruhe which shows Ares intimate with Aphrodite is more directly related to the Apulo-Tarentine tradition of vase-painting than the Sicilian lekanides out of tomb 313 Lipari, which continue to associate her with Dionysos, there as manageress of a certain place of bathing which is preliminary to his paradise, yet not really comparable with the infernal bathrooms, un-Dionysiac, in which Aphrodite appears on Apulian vases in London (Pl. 5) and Leningrad (fig. 4)." But while it is incontestible that the Primato Painter, decorator of the nestoris, has in his debt to the Tarentine Lycurgus Painter, remarked by Trendall (*LCS* p. 159), a relation in the Apulian tradition closer than any claimable for the Cefalù Painter who designed the sequence on the Sicilian lids (pl. 22a-f), it is really more interesting — because bearing on the theory, or guesswork, about "evictions," stealing of heroa, by Aphrodite or Ares — that there are late Apulian vases on which *part* of the irresistible symbolism denoting Aphrodite in that Sicilian sequence is introduced into a woman's heroon. In the light of the distinction already understood, between on the one hand "dead" and essentially ambiguous attributes of Aphrodite, the things she only has as her distributable gifts for women, and on the other her live and normally undistributable belongings, the two birds and the bird-boy, contrast the following vase-paintings, pair with pair.

Richness is rhetorically desirable, for present exposition highly opportune, ambiguity is the interest of the first pair, the obverse picture of the volute krater 568 (Palagi 912) in the Museo Civico of Bologna and the comparable obverse of an amphora from Ceglie del Campo, no. 242/7014 in the Museo Nazionale of Taranto (*CVA* Italy 12 IV Dr, pl. 7, 3, and *CVA* Italy 15 IV Dr, pl. 14, 1). Comparable pictures, because the figures in the respective heroa, though having altogether different attributes, could both pass, perfectly well, for Aphrodite, yet are both ambiguous, for more good (that is, engaging and work-making) reasons than can be set down all at once, but in the first place because none of the live and decisive denoters of Aphrodite is to be seen within either heroon. I have not failed to notice the bird perched on a convolvuloid flower on the shoulder of the Taranto amphora, but am much less sure that the painter meant it for one of Aphrodite's two birds, her dove, than I can be about its perch, recognizable as the bindweed which is a favorite of this ware's naturalism, and in any case the matter of Aphrodite's presence or influence on the shoulder or neck of a vase belongs to a question really separate, except perhaps in regard to my Holstein-Berge Painter. He is such a compulsive repeater, doubling even the (already superfluous) loops of the washpan symbol, that a probable Aphrodite in any of his neck-strips is almost enough for our suspecting a possible one in the heroon below (as on Milan 225, pl. 28 after *CVA* Italy 31 IV D, pl. 6, 1). But of the two pieces of the present pair it is not the Taranto amphora but rather the Bologna krater that recalls his style. Before passing to the other pair of vases, contrastable with the first in their own "live" symbolism, I have to give more precise explanation of the warmth with which for the first pair the ambiguity of their "dead" symbolism and of other traits was welcomed. It will not be quite enough to say that this study has almost reached the stage, at the entrance to an entirely public garden of engaging problems, where its writer's duty must become simply incitement, goading of others to be enterprising in enjoying opportunities, unexpectably curious and attractive, for the newest resources of enquiry. Doubtless, recognition already made of a certain particular debt to Patroni's eschatological insights should be of help towards a more general sense of his good example as rebel against an influence not tending to a finding of pleasure in the resolution of ambituities, namely that of Heydemann's repressive agnosticism: a force still blightingly at work, for incuriosity about the *meanings* of Apulian red-figure is (even by specialists) very readily excused, if no longer preached. But, for me at least, the right last words to say in transition from the heroa, not yet bird-invaded, of Bologna 568 (Pal. 912) and Taranto 242/7014, are not that they (with so many others) belong to the lining of what, for lack of such interest as was shown by one or two pupils of Patroni in all the fluctuating (developing?) variety of *persons* and *things* iin and about such structures, has been an avenue of sleep-walking. What rather is demanded is a certain sacrifice, of my own strong opinions about the obverse pictures of these two vases, to the new rigor, if it exists and I have not absurdly overestimated the powers of good computers well fed, that is, by fully instructed observers enabled to range exhaustively. As far as I can see in regard to some matters among those which are to get their due subsequently, for the proposed "benching" of Aphrodite and not till then, particularly a certain scale of varying importance in her "dead" attributes and certain natural factors of change in the design of funerary vases, I must judge that Aphrodite is to be recognized in the two *aroused* and backward-glancing figures in heroa, the one seated on a wardrobe-chest and the other with an equally telling (and longer established) attribute, the sunshade, paradoxically up and open in her shelter. But my best use for the two pictures, here and perhaps in any recurrence, is to illustrate and accept conditions under which "and please take over!" has to be said instead of "am I not right?" At the same time, for our present transitional business, concerned with some final considerations about the range and also the efficacy of symbolism, it is immensely important to grasp why no one's assistance or approval needs to be asked for the interpretation which we have already accepted of the neatly eloquent sequence of the

Sicilian lekanides of tomb 313 Lipari (pl. 22d-f). The immediate certainty that there the presiding figure with fan and thyrsos is Aphrodite is mainly the result of lavish completeness in providing her most properly character- istic attributes, absolutely sure signs of her when they are all present, dove, waterbird, Eros. But moreover this is reinforced with a most intricate contrivance of supplementary and complementary symbolism: not only the scrupulously *successive* signs of Aphrodite's work for the dead girl who is her present client (first, mirror of nubility, next, laver of cosmetic preparation, then fan of the new status thereby gained, last, timbrel of the wedding festivities), but also other symbols for three more gods, Dionysos, Aphro- dite's here invisible coadjutor, and Aphrodite's friendly opposites, celibate Apollo and virgin Artemis, no longer the living maiden's protectors and only able, now, to commend her to Dionysos and Aphrodite, proper patrons of the beginning of her new existence, its *dis manibus* (if convenient Latin — convenient for its implication of special and particular benevolence — may be borrowed without imputing to Roman thought the idea of eschatogamy).

Of almost inopportunely great interest in the whole setting pertinent (since this would include much more than my tentative Aphrodites at Bologna and Taranto, with their contrastingly "dead" symbolism) are the two vases of the pair which I have held back rather too long. Their obverse pictures have "live" symbolism in the waterbird perched on a woman's lap, but only — in this swan or goose — one-third of the winged company which when mustered fully (as in the Lipari sequence, Sicilian) or with effective substitutes for an absentee (as on the San Simeon pelike, Apulian, of my pl. 16a with live Pan, and much else that is lifeless, to make up for the missing dove) suffices to denote Aphrodite. "Aphrodite, or now rather Leda?" This I borrow from Madame Massoul (*CVA* France 13 p. 75) as at any rate the first of questions to be asked about the new pair, a volute krater in Sevres (Mus. Nat. no. 1, *CVA* France 13, pl. 37, 1 and 3) and another in London Br. Mus. F 286: here pl. 27 after cleaning; in *Antiken und Abend- land* 10 [1961] pl. 18, fig. 34, not yet cleaned, but K. Schauenburg's publi- cation there is important, because of the opportune context provided in his pls. 16 and 17, figs. 31 and 33. The latter illustration is quite exciting in the suggestion offered on this Liverpool bucket of a *paredria* of Aphrodite and Dionysos more literal (D's partner being seated) and more explicit (because she holds a waterbird, not mere pastry, and Eros too is present) than on another abosrbingly interesting bucket in Bologna, 631 (Palagi 708), pl. 29a after *CVA* Italy 12 IV Dr, pl. 35, 17. This Bologna vase I would attribute to the same hand as the one in Liverpool;[1] in any case, the head of its other side, *ibid* pl. 34, 13 should put it in A. Cambitoglou's Amphorae Group (*JHS* 74 p. 120), which for our concern with Aphrodite will be found not much less important in its own curious way ("gone native", we shall discover, on two or three pieces) than my Holstein-Berge Painter's excesses.

---

[1] The Liverpool article is by the Ganymede Painter, but *not* the Bologna one. [A.D.T.]

But Madame Massoul's dilemma, "Leda, or Aphrodite?" is an invitation to stray digressively in a particular Campanian byway, among swan-burdened laps (and these not exclusively female) of the Boston Ready Painter's repertory (cf. Trendall, *LCS* pls. 201-203). At present I can only answer her question with a provisional preference for Aphrodite, until it is shown (by reference to Campanian practice or otherwise) either (1) that the myth about Leda's *violation* belongs (as the myth about Europa's *abduction* certainly does) to one of the kinds of legend within the range observably natural to the funerary purpose of Apulo-Tarentine vase-painting and to its eschatogamic assumptions (for in a matter where far departure counts it is not quite enough that the delightful surprise, *uxorem Iovis esse nescis*, can be appended to both stories). Or (2), that such persons, entertainers or possessors of big waterbirds, are after all not subject to that dilemma, if Apulian symbolism can (with the help of Campanian or Sicilian conventions?) be shown to allow their being simply brides, bathed and ready. At any rate, the propulsive considerations, with (as it were) the effect "yes, you are on a train; no, you are not on the wrong one, for the clearing right for your proposed amenity or facility, the paradise of ampler problems, is already in sight," are those now following.

Questions Raised by the Enshrined Aphrodite: Some Tentative Answers

(1) THE QUESTIONS RAISED by both sorts of enshrined "Aphrodite?" (thus taken together) are in a most precise way timely. For whether the person in the naiskos has an *impressive* allowance of the *lifetime* attributes which often in fact (and no more than a few at a time) do denote the goddess without ever being hers in a fully natural, essential, original sense, or has, instead, a *short* allowance of the live attributes which in their full complement would be conclusive designation of Aphrodite, the problems actually posed by this "evicting?" kind of possible Aphrodite — not to enlarge upon other kinds ambiguous because (again) of isolation or in spite of scampering company not unsuggestive — show the need of some tidily work-promoting arrangement such as my word "benching" at least promises. In themselves, they are quite good enough specimens of the material for arrangement. Given (in pl. 19), as godsend for some preliminary probings or shiftings of it, the Cleveland Aphrodite better than "possible" who is in the open but indeed benched — on the wardrobe chest which (in or out of heroa) has so often interested us as a nuptial symbol, and once at least in a connection

(fig. 8) with the mirror of nubility which she seems to be testing here — moreover with Eros from the other category of her attributes facing her, and just behind her an inscribed shaft *naming* her, who now shall say that it is not a matter for curiosity, not a problem, not a quite general invitation to enterprising research fully resourceful, that within an archaeological situation already casting doubt on the historical reality of even the heroa with domestic groups comparable with persons on Attic stelai there should happen such a change as now we can be invited (at least) to observe? A development, that is, from domestic to divine, one that installs in the heroon a goddess of the affairs — rather variously, love affairs — which are now quite often depicted taking place near such structures. Certain Campanian curiosities, no doubt more than merely the lap-swans already glimpsed in a side-glance prompted by Madame Massoul's hesitations about a krater in Sèvres, need not be distractions from this Apulian problem about fresh encroachments of Aphrodite. That, instead, they are enrichments of it is what we can hope to find, once past the point to and beyond which the following should give headway.

(2) We shall not be ready for even the most modest ushering and benching of personages (an undertaking that only seeks to put Aphrodite and her company, some gods and a prophet, in a light good enough for others' study of their natures and relations according to the purpose of late Apulian red-figure) without now more work, enough for at least opinion-making, upon some symbols in the language of that purpose which though not abstruse still remain difficult. I do not mean merely that there should be no sign in its extensive code of chattels which we have not tried, with some at least provisional result, to read. Perhaps there would be affectation in any more talk of moods and tenses imputable to that language. But there is certainly some practical need of drill in appreciating the means, including means of respect for time, by which symbols can be put to make statements. Let me give a few instances, very few, to avoid trenching on the next chapter's business with great personages. What indeed, with due account taken of considerations of space and time, are we really ready to make of combinations in the things, for the most part seeming quite commonplace, carried by (or besetting) the following?

(a) Hurrying figures, a possible (probable?) Aphrodite and Eros, in my Holstein-Berge Painter's obverse picture for a column-krater in Bologna, 583 (Palagi 955); for her, washpan, deep cylindrical basket (hereinafter d.c.b.) garnished with a flower or two, tainia; for him timbrel and bunch of grapes.

(b) Two hurrying figures (the male in Apulian hat and shirt), by an artist of Cambitoglou's Amphorae Group who is intimately related to Trendall's Baltimore Painter if I am not mistaken,[1] on the obverse of the bell-krater from Ruvo numbered 774 in the Museum of Lecce (my pl. 29b); for him,

---

[1] It is the Patera Painter. [A.D.T.]

mirror(!) and "horned wreath" tainiaed; for her tainiaed thyrsos and d.c.b. carried on phialoid dish as by a female figure (probably Aphrodite?) facing Eros on a bell-krater in Karlsruhe painted by the same hand (B 218, *CVA* Germany 8, pl. 23, 1). This is one of several pairs of persons, not all of them in the same neighborhood of Apulian vase-painting, for which the interpretation "*Ana Aprodita* and Italic Mars" is at least arguable. But that is not this picture's chief importance, which I must leave to develop naturally, out of what we can properly make of the combination thyrsos, basket with overlapping lid, and mirror so strangely held, by a man and as far as possible from its due (?) face.

(3) Six persons, all female (my pl. 28a and b), on my Holstein-Berge Painter's[2] volute krater Milano 225. Obverse in the neck-strip, protome beset by two flowers rather like the spike of bloom garnishing the d.c.b. of the washpan brandisher on Bologna 583 (Palagi, 955), and by two balls recalling Aphrodite's present to Europa (fig. 16) as well as the provision for Andromeda (Naples H. 3225; cf. M. Schmidt, *Der Dareiosmaler und sein Umkreis,* Pl. 13) which are repeated (as if for linkage?) as soon as possible in the picture below. There the woman or goddess in the naiscoid structure holds in the same hand a notably slender wreath and d.c.b. topped with pellets of pastry; the women flanking the heroon or shrine are interestingly distinguished, for while both hold a gabled dowry-box, the mirror of nubility which the woman at the left has in her other hand changes, opposite, to a phiale garnished with an ivy leaf, and from this other woman's right hand, below this dish a swag of great flowers dangles (when no. 4 of the present list has had its turn, even sooner if the transaction on the London askos pl. 7 has not been forgotten, it may seem that this woman on the right is a little nearer marriage). But on the shafted and really sepulchral reverse, with no "possible Aphrodite" to confuse any issue of interpretation, its two women are not less interestingly *uniform*, each hurrying to this graveside with the same three things in hand, timbrel, swag (again) of flowers, and a receptacle which is like the d.c.b. of the obverse only in having a sprinkling of pastries on the lid, and this one matter of very strictly *superficial* likeness between circular basket with amply overlapping lid and angular box with resting lid need not imply similar contents for vessels so elaborately distinguished, especially here where white triangles reinforce the effect of the criss-cross.

The cross is itself matter for a computing-team; I only dare say that it cannot mean any confining contrivance of strings, that evidently it is not quite incompatible with (though not well adapted to) a rounded surface, that it most resembles an effect which perhaps every one has seen in carved wood, but perhaps only tells that the thing's lid does not overlap, that it is not difficult to think of a possible reason for it, interesting if it was

---

[2] The reader is again reminded that the vase is *not* by the same hand as pl. 26 (Berkeley 8.62). [A.D.T.]

important to this symbolism to distinguish basketry from solid wood; especially interesting, if a distinction of content were implied, clothes or bedding in the wicker d.c.b., food in the more solidly wooden box or tray. For that could be given immediate application to the order of things (left to right) in no. 1 of the present list, making sense of it in sufficient accord with the sequence on the Sicilian lid already so much discussed; though on the Bologna column-krater Eros' timbrel does not come (as there) quite last, it is roughly the same tale on both, bathing, *robing* of course next, then festivity. Sense, moreover, that is not in disaccord with the reverse of the Milan volute-krater. There the note (if I may use the word of pictures where none of the three *timbrels* involved are actually struck) would be correspondingly festive; in the Bologna scamper of deities, *two white tainiai,* in the Milan arrival of two women, *three* (including the tainia loosely inserted in the black one more firmly fixed, for mourning, on the tombstone), and *food* not less agreeable than the grapes carried by the Bologna Eros, according to a guess which I can allow to be reasonably penetrating in regard to the Milan boxes. It is not to us a new idea that festive grapes or raisins imply complementary pastries, and if in fact we got it from contemplation of Campanian vase-paintings, there is now the aptest possible illustration of it at hand in Apulo-tarentine work by an artist of the Amphora Group, not unrelated in its own shades of style to the practice of my Holstein-Berge Painter and like him suspectable of theological innovation, very nearly the same one, an adjustment *à trois* between Aphrodite, Dionysos, and Italic Mars. See *CVA* Italy 12 IV Dr, pl. 35, 17, obverse of the Bologna bucket (631; Pal. 708, my pl. 29a) which has on its other side a head in the most strictly characteristic manner of Cambitoglou's Amphora Group. Most characteristic, that is, in the sense of being longer recognized for it (*JHS* 74 [1954] 120) than the nevertheless equally distinctive styles of mantle-folds and diptych in the palaestric reverse of those of its vases, mostly to be kept for the next chapter, which might be thought responsive (by various oddities of "local color" in their obverse pictures) to uplanders' pressure for more recognition of Italic Mars as *complementary* patron, on the male side, of nubile maturity.

But the Bologna bucket, 631 (Pal. 708) does not belong to that "gone native" division of the Amphora Group, where males in the guise of Apulian soldiers or unarmed yet recalling a partly disarmed Lucanian Mars consort with women whose attributes (washpan and thyrsos) invite curiosity. On the front side of the bucket the companion of a person in whom I am quite ready to see Aphrodite, possessing a thyrsos but in this quite like the Sicilian Aphrodite at a place of nuptial bathing (pl. 22e), is unquestionably Dionysos. My present point in regard to this pair is not simply that in a certain festive nexus already familiar yet still in need of emphasis her pie-like pastry *completes* his bunches of grapes. For now (in our situation at no. 3 of a list) I would invite notice, first, of the criss-cross pattern with white reentrants on her "piedish," answering to the ornamentation of the boxes exhibited (rather than offered) by two women at an ancestor's tomb on the reverse of the Milan krater, which do not (in my conjecture) hold things for them to put on or sleep under. And next (Bologna 631 again), of two sorts of flower which garnish her "pie," matching the two sorts seen on the lid of the deep cylindrical basket (this, on the contrary, holding things less edible than wearable?) carried at no. 1 of this list on the Milan column-krater by the woman or goddess whose washpan suggests bathing and the sequel of bathing. One of these blooms is a mere triad of dots; the other is spiky like many flowers of Italy and Sicily, including certain terrestrial orchids which like those of Shakespeare and of Mathew Arnold are of this very color, such as (at their season) one may see from the Palermo-bound train as it climbs up towards Enna. Those little purple orchids are worth this mention, if only as part of a by no means misplaced gesture of moderation; their erotic connotation, though surely no less obvious to Italiote vase-painters than to modern taxonomists and to Shakespeare, preaches scruple, as example of a firm fact which it would be disastrously absurd to stress. Much more important altogether, subject to what computers may do with the widest possible harvesting of relevant evidence, we may hold the foregoing observations good for three conclusions: (a) that the play symbols in four pictures[3] refers to successive stages of the same sort of affair, nuptial; (b) that the chief value of the whole aforesaid series is as means for our distinguishing that affair's anxious beginning (making sure of the dowry and the needful accumulation of *hedna*, making sure of ritual purity and cosmetic perfection) from its later and enjoyable development. Having used the means, having appreciated the parts which the most arbitrary symbol, the sign for bathing so disguised for our own vision by an intensifying conflation, and another the most impenetrably cryptic one, the gabled box for the husband's dowry, so luckily played in launching us to the distinction now arrived at, we are in a position to take some enjoyment for ourselves — in savoring a certain elegance of irony in late Apulian red-figure that is more than just intrinsically *pervasive*, objective of course and inherent yet not failing to flavor any serious concern with it.

Moreover, (c) certain intelligible causes of complication need not be allowed to make distressing confusion. Already we have had much more of Theran Epikteta and Aeschylus' Electra than is enough for useful understanding of ancestors' stake in descendants' love and marriage, and so too of the place which this earthly subject is allowed to gain and even extend

---

[3] Volute krater, Milan, Museo Civico Archaeological No. 225 (*CVA* Italy 31 IVd, pl. 6) observe and reverse; column-krater Bologna, Museo Civico 583 (Palagi No. 955; *CVA* Italy 12 IV Dr, pl. 20.1) obverse; bucket, Bologna, Muser Civico 631 (Palagi No. 708; *CVA* Italy 12 IV Dr, pl. 35.17) obverse.

All from the workshop of the Patera Painter. [A.D.T.]

usurpingly in a funerary art based on unearthly, Elysian, love and union. There may be more difficulty in a certain almost absurd trifle — the "pilled" hamper of the obverse of Milan 225 — than in having to concede that probably nothing suspended for or carried by the living women on the obverse of this vase is an offering for the dead, and that possibly the figure enshrined between them is not an ancestress equipped as Elysian bride but the equipper of all brides, Aphrodite, whom these girls, for merely earthly prospects manifest in everything they carry and even in the suspended scarves and balls, have every reason to court. But what of features perhaps premature, the four white pellets on the central d.c.b.? Assuming, easily enough, that the picture shows Aphrodite, Aphrodite now "in full," courted just under her mere protome by two nubile girls, with so far less effect on the left than of the right (where, cf. pl. 28b, exchange of mirror of mere nubility for garnished phiale and swag of flowers, without surrender of dowry box, might be read, I agree, as "have suitor, but not yet husband"), can we after all retain a distinction that was beginning to seem important for practical alertness to certain messages of timing? Namely, an assumption that the deep cylindrical basket was required for things of a sort soon needed but not soon consumed, *hedna* more substantial than those fit to be stowed in another familiar receptacle, the little trinket box with hinged lid which (as we know from ribands or scarves rather surprisingly emerging) can take some woven things, but not of course clothing or bedding. We saw, or thought we saw, how a master of narrative symbolism (my Holstein-Berge Painter) could make such a clothes-hamper say, just in passing, "here comes the wedding dress," and this by his cleverly contrived contrasts: one which by means of an Eros following suggested that the holder of the basket could well be Aphrodite, another which made it, even as held by this leading figure, *subsequent* to something else in her other hand, sign of the nuptial bath, a third contrast which gave the Eros behind her things to carry which were not preliminary but fully festive. But there is a fourth contrast to face, before the flower-garnished and preliminary d.c.b. of the supposed Aphrodite on the Bologna column-krater and the pastry-topped one of the enshrined person on the Milan volute-krater decorated by the same artist, and in her shrine so much easier, because of the Bologna scamperer and her basket, to read as Aphrodite. Is this formidable, a stultifying clash between bath-time and snack-time, making reckless nonsense of all our fine measurement, now that we have descried (out of place, out of timely sequence too?) four or five edible morsels on the Milan person's basket? Can we reconcile our idea of *its* being (importantly!) a clothes-basket with *their* appearance of having come, in a usurpingly backward trespass, from the garnishing layers on the tops of the criss-crossed boxes of food on the reverse of the same vase? Those should be so *final*, it they are containers of consumable good-cheer which in conjunction with the woman's gay tambourines mark the festive climax — delightful, naturally to that ancestor underground now reasonably sure of the line's further perpetuation — of the simultaneously nuptial affairs which for the same women (as I would not deny) began, rather anxiously, on the other side of the vase. Is this perhaps after all another opportunity for the good work of preaching to computers and their teams, if through sticking much too long to reasoning and measuring — long after all should have been turned over to the new specialists? — we are now at a rather meanly banal impasse?

All I may say at present without breaking off the particular survey undertaken, of a few compositions eminently useful for the exercise naturally last in any study of a symbolism, practice in its grammar of expressive connection, can only make two points. First, that I must allow the various garnishings of symbolic vessels (as well as a certain refusal to garnish) to be important in that grammar, enough so as to require discrimination presently between a good direction for computer-work, and another less worthwhile which would probe the antecedents (in one fork of history) of importunately festal confetti and (in another) of the sudden crop of Christmas comfits which seasonally spreads itself in offices of North American business. Second, that the idea mainly at stake in the present alarm is the hypothesis that almost all the vessels distinguishable in this art's code have their *distinct* values of symbolism: not quite all, because the dish for which the word phiale is fashionable is a vessel of many purposes, for reverent libation, for drinking, for passing food. It is to the meanings of phialai that garnishings should matter most; yet it would be to a phiale, in the Lycurgus Painter's "Naked snack," *impossibly there* serving for a drink and *at the same time* for solid food (pl. 18b), that I would appeal in making the counter-objection, that in the affairs of a wedding nothing, even reason, can prevent food of that kind in that form, a row of comfits, little white pastries or sweetmeats globular or piriform, from appearing on anything that passes and has a surface flat enough to carry such pleasantly pilferable pretty embellishment of the passing.

Methodological Questions;
the "Elep" Hypothesis Again?

THERE IS SOMETHING opportune in all this, and I do not particularly mean an opportunity to snub anyone seeking with just the observation "that's no clothes-hamper under these pills" to demolish a chain of systematically good ideas, nor even the opening for obtrusion of a really captivating coincidence, that Latin recognizes just such comestible "prettifications" of semi-religious occasions (even preparations for a birth) with the word *bellaria.* Rather, it is my own opportunity to offer "good ideas" as a technical term of the new rigor, meaning a proposition worthy of its testing, one that is arresting from the very beginning, able to show some likelihood of its turning out true in good measure and at all events of gaining in propulsive interest, suggestiveness, in the course of the test. We can usefully grant that there must, in practice, be degrees or shades of such goodness. In fact, my own interpretation of the principal picture on the obverse side of the Milan volute-krater no. 225 would have to be rated rather patchily, in part perhaps as "at worst not bad, immensely work-making." But as excellent on the left in its discerning a girl just nubile, if my decidedly confident reading of gabled boxes is not a delusion; for then the mirror shows her ripe for her husband, and the already boxed dowry is information that her parents can well afford her one. On the right, the idea that this other girl is already betrothed is not much less "good" in the present humbly tentative sense. For we know many vase-paintings in which a phiale thus garnished with foliage of the sort interestingly taken up in Latin as *verbena* (and associated at least once with *bellaria* comfits! Plautus, *Truculentus* 2.5e 480) belongs to the preliminaries of marriage, and one in particular (pl. 28) where it might seem to be given, "issued," by an outfitting Eros to a girl just ripe for marriage, at any rate seen showing him the very two things, mirror and dowry box, which in this picture on the obverse of Milan 225, are handled by the figure to left of the heroon or shrine, wherein there sits someone for whom two or three ideas compete. Ancestress, represented as a bride? Lamented maiden aunt, incapable of posterity, but (given that comfit-strewn clothes-hamper) duly consigned to eschatogamy, a compensating union in a further world which Dionysos perhaps owns but Aphrodite seems to manage? Or Aphrodite herself, on whom all cohabitation here or there, depends? How good now, in the technical sense of computer-worthy, is the most novel of these notions, which (unless compromising implications of Italic Mars for males of other heroa forbid?) would let us give the *present* edifice full rank as a shrine? Its occupant would then be the mother and senior partner of the outfitting Eros aforesaid, housed as deserved doubly, by her divinity, by her seniority in the business she shares with him and to which (it is urged) there can be neatly pat allusion in the big but light basket proffered by her right hand? For to penetration sharpened by no. 1 of the current minimal survey of transitional things indispensable to the finally practical best we can hope to do with the symbolism of the vases should not this imply "and here, inside this round wickerwork, I hold what these two girls need *next*"? That is, their respective wedding dresses.

So it is, at any rate, if we may favor the interpretation of the whole vase, that is most flattering to the painter's mastery of narrative symbolism. In this view and estimate of the whole affair he would get great credit for not letting the two twins (or cousins, rather?) proceed quite *pari passu* to the destination of both at the back of the piece, their parent's or grandparent's tomb, which they do after all reach in a dead heat, giving the buried woman (or man, as with Aphrodite in the ex-heroon he is now free to be!) simultaneous good news, by their having now finally festive things to show, for two more descendants' marriages accomplished. But credit only incidentally given as we turn the Milan krater round, allowable meanwhile for adroitly tactical variation quite admirable in a compulsive duplicator but less important for our impression of this instructive artist than the opportunity which we are given to acquit him (with great advantage to our own training?) of the vainest conceivable repetition in this sequel. For that would have been a fair charge against what follows in his reverse picture for the Milan krater's sequence if, by way of "glad and gladdening *showings*" there were not a loophole of escape from our having to register "hysterical foistings of *offerings* madly excessive and unsuitable."

That is not uninteresting, especially to anyone able to flavor the incidental lesson (that we should educate ourselves out of seeing mere showings as offerings duly passing) by ironical recollection of the back of the Leningrad krater St. 420 (pl. 2). There a timbrel like the two at the graveside on Milan 225 was shown at a youth's heroon, in a context that made more than mere showing of the fact of a certain bystander's being seen to hold one. For another picture just above, on the same vase's neck, could be taken as (aware of verification soon to come) I would still take it, for voucher of that very youth's *receipt* of this tambourine in another life. Such an occasion of contrast should be welcome perhaps, if now (as exercise for sometimes idle computers?) contradiction or muddle can be more than ever the subject of briskly remedial scholarship. I can foresee that after more urgent business of reappraisal of an idea which allowed a perhaps compromised, Mars-encumbered, Aphrodite some means nevertheless of seizing the heroa of the dead for herself, there may be better opportunity of advertising that curious example of such confusion which presents itself now in a capacity-incapacity of tambourines for double life, on either side of the grave. There should be something to be made of this notion, given in the first place what we have already accepted, a new and relieving view of heroa (that perhaps they and their visitors need not be so "realistic" as graves and theirs) and then, presently, a certain opportunity to complete this present education in exploitably distinct categories of nuptial symbols. I mean one that is available in the light of quite a constellation of these signs. Luckily with an actual line to divide the "anxious" from the festive category and with an immediate importance, luckier still, for theological questions already incurred in our benching of Aphrodite, and with no shortage moreover of savorable irony, on the London amphora F 332 (obverse, pl. 5 K. Schauenburg, *JdI* 73 [1958] pp. 63-64, fig. 9).

Male Heroa Do Not Show Ares as
Aphrodite's Counterpart

MEANWHILE, AS NOT inconceivable corollary of an exceptionally intrusive yet quite likely Aphrodite, an Italic Mars capable of usurping heroa is rather a nuisance from my chief point of view in regard to Apulo-Tarentine art, which I can only explain as a quite peculiarly intimate compromise between certain gifted Greeks and certain rich neighbors, uncommonly exclusive, therefore of merely random influences. And just so we should treat him. But not of course without such respect as may be deserved by his possible relevance to the provincially dressed man with very paradoxical mirror (not, certainly, for present courting, for he holds it well away from his companion?) in no. 2 of the present short list, the bell-krater in Lecce, no. 774 (pl. 29b).

For this rustic, on the whole and with sufficient consideration of other associates of surmisable Aphrodites in the same Amphorae Group (males only a very little less Italic-looking because more martial, wearing shirts just as gay but helmets instead of an uplander's wooly hat), may be said to *seem* related to the sure Ares also handling a mirror in the presence of an Aphrodite surer than that rustic's companion on a vase of provincial shape ("nestoris") in a picture by the Lucanian Primato Painter. I can imagine certain Campanian enigmas being adduced in an effort to make the utmost of this, groupings in which there is no queer play with a mirror but a man or god in armor is shown consorting with a woman of goddess whose Dionysiac pelt (as in Trendall's *VIE* pl. 18a and also his *LCS* pl. 175, 3) can indeed claim some correspondence with the thyrsos carried on Lecce 774 by the companion of the Apulian man in the fleecy hat, and with another thyrsos which helps to confer on one of the persons attending the helmeted man on a column-krater of the Amphorae Group (*VIR* pl. 32g) her resemblance, in two of her three attributes, to the most notable of all Dionysiac Aphrodites, the thyrsos-bearing, fan-awarding supervisor of baths in the Sicilian Cefalù Painter's Lipari sequence (pl. 22).

One is not comfortable with the idea of a chthonic Aphrodite shared by Dionysos (her landlord, as it were) with an Italic adaptation of an old, Homeric, flame of hers, Ares. Yet in the abstract and apart from the real symbiosis of Apulia with Tarentum and its real accompaniments or consequences in funerary religion and art this is not an inadmissible thought. It is much less thinkable, however, that in the armed youths of some heroa, those edifices not occupied by a person with one or two or three of the attributes capable of denoting Aphrodite, the Tarentine artists meant to depict not the dead man of some future burial in Apulia but an intrusive god. Intrusive in a more violent and anomalous sense than the local goddess Aphrodite-

Aprodita can be thought to be, even if we should have to think of her as in vase-painting an invader of monuments; it would never do to forget K. Schauenburg's demonstration (*RM* 64 [1957] pls. 33-36) that some vases have them almost wide open to her already, with no ancestor, only the back wall's floral ornament, requiring eviction.

Enshrined Aphrodite
Takes over a Former Vacuum:
Ares Has No Place

To us, FRESH from the volute-krater in Milan, the krater "im Kunsthandel" of Schauenburg's pl. 36 is a perfect godsend of timeliness, all the more so for seeming attributable to the same decorator. On the left we are shown a monument of that vacant type in a picture which leaves some curiosities unsatisfied but, as regards the chief of them, propulsively so; the question "are those beflowered monuments for women only?" adds immense interest to excavation reports which have tomb-groups like that of grave 2 at Monte Sannace to publish (Scarfi, *MonLinc* 45 [1961] fig. 9; indeed for a woman, with terra-cottas to be presently not less arresting — in their own connection, with the "anxious-festive distinction — than this tomb's amphora with picture of such a "vacant" monument). But on the right of Schauenburg's pl. 36 not only is it as if Aphrodite, very nearly as we are about to see her (fig. 5) at the cosmetic stage of an august but exceptionally stressful wedding, had blacked out the flowers and moved in; no sooner is she thus enshrined than a love affair develops in her neighborhood, and this is remarkably like a supplement to (or a missing link for?) the affair of the leftward of the two "cousins" on the krater Milan 225.

The Milan vase gave me some practice in *inferring* suitors (from a swag of flowers that supervened, and a garnished phiale that banished the mirror of mere nubility but not the dowry box!); some also in surmising husbands (from the equivalent of modern wedding-cake and modern wedding-music exhibited as matters of good news for a deeply interested ancestor, but also from the final vanishing of persistent dowry boxes when the boxes of food and the festive timbrels made their appearance). This is in notable contrast with the both cousins' having retained (or having refreshed) their betrothal swags. But on Schauenburg's lucky find "im Kunsthandel" the painter *shows*, does not leave to inference, the suitor of the woman who there now so much resembles the more "anxious" of the two nubile girls at Aphrodite's shrine on the Milan vase, the one farther from marriage, having only the barest certification of ripeness and readiness, mirror and dowry. There is no very momentous point to be made of the present girl's wearier waiting at the present shrine, since at the back of the same vase, Schauenburg's krater, there is a girl at the mere monument not less languidly posed. But the former does answer very nicely to the suitor's brisk stride as he comes in towards her from the right, and whatever it may be that he has in his left hand (tainised palm of highly "eligible" victor?) there can be no doubt of the destination and perfect timeliness of the swag of great flowers in the other.

It must now seem plainer than ever that we can acknowledge an enshrined Aphrodite on Apulian vases (if there she just takes over a traditional vacuum) without now having to suspect that their heroized men are breaking the tradition which they are seen continuing. No doubt the false half of the impression "there is Aphrodite and here is martial Italy's naturally glad welcome of her old Ares" can be made to pay for brief lodging, if it very soon causes profitable reflection on the fundamental data of all study of late Apulian red-figure, namely Apulo-Tarentine interdependence and the great strength and reach of Tarentum's influence for diffusion of the funerary art which resulted from accommodation to that symbiosis. The notion of the rustic Mars of Lucania or Campania reaching and penetrating some crack in the cement is really fatuous, but it is by no means a waste of time to test it objectively by Trendall's documentation of the effect of Apulo-Tarentine vase-painting on Lucanian, Campanian, and even Sicilian red-figure (*LCS* pp. 158-165, 452-453, 579) The best lecturer and demonstrator on what is after all a question of traffic would be the transvestite Eros of a Sicilian master-piece (pl. 22d-f), if he could step out of the elegance and wit of his setting (which includes pl. 22a-c) to point to his bonnet and say "if you don't understand how an Apulian fad, even a crass one, could infect Tarentine art and the prestige of Tarentine example diffuse it, look here!"

The Marriage of Hades and Persephone

(4) FOR END OF what I started and must not delay to finish, a list of groupings indispensable for the minimum experience of *construction* in the symbolism pertinent to an affair humbly practical, task of merely menial clearing and benching for others' better use of opportunities in, now, the *theography* of Apulo-Tarentine red-figure, may I choose the three figures seated in the obverse "basement" of the London amphora F 332 (pl. 5) rather than the two scamperings on the obverse of a bell-krater in Karlsruhe (B 215, *CVA* Germany 9, pl. 67)? I could not afford the choice if it meant sacrificing altogether the evident fitness of the man and woman of the

Karlsruhe vase to supervene after the two women who appeared – and reappeared – on the Milan volute-krater no. 225 (pl. 28). So it is fair to call attention in passing to the relevance of Karlsruhe B 215 in regard to the drill in divining unseen suitors or husbands which Milan 225 let us practice, as well as the bearing of both vases upon a matter which came in view at the beginning of this listing – mysterious hurry in Apulo-Tarentine vase-painting (for Gerhard of course, especially in no. 2 where the man's mirror invites teletic fancies, it would have been mystical). On the Karlsruhe vase it is almost as if either one of the two simultaneous brides of the Milan krater had chosen her husband, not her co-bride, to accompany her to the ancestor's grave, so that the signalling of her good news for the dead, the solemnization of her marriage, could well *dispense* with one-third of the appropriately festive and final signs, the timbrel, *retaining* swag of flowers and criss-crossed box of pastry as quite enough. But that is too much of an improvisation to be applauded as a good idea in the practical sense just distinguished. Yet it becomes something to work with if it may be revised to say "enough in the circumstances, the quasi-grammatical circumstances given by what the bridegroom has, first the sapling of respect and second the garnished phiale of betrothal, for a much less fanciful signal, from shop to bereaved customer, of rich and *orderly* nuptial allusion."

Need I add, nuptial in this ware's commoner and eschatogamic sense? That is, like all that makes up now the meaning of the two principal pictures on the obverse side of the London amphora F 332 (pl. 5a): not only the marriage of Persephone, but also the dead man and dead woman in Love's care below; what, on the other side of the vase (pl. 5b) certifies the lovers dead (a tombstone and survivors) is less to my present point than the respect in which the symbolic apparatus of the group at rest on the amphora resembles that of the hurrying pair on the Karlsruhe bell-krater. For it must not go without further remark how closely, through their women's attributes, criss-crossed box and swag of flowers at Karlsruhe, similar box and timbrel in London, both these Elysian scenes are bound up to one *not* Elysian on the Milan volute-krater No. 225 (pl. 28) where the earthly brides showing themselves at an ancestor's tomb have each all three things, swag, box, tambourine. This of course should be one more occasion for steadying use of the advantage, the hold which we possess through having sought a concretely historical apprehension of late Apulo-Tarentine vase-painting, done for upland burials by Greeks quite incapable of not enjoying themselves in any art they had to make, as also of not exploiting every opportunity to please, to flatter, the affluent living.

It is a pity that the most concrete manner of closing on this hold requires rather oracular directions, if what I have to say is that Aphrodite, Aphrodite simply and not some specialist for undertakers like the Roman Libitina, is naturally and inevitably cardinal to this Apulo-Tarentine art for the dead – *such* dead, peculiarly loving in their own world and (by a less peculiar desire of posterity) love-encouraging in this other. At any rate, upon the Power on which it all turns no captious rule objecting anachorism, no "down with you and stay chthonic," can be enforced by academic interpretation of the vases, however secure this may after all be in its assumption that no Apulian red-figure vase was bought for a wedding and could have spent some small fraction of its long existence decorating a house of the living. As those to whose personal environment Apulian vases visibly or lurkingly belong are among the readiest to assume; "tutti essi hanno *carattere* funebre, e quand' anche non sapessimo che derivano tutti da tombe" are words all the more interesting for their writer and their place, M. A. Micalella, *Apulia* 3 (1912) p. 4.

Thus no one whose main undertaking is to defend Patroni's insights can afford to underrate the bewilderment and irritation only too naturally resulting from the shift sooner or later required of the defense, to unexpected insistence that on funerary vases of various sorts for various reasons, perhaps not quite all comprised in those which Athenian Aeschylus and Theran Epikteta would have understood so well, nuptial love may sometimes appear as simply general, not eschatogamic: this to an extent which Patroni's immediate pupils did not, in their time at the beginning of the present century, fully appreciate. It would be absurdly flighty if I were to make the present feast of arrestingly suggestive detail (pl. 5a and b) on the quasi-panathenaic amphora London F 332 an excuse for quite digressive rambles through the extensive typology of another kind of Apulian amphora, the pelike, where on some very elaborate examples unearthly love is accommodated at the back of the vase, in demeaning contrast with earthly love or love in general at the front (e.g. Torino 4149 as published by Felice Gino Lo Porto in *CVA* Italy 32 IV D, pls. 13-15 and p. 9, with its two sides distinguished, not unmomentously for Italiote studies, as "nuziale" and "elisio-dionisiaca"). However, after our recent poring over tambourines, again and again found obtruded as nuptially *final* things, and with our continuing preoccupation with Aphrodite as a person to be recognized and correctly related, given never less than her full due of interest wherever she occurs on this pottery, there might be a good exercise in counting, and accounting for, the Aphrodites on that pelike at its "merely nuptial" front (four altogether? two of them with a tambourine, one more tritely denoted, benched on a wardrobe chest?).

A good one, at any rate, for setting to any eyes there may be which demand further training for the scarcely athletic feats of recognition or response to timing required for reading what is said with symbolism (Aphrodite's own) in the three most legible of the four compositions on the London amphora F 332. For present purposes with those three, a convenient order of introduction would begin: (1) the pair of "finished" mortals on whom perhaps one might say (if he cannot deny himself the nearly worthless flourish) that Love is seen to have flowered for them (pl. 5a): what is really there to be remarked is rather that thanks to this manifest agent of Aphrodite they are in possession of the final things of their affair of mutual completion in a second life, the very things addressed to the dead girl and her eschatogam by the two maidens surviving opposite, timbrel, box of pastry, bunch of grapes (pl. 5b). (2) The scene (pl. 5a), not quite so formally final, but no less eschatogamic, since the principals are Hades and Persephone, just above the one first taken. It is quite important to remember that unless the present state of the Naples Nekyia (fig. 11) is thoroughly untrustworthy, there does exist, for their affair too, a more serenely conclusive ending, told in terms of chattel-symbolism very much like the combination so hard worked in the two low strips on the London amphora; but the timbrel has been hung up, the pastry has been unboxed and dished up, the grapes have yielded wine. Without the Naples Nekyia (including its figure of Orpheus) as foil, full response to the time-play of the London amphora is scarcely possible. At least, without the contrast of my fig. 11 for the Naples vase to my pl. 5 for the London vase, reinforced by my fig. 6 for evidence at Leningrad that there was someone, in fact the painter of that London piece, who knew an Orpheus resident and *available* for the epithalamium of Hades and Persephone, the impression made by these merest preliminaries in a now double bathroom, with Aphrodite still seated for some remainder of cosmetic niceties and even Hermes lingering, would not have been so useful. Perhaps it might go without saying that to show, more than show, to make acutely felt, the usefulness of attention to symbolism, belongs to the business of the present transition to larger matters, such as (for example in passing) may soon loom from the present artist's picture (fig. 6) of a younger and still bachelor Hades letting a very similar Aphrodite – on duty in an infernal laver yet inseparable from an open parasol – lecture the all-influential prophet Orpheus and his dead Eurydice on the timely advantage, for them, of eschatogamy. But at all events one has not exhausted the lessons of the London bathroom when he has mastered its beautifully analytical demonstration of the washpan symbol for *perfection* of cosmetic purity, here *put* under a laver for truth to a special function of scooping out water and sluicing the head and body, but *happening* to be opposite a footbath much more properly entitled to *its* arched handles, this for our own grasp now of the symbol's telling element of untruth – telling for the idea of perfect thoroughness, head and foot, false to the actual form of scores of extant scoops, all with a single axial handle. Should there not be this further result, a keen feeling of humble gratitude for one of those lucky escapes from fatuity which can reward determination to respect both what is systematic in the functional symbolism of Apulo-Tarentine eschatography and what is organically personal in the ways of the eschatographer? Just as it should be impossible for anyone accustomed to the professional dialect and private propensities of another recent acquaintance, the Holstein-Berge Painter, to be snared by a now respectably traditional but quite anachronistic interpretation of part of my plate of amphora Naples H 1765 as Paris (and the pastoral dog of his earlier life) settled by Hermes in Helen's Sparta bathroom, so "Preparations for Persephone's Leave of Absence," a still current titling of picture 2 on the London amphora, should be too desperately difficult for acceptance by anyone duly guarded. That is, anyone who has fully analyzed and duly related pictures 1 and 2 on the London amphora (pl. 5a), and knows moreover that they are works of a man firmly anchored to the idea of eschatogamy, by no means a natural truant to love in general, the Painter of London F 332 being in fact the very person who paid the most eloquent of all tribute to the loveliness of Hades' realm, Aphrodite's *detention* of intruding Orpheus on Leningrad St. 498 (fig. 6).

It would however be very rash indeed to infer that the vase-paintings of Tarentum did not know of any return of Persephone to her mother, or even that for reasons indeed fully sufficient in themselves, for one reason the legend's element of savagely unnatural "momism" (if for the classic case I may economize with the trenchancy of Wylie's word), but for one much graver its mockery of a fabulous investment of optimism, they just shut their minds to it. I know that it is not impossible that there was even drastic tampering with the Eleusinian myth by certain eschatographers, and because this possibility depends on a matter of symbolism, shifts of meaning for the cross-headed torch, it must have brief consideration, if I am not to shirk some constructive, sufficiently exact and work-promoting, admission of the *limits* of present penetration into the code's system of eschatogamic signs. But much more urgent is the hermeneutic matter of principle (or principles, for it is rather complicated) arrestingly raised for us by Konrad Schauenburg in his comments on a vase-painting which deserves collation with the preliminaries of Kore's wedding as they are shown on the obverse of London F 332. This is the most unrapelike "Raub der Kore" in Geneva which he published in *JdI* 73 (1958) pp. 57-58, fig. 6 (cf. my pl. 14).[1]

Reconsideration of the Iphigenia Krater in the Light of Recent Discoveries

WE HAVE HAD some preparation for features of it which understandably troubled Schauenburg, in our own noting of the very nearly cordial behavior of celibate Apollo and Artemis at the nuptial preparations of a dead girl in a masterpiece, both erudite and sensitve, of the Cefalù Painter, a Siciliote Greek (pl. 22a and b). Accordingly, if the first principle of objectivity for

---

[1] Much of this vase has gone in the process of cleaning. [A.D.T.]

our interpretation of Tarentine vase-painting for bereaved Apulians trusting in *Aprodita* should be this, never to underrate the Greekness of Tarentines, their Greek canniness in trade with quite exacting neighbors as well as the fulness of their Greek culture and of their share of mere nature's good gifts to Greeks, then we can begin by being glad that at Geneva we need not starve the surely participant Apollo of meaning, by having to treat him "nür als Fullfigur, aus einem anderen Zusammenhang übernommen," and can go on to acknowledge that the whole hellward sendoff, better than cordial, with Apollo, Artemis and above all Demeter approving, does presuppose Persephone's return to Olympus and her mother. Not necessarily, be it remarked, more than one return in either direction. The proper inference is not "see, for all the heavy load of *Aprodita*-blest eschatogamy on half of London F 332 (pl. 5a), how Geneva MAH 15043 shows that even Apulian Persephone is subject to the annual back-and-forth of Eleusinian tradition and the Homeric *Hymn*." Rather it would be this, that it is one and the same thing, a funerary art's commitment to loving union after death, which for us on the one hand forbids even the most contemptuous, cat-and-mouse, dallying with any alternative to the simplest idea of Aphrodite's cosmetic work for Persephone and Hades on the London amphora, yet for the Tarentine potters catering to Apulians made the legend of her return to Olympus quite usable — as an opportunity to show gods of celibacy blessing her resumption of infernal marriage and Eros himself impelling Demeter (pl. 14 upper right) to belatedly eager performance of the torch-work expected of a bride's mother (as by Clytaemnestra of herself according to line 732 of Euripides' *Aulidensis*; her first thought, on hearing herself dismissed from the place of her daughter's "wedding" is τίς δ'ἀνασχήσει φλόγα).

We undertook to give the three most interestingly definite of the four large pictures of London F 332 (pl. 5a and b) a certain serial consideration. But before our exploiting no. 3, the graveside group on the reverse, not necessarily a stale anticlimax because it portrays the earthly senders of the good things shown as duly delivered in the corresponding strip of the obverse, I must not fail to say for what I most value K. Schauenburg's publication of the Geneva amphora MAN 15043. This is its suggesting the afterthought, perhaps quite preciously corrective, that anyone's taking the Geneva Apollo for an insipid stopgap may be the merest venial oversight in comparison with my own failure to recognize one more cosmetic Aphrodite on the Iphigenia krater in Leningrad (fig. 2), in the person possessing two of the things which notoriously can be attributes to denote her, and surrounded by others of more or less the same order. This was the woman, holding complexion-saving parasol and deep cylindrical basket, found sitting on the abverse of Leningrad St. 420 among Taurians and various ablutionary vessels, lavers and three-handled waterpots, perhaps capable of double meaning anywhere in this irony-loving art but for once not obviously nuptial. Like another vessel also to be seen, Iphigenia's sluicing scoop for use at such lavers, shown as in reserve in the little temple of her goddess, they were for the grimmest possible work, lustration before human sacrifice. It once seemed (p. 190, so before certain distinctions recently drawn) reasonable to take the hint that seemed to be offered by a certain symmetry in the foreground.

There on the one hand, to our right, a Taurian man held out his own festal wreath to one of Artemis' deer in an unmistakable offer of festive refreshment, an invitation to nibble. To our left that woman with the parasol, not less involved in the sinister feast (by wreath handled and hydria of lustration nearly sat on), held out her basket to a Taurian man, in a certain sense the most distinguished of the three present, the most formidable anyhow, fully armed, with spear and shield. Invitation to share its contents in a holiday picnic? That idea had not then to cope with the challenge to be more concrete which now comes from containers of a *contrasting* sort in both the low pictures (pl. 5a and b) on the London amphora F 332 with the backing of perhaps countless criss-crossed receptacles of *food* solider boxes or trays. Backing, even, of some deep cylindrical baskets, notably the one that in a work of my Holstein-Berge Painter which is characteristic of his three zeals (for Aphrodite, for reduplication, for telling order) came, in a certain streak of nuptial symbolism, just where the basket for a change of clothes should come; that is, *before* two symbols of final festivity and *after* this painter's equivalent of the very symbol of thorough purification seen standing for Iphigenia's principal duty in the Leningrad picture, the HBP's typical liberty of alternation (doubling the loops of the pan's handles) working as actual reinforcement of the disturbing likeness. For it is especially his Aphrodite of Milan 225 with washpan and clothes hamper that now suggests a little discontent with what was guessed, namely that this other craftsman's professional obsession with customers' *Aprodita,* natural enough, might fully account in the hostess of a Tauric picnic for two traits like Aphrodite's (parasol and basket) and one like a Danaid's (the hydria nearly sat on); it being true (as I still agree) that the painter of the Iphigenia krater (fig. 2, pl. 2,) was also the decorator of one of the most phenomenal symptoms of Western devotion to this goddess, the krater Leningrad St. 426 which more emphatically than any other work of painting or sculpture serves notice of the West's cancellation of the Danaid's impunity for their offense against Aphrodite (pls. 4a and b, fig. 4). We have at any rate to recognize a really wholesome crisis of method in what finer discrimination of rather similar symbols has brought about, a conflict of good ideas, "good" in the new and modest sense.

What does the new rigor require of us in regard to the fresher one, this? "In an affair where concreteness is everything, a task of interpretation, your attempt at it, though not unexemplary in its rather close scrutiny of a foreground, was not nearly concrete enough. Even in that part of the Tauric scene (fig 2) it could suggest no connection, no use, for the waterpot which is too near the supposed 'hostess' not to be hers, and in some way, important to the whole nexus, definitely functional. In its observation of her still closer belongings, the things held, there was quite a balance of inattention. No one with a mind for the most relevant precedent, the sunshade seen among the spectator gods of the east frieze of the Parthenon, could lightly make a mere 'Aphroditoid' of a high personage parasoled on a great religious occasion. Next, and surely worse: anyone imputing a picnic lunch to the receptacle extended in her other hand is either unobservant of its obvious material, wickerwork, or an irresponsible sloven indifferent to an actual and quite promising effort to distinguish kinds of container, tending already to show that food comes in X-marked trays or boxes, and only wool or woolens in baskets, open and flaring for wool unworked, closed and cylindrical for textile goods. Here, then, was negligence of symbols inducing blindness to persons. For while the "distinguished" Taurian is doubtless King Thoas, if not too young for that part, it would be an affront to the text of the play (630-632 on a cosmetic matter) to guess that his neighbor was only his Queen, with their lunch. This figure, *once connected with her cosmetic hydria* (cf. figs. 6, 11), can only be Aphrodite, in her funerary and eschatogamic aspect saving for Thoas, not such a savage after all as long as she is there to bless his victims with her happy, so naturally happy, eternities."

Should I hope for the new rigor's leave to laugh at this, or is it just that a problem has improved, all the prettier for maturity, which now has ripened it to a dilemma: an overworked craftsman's significantly Aphroditoid wife for a Thoas rejuvenated, or a not less significantly interpolated Aprodita? Served (as just now) with a coolly businesslike reference to lines of the *IT* which brings Iphigenia's scrupulous κόσμος for her dead victims to mind and that word "cosmetic" to mouth, we could not expect much success in deprecating the new suggestion as objective scholarship in a seizure of self-parody, over-interpretation done at some somehow vicious opposite of certain attitudes to funerary vase-painting which are only too actually torpid, in various respects and degrees failing in both sympathy for the bereaved and empathy for their purveyors, the merchants and the decorators of pottery for burial — besides altogether neglecting the last as *persons,* individuals who were contemporary and neighbors of one another and (in the very nature of their art for the peculiar exigencies of Apulian burials) uncommonly harnessed to a single drive, yet with the traits and predilections which already have begun to attract absorbed connoisseurship. However, with all the right resistance ready for any invitation to wince now at my own past phrases in preparation for "pretty" problems, I have to recognize that in the actual situation there are, for the best sense imputable to the first half of the question which was just asked, certain alternative words. Should an all but octogenarian allow himself any hope of surviving to see the exhaustiveness of the new, accelerated, research either confirm or stultify a proposable scale of receptacles varying in shape according to *successive* function in the serious-to-festive course of weddings earthly or unearthly, the mere proposal of which, cosmetic with a vengeance, would so notably increase the practical fascination, as of a "problem picture" inviting work, exerted by the Tauric scene on the obverse side of the volute krater St. 420 in Leningrad? (fig. 2).

More Reconsiderations—
The Munich Krater Re-examined

I THINK THAT this can be judged a quite generally useful question, even if the right answer, allowing both for the certainly great importance of the idea's bearings and for its test's long laborious difficulty, should have to be "*alas, perhaps not.*" There can be quite a welcome for the first of the three words if it implies a reflective preestimate *awarding* that importance, not just enthusiasm for the elegance of certain favorable patterns within the configuration of evidence.

Doubtless one might claim that among the minor amenities of our whole great field, Classical Studies, none is much more elegant than the prettily compelling evidence of a thing unseen which causes us to divine a dowry in the "sharp box," whether sharp-edged between two gables as commonly in Attic and Apulian vase-paintings, or sharp to a point as in the astounding byway of immensely distant connection discovered in Kyrle M. Phillips' collation of an Attic vase with medieval manuscripts of later (cf. once more Phillips' article and illustrations, *AJA* 72 [1968] pp. 18-20, pls. 6 and 7, figs. 16 and 17 and pl. 17, figs. 53 and 55). But may the divined truth (as I grant it is) claim importance, even in that application of it which upset a traditional interpretation that on the London calyx-krater F 272 had mistaken a grieving widow whose name was not many centimeters away, Laodameia, and so loyalest of all *young* wives, for an incestuously love-sick stepmother, Phaedra. Momentous importance, making a clearance of false and obstructive pedantry, would certainly have been easier to claim if what is doubtless true – that the meaning corrected would have outraged eschatogamic sentiment – had been easier to argue than actually it is in face of two awkward considerations, of which the second is certainly concretely practical. I must acknowledge, first, that for Hellenistic sarcophagi at any rate there was no ban of sentiment keeping Phaedra off; next, that given the system and scale of the grandest Apulian burials we cannot rule that some play of contrast in the tomb's planned eschatography might not have let this bad wife in. We have to be in the most exact sense circumspect in all thought given to a topic which is certainly before us and demanding some, namely fitness or (more objectively) *tact* in the mythography designed at Tarentum for the exceptionally sumptuous and roomy buryings customary among its best customers, rich pastoral Apulians. I hardly need to hammer at the truism which has never needed any special Etruscan course in it to make it more familiar, the principle that worse can be good consolation for bad. There is more force, circumstantial, in the reflection suggested by particular horrors (Medea's havoc in two families, also the fate of Lycurgus' wife and children) which came to light in Caroline Bonaparte's mining of Apulian Canosa together with the great classic of reunion eschatography (pl. 1a), the "Happy Family, Happy Again" that in Munich still keeps those others company (Jahn, nos. 849, 810, 853) and was from the same room of the same tomb as the pregnantly sinister picture which besides exhibiting two of Medea's crimes contrives to suggest her impunity for all of them (FR 2, p. 161, pl. 91). In fact the great interest of the Laodameia krater in London, its useful bearing on more important compositions in which a really religious question turns on some fine shade of the progressive spectrum of symbolism, lies in this, that the right interpretation of the bedroom scene is open to counterattack from the Phaedran side of the dispute, quite pretentious in its means of objection to the argument from the dowry box visibly awaiting disposal, sign of a fresher wife than Phaedra (Trendall, *SIVP*, pl. A at p. 16). For it can adduce lexica, Hesychius' and the *Etymologicum Magnum,* for what they say about Κοιτίς, decidedly a box for *matrons*' bedrooms if the compilers of the *EM* were right in explaining it by Κοιταζόμεναι, and so as the place where the personal jewelry of a woman entitled by age and status to wear it would spend every night. But this onset can, as we shall see, be so decisively routed by the right notion about the box in Laodameia's room that it will seem fair to let notions more provisional, about the position of other things in the anxious-to-festive scale of nuptial symbols, have some benefit (pending computer work) from an *aristeia* of this thing, gabled box for husband's dowry, so very well able to defend its own place in the early and thoughtfully serious part of the matter's temporal scale. At this turn, of course, even the most parenthetical evidence of trust in, and coming appeal to, the new rigor's newest resources implies confession. It amounts to admission that this scale itself belongs to the same category − of things at best obscurely evident − as the meanings of some of its constituent or collateral items, the cross-head torch, the horned wreath, the bandoliers and bracelets of wool, the "ladder of sounds" even also, if only in certain circumstances, the particular signals intended by representations of things quite lucidly self-explaining, mirrors, sluicers. Thus, some preliminary hint of what (for any practical issues) may be at stake is indispensable.

This can best be given if I myself adduce three things. First, let us have once more the column-krater Bologna 583 (Pal. 955) to redisplay its not unverifiable glimpse, brief and electric but valuable, of the actual run of that scale. The symbol of nuptial bathing is followed immediately (in Aphrodite's other hand) by a basket of the sort that should be symbol of nuptial vesting, itself followed (to close) by timbrel and grapes (no pastry, so only two-thirds of the conventional symbolism of wedding festivity). I must hope that leave for this will let me include reference, at least, to the even more strikingly final timbrel of another (but Sicilian) Eros attached to another Aphrodite in another serial matter that also begins with bathing. Next, for stronger and more concentrated light on the scale (at its "far" end) we should take advantage of a cup in Bologna 669 (Pal. 841) (*CVA* It. 12 IV D r, pl. 33, 8). Inside it there is a figure of Nike, Happy Ending indeed, with all three signs for the final festivity of marriage: besides timbrel and grapes now some pastry, and this in mercifully plain sight, not inferred from (wicker-denying?) diagonals on a closed box but exposed in a criss-crossed tray. This is the place, before an ordeal of difficulty beginning with the next and final exhibit, for the present hypothesis to plead good works.

Certainly, it has already been good for something, namely improvement of two tolerably good ideas. It was remarked earlier, not unpropulsively then, that in the little procession on the first of my present exhibits (Bologna 583, Pal. 955) it was as if the woman of a certain newly published lid in Heidelberg were being steered by that lid's own Eros to the tryst with a man (brandishing such a pan as hers) depicted on a newly excavated bell-krater in Bari 20217 (Miss Scarfi's fig. 56, col. 213, *MonLinc* 45). Having in the meantime detected on the Bologna piece the style of one given uncommonly to Aphrodite, my Holstein-Berge Painter, we have now learned that "woman" would be an unguarded word for the probable goddess who is ahead of Eros in that procession. Moreover, if the tentative scale of nuptial stages and corresponding symbols was not mistaken, we are now finding that the former comparison has broken in pieces, because the old connection of two terms, pan and container, has come apart. What pan and clothes-basket meant in Aphrodite's two hands is not what criss-crossed pastry-box and pan mean as divided between two lovers on the bell-krater from Miss Scarfi's excavations, and a certain similarity of ingredients still remaining between the two compositions, in the Bari man's having in his other hand what came last in the Bologna streak of symbols, bunch of grapes as dangled by Eros there, only reinforces the general difference of the respective messages; that is, between the Bologna krater's telling us "according to Aphrodite's rules, the bride will have to bathe scrupulously and then vest elaborately, but general festivity and the principals' beginning of love will follow" and the Bari krater's "now those two can enjoy themselves; to judge by what the Munich widower (pl. 1) had to get in the ante-region (fig. 1b), bunch of grapes and bath-certificate, just like that pan, these lovers are wife and husband reunited."

Especially because these latest afterthoughts, suggested about familiar objects in Bari and Bologna by that emerging theory of a scale, have a bearing on the difficulties and the opportunities of the "Reunion" (or "Nekyia") krater in Munich, an eschatographic monument of the highest order of interest, they now have certainly earned a welcome. It should not be less warm than that deserved by another afterthought which was similarly prompted, the dilemma "Taurian hostess, amusingly, or (through what her quite special basket does to the already warning parasol) Aphrodite, solemnly and not inappropriately?" by which the interest of an illustration of Euripides' *IT* (fig. 2) was enriched: this so measurably, in a new degree beyond its almost banter-deserving values for pleasure of ἀναγνώρισις, mere or nostalgic ("in Chipps' form, remember, that hot May?"). It will now be of some practical importance, for others' convenience (those drawn, as we must hope, to put their better resources to a test of the hypothesis in question), to indicate the two respects, in regard to a certain basket, in regard to a couple of sluicing-pans, in which there is an *exploitable* connection between the two improvements. For me this should be cue for adducing the promised third exhibit, in what of course is not its first appearance here: namely the Dionysiac strip (fig. 1b) of the "Reunion" krater in Munich in its organic connection (if one can be found) with the rest of the vase (pl. 1a-b), but anyhow in relation to possibly embarrassing development of a fact which the Bari bell-krater (20217) from tomb 17 at M. Sannace and the Munich strip combine to establish, our spectrum's uroboric capacity for uniting head and tail; both extremes of a scale of symbols supposedly *serial* are only too easily caught occurring at the same moment of a single affair (initial) pan with final pastry-box and final grapes in the Bari love-affair, pan with grapes and a personification of final success in the Munich widower's effective preparations for reunion.

It is not *round* the Munich krater (pl. 1, fig. 1), in a B to A direction according to the usual notation for this vase, heroon to hellscape, that there is any difficulty of tracing connection. Especially after what was made out in some other neckstrips of volute-kraters, it is not hard to suppose that the mortal in the Dionysiac limbo is being prepared for his reappearance on the other side of the vase at the judicial and executive heart of his second world, there to be reunited formally with wife and son, and though both ends of the scale of renuptial symbols are shown, here at any rate they have not been tied in an obstructive knot. No objection to the phrase "bath certificate," no difficulty with its idea, can be excuse for supposing that the satyr's brandished pan means interference ("the man is not even clean yet") with Happy Ending's provision of the wreath with which this mortal will crown himself on the other side, and that it also portends veto of the gift to follow, the bunch of grapes from our standpoint almost uncomfortably apt; dizzying in the trick it plays us of recalling *not only* Apulo-Tarentine pictures just recently reviewed — the Bologna Nike and the grapes that came with her "pie" and timbrel, also the Bari lovers and the things (including a brandished pan) of their picnic, as well as the London couple with grapes, pastry-box and timbrel at a more settled stage of their affair than Hades and Persephone in theirs just above, where the picture of them (pl. 5a) in comparison with the Naples Nekyia (fig. 11, with pastry, wine and timbrel provided) amounts only to a bath certificate, double. For the Munich "trauma room," taken with its joyful sequel (pl. 1b) on the other side of the Munich krater, cannot but remind us of a late Campanian vase-painting in Vienna which was decorated by Trendall's Rio Painter (pl. 21) most uncanny of all reunion groups, where the entranced, all but frozen widower somehow retains firm hold (in yet another conjunction of opposites?) of a bunch of grapes and a mirror, while the dressy little boy, a rather formal figure in comparison with the toy-trundling Munich child, waits for his mother's already caressing touch to revive his father. But while there is all this encouragement to run a thread *forward* from the Dionysiac antenook at the back of the Munich krater to a group of three figures in the principal picture of the other side, reunited in a vastly more elaborate and public setting than the Campanian vase in Vienna provided, the matter is rather different in a nearer direction. That is, between the Dionysiac picture on the neck and a separate composition just under it (pl. 1b), of altogether eight figures, two (a young and an old man) in a heroon, four flanking it (this in a notably chiastic alternation of sexes), two below it (significantly nubile youth and girl; his armor does for him what signs of athletic maturity, stlengis or aryballos, did for Apulian young men in more peaceful times; on her mirror and clothes-basket there should be less need to remark, perhaps).

How would an alert, soundly briefed, team of new-rigorists collecting for their machine, set to work for their own intention of thoroughness, at first sight of this picture? That is a question which a student of my generation could not usefully try to answer — unless there would be some use in his not keeping some hopes unsaid.

This for one of them, perhaps: that the aforesaid platoon of an army for a great conquest of objective truth in a major department of Italiote studies would not lack opportunity to note quite fully how disappointingly this side of the Munich "Nekyia" krater had come off in the publication of that vase (FR, 1 pl. 10, pp. 47-52) by the very discoverer of its ware's chattel-symbolism: for so, in spite of frustrating reticences ("offerings" cryptically "usual") in his Berlin catalogue, Furtwängler does deserve to be reckoned — by right of the specific enumerations on pp. 60-61 of his *Eros in der Vasen-malerei.* It is certainly a matter for someone's rumination (though not our own particular business) that the vase's stale but picturesque mythology, mere *setting* of the theme humanly interesting, a family's infernal reunion, but in actual fact making a vast, ingeniously arresting hellscape of the other side, captures so disproportionately much of his attention. This in six pages had only seven lines for the present heroon-centered aspect (pl. 1b), displaying in its main picture an absorbingly curious pattern of *figures*, perhaps reducible to a much less numerous arrangement of *persons* (from eight to only three?); those seven lines and half a small drawing, which sacrificed figured matter to floral ornament, not indeed wantonly but with the practical effect that with the vase so turned no figure to our left of the heroon could even appear, however inportant to the whole surely significant pattern its sex and its attributes happened to be. For one thing we must indeed thank Reichhold's sketch; it did catch and can still serve as an alerting reminder of a fading feature which is rather easily overlooked in a photograph, the ladderlike symbol hanging up below the heroon between the young soldier and the girl who in fact (though not clearly in that sketch) holds two other symbolic things, these belonging to the beginning of our scale, for they are clothes-basket and mirror. If I am not mistaken, advantage may come presently of our now recalling, in their own contexts, two very similar ghosts; first, another such instrument, however we should name it (Archytan *platage*?), barely visible in the background of a Sicilian bride who is concluding the anxious (cosmetic) part of her wedding (Trendall *LCS* 2, frontispiece); one more, still fainter, on the wall of the bedroom on the Laodameia krater in the British museum, together with much more conspicuous symbols from the same code, ball and dowry box. It is of course involved with them (and with the *paidagogos* as bearer of bad news and the Eros who would be so apt for Patroni's *amore funebre* as distinguished from *amore elisiaco*) in the question at stake there: the just married, just widowed Laodameia as written (a little out of place), or after all Phaedra? By no means ghostly, according to the publication on pl. 16 of E. Gerhard's *Apulische Vasenbilder,* is the showing the same thing makes on a nuptial loutrophoros in Berlin, F. 3262 (cf. Karl Anton Neugebauer's *Führer durch das Antiquarium* 2, pl. 83, p. 158) where its occurrence is rather opportune, as is at once obvious (since also there the "ladder" occurs between the youth and the girl of the underparty and she there too holds a clothes-basket) the *upward* pattern of symbols as distributed within the pattern of men and women is interestingly related to the very striking and suggestive scheme set U-wise about the heroon in the Munich "Nekyia" krater (pl. 1b; all the more usefully so, perhaps, for its being impossible to think that this and the Berlin loutrophoros were decorated by the same hand; the latter's style is much more like that of the "Orpheus" amphora, Bari 873, pl. 23).

What is most urgent now is my promptest possible accounting for rather warm words just used about the U of some ten symbols, six figures, but perhaps only two persons, in which the heroon of the Munich volute-krater is set. But I cannot see that it will interfere with this if we take the present opportunity of adjusting the "ladder of sounds" (a linguaphone if I may suppose that pluckable tabs made up the operative part) and its more or less correlative symbol the quartered ball, *pila picta,* to their proper place in relation to the scale we already have in a series that begins with signs which we may call, rather lamely, meticulous, standing for scrupulous care taken of the bride's preliminary needs (these largely, but not wholly, cosmetic), and is continued at the proper point by others of another character, evidently festive. It is prudent to recall that though (thanks to a most eloquent group of Europa mythographies) we may feel that we understand these two symbols, "ladder" and ball, well enough, as nuptial in a peculiarly trailing way (representing things of girlhood *renewable* at marriage), we are far from understanding this art's need to make so much of the objects in question. Yet, though they hardly seem matters for anxiety like the bride's not falling short in dowry and *hedna* and her appearing at her very best on her wedding day, it is not surprising when either ball or the runged thing which we may wish to call Archytan *platage* occurs with symbols belonging to the dotal-cosmetic end of the time-scale. On the Munich krater, pl. 1b, the *platage* is exactly at zero if there the symbols run upward in their temporal order, as seems guaranteed by wife-making fan (and not inconsistent swag of flowers) for top woman, and wedding-cake (and not inconsistent sapling of respect) for top man. My phrase for the things place applies even more strictly to the Berlin loutrophoros, where the *platage* has not left the renewer's person. As to the ball symbol, on the obverse of the London amphora F332, pl. 5 where it appears twice, both examples are on cosmetic Aphrodite's part of the surface, one of them (this for the renewal?) being in her actual possession, the other suspended, with the effect altogether of their recalling the fittest of all occasions for hyphening "dotal" with "cosmetic," the visit of a girl with dowry-box and mirror to Eros' ball-shop on the British Museum's askos 1928.1-17.68 (pl. 7). But on the other hand it would be cheating, as well as fickle repudiation of a value (in suspense) which already I have conceded to be one of the proper pleasures of scholarship, if I did not here emphasize that, as long as there is the least doubt or embarrassment in or about our respectably commonplace interpretation of ball and "ladder," both symbols must remain at least a little exposed to Orphistic wrenching, that is, to the preferences of scholars collecting tokens of mystic redemption from original sin; the ball because the most notoriously redeeming *telete* of the Orphic scriptures did require one, the supposed *platage* because it can be argued seriously (to my mind, quite validly) that we have Archytas's own certification of his interest in the noises of that very rite. I need not hark back to the unlikely contingency which would of course render that exposure more than slight, an improbable but not quite unimaginable find of inscriptions that would both reinforce the not quite negligible signs (in an inscription extant) of a chthonic cult of an Orphic daimon, bisexual Mise, in southeastern Italy and also identify this her-or-him with the excessively effeminate Eros of a late phase of the religions's vase-painting. But as we ourselves approach the pleasure which (in a range of material that he had almost made his own) Furtwängler had to forage, namely of attention to the absorbingly curious zig-zags of symbolized meaning, man over to man and woman over to woman, in the two stacks of figures enclosing the heroon forkwise (pl. 1b) on the Munich "Nekyia" krater, we should miss a great deal (including preparation for some theological issues of the next chapter) if in making out these interesting diagonals we could not recall, at least, a rejected line of interpretation, Orphistic, which I dare neither practice nor forget. At any rate there will be advantage in reflecting that it could not intervene now, amusing itself with the mirror (prime Zagreus bait!) and the plausibly "Orphic" horned crown and the "mystic" receptacles in that which I would reckon the first of the four slants in the whole of the latticed pattern, since it runs from the lowest female figure to another half-way (all three, I am supposing, represent one *person*). Or, in terms of their respective chattels, from the mirror and clothes-basket of the woman in the underparty exchanging glances with the soldier who (in the male line) is co-starter in the criss-cross, over to the horned wreath (tainiaed like the aforesaid basket), and also trinket box, of the woman standing at the same level as a male figure opposite, who is bending forward with a phiale extended in his left hand (as if abetting the action which is to be thought carved or depicted in the heroon). The same has a sluicing-pan (one more bath-certificate?) hoisted, very conspicuously elevated, in his right hand. Thus it is held as the "Happy-Ender's" attendant satyr in the little picture above holds his, in the like hand, nearly vertical, and with the bowl's convexity outward (pl. 1b, fig. 1); the resemblance was noted and illustrated by Mrs. G. Schneider-Herrmann in *BABesch* 37 [1962], pp. 43-45, figs. 5-7 (cf. her fig. 5 in *ibid* 38 p. 95) in passages perhaps too deferential to one-sidedly *Dionysiac* "Orphism," yet important to us in their seeming to favor a distinction which, as I have betrayed, I should not be sorry to see recognized, between offerings and showings, things the dead must get and things of which they must be notified.

But for the present this figure midway in the male zig-zag is, together with his fellows, not more interesting than the three neighboring women or repetitions of one even if his phials should identify him with the youth of the picture-within-picture, shown in the heroon with wine (in a similar dish in his own left hand) for an older man's libation, even if his hoisted washpan is reporting progress comparable with that of the *reunion*-bound pilgrim of a separate neck-strip just above, but earthly: on the way, that is, to wedding-cake (high right) past, already, the nuptial bath from which, as Tarentum's vases for wool-enriched rustics note with some insistence, Aphrodite and her prophet Orpheus have not exempted men, even the most primitive (pls. 11a; 12, figs. 6, 13). Thanks to vivid lessons from the Siceliote Cefalù Painter as well as from Tarentines, we can apprehend that there is a corresponding passage of meaning, nubile to wedded, from low end (bride's mirror and clothes-basket) to high end (wife's fan and swag of flowers) of the female line of this anfractuous business — if "business" has not, meanwhile, become inept.

For while it is certainly my assumption that the vase-painter has undertaken to carry one person, his hero, through *all* three stages apparent on this vase's surface, and so first, as mortal youth, to a marriage celebrated with due veneration (*ELEP*) of his own father, next, as dead at last after loss of his wife and infant son, to the crowning success of beatification, then, as thus beatified (pl. 1a, fig. 1b), to reunion with them in the most august and telling circumstances imaginable, nevertheless I must not suppose that his hero's wife is part of the theme, of the eschatographer's professional job, in quite the same continuous fashion. On the one hand, therefore, I can find no difficulty in identifying the just dead, just beatified *thyrsiger* of the neck-strip with the living bridegroom below him who is denoted directly by the wedding-cake and the sapling, indirectly by the attributes, fan and swag, of his own wedded bride, seated opposite. But if I were ordered to give, with the means at hand, illustration, conscious illustration, of a term once or twice used already, "overinterpretation," could I do better than by prolonging the female line of the lattice of zigzags into the neck-picture, to end at the figure holding a tainia for the beatified hero? Geometrically that would achieve a great triumph of final symmetry. But really, that is to say mythographically, it would be a sin against symmetry as experienced, divorcing the ministering satyr of this neckstrip of a volute krater from the nymph we have learnt to expect, in such a place at such a task, as his partner (pls. 2 and 4b for Leningrad St. 420, St. 426). The vase, as we have begun to see it, cannot be integrated without several appearances of one and the same woman, but four are enough, three by the heroon to mark her way from nubility to marriage and the last on the opposite side of the vase, for her reunion with the man who by my reckoning (which would include the younger of the two figures in the heroon) is shown six times altogether. To a claim of integration so urged, with earthly marriage and infernal reunion for its nexus, no bar can fairly be made out of a picture intervening (FR 1 p. 51) but scarcely interrupting, namely the nuptial astronomy of the mere neck-strip let in above the great Nekyia which is the reunion's setting. Where is the telling part of this upper and incidental composition, which puts Sun and his chariot-team behind, Moon and hers ahead, and the Evening Star in his proper place as her harbinger, but dangling something hardly needed for that work, a tainia of favor? The man or woman painting this vase reveled in meaning, densely packed, as long ago (p. 147) we began to learn; but let us make least of whatever may be appositely meant in the contrast of Day with Night, more of winged Hesperos' intrinsic likeness to Eros, and most of the feature (that tainia) by which the painter, nearly as much as Catullus in his pastiche of a Greek epithalamium (62, 35), puts him to sharing the nuptial work of Eros.

I have not yet, I know, made fully good my implication that (for some of our concerns)the mortal woman of our integration, only fourfold, is more interesting than the sextuple mortal man. But already this is the practically proper place for offering our novelty (as any integration of Munich 3297 certainly is) to the new rigor's operation, hoping for the best. That is, for the idea's acceptance in more or less these terms: "perhaps not right, of course not bright; but, as something which has seemed to work out, in a circumspect effort of proof, peddling no unreasonable nostrum and compromising no related problem, it is, in a priming way, testworthy, as itself work-starting for our better means and grander range." In this submission would there be more involved, more for testing, than the scale of nuptial symbols according to temporal order of the real object's use or enjoyment, which besides giving us for the really difficult side of the Munich krater the all-important signal "read *up*, and obliquely, had seemed to make sense of horizontal enigmas of Milan 225, and had seriously enriched the interest of an illustration of Euripides *IT*, by offering for its foreground a closer relation both to the text of the play and to the funerary religion of Apulia at such slight cost, the low price of parting with some questionable "iconography" and half a vapid jest?

Some Objections and Alternatives— Support for the "(Re)union Hypothesis" from Multiple Burials

WELL, THERE ARE some assumptions which we are not surrendering unreservedly for question; one is this, that the idea of an Apulo-Tarentine ware made as I have supposed, that is, decorated in advance of funerary need but by the most sophisticated of Italiote Greeks for the not-Greeks most conditioned (by an exceptional symbiosis) to be exacting customers, should suffice to make ignorable, if not yet, perhaps, unsayable, such words as "the more fool you, if you expect integrated sense of an *Apulian* pot, especially any monster big one." Nor are we meekly exposing for unsparing criticism — except for the uncouthness barely tolerable in their convenient labels — either the general notion eschatogamy, or a certain freedom, for which (all too compendiously) the simile *ELEP* lends label and gives justification, the liberty at monuments or even tombstones to prefer (when the right signs are really there) the conclusion "no, not a funeral, a wedding, in the well-attested detour of ancestor-worship." But there would have been indescribable impudence in the particular overture just made to the machinery of the next exhaustiveness, proposing for its early (perhaps priming) acceptance a confidently single thread of meaning for the entirety of the "Reunion" (rather than "Nekyia") krater Munich 3297, if there had not been, with my making it, a duly abashed sense that hereabout, in the subtopic of reunion, was the most exacting part, archaeologically, of the whole eschatology of completion as scholarship has to cope with it.

This is not an admission that any corroboration is needed of views already taken of actual groupings on certain vases, confidently seen as families reunited in a new life. Even in the most important and absorbing of the theological questions known to be ahead of us, about a chthonic partnership of Dionysos and Aphrodite, there could be no excuse now for even the briefest flirting with Winckler's reading of the anonymously happy Munich triad (fig. 1a) as Dionysos with Ariadne and son, though there is a sense in which it is true that Aphrodite must be recognized as applicant for the place which the old catalogues used to let Ariadne have, before it was seen how inexorably (p. 75ff.) the Hesiodic heresy of Dionysos' full acceptance of her had been excluded by red-figured vase-painting, indeed by Greek and Hellen-izing art altogether. I cannot imagine any objection to the interpretation, dazed soldier reunited with wife and shyly filial boy in an evidently Dionys-iac paradise, which we found inevitable for the reverse of a more consistently eschatographic, on both sides quite unearthly, vase in the Jatta collection at Ruvo which was range-extending, being a good deal earlier than its Munich counterpart (Jatta no. 1094, Sichtermann no. 36, pp. 33f, pl. 54, here pl. 18b). Nor even much, perhaps, to what I have rather gropingly to make of a blend of themes, earthly marriage and infernal reunion, divinable in Stephani's description (*Vasensammlung der Eremitage* 1 no. 421) of a piece which I do not know by sight, but nevertheless must beg leave to reserve for some notice presently; there is a point which it can give for affixing to what perhaps is not yet, as an energizing goad behind the new thoroughness, quite sharp enough, my ventured integration of the sense of Munich 3297 on the rod of one man's three experiences, of conventional marriage with ancestor-worship (*ELEP*), of solitary beatification in a Dionysiac anteparadise, of acceptance by the Highest Authority for reunion with wife and son. But obviously it is in this guise, wearing its full untidy trappings as "supposed (re)union eschatology," that the eschatogamic hypothesis cannot avoid invit-ing the controls of real pick-and-spade work among the sometimes doubled dead. Thus on the Patronian cause in general, if not (I must hope) upon every defender of it, there is imposed an obligation of perpetually alert scrutiny of the areas of discovery (fortuitous as well as planned) in southern Italy and Sicily, and evidence of faith in reunion will indeed be less than half of its concerns.

The new vigilance will need to be much more than just a sharper eye for "letti matrimoniali," ledges twin (as momentously for Campanian eschatol-ogy in Gabrici's wonderful T. 185, *MonLinc* 22, cols. 644-647 of his *Cuma*) or exceptionally broad (as at Canosa in the second Scocchera tomb [T. A], one rather teasing for the topic of reunion, Andrew Oliver, Jr. having shown in his *Reconstruction of Two Apulian Tomb-Groups*, p. 5, fig. 1 that the male skeleton with armor on it had two adult bedfellows). But at all events it is certainly for Italiote studies to recognize that physical reunion has quite an archaelogy of its own. Here, then, there should be better than perfunctory acknowledgement of some scholars' recent contributions to it which are especially welcome because especially work-making. One is Oliver's retrieving and reuniting in his pl. 5, 1-4, a long separated pair of kantharoi which once belonged (with others) to T. Scocchera A at Canosa, vases which raise the question whether the plural designation, "Warriors' Tomb," proposed (or rather, aired) for this burial, should really be allowed to settle there, on a *corredo* which had plenty of armour but only one of its three skeletons *wearing* any of it. Besides, in another direction altogether, the two aforesaid kantharoi suggested eschatogamy, matching together as if they were the "his" and the "hers" of a wedding (see not only the nuptial pair in pl. 15 of Gerhard's *Apulische Vaseubilder* but also the two nuptially complementary sides of the single kantharos Mannheim 46 in *CVA* Germany 13, pl. 42, 4-5). In the same grave some reinforcement of this hint was given by a remarkable basin very opportune now (Oliver's pl. 8, 3). For not only does it have "nuptial astronomy" recalling the Munich "Reunion" krater (fig. 1a) but the thing itself is variant of a type of vessel also illustrated by the footbasin occurring near the "his" laver in the double bathroom for the London "Wedding of Persephone" (F332, pl. 5a) as well as by the tripodic example in the most instructive litter of Thersites' interference with the necrophilia of Achilles on the colossal volute-krater in Boston (J. M. Paton, *AJA* [1908] pl. 19).

This basin from the alphabetically first on the Scocchera burials (second in order of disclosure) can be seen in the Art Gallery of Yale University at New Haven, a loan there from Thomas H. Watkins, II. Oliver's service in publishing it (pl. 8, 3, with commentary on pp. 12-13) is an appreciable part of the grounds for ranking his book, as an archaeological revelation, on a level with Miss Scarfi's "Gioia del Colle" (*MonLinc* 45, 145-332), Mrs. Fernanda Tine Bertocchi's *Pittura funeraria Apulia* (1964), and the fuller transpiring of the significance of E. Gabrici's account of a grave of husband and wife at Cumae (*MonLinc* 22 644-647, t. 185) after A. D. Trendall's illustration of it and correct resexing of some of the persons on its vases (*LCS* pls. 187, 3 and 4, 188, 2-3, 189, 6-7, pp. 486-490, nos. 331, 332, 342, 367; banter by me of Gabrici's mistakes of sex would be risky, courting nemesis, for I have not reached agreement with Miss Scarfi (cf. her col. 154) about the maleness of the bather in the woman's tomb 2 which so interestingly adjoins the man's tomb 3 at only a few centimeters' distance (her figs. 7-12, 30-33), and under the influence of Selene or Evening with Hesperus at Munich, I should like to think the heavenly body or season in the basin too bosomy to be Oliver's Helios).

More Nuptial Symbols—
the Garnished Phiale

HOWEVER ALL THAT may be, unless I am altogether mistaken in my idea of the associations of this type of basin, nuptial, as well as in my reading (as epithalamic Herperus) of the one sure star, rayed, ahead of the horses in the picture's field, there is timely interest in what we can see in the rather leaky exergue below the driver's horses; in Oliver's description (pp. 12f) "two seated figures: Eros with a fan, and facing him a woman holding a phiale and a situla; at the right, behind the woman is a bird." At any rate, that is not inopportune to the turn which this merely ancillary study of a funerary religion must for its modest purpose take as soon as possible, from the code of the religion's symbols to the society of its Personages. Are there symbols present exalting for that "woman," urging her promotion to the rank of Personage which Eros has and certainly also the driver, whether female as the Moon or Night, or male as Oliver's "Sun"? For precisely that question, what now is the value of her position, seated on what is not a tomb or altar but the reerected top of a ruined Ionic column, between Eros and a nameable bird (a dove, is it not?)? And also of the distribution between her and Eros of chattels certainly belonging to the nuptial code, all three of them, the bucket (whether it is for filling preliminary bath or for providing final wine), and fan (so preeminently the matron-making thing), the phiale? Especially the phiale, for being garnished with leaves it recalls one that was so interesting for our scale-making within the system, on the British Museum askos 1928. 1-17. 68 (pl. 7a); there an evidently outfitting Eros had a ball but also a phiale, garnished with foliage and other things, for a girl who by what the rest marked was so measurably only at the beginning of her way to marriage; like the at first more backward of the two "cousins" on the obverse of a krater in Milan she had only the mirror and dowry-box of a portionable maiden's mere nubility. And in Mr. Watkins' basin at Yale does it matter that unlike the vaguely flowery foliage in the phiale for Eros' visitor on the London askos the garnish of the woman's dish is definitely ivy? Dionysiac? Do the three ivy leaves, one frontal, two sideways, certify one more Personage for this eschatotheology, Dionysos? Is there any fine shade of emphasis in there being two *more* ivy leaves than in the phiale acquired by the (at first) speedier of the two girls bound for marriage on the afore-said krater in Milan, at the front of it, standing by something which we thought less like a gradmother's heroon than like a shrine of the chief, perhaps, of all the Personages of this department, Aphrodite-*Aprodita.* Is it emphasis or *reassurance?* Is it as if there had been written, with triple underlining, the following, "don't waste pitying concern on Dionysos; he is as much in this as ever"?

Perhaps in any case there is some stress for our *use*. if only subjectively, for it is now inevitable that the topic of garnished phialai should recall a monument from before the time of Aphrodite's primacy, the front picture of the Hoppin Painter's bell-krater 620 in Lecce (pl. 8b) where Dionysos, quite unmistakably denoted (by proper headdress, proper hair, as well as by thyrsos), is about to bless a girl's marriage to a youth less soldierly than the bridegroom at the beginning of the lattice pattern of figures on the "Reunion" krater in Munich (pl. 1b); as with the satyr-abetted suitor on a hydria from the Degrassi grave at Heraclea-Policoro (Trendall *LCS* pl. 25, 2), his badge of maturity is not armour but an athlete's stlengis. No doubt there is matter, chronological mainly, for rumination in that difference and that likeness, especially if the "ladder of sounds" to be dimly seen between soldier and bride on the Munich krater and comparable with one fingered by an unarmed man on the corresponding part of Berlin F. 3262 is the sub-musical *platage* of Archytas whose death or retirement can be thought to have brought the loss of Heraclea and a Lucanian war upon Tarentum and its allies. But much more interesting (if not almost too elegant for acceptance and confident application) is the theological-*cum*-botanical *chiasmus* between the perhaps myrtled phiale of the unarmed youth on Lecce 620, at his marriage by grace of Dionysos in a work of the comparatively early Hoppin Painter, and the certainly ivied phialai of female figures respectively later and later still, the bride whom we regarded as conspicuously dependent on Aphrodite at the right of the abverse of Milano 225, and the "woman" whom we are almost ready to hail as Aphrodite herself, awaiting with her son and her dove the evening's nuptial work, in Mr. Watkins' basin.

At all events it is a small part of the immense importance of the matchmaking, still by Dionysos, taking place in my pl. 8b for the obverse of Lecce 620, that the phiale for it has garnish from neither of Dionysos' plants, grape or ivy, and that the densely pinnate leafage offers itself to be understood as cut from one of Aphrodite's – myrtle. The three Bacchic ivy leaves so curiously arranged on the phiale of Mr. Watkins' Aphrodite must not steal excessive attention, but in any we give them we are more or less close to momentous questions. In theoretical importance at any rate no matter of this study ranks above what, without giving the least countenance to Orphistic speculation which now threatens recrudescence but using what is actually Orphic language adapted from a Pergamene scripture, we may call the *paredria* of Aphrodite with Dionysos, aware of course that Patroni's insights are included there. Of more simply practical importance is common respect for phaseology, a word that just here is less question-begging and trouble-inviting than "chronology," especially since Oliver has shown that even the helmet of Celtic pattern in this Canosa tomb is not a thing out of which serviceable dates in figures B.C. can be conjured (pp. 15f). One consideration really useful is that insofar as the surface of the basin is antique and good for inferences (less than altogether?) the dry style of the drawing on it seems appreciably later than the exuberant style of Milan 225 (pl. 28). Thus on the one hand it will be prudent, at least, to see no more than an arid little quirk of sophistication ("do you 'get' my clever profiles?") in the multiplication of leaves, three instead of one, while on the other it will be rather more positively creditable if one does not fail to observe and exploit a startling lack in the basin's type of Eros.

The New Eros Again;
More Reconsideration of
Nuptial Symbolism

THIS HAS LOST something of indeed rather more than simply phaseological interest and convenience, the womanish bonnet which most conspicuously (most so of several simultaneously sudden turns to specifically transvestite effeminacy) marks a derangement which for all its triviality could be reckoned almost seismic: so concretely (even if undatable) does the artistic and religious alteration pertain to the stuff of political and economic history. That is, of course, if I am not mistaken in discerning that the debauching of Eros in Tarentine vase-painting came about when (somewhere in the career of Tarentum's Lycurgus Painter?) a certain point in the symbiosis and mutual acculturation of Tarentum and Apulia was reached, at which an Apulian agency dared to demand and a group of Tarentine potteries had to stomach an assimilation of the type of Eros to the established type of Aphrodite as far as possible, and thus from the neck upward. At our own present pass, I know that I do not have to plead that there is nothing fantastic and unwarrantable in the idea, already aired more than enough, of such an ultimatum and its acceptance. But because we need to keep the new integration of the Munich "Reunion" krater in view during the little that remains to be said about the Watkins basin as (in its own way) another of our time's archaeological novelties, inviting the new rigor's useful application, it is not digressive (or slackly repetitious) to add that besides the new Eros there is a new satry — such as we see in that part of the Munich krater's neck that is not astronomical but Dionysiac — better than merely mild, better than just safe for the dead daughters of upland probatocrats; for there on this important vase he is not less benignly employed than a modern orderly assisting nurses in a post-operational recovery room (fig. 1b, pl. 21). In other circumstances, with more direct bearing than quite at present on the chthonic *paredria* of Dionysos and Aphrodite, one might welcome, as an opportunity delightfully work-making, the question how far the two are really comparable in their origins, on the one hand the new and unrandy kind of satyr that in the Degrassi grave at Heraclea seemed very new indeed but to which we have become accustomed in Apulo-tarentine neckstrips, and on the other the remodeled kind of Eros which, surely, we must be surprised *not* to find in this basin from one of the latest tombs of Canosa. Surprised in any case, but especially if on oinochoai from the same grave published in Oliver's pl. 3 we must now pronounce the two Erotes to be fully transvestite, betrayed by the hollow loop and pair of long streamers belonging in each example to perfectly normal cap-strings; what is not normal on those oinochoai, and may be in its own measure significant, is the dark color of the womanish bonnets, in curious contrast to the immediately tell-tale white (evidence of almost paradoxically strong Apulian influance) that catches the eye of any one thumbing through Trendall's examples of Sicilian Erotes (*LCS* pls. 238, 240, 243, 246-248). The surface is light if perhaps not white, thus at any rate not assimilated in tone to the god's dark hair and so quite undisguisedly effeminate, on the head of the Eros belonging to the Dionysiac Aphrodite of the sequence of pictures which on lekanides of the Sicilian Cefalù Painter (pl. 22) we found to be so powerfully eye-sharpening in regard to temporal and other fine distinctions of symbolism. It is fair and quite safe, most unlikely to snap any thread which we must keep in hand, to reflect how much of our actual trust in their practical value we owe to this not-Tarentine: I have certainly to confess that such confidence as I can feel in my integration of the Munich "Reunion" krater, faith in its being able presently to defy Orphistic mutterings, depends on belief that part of the composition about the heroon (pl lb) probably exhibits what the Sicilian sequence incontestably implies, progress from mirror of nubility to nuptial fan.

Even more direct and irresistible is the bearing of this Sicilian sequence on the population, the *cavi personae,* of Mr. Watkins' basin. We very well remember how brilliantly the Cefalù Painter contrives that the Dionysiac thyrsos of his fan-awarding Aphrodite shall mislead nobody (not even, posthumously, the most compulsive "macnad"-hailer?) by providing the full foolproof complement of her live attributes, and lively things to be done by all three, by the bird-boy, by the dove, and even (defensively) by the less agile water-bird. With only two of the three now present to warn us "no, not impatient bride at nightfall," the provision in the basin falls short of that. But with the Sicilian to prompt us we shall not mistake any part of the Apulo-Tarentine artist's meaning, and shall quite appreciate the difference of stress in the latter's version of the common theme "final fan — before long — for bride." For the former devotes almost all his resources of symbolism to what I have had to call the anxious or scrupulous or meticulous part of the affair. Almost one might hope to provoke objection to that phrase, a charge of affectation ("what's formidable or even worrying in bathing and vesting and perfuming?"), for the pleasure of calling as witnesses for the defense the Cefalù Painter's animals: not only Aphrodite's quite threatening bath-guard, the neck-craning swan, but also (if a shade unfairly?) the hound which Artemis has to restrain with a precautionary hug. Perhaps presently, against carpings of a certain other sort, there will be comparable use for Mr. Watkins' basin, if (subjectively but not unreasonably) we may treat its exergue (Oliver, pl. 8, 3) as explicitly festive embroidery of ideas expressed respectively in the nuptial astronomy on one side of the neck of the Munich "Reunion" krater and the decoration of gravemates of the basin, the twin oinochoai of Oliver's pl. 3. But meanwhile, at any rate, note that on the krater (fig. 1a) the tainia of favor dangled by the Moon's harbinger Hesperus only tells "tonight someone is somebody's darling." The basin, where the Moon's Hesperus cannot be given anything to do (since the star is unpersonified, a mere asterisk ahead of the horses), would have had even less to say – only the message completed by the thing's shape as merely prenuptial wash-pot of earlier in the afternoon – without the contribution from below of matters less preliminary. I mean Aphrodite's bucket of wine and garnished phiale for the wedding's main act of religion (still a libation, as under an earlier dispensation in my pl. 18b) in that part of the whole affair for which the evening sky now gives signal, as well as something perhaps still more terminal, Eros' status-conferring, matron-making fan. But as it is altogether, including the exergue, with deities of marriage there to get the signal, the composition in the basin has meaning to spare, helping to charge with fuller significance yet another combination of driver with harbinger, triumphant Nike and festal Eros (festal with wine in decorated bucket!), on the almost identically twin oinochoai out of the same tomb (Oliver, pl. 3). And this in a most acceptable connection (thanks to their Nikai, thanks to the basin's Moon and Evening Star) with the Munich "Reunion" krater; for since the krater's integration according to a perceived scheme in which Nike is cardinal, she being the operative factor "Happy Ending" at a hinge of Dionysiac beatification between the themes "Stages of Earthly Marriage" and " Magnificent Reunion," that vase's luckily monumental show of symbolism no doubt affords our own best means of keeping our present considerations propulsively yoked and harnessed (pl. 1.a and b; fig. 1a and b).

From Symbols to Personages— Aphrodite, Not Ariadne, as Partner of Dionysos—Some Consequences

THE CHIEF OF these is an affair of expository transition, from a religion's system of symbols to its system or society of powers and personages (if I may continue to use the word which would let me include Orpheus and Triptolemos if they should deserve it). If (as I fear is true) Orphistic counter-interpretation of the symbols has still to be reckoned with, cannot quite yet be safely ignored as a chimera which should have died of attrition at an earlier page, there is need of every precaution against clogging, blinding, diffuseness. For one, may I show already, in very plain sight at fig. 3a and b, what from a standpoint taken at the ample but not exhaustive symbolism of the heroon side of the Munich "Reunion" krater (pl. 1b, fig. 1) I can discern at the far and theological end of the bridge now to be crossed with the least possible molestation, namely a satisfactorily vivid document of the partnership (as powers for eschatogamy) of chthonic Dionysos and chthonic Aphrodite, on the bell krater St. 1427 in Leningrad, published by L. Stephani in *CRPétersburg* (1863) pl. 5, 1-2. Because the symbols in the field of its obverse picture are so necessary to our business of *finishing* with the lattice pattern of an (at first!) earthly couple's nuptial symbols on the Munich volute-krater 3297 (pl. 1b), we already need a glimpse, though I cannot yet afford very full discussion, of the major composition on the Leningrad vase. There we can see Dionysos and Aphrodite together in an embowered chariot drawn by a pair of deer and attended by their respectively natural satellites with the respectively proper symbols in a markedly clear division, hers above and his below (fig. 3b). Above from right to left there is, first, an Eros with swag of flowers (as held by the bride at the uppermost and ultimate of her three stages of nuptial progress on the Munich krater, pl. 1b) and also a "ladder of sounds"; this second thing could be momentous here if it is really an Archytan *platage,* and so able to abet certain Archytan associations of the *rhombos* of the other Eros in forcing us to accept reintrusion of teletic issues appertaining to a blackmailing religion of terror condemned by Archytas' friend Plato, and perhaps even more directly known to Archytas himself; at any rate, it was at *teletai* of some branch of it, Orphic or Eleusinian, that Archytas intently studied the rumble of the rhombos (*supra*, pp. 102, 109, 254). But for the present let us only note that in the apparently graduated scheme (pl. 1b) of the Munich "ascent to marriage" the possible, probable, *platage* was far away down at zero precisely, between the bride shown about to vest and the bridegroom shown disarming and in fact about to bathe). Next, not in flight but seated on a ledge of higher ground with the effect of indicating that the chariot will presently veer right to reach the flaming censer further left, is seen another Eros, and again the things which come together in his hands are from far apart in the scale of symbols. We know another use, indeed other uses, respectively Orphic and Eleusinian, for the rhombos rumble-wheel which he holds in his left hand, but if here it means the love-charm iynx, from before any suitor's courting, then it is a symbol from *below* zero in our scale. Yet the tainiaed sapling of respect in the same figure's right hand belongs to the pomp and circumstance of a grand wedding, as the weddings of both Hippodameias in their respectively strange ways certainly were (it does not matter much that the centaur's sapling for one has lost the tainia which Pan's sapling for the other retains, pl. 24, M. Schmidt, *Dareiosmaler* pl. 3). Except that for a nuptial purpose which is already quite familar to us (pl. 8b), Aphrodite is about to borrow the satyr's torch, the various persons and things of the lower level, nymph and satyr, three thyrsoi, a timbrel, and a travelling grape-arbor, belong to Dionysos' share.

I do not need to argue, now or later, against the old view to which time and accumulating inscriptions have been so merciless, the opinion which took Dionysos' companion in the stag-drawn chariot for Hesiodic Ariadne. If I need to prove at full length that she is not Pindaric Semele, fetched up by her son from the dead to rejoin Zeus as his continuing paramour, that should be done elsewhere. But perhaps it is already enough — after first pointing to the censer as possible destination much nearer than Zeus's Olympus — to turn the vase round, to where amply (fig. 3a) there is human material for an infernal wedding, with even a "best man" available for the couple there, perhaps actually of opportune interest since he holds what can be recognized as raw material of the horned wreath seen as looped to completeness and provided with a streaming tainia in the right hand of the Munich bride at half-way, only half-way, in her ascent to earthly marriage (pl. 1b). But there are some aspects to be exploited at once in this bridgehead view *a citeriori* of Dionysos and Aphrodite in quite unmistakable partnership, caught setting out for what seems to be an appointed affair of mortal eschatogamy.

I must hope that in point of useful novelty this recognition of Aphrodite as Dionysos' companion (instead of Ariadne) in the chariot on Leningrad St. 1427 can rank as of not lower degree than the revelation that Iphigenia's pan on Leningrad St. 420 (fig. 2) was a specific vessel of ablution, having nothing to do with wine and libation but belonging, instead, to any use (in the act of lustration or the process of bathing) of the stemmed lavers with which it was associated in a bathing-place on London F 332 (pl. 5a), as well as at a temple notorious for sinister ablution on Leningrad St. 420 (fig. 2). It may be that a rather high price, in exposure to Orphistic reinfection, will have to be paid presently for this novelty of quite the highest rank. But it is not just a very lucky hypothesis, not an idea in fact invulnerable but nevertheless not *cryingly* true, not a conception like that which was safely risked in admitting cosmetic Aphrodite to the foreground of fig. 2. Still less is it only a promising but perhaps in the long run expendable tool such as we were given in the temporal scale of nuptial symbols. This scale is still far from full verification yet has been truly useful, even if in shaping a whole new meaning for the Munich "Reunion" krater by integrating the heroon with the rest of that vase's decoration it has furnished the new rigor with only rather less than a tool: mere priming, that is, for the exhaustiveness of a more perfect scholarship's most formidable duty, that of getting fully intelligent and therefore richly exploitable mastery of the scenes at heroa and graves in their whole computer-tasking variety, *nearly infinite* in its material and spatial permutations.

In fact this new bit of certainty behind the harnessed stags, which is only not quite exactly the Orphic *paredria* of Aphrodite and Dionysos because they have to stand up together in their traveling arbor (fig. 3b), might already be thought to be affecting, infecting, destroying the interpretation suggested and still maintained by me for the alternation of sex and succession of attributes in the pattern of six figures for a couple of persons which embraces the heroon on the Munich krater (pl. 1b). There is of course no surrender to anything sinister in that recent fitting of "Orphic" to *paredria*; by definition there can be nothing that is not Orphic in any scripture, however late or local, that was attributed to Orpheus in a natural borrowing of his decisive authority. Nor does a gap of several centuries (five?) lessen the great significance of Ariadne's exclusion from the *Orphic hymns,* any more than it spoils the interest, merely topical in passing, of two phrases which could be borrowed from successive lines (7-8) of *Hymn* 55 to Aphrodite for rather neat annotation of my fig. 3b (σεμνὴ Βάκχοιο πάρεδρε and γαμοστόλε μῆτερ Ἐρώτων). Not only is it that, of course, Aphrodite on Leningrad St. 1427 would be so "paredric" if she could only sit down with her present fellow-traveller; there is further this, that she could not have more precisely "gamostolic" employment for her children than here, where both Erotes have their hands full for their parts in a comprehensive mission of eschatogamy. It may be that one of the good results of a recent demonstration by Kyle M. Phillips, Jr., already commended, of the long life uncorrupted of abstruse and intricate refinements of mythography (from the fourth century before Christ to the twelfth after and beyond) will be that citers of the *Orphic Hymns* can be less and less in fear of hearing (as merely impulsive extinguisher) a patronizing reminder of the date and place of these Pergamene litanies of the third century A.D.

But no good resolution to be rational about them, to require some actual and definite effort of mind in any impugning of their authority as a museum of theological embroidery mostly quite old, should impose more than the minimum of prudent patience with either an Orphistic interpretation of the outing of Dionysos and Aphrodite on Leningrad St. 1427 (fig. 3b) or Orphistic objection to the scheme of integration ventured for the Munich "Reunion" krater (pl. 1b, fig. 1a and b), while "Orphic" in its covering all that pertains to Orpheus includes naturally everything, whether scripture or institution, attributed to his creation, "Orphistic" has thus far meant for us "satisfactory to any of our contemporaries who believe in the historical reality, at the place and time pertinent, of 'Orphism,' a supposed religion of redemption from original sin, with some taboos (against animal food, against wool for the dead) but these less relevant to Italiote vase-painting than the symbols involved in its teletic character, its dependence (in a manner not very clearly definable) on celebration of a mimetic rite attributed to Orpheus, a *telete* (effective ritual) enacting the primal cause of original sin, namely the Titans' trapping, rending, devouring Dionysos." Apart from our interest in Patroni's ideas, especially his detection of an eschatology of completion in 'Elysian love,' we should have had none in the Orphistic point of view.

This has only been of concern to us because it has been the fate of Patroni's insights (especially as developed here in their bearing on the vases' systematic symbolism) to become curiously subject to Orphistic wrenching. At our present stage, with a bridgehead reached that is leading away from symbolism to an evidently livelier region of inquiry, it is too late for any reiterative contesting of this. But, equally, it is urgent that timely advantage should be taken of unquestionably sure aspects of the situation thus caused, for purposes which we can expect them to serve, our discovering any forbidding limits to, or facing usefully confessable failure in, mastery of the nuptial code. Some recent publications, already named as making disclosures in which the new rigor (as it girds for its operations) must be pressed to recognize momentous novelty, might even suggest that one of the symbols least fully understood is actually that which, in its use as sign of nubility in special antithesis to the wife's fan of status, I have been treating as pellucidly elementary, the mirror. And not without corroboration of the postulate, for the antithesis is so pointedly taken for granted by the Cefalù Painter in his composition for the lid of Lipari 749B (pl. 22d-f) — whatever shifts Orphistic objection may have ready for precisely this pointed contrast where it occurs between bottom and top of a zigzag of symbolism, pl. 1b, on Munich 3297. But, it might be said, the Cefalù Painter is only a Sicilian, and does not one of the Munich women invite this comment "no, not bride with the mirror and basketed clothes of her toilet for her wedding; surely woman initiate if not initiand, with part anyhow of the customary bait for the Titans' victim, that mirror, in her right hand, and at least some of the rest in what she balances on the other, that deep cylindrical basket, which is of just the right shape for a *cista mystica*"? And the other this: "no, not wedded wife with the ceremony's fan and swag of flowers; surely, in that position at the top, a woman purified by the *telete*; if purification of fanned air (cf. Vergil, *Aeneid* vi. 740f) is too Roman for you, think of Sophocles' naturalization of Eleusinian Iacchos in southern Italy (*Antigone* 1119-1151), think of the Eleusinian torch in a Tarentum grave which one of those 'momentous' publications, Mrs. Tine Bertocchi's *Pittura funeraria apula*, has provided (her fig. 71) as happy complement to the Messapian series remarked by Whatmough *PID* p. 354, and then look across this vase-painting to the man opposite the aerated woman, the youth possessed of an Eleusinian bumpcake, veritable *popanon*"?

Reconsiderations of the Problem of Possible "Orphic Symbolism"

WRENCHING? CERTAINLY, BUT just in passing, it must be said that this was not the word for Miss Erika Simon's quite properly finding a teletic point in the mirror brandished by ecstatic but nymph-ignoring satyrs on Roman plaques not far from contemporary with Cicero's allusion in *De Natura Deorum* iii. 58 to *sacra Orphica* that were celebrated in honor of the fourth Dionysos surprisingly distinguished by him as "son of Jupiter and Luna." I should be the wrencher if I could not see that in Roman reliefs this sculptural allusion to an Orphic *telete* about outrageous Titans (the meaning we have already admitted those paradoxical mirrors of satyrs to have) belonged to a matter quite separate historically, namely conjecturable influence on Roman art of Cicero's own time or a little later of more than one Greek *telete* concerned with a suffering or endangered Dionysos. That Roman question is of course not a topic for this side of the present bridge. Its need for any consideration even over there across it, somewhere in Orpheus' division of the problems about Personages, would be contingent, I suppose, on assuming obligations which it would be rash as yet to acknowledge, any duty of discussing M. P. Nilsson's idea of the relation of the winged figure (Dika, or Nika?) on the Fenicia fragment of an Apulo-Tarentine Nekyia to the immortal teazed at the Villa Item and elsewhere (his *Mysteries* p. 125), or of really full inquiry, palaeographic but also physiological, into the failure of sight or hearing which brought about Cicero's scarcely credible Luna as name of the mother of his fourth Dionysos, who should be (and by independent testimony must be) the Theban one, son of Semele, not Selene. It is true that only from Berkeley, by someone who was in actual attendance upon Nilsson during his inspection of the Semele hydria there[1] (*CVA* U.S.A. 5, pl. 48), could there be fair and excusing explanation of his paradoxial preference of Justice to Hera's sinister Iris for the part of the winged person *humiliated* by friends of Dionysos, human or immortal, in several Roman works of art besides the very famous painting at the Villa Item (his *Mysteries*, figs. 10e, 31, 33, 36). But what we have imperatively to face at this turn is a bracing last challenge, from a certain combination of novelties, of the truth and usefulness of such equipment for assistance of others' future work as we have acquired, altogether, in the fullest impression which we have been able to gain of the nuptial symbolism of the vases.

Bracing, it may have seemed, is not unneeded also on the Orphistic side of present questions, those which are beginning again to have one. Yet it would not quite do to dismiss, as only randomly compulsive rattle, what has just come from that quarter in criticism of a consistently nuptial reading of the pattern of figures and chattels which nearly surrounds the heroon on the Munich "Reunion" krater (pl. 1b): a revision tending to substitute reinterpretation in terms of the saving apparatus of two allied religions of mystic reassurance (as I must say if I have already staled the phrase "holy terror"). Only tending, so far. For the critic forbore to search the halfway figures of the Munich lattice for symbolism of moral purgation and its reward. He availed himself neither of the man's washpan, nor of the woman's peculiar

---

[1] Cf. H. R. W. Smith, *BABesch* 45 (1970) p. 76, n. 44, where it is explained that Nilsson mistook a detail of the background for a needle in the winged figure's hand, and supposed that the purpose was friendly surgery on Zeus's thigh.

wreath, of the horned kind not meant for putting on the head and therefore in this example lending itself to comparison with the crown *raced to and raced from* in an Orphic tablet concerned with purgation (Kern² *Fr.* 32 c 7 and 9); besides, it is of the same form as the wreath which might seem to mark a point (ahead) in the blessed progress of a certain woman purified by water. I mean the "not Danaid" infernally sponsored by Eleusinian Triptolemos as well as by Aphrodite, awaiting her turn in their company opposite Orpheus in the Karlsruhe Nekyia, fig. 17.

For a last alert there may be considerations worth developing in this. Meanwhile, for debating points which (if only for our own chastening sense of limits) we can certainly encourage it to seek, the Orphistic case has most to gain by boldly enterprising advantage taken of some not very conspicuous accessories high up in the picture of the outing of Dionysos and Aphrodite on the bell-krater Leningrad St. 1427 (fig. 3b). Even this may involve some wrenching treating the prestige of Archytas as if it were very nearly the same thing, practically, as the prestige of his friend Plato. But in any event the special weakness of the Patronian case, or rather its most embarrassing circumstance, is that any resolute bully, if he minds his tone and makes it vehement enough, can out of material only too accessible in the second book of Plato's *Republic* (363-366) find means of molesting it quite cheapeningly: "hell and damnation, not eternal loneliness as some soft Protoproto-Swedenborg (idealizing, like the bachelor S., domesticity he never had) might have felt about it, was what the fourth century of that era dreaded, and we have Plato's word both for the fear itself and for the scale on which it was exploited."

Annexing that bell-krater, he can go on to add: "welcome to *Ana Aprodita,* quite subterranean enough in her inscriptions to be partner now of the chthonic (by no means Theban and so never Olympian!) Dionysos of Orpheus' Dismemberment *telete,* that Dionysos who indeed, as we have known for some time (pl. 12, fig. 13) shares Orpheus with her. How delightful it is now, and against ignorers of Plato's authority how opportunely trenchant, that in fig. 3b one of her children hands us something to ply as a three-edged weapon for their discomfiture, the *rhombos* rumble-wheel, *volubilis rota.* For was not this (1) regularly part of the god-bait for the Dismemberment *telete,* not less so than the mystic mirror which is so obviously important for the vases, yet (2) also a noise-maker of the Eleusinian religion from which (as you should have been able to see!) the fancied husband, your graduate "bridegroom" past fuss and now at fun in your supposedly relaxed and festive phase of the affair, in fact got his bump-cake (pl. 3) — the very branch of soul-saving mysticism from which other Erotes of yours (pl. 25) got their crossed torch? And (3) was not the religious *rhombos* studied intently, at Tarentum itself where this bell-krater was made, by Plato's friend Archytas — whose own *platage* the second Eros of this vase is actually holding?"

Restatement of Evidence
Supporting the (Re)union Theory

PRESENTLY, IT WILL be fair to let the Orphistic interpretation of the Lenin-grad outing register such support as it can fairly claim from the paradoxical scamper on the bell-krater Lecce 774, the interest of which (for us) has been meanwhile ripening: its final and general importance will depend, I suppose, on its relation to a fabulous vase in Baltimore to be published by Trendall. After the turn of Lecce 774, it should then be the right stage for something indispensable to our overdue change of subjects, the only means of making the actual farewell to symbols useful. That is, a concisely conspectual operation in that department of mere chattels for which "tabling" should be as apt a word as "benching" seems already to be for the ulterior department of Personages, if in regard to the latter it is not unsafe to reply on a Paris bell-krater published by Millin (2, pl. 16). In any case this vase in the Louvre should be opportune now even in its not quite unquestionable showing in an old book, for it can furnish an Apulo-Tarentine pairing of Aphrodite and Dionysos more exactly paredric than was their stag-drive, so erectly together, in fig. 3b, and this now after a fashion which should have made even the old unguarded scholarship pause before taking the goddess to be Ariadne; the bench they share is an altar. Such trouble as there is with the drawing furnished by Millin is no doubt in the copyist's failure to capture authentic style rather than in the evidence given of the vase's having suffered some corruption of original detail. On the left it is especially reassuring that the *platage* assigned to this Aphrodite (as to others whom we know) for distinctive attribute does not lack the median dots, features about which (even in the very little to be told at the thing's tabling) there will be more to say; further to the right, curiosity already indulged about the garnishing of phialai for weddings pays off in detection of a little mischief at the level of Eros' dish. Its garnish is sailing off into the void in a configuration only a little less bogus than the rendering of one of Eros' wings still further right. It is almost fortunate that the drawing in Millin's book is not wholly credible, for this has an astringent suggestiveness tending to keep our novelties together and addressed to their target, the new thoroughness which will so soon have the means of exploiting them. Here it makes against the chief enemy, grasp-loosening diffuseness, to be reminded now, by an absurdity of restoration in the slide-away garnish which Millin's book records, of re-sources still in hand from Andrew Oliver's Canosa disclosures. I mean much more than just the foliage, sophisticated in a more innocent sense, on the phiale held by Aphrodite who with her son (again) but no Dionysiac company is awaiting work of the sort which impends for those larger wedding teams, stationary and self-concerned in the Louvre or, on the way

272 /

to a task, in the Hermitage. For the first point of perhaps many, it is part of the special curiosity of Mr. Watkins' basin, published in fig. 3 of Oliver's pl. 8, that less grossly but perhaps more interestingly than the setting of the Louvre *paredria* it is relevant to the second and expurgatory concern of the new exhaustiveness, which is to ensure us the whole truth and (more laboriously still?) nothing but the truth. No one is going to ask, about that Louvre Eros, "can it really be true that, on this bell-krater as it honestly is, Aphrodite's boy is wearing that girlish bonnet?" On the contrary, we should be surprised if a cleaning of the vase altogether did away with it, since what is odiously there we thoroughly understand; there would be more reason in this drawing, pl. 16 of Millin's second part, to suspect its Aphrodite's caplessness. For, as we know, the caps of Apulo-Tarentine Erotes result from the goddess's usual headdress, in an Apulian reaction against the hulking, sometimes vehement and grabbingly Death-like Loves of earliest Italiote red-figure, which causes a demand that Tarentine Eros should resemble, even if sickeningly to the Greek decorator's taste and past the point of trans-vestism, the goddess whom for the great improvement of death neighbors of Tarentum adopted as *Ana Aprodita.* On the other hand, given leave to imagine some exploring scholar from Europe or the Southern hemisphere perusing Oliver's recent book in a train between the satisfactions of New York and the promise of Boston, and turning from its pl. 3 (bonnets gone black) to its pl. 8 (bonnet quite gone) and back again, fancy could well go on to add an unplanned descent at New Haven, result of the north-bound traveler's interest to the point of impatience in the sudden question "can it really be that after corrupting even Sicily in this matter Apulian red-figure sickened at last of the effeminate type of Eros forced on, or rather from, Tarentum?" Well, it was so if the uncovered (merely ribboned) head of Eros on a certainly very late piece, the basin lent by Mr. Watkins to the Art Gallery of Yale University, has not been repainted over a crack.

Perhaps there could not be a fitter cue for the reappearance of the bell-krater Lecce 774 (pl. 29b) than the present conjuncture of matters, the topic of mutual acculturation between Tarentum and Apulia having com-bined itself with our welcome, for its exciting disclosures, of Oliver's *Recon-struction of Two Apulian Tomb Groups.* Nothing could be more conven-tionally Hellenizing than its reverse, the ware's stale "pair of youths with symbols of their education, not merely gentlemanly but Greek, in μουσική balanced with γυμναστική. Nevertheless, its style, once mastered by seizure of what even random comparisons can reveal to be characteristic detail in the diptych and the drapery, can direct us *via* the column krater Vatican V 44 (Trendall, *VIE* 2 pl. 33 g then pl. 32 g) to a family of vases which (on the obverse sides) exploits the decorative value of the Apulian "step-in" shirt, and moreover (with quite a wide choice given) prefers for it patterns from the same *particular* system and range of gay striping as that which furnished the "yoke" and the verticals in the shirt of the arrestingly striking man in the

obverse picture on Lecce 774 (pl. 29b), less curious however for his uplander's hat, shirt and belt than for what he carries and at what and at whom
he looks back. As a suggestive control here Oliver's pl. 5, 4 for the "action
side" of a nuptial kantharos (one of a pair from T. Scocchera A at Canosa,
the "his" one) becomes invaluable, for me at least, if I am to say with the
least ceremony how I read the Lecce krater. Roughly speaking, and without
refining about types of wreathing (slender, coarse, plain, horned, tainiaed),
may I not describe my almost excessively Apulian man on Lecce 774 as
having in his right hand what Aphrodite on the Canosa kantharos has in her
left, a wreath, and certainly (however surprisingly!) in his left hand what she
proffers in her right, a mirror? I cannot imagine any conference of persons of
long experience in Apulian red-figure waiting for anyone's leave before
recognizing Aphrodite on that kantharos, in the female figure stooping to
offer mirror and wreath to the male in whom they would recognize a nearly
ready suitor, or (if this is better wording for an eschatogamic situation) a
bridegroom with some final wooing still to do. He has his own wreath, and
two phialai for the formal religion of the affair, one of them garnished, I
think. That he should have use for an extra wreath in the final overtures of
eschatogamy, we easily understand, why he needs a mirror we have seen
(pl. 8a for Lecce 623) and could reillustrate again and again (Lecce 777 in
CVA Italy 6, pl. 22, 6; London F361 in Walters, *Cat.* 4 *ad num.*) if in regard
to Lecce 623 it should be objected that the combined courting-reviving by
mirror of the dazed girl dumped *in loca senta situ* is an affair weirdly
exceptional, belonging moreover to an earlier dispensation in which it is not
Aphrodite but Dionysos in person who deals out eschatogamy. So, if I may
judge the newest available tool, that Canosa kantharos with Aphrodite
pressing a mirror on a nubile man, to be really better for our deciphering my
pl. 8a than even a composition on a Verona pelike (Stet. Ce) which formally
bears more resemblance to the Lecce scamper, than my interpretation of the
front of the bell-krater Lecce 774, a really propulsive and end-hastening
piece, can be as follows, at little risk save of Orphistic displeasure. The rear
figure holding in her right hand a thyrsos of the peculiar type (with flowers,
and these dishlike) to be found on vases of the family which connects
Cambitoglou's modest Amphora Group with Trendall's rather staggering
Baltimore Painter, is Aphrodite in that Dionysiac aspect of her which was
first revealed to us with overwhelming certainty in a piece that was Sicilian
(pl. 22) but is just as surely established for Apulo-Tarentine red-figure. For
the connection with the Baltimore Painter, as well as for some already
obsessive topics of theology, it is important that we can feel certain (if we
start with the female heads and work patiently with proper foils through the
rest of the configured detail) that one and the same hand painted the front
of the Lecce krater 774 and the side of the Ruvo column krater Jatta 808
that was published by Hellmut Sichtermann in his pls. 96 and 98, K 59.
Because, in this art for the dead of the wool-wealthy, Pan (for reasons

mastered already) is rather steadily the companion of Aphrodite (pl. 16) it is arguable that this goddess should be recognized in the central, most dignified, and altogether dominant figure of the Ruvo triad, the one with attributes (tainiaed sapling and timbrel) not unfitting Aphrodite and now turned to talk to Pan, A's established colleague. But unlike the figure with phiale and basket for *hedna* who follows the Apulian rustic on the bell-krater Lecce 774 she is not herself equipped with a thyrsos. We are left to make what is on the whole reasonable of her situation as neighbor and superior of two figures who each have one, Pan and a nymph, and to develop a contrasting aspect of this idyll of three immortals which should be suggestive for completing such description and brief comment as the front of Lecce 774 requires at this turn. We are to remember that the two vases represent not only the same decorator but also the same "public," the same place's demand; Lecce 774 is not, like so many of the Apulian vases in its museum, from Rudiae-Rugge in the Messapian heel of Italy; not less surely than the Jatta krater it is from Ryps-Rubi-Ruvo near Bari (P. Romanelli, *CVA* Italy 6, text p. 13). All the stronger now and more notable is the unidyllic, unmythic effect of the person rather incongruously ahead of Aphrodite in this scamper (pl. 29b), in such company, august, divine, this man's steeple-hat with the wool left on and his gay but almost laughably prudish tunic seem clashingly bizarre, hardly less so than his womanly yet womanless mirror. As to that, it would be stupid to forget the mitigation Oliver has provided for the present paradox in the contrastingly stationary group, Aphrodite equipping suitor with a mirror for courting, on the kantharos from T. Scocchera A at Canosa published in his pl. 5, 3. One of our reasons for making the obverse picture of Lecce 774 so welcome now, for treating it as specially opportune, is in its effect for timely concentration, rallying back to us some considerations that have had time to become distant stragglers (for one, the sampling of Dionysiac recovery nooks which took in a good deal more than the back of the neck of Munich 3297 [fig. 1b] and now as it comes to mind implants the scruple "How do you know that this 'Aphrodite' is not one of those thyrsigerous nurse-nymphs expediting a forward transfer?"). But also permitting some raking-in from ahead. "Ahead" (in more than one shade of meaning?) is where I must leave, awaiting his impresario, Trendall's Baltimore Painter, in whose manner (to say the cautious least) the obverse picture of the present vase, Lecce 774 is painted. Though neigher scholar has interposed the least restriction, the reason that was good against anticipating Boulter's publication of a showy, important, and quite difficult oinochoe in Cleveland (pl. 19; landmark of a certain pass) holds against my publishing photographs (these generally available but unpublished as yet) which I possess of the colossal crux that is the artist's eponymous piece, the volute krater 48.86 in the Walters Art Gallery, Baltimore. It is now one of Trendall's best opportunities for his work in progress on ornate Apulian styles; I must not spoil, but may hope to better his sport. As I reckon, there are at least three respects in which concentration, the bracing or binding or linking of ideas already present to us, could be served by even rumors, only, of Baltimore 48.86.

Here and now we may not ask very much more of it than such help as it can give, from its place in the background of Lecce 774 for our finishing, effectively, with symbols. We must hope for better — if possible — than mere stop-signs, limits of exploration, signals flashing the message "here your ignorance begins to be invincible," though if Baltimore 48.46 offers any, either in the persons and things flanking the heroon which shatters precedent by the Apulian dress of its tenant, or on the other and mythic side of the vase where overtures of trousered women to Greek warriors would suggest Lemnian viricides making up to Argonauts if only the queenly woman pavilioned with Hermes fitted better than at present some situation of the Lemnian princess Hypsipyle, then the sooner those signals are seen and acknowledged the better.

So let it be registered at once that on the Baltimore krater there is triple occurrence, no less, of the minor component of a paradox of seeming effeminacy in pl. 29b for Lecce 774, namely the *deep cylindrical basket with overlapping lid* which the Lecce vase showed us carried on a phialoid dish by a woman (if not goddess) who had also a thyrsos, behind (and *for?*) a man in Apulian dress who had the major component of the surprise, something more glaringly womanish, a *mirror,* and also a wreath (horned, tainiaed). Twice, twice only, such a basket is seen on the Baltimore krater in an "easy" context, not inconsistent with our provisional idea of the specific purpose of such baskets and of the value resulting for them in a code of nuptial symbols adjusted to the stages of a wedding. The first of those baskets is on the mythic side of the vase in the "underparty" (below the queen's pavilion) consisting of three armed Greeks and two unarmed women, who in spite of their caps and trousers are not really Amazonian; the thing in question is certainly part of the overtures of the rightmost woman to the rightmost Greek, to whom she is showing it, as also is the oinochoe in her other hand, with wine for his phiale, which is not the only responsive thing on his side, for his other hand holds a wreath. Very nearly the same nexus of symbols, at any rate deep cylindrical basket together with wreath and phiale, offers to make bride and her bridegroom of another pair of adjacent figures, on this volute-krater's other side, where there is a heroon and no myth. This is at the top of the stack of figures in very settled poses to left of the heroon, and no eye, crossing the heroon and its very uplandish hero to light on the stack of persons opposite, could fail to take, *at first,* the impression "here they are again, the same two who were seen on the left at the somehow larval stage of their affair, marked there, just as was the similar stage of another among the near-Lemnians and near-Argonauts of the other side (not to mention the heroon side of the Munich 'Reunion' krater, pl. 1b), by the thing which much more than the mirror of nubility, even more than the mirror to go wooing with, is the great starter, namely the basket with the woman's *hedna,* especially the textile things, her clothes, their bedding." Till the same glance catches the last of the three baskets, a little lower on the right side of the picture, it might well seem that the two figures recurring or seeming to recur high on the right respectively "fulfill" the two high on the left. As eschatogams, it would have to be, in view of what the man has, thyrsos and grapes. While the woman's promotion from ready bride to matron (marked by a fan) is quite according to the structure of successive symbols used for the stages of what we had to suppose an earthly *ELEP* marriage on the Munich "reunion" krater (pl. 1b), with the man it is otherwise, almost exactly as if he had been passed through the Dionysiac recovery nook which (as a separate picture) is on the Munich krater the hinge between the theme of earthly marriage and the theme of widower's reunion (pl. 1a, fig. 1b). The woman top right on the Baltimore krater, if we are to reckon that she has come there from top left of the same side of the whole vase, has given up in her easily imagined crossing two preliminary things, *hedna* basket and tainiaed wreath (cf. pl. 29b for Lecce 774 as well as pl. 1b for the Munich krater) in fair exchange for two nuptially final things, two (matron's fan and festive pastry) that can in fact be collected from opposite sides of the climax of the Munich ascent of two persons to their marriage on earth. If (under her) the man on the right of the Baltimore heroon has made a corresponding crossing from the left side of it, his exchange has been of simple cane to thyrsos and of phiale for bunch of grapes; if there were not, just below him, a deep round basket to trouble us (*hedna* hamper out of place?) we might have explained him, point for point, in terms of the already emparadised but transient widower of the Munich krater: "of course the Baltimore man could not keep his mundane stick when he received, like the Munich man, a thyrsos; but, as the Munich record of all that the transient had shows (fig. 1b, cf. pl. 1b), the phiale will have been useful in transit; the Baltimore man's acquisition of grapes as well as thyrsos and his discarding of phiale are explained with not inelegant precision by the final transaction in the Munich trauma room, where the man just beatified will (if he is to keep the thyrsos) have to put away the phiale when he accepts the grapes which Happy Ending is about to proffer him."

The "Orphic" Solution Not Adequate; Possible Directions of Future Research

BUT AS IT IS, between the thyrsigerous man's round basket on Baltimore 48.86 and the thyrsigerous "woman's" round basket on Lecce 774 by the same hand, both with the overlapping lids characteristic of the *cista mystica* in the shape that come unquestionable (with snakes erupting) on Hellenistic coins, what recourse have we against Orphistic objection's extreme of scorn: "will you never learn?" It is of course the conjunction with Lecce 774, an inexorably objective matter of shared style, which forbids us to make light of this, for there (pl. 29b) we cannot refuse to recognize presence of a feature — "targetless" mirror held by a male in female company — which in a more orgiastic setting on Roman plaques implies allusion (we have conceded) to the rite with which (because it cancelled sin) Orphistic reverie is still most preoccupied, a *telete* which enacted the Dismemberment of Dionysos. Mirror for trapping Dionysos on Lecce 774, grape bunch ready to be rent and consumed as Dionysos on Baltimore 48.86, combination of thyrsos with *kiste* on both: here, in a contemporary setting which includes *telete*-implying talismans not unconnectable with the presence of an army allied with all here concerned and commanded by the brother of a woman, Olympias, notoriously given to the kind of ritual reflected on cistophoric coins, are data for which an Orphistic explanation is obvious, at least in the sense that it is the one soonest and most glibly improvised.

I believe that with sufficient pains taken it can be refuted, thoroughly and so profitably as to make such recrudescence of Orphistic obstruction almost worth a welcome. One result of refutation should of course be practical knowledge of the limits, the safe limits, of our actual insight. It can only be a practically good thing, work-making for abler workers, if I may make public confession, presently of uncertainty about the Baltimore Painter's meaning in his use of the two signs, lyre and also cross-headed torch, as nuptial symbols, I perhaps can hope it may be interesting that confidence of his at least meaning them nuptially is given us by his making them neighbors of something already promised an *aristeia* of meaning, meaning to the rescue, namely the inscrutable but steadily dependable dowry-box (the occurrence of all three together is on Mrs. G. Schneider-Herrmann's already celebrated fragment, published by her in *BABesch* 36 [1961] pp. 64-70; see especially her fig. 2). But attention to business — I mean that which is most immediate, of leaving the data of eschatographic symbolism in fair workable order for at least late Apulo-Tarentine red-figure, with only perhaps some Campanian *desperanda* altogether shelved — need not preclude some awareness and enjoyment of the view, from our place of work, of Tarentino-Apulian culture, my reversal implying distance and difference. This is a prospect which meanwhile is appreciably clearing, thanks to interaction of considerations revealed respectively by Oliver's light on the sick taste of bereaved Apulians as imposed on Greek potters of plastic vases and Trendall's detection of the Baltimore Painter, eminently a flatterer of rustics, perhaps at unsuspectedly short range, yet a colossus in his way. And that (apart from restorer's mischief) was not un-Greek. Our exploitation of novelty, novelty in the sense of newly available stuff, any usefully fresh occurrence or improvement, must not be too self-conscious; it is only the drudgery of purveyors to purveyors, for what, near the end, machines will make of it all.

But it is so instructive, and as tending to a relievingly half-absurd anticlimax to scholar's agonized controversy about the red-figured ware's location so delightful, that for comparison with something new from Sichtermann in a familiar vein of Apulo-Tarentine grandeur, namely improved publication in his pls. 123-127 of the Baltimore Painter's 'Niobids' volute-krater at Ruvo (Jatta 424, Sichtermann K 73), we have something fresh in a familiarly opposite line in Oliver's suggestively circumstanced showing of a local askos from his tomb A (his pl. 7, 1, merely painted, nothing plastic) which is ugly in a way quite perfectly childish.

This way, however well known from other publications of very feebly rustic examples of upland pottery, is not numerously represented in the whole haul retrieved by Oliver from the dispersal of two Canosa tomb groups, in which there is no lack of the dislikable (his pl. 1, 7-8; pl. 10, 1; pl. 11, 1-3; pl. 10, 3?) but a dearth of the simply pitiable (besides his pl. 7, 1 only pl. 7, 5?). Because also at the other extreme of the present antithesis, the pole of it that belongs to the Baltimore Painter, so grand and Tarentine yet uncommonly aware of his neighbors, we shall have to take account of an interesting factor of variation, different except that it too is quite practically related to the master-topic of Apulo-Tarentine symbiosis, we need now to be better than vaguely aware of a mixture of quality in the ceramic material of the two Scocchera tombs, A and B, at Canosa. The red-figure which we have already sampled "shows its age," but no enfeeblement (still less barbarization) of ripe Apulo-Tarentine style, any more than its tiring of an appeasingly Apulianized but really stupid type of Eros marks erosion of the importance of Aphrodite in the eschatology or (to respect a valid distinction) of her primacy in the actual eschatography. Structurally, in their excessively bloated or flaring shapes (to say nothing of defects in integration), most of the larger plastic vases seem out of taste with the tradition of Greek pottery, but such charm as they now and then happen to have in sculptural detail is Greek enough to be decidedly presentable; that is quite safe to say, since part of one of them provided Oliver's book's cover with its only decoration, though there the decision so to use the attached figure involved suppression (or rather relegation, pl. 8, 1) of the pitcher itself. We shall lose our way (and quite hopelessly) if at any sudden opportunity of a wider view we forget that our simultaneous involvement with the Scocchera tombs and a vase-painter not even represented there, the Baltimore Painter, has happened because symbols on an Apulo-Tarentine kantharos from tomb Scocchera A at Canosa have offered, on Oliver's pl. 5 at fig. 3, to remove an obstruction of the way threatened by symbols in a work of the Baltimore Painter as I judge it to be, the obverse picture of the bell krater Lecce 774. For theological agenda of my closing chapter the female behind the doubly curious male, the man in full Apulian dress and clutching a mirror as well as a conspicuous wreath, is precious. But only if she remains a Dionysiac Aphrodite of the afterlife, guiding (or rather, steering) a man who died unmarried to the mate whom he is to woo so flatteringly with that mirror. Of course I lose her if (as can so glibly be urged, we know) those two persons on the Lecce krater are only a couple of upland rustics on their way to the principal service (Dismemberment *telete*) of an unwholesome but interesting religion, the venality of which distressed Plato while its incidental noise was of scientific importance for his Tarentine friend Archytas. There her thyrsos, and his god-fooling mirror, not to mention gear silent or noisy out of sight in the thing answering so exactly to a *cista mystica* of the cistophoric coins, would have momentous, soul-saving, work to do? But I may keep her, I can hope, if in a tomb-group certainly redolent of eschatogamy, the person proffering a man a mirror and a wreath in Oliver's pl. 5, 3 is Aphrodite, who is sufficiently Dionysiac there too if the ivy below her may count. But no doubt it is lucky — sensitizing and touchstone-making for work of historically concrete observation perhaps superior to any ancillary symbol-reading — that simply rustic ware, unaffected by contemporary Greek taste, was not quite lacking, and that its representative in tomb Scocchera A was the askos of Oliver's pl. 7, 1, which he has made doubly serviceable by his discovery and publication of a pot decorated by the same hand, a funnel-mouthed (to elderly North Americans spitoon-like) vessel now in the Folkwang Museum of Essen (his pl. 7, 5, p. 12).

Taken by itself, the askos from tomb A is exemplary in the extreme for the question of origin and continuance that of course lurks in every application of the phrase "Apulo-Tarentine," for nothing could be more rawly Apulian than this. By a standard sufficiently objective, set by the rest of the pottery published in Oliver's book, including the piece in Essen, the shape is utterly graceless as well as quite unhandy; to the painting on it grim justice can be done at a glance, thanks to Oliver's showing the Essen pot on the same plate. The former's silhouetted rabbits and birds and its sprays of floral and wisps of linear ornament amount to a merely puerile romp by a hand which indeed (though commanding only the humblest resources) could nevertheless make really decorative use of them on the tauter form of the thing in Essen, which is only subjectively and unfairly, to just a few long-memoried Americans and Canadians, absurd or worse. For any important but subtle and perhaps teasing distinction, such as between Apulian quite simply and Apulo-Tarentine hyphenated for an interaction not quite constant, there cannot fail to be some useful elucidation in a single pair of crying examples, one on either side of the difference. But it is even better with several, and with some modulation, up or down, in the crying. As we are finding the bell-krater Lecce 774 so propulsive, both towards our prospective duty to chthonic Aphrodite in her various correlations and for our more immediate duty against unfairly Orphistic interception of her symbols, it is not unfortunate that on the Apulo-Tarentine side of our present affair of contrast the example extremely telling, with the liveliest symptions of interaction, is work which I must judge to be of intimately related style covering both sides of the Baltimore Painter's volute krater in the Walters Art Gallery of his city. I must leave this to be confirmed by Trandall's publication of it.[1]

Then everyone will get his sight of Apulian male costume caught at an extreme of intrusion, worn even in a heroon, and also (unless T. shall have settled the enigma for us in the meantime) his opportunity of three guesses at the myth opposite. Argonauts in Lemnos according to the vulgate tradition as followed by Apollonius and Valerius Flaccus in their turns? Or, since that does not tell of any intervention of Hermes with the women's queen Hypsipyle, then the same story according to the lost *Argonautics* attributed to Orpheus (Kern² p. 65 *Test.* 224), of which we know at least that it did not shirk the Lemnian interlude? Or, with frankly Apulian reference and deference, Diomed's Greeks made welcome in South-Eastern Italy? As mean of a matter of mutual acculturation in the Baltimore Painter's group (which already seems to furnish three examples), the obverse of Lecce 774, should serve, if for present purposes it may be seen as I would still indeed explain it, underworld Aphrodite-*Aprodita* matchmaking in very much the former way of the partner to whom her thyrsos alludes, underworld Dionysos, but with ampler means, the old "mirror to woo with" being supplemented with a whole basketful of suitable things (cf. Lecce 774 with Milan 225). Making it the middle term takes account both of its mirror-borrowing suitor's completely Apulian dress, now including the national hat, and of the definite compromise with Apulian religion exhibited in this eschatogam's being ward of an *Aprodita* who however remains Dionysiac, having to carry a thyrsos. At any rate those features must be understood in duly measured relation to the vase most fit, as *least* restically Apulianizing, to be significant third

[Here, in the middle of a sentence, Smith's typescript ends. It is beyond the editor's capacity, and would be an impertinence were he to attempt, to impose an artificial conclusion upon a work which the author himself regarded as inconclusive.]

---

[1] It has been published by K. Schauenburg in *Opus Nobile,* pl. 21.3. [A.D.T.]

APPENDIX

A New and Unimpeachable Bronze for the Reggio Group of Android Handles

MUSEU NACIONAL 75. Pan handle, Greek work in the manner of Tarentum in southern Italy, of date not later than in the second quarter of the fifth century B.C. In the form of a nude youth, posed tiptoe on the palmette finial in seeming support of the hollow round of the shallow bowl originally soldered to the present superstructure (that this tectonic illusion would be lost in horizontal use of the pan raises a problem discussed below). For the complete effect, with bowl aloft, see K. Schefold's publication of Karlsruhe 573, from the same workshop and fully preserved, *Die Antike* 16 (1940) 27 fig. 21 (its side view is shown by U. Jantzen, "Griechische Griffphialen", *Berliner Winckelmannsprogramm* 114 (1958) p. 5).

Height of the present remnant, 21.2 cms; greatest width, 11.0; height of the figure, crown to toes, 17.2; its thickness (at buttocks), 1.9. Brief mentions by: A. Childe, *Museu Naçional do Rio de Janeiro (IVª Secçâo) Guia das Collecçoẽs de Archeologia Classica* (Rio de Janeiro, Imprensa Naçional, 1919), 63; H. R. W. Smith, *Year Book* of the American Philosophical Society (1960) 572, and *AJA* 66 (1962) 323 n. 1.

The lion's mask at the back is merely for outer ornament of the concave tongue which gave firm and becoming attachment to the bowl cupped against its plain side. Childe in his *Guia* can be excused for over-interpreting it (as an attribute of the figure, part of a pelt denoting Herakles), for he had not the benefit of Mogens Gjødesen's comprehensive study of such handles, *ActaA* 15 (1944) 101ff, now available for determining the sculptural type and for retrieving from it the detail obscured in this specimen by corrosion or incrustation. The uncommon posture of the hands, quite vertical with palm inward, at once relates this specimen to one of the choicest varieties of Greek panhandle, of severe but very subtle design, Gjødesen's type I/D for his Reggio Group (*ibid*. 113-116, 137-139); published examples: (1) Reggio-Calabria, Museo Nazionale 1763, R. Putortí, *L'Italia antichissima* fasc. 2 (1929) 99f fig. 1 a-b. (2) Karlsruhe, Badisches Landmuseum 573, K. Schumacher, *Beschreibung der Sammlung antiker Bronzen* pls. 5, 1 and 12, 2, and the publications by K. Schefold and U. Jantzen already cited. (3) Till recently at Northwich Park, Blockley, in the collection of Captain E. G. Spencer-Churchill; sold to a Mr. Bickford-Smith at Christie's London auction of June 23 1965, no. 469 in the catalogue, the compiler of which, quite unacquainted with the typology of panhandles, offered his well-meant caution that "this would seem to be a copy of the example in the Louvre (no. 3021) or at least a bronze virtually identical to it" – but Louvre 3021 is of quite another pattern, being Gjødesen's no. 28 on the fringe of his Acropolis Group, type I/B, *ActaA* 15 p. 112. The Bickford-Smith handle was published by C. H. Smith and C. A. Hutton in their *Catalogue of Antiquities in the Collection of the late W. F. Cook* pl. 37 no. 52. (4) Douai, Musée, S. Reinach, *Répertoire de statuaire grecque et romaine* 3 p. 25 fig. 1. (5) Berlin, Antiquarium Fr. 1478, Gjødesen, 115 fig. 4. Much of the system of detail that is uniformly characteristic of this Reggio Group can still be made out on Rio 75, enough for a confident attribution: as finial below, an inverted palmette of seven leaves between volutes; under the curved "saddle" made to fit the bowl's rim, a winglike spread of two half-palmettes of five leaves each; next inward, the volutes of an Aeolic (or "Proto-Ionic") capital, the youth seeming to steady this burden with his fingertips, which touch the outer extremities of the volutes just short of the first leaves of the half-palmettes. The grooves between the leaves have almost filled up, and the upper curves and inner detail of the volutes are nearly effaced; originally, each volute must have sprung from a horizontal collar (probably with angular chasing), and the small palmette of three leaves that flares upward between the volutes on fresher specimens of the type cannot have been lacking (in the handles of the Reggio Group this little feature plays, inconspicuously, a quite essential part in the whole elastic design, resuming the upward thrust, yet beginning its horizontal dissipation). To the youth's diadem there has been less damage, and the central flower of the three set in it (in the fashion of Tarentine terracottas) is still a conspicuous knob. The contours of the fall of the hair are no longer distinct, and the once crisp detail of fall and fringe have caked over; but at the back there remain clear traces of one of the two tyings that shaped the fall (compare especially the handle from Locri at Reggio, in Putortí's fig. 1b). All publications of handles of the I/D-Reggio type show a peculiar rendering of the collarbones, so angular that it might almost be mistaken for the taut string of a heavy pendant; traces of such a V, dim but as I judge certain, remain on the Rio handle. On the other hand I could see no sign at all of the chased detail to be expected above the lion's mask (cf. Putorti's fig. 1b), as rendering of the fluff of the mane. But that lack, superficial, is less important than the positively characteristic form in which this tongue for seating and attaching the bowl is cast, namely the lion's pelt of the Reggio Group, not the palmette of most other patterns.

It is not unimportant — especially to the question of function, as we shall see — that the whole Reggio Group of panhandles remains essentially true to the archetypal design for such things, as preserved for us from the late sixth century in the Trebenischte example (Filow, *Die archaische Nekropole von Trenbenischte am Ochridasee* pls. 12-13, H. Payne *Necrocorinthia* pl. 46 fig. 6). No argument from design to function would have been allowable if the present handle had belonged to one of the interpolated (ram-muddled) types. But as it does not, such a line of inquiry, if not of argument at first, is already open. I propose to follow it presently, if I may assume that while Greek design (notoriously) admits *monstrosity* and of course is subject to deterioration of every natural sort it does not *conceive* in *forms* of mere muddle, mere ineptitude.

The condition of the piece, however deplorable, is interesting. I need not apologize for publishing my unflattering record of the thing as I found it. Much thought, I know, has been given to the problem of restoration, and much advice asked about it. But photographs taken after the treatment would have had less value in certain respects. Less, in the first place, in regard to that cloud of suspicion under which, ironically, the Reggio Group once lay, as too minutely uniform in style, too sleek in condition, to be altogether true: suspicion perhaps even now not entirely dispelled by Putortí's publication of an excavated piece. That of course has vindicated the *type*, but not all the specimens of it. When Gjødesen wrote his monograph the Berlin example was still imputed to a forger, K. A. Neugebauer having withdrawn his former defense of its antiquity (*BerlMus* 45 for 1924 p. 35 n. 1, in opposition to A. Furtwängler, *KlSchr* 1, 397). It is only a little that the Rio de Janeriro handle can do to support Gjødesen in his cautiously favorable judgement of the Berlin one (pp. 115-116) and in his unhesitating acceptance of the Cook-Churchill-Bickford-Smith handle. But at any rate it takes a better than respectable place, criterion-making, in the group it joins. Besides the handle from Locri at Reggio it is the only specimen of its type that presents *credentials* of its antiquity. That is not to claim that the piece has altogether escaped modern tampering. Childe, wrong partly in his judgement of its condition (he thought it a miscast), was perhaps right in detecting signs of tooling; at the back, between hair and shoulders, there seem to be traces of an attempt, begun but soon abandoned, to clean the figure mechanically. This in some workshop of the Museo Borbonico at Naples? Many things now in the Rio collection are known to have passed through its storerooms, reaching Brazil finally as presents to the Emperor Dom Pedro II from Ferdinand II of Naples, his cousin and brother-in-law. Unlike an also Italiote, also fine and important, also rather sadly damaged object recently published (the phlyax krater Rio 1500), and indeed several other vases in the same collection, the present bronze cannot be run down in any inventory or catalogue of the old Museo Borbonico. But taken together with its Italiote style, its combination of good quality and bad state is, I rather confidently judge, presumptive evidence that the panhandle Rio 75 belongs to the Ferdinandian stratum of the Greek and Italic collection at the Museu Naçional. There almost everything is interesting; but by the condition or by the character of many of Ferdinand's presents to the antiquarian "rei filósofo" we are reminded of his taste and talent for disconcerting. "The best of his family," as De Cesare was inclined to rate him (with injustice, doubtless, to a sister, the Brazilian Empress), Ferdinand was no monster, nor even, on the whole, a disaster. But, as Harold Acton's rehabilitation concedes, he was a compulsive *farceur,* and no doubt there was a target set for him in the young Emperor's touching seriousness, the bent which was finally to seem, to some detractors of this admirable man, a hobby of omniscience. At any rate, no one privileged to have gone studiously through the Greek and Italic collection at Rio to its arcane anticlimax, a certain remote drawer of foolish obscenities from Naples, can acquit Ferdinand of mixed intentions in his discardings from the Museo Borbonico; it is, then, a little bonus of modern history in the Ferdinandian layer of the antiquities at Rio that this is such a characteristic mixture of pleasing, teasing, "shocking" things. More-over, since the flow of antiquities from Naples to Brazil began, in 1843, with a wedding-present, the ten second-rate bronzes (mainly Roman pantry-ware) which the King packed in his sister's *trousseau*, there is some thread of at least incidental connection between Ferdinand's ambiguous munificence and the only one of his practical jokes which was historically momentous: something beyond the mere antics of chair-pulling, wig-snatching, stealing and burning of hats, recorded by the Italian writers. These seem not to know of the trick, a thoroughly mendacious portrait of the proposed bride, by which the negotiations for Pedro's marriage to Teresa Cristina were clinched (it is just to allow that a determined apologist for Ferdinand could scrape material even here; the trick was played for his lame sister's sake; there was Brazilian collusion; the marriage, which the bridegroom's disappointment all but broke off, turned out a happy one, and in later life Teresa's sheer goodness brought her quite a measure of beauty and dignity).

Select Bibliography

Aeschylus, *Agamemnon*, ed. Eduard Fraenkel. Oxford: Clarendon Press, 1950.

Albizzati, C. "Saggio di esegesi sperimentale sulle pitture funerarie dei vasi italo-greci," *Dissertazioni della Ponteficia Accademia Romana di Archeologia*, ser. 2, xiv, pp. 149-220.

Aurigemma, S. *Scavi di Spina* I (*La necropoli di Spina in valle Trebba*). Roma: "L'Erma" di Bretschneider, 1960-1965).

Bartoccini, R. "Taranto — rinvenimenti e scavi (1933-1934)" *NS* ser. 6.12 (1936) pp. 107-232.

Bernabo Brea, L. "Rilievi tarentini in pietra tenera," *RivIstArch* 1 (1952) p. 432.

Bertocchi, F. Tiné. See Tiné Bertocchi, F.

Boehringer, E. *Greifswalder Antiken*. Berlin: W. de Gruyter, 1961.

Brunn, H. and G. Körte. *I Rilievi delle Urne etrusche*. 2 vols, Rome: Deutsches Archaologisches Institut, 1870-1896.

Cambitoglou, A. "Groups of Apulian Red-figured vases decorated with heads of women or of Nike," *JHS* 74 (1954) pp. 111-121.
    . "The Lampas Painter", *BSR* 19 (1951) pp. 39-42.
See also under Trendall.

Chase, George H., Cornelius C. Vermeule, and Mary B. Comstock. *Greek, Etruscan and Roman Art: the Classical Collections of the Museum of Fine Arts, Boston*. Boston: Museum of Fine Arts, 1972.

Chieco-Bianco Martini, A. M. "Conversano (Bari). Scavi in via T. Pantaleo," *NS* 18 (1964) pp. 100-176.

Childe, A. *Museu Nacional do Rio de Janeiro (IV^a Secção) Guia das Collecçoes de Archeologia Classica*. Rio de Janeiro: Imprensa Nacional, 1919.

Ciceri, P. L. "Le figure rappresentate intorno alle tombe nella pittura vasicolare Italiota," *Rend Linc*, ser. 5, no. 22 (1913) pp. 109-136.

Collignon, M. *Les statues funéraires dans l'art grec*. Paris: E. Leroux, 1911.

Cumont, F. *After-life in Roman Paganism*. New Haven: Yale University Press, 1959.

Degrassi, N. "Il Pittore di Policoro e l'officina di ceramica protoitaliota di Eraclea Lucana," *Bolletino d'Arte* 50 (1965) pp. 5-37.
    . "Meisterwerke Frühitaliotischer Vasenmalerei aus einem Grabe in Policoro-Herakleia," *RM* Ergänzungheft 11 (1967) pp. 193-231.

Del Chiaro, M. A. *Greek Art in Private Collections of Southern California*. Santa Barbara: University of California, 1963.

Dieterich, A. *Nekyia: Beiträge zur Erklärung der neuentdeckten Petrusapokalypse*. Leipzig: Teubner, 1893.

Durm, J. W. *Die Baukunst der Griechen*. Leipzig: A. Kröner, 1910.

Festugière, F. "Review of Guthrie, W. K. C., *Orpheus and Greek Religion*," *REG* 49 (1936) pp. 306-310.

Filow, B. *Die archaische Nekropole von Trebenischte am Ochridasee*. Berlin: de Gruyter, 1927.

Fränkel, Charlotte. *Satyr und Bakennamen auf Vasenbildern*. Halle a. S.: M. Niemeyer, 1912.

Furtwängler, A. *Berlin: K. Museen. Beschreibung der Vasensammlung im Antiquarium*. Berlin: W. Spemann, 1885.

. *Kleine Schriften*, 2 vols. München: Beck, 1912-1913.

Gabrici, E. "Cuma: capitolo quinto; l'invasione sannitica e la dominazione romana," *Mon Linc* 22 (1913) pp. 586-766.

Gargallo-Grimaldi, Filippo. "Dichiarazione delle pitture di un inedito vaso fittile greco del Museo Jatta," *Bull Nap* 5 (1857) pp. 153-155.

Gerhard, E. *Apulische Vasenbildeer des Königlichen Museums zu Berlin*. Berlin: K. Museum, 1845.

. *Etruschische Spiegel*. 4 vols. Berlin: G. Reimer, 1843.

. *Gesammelte akademische Abhandlungen und kleine Schriften*. Berlin: G. Reimer, 1866-1868.

Gervasio, M. "Scavi di Ceglie," *Iapigia* 1 (1930) pp. 263-272.

. "Thurii e Thuriae," *Iapigia* 3 (1932) pp. 283-292.

Ghali-Kahil, L. *Les enlèvements et le retour de Hélène dans les textes et les documents figurés*. Paris: E. de Boccard, 1955.

Gjødesen, M. "Bronze Paterae with Anthropomorphous Handles," *Acta Archaeologia* 15 (1944) pp. 101-187.

Guthrie, W. K. C. *Orpheus and Greek Religion: A study of the Orphic Movement*. 2nd ed. New York: Norton, 1966.

Haas, O. *Messapische Studien*. Heidelberg: C. Winter, 1962.

Haspels, C. H. E. *Attic Black-figured Lekythoi*. Paris: E. de Boccard, 1936).

Heberdey, R., and W. Wilberg. "Grabbauten von Termessos in Pisidien," *ÖJh* 3 (1900) pp. 177-210.

Heydemann, H. *Die Vasensammlungen des Museo Nazionale zu Neapel*. Naples: Museo Nazionale, 1872.

Hoffmann, H. *Tarentine Rhyta*. Mainz: P. von Zabern, 1966.

Holwerda, J. H. *Die Attischen Gräber der Blüthezeit*. Leiden: E. J. Brill, 1899.

Jocobsthal, P. "The Nekyia Krater in New York," *Metropolitan Museum Studies* 5 (1934) pp. 123-145.

Jahn, Otto. "Die Entführung der Europa auf antiken Kunstwerken," *Denkschriften der Kaiserlichen Akademie der Wissenschaften; Philosophisch-Historisch Classe* 19 (1876).

Jantzen, V. "Griechische Griffphialen," *Berliner Winckelmannsprogramm* 114 (1958).

Jatta, G. *Catalogo del Museo Jatta*. Napoli: Ghio, 1869.

. *I vasi italo-greci del signor Caputo di Ruvo*. Napoli: Testa, 1877.

Jatta, M. "La collezione Jatta e l'Ellenizzamento della Peucezia," *Iapigia* 3 (1932) pp. 241-282.

Johnston, M. A. "Etruscan Collections in the Royal Scottish Museum, Edinburgh and the National Museum of Antiquities of Scotland, Edinburgh," *StEtr* 11 (1937) pp. 387-406.

Jucker, H. "Das Bildnis im Blätterkelch," *RendLinc*, ser. 5, no. 22 (1913) p. 37.

Kerényi, K. "Bildtext einer italischen Vase in Giessen," in *Hommages à Jean Bayet*. Bruxelles-Berchem: Latomus, 1964. Pp. 334-348.

Kern, O. *Testimenta Orphica, in Orphicorum Fragmenta: pars prior*. Berlin: Weidmann, 1922. (= *Test* and = *Fr.*)

Klumbach, H. *Tarantiner Grabkunst* Reutlingen: Gryphius Verlag, 1937. (= *TGrK*).

Kraay, C. M., and Max Hirmer. *Greek Coins*. London: Thames and Hudson, 1966.

Krüger, A. *Quaestiones Orphicae*. Diss. Halle, 1934.

Langlotz, E. "Eine Apulische Amphora in Bonn," in *Anthemon in onore di Carlo Anti*. Firenze: G. C. Sansoni, 1955. Pp. 73-81.

Lattimore, R. A. *Themes in Greek and Latin Epitaphs*. Urbana: University of Illinois Press, 1942.

Lenormant, Ch. *Élite des monuments céromographiques*. Paris: Leleux, 1844. (= *Él.Cér.*)

Libertini, G. *Il Museo Biscari*. Milano e Roma: Bestetti e Tominelli, 1930.

Linforth, I. M. *Arts of Orpheus*. Berkeley and Los Angeles: University of California Press, 1941.

———. "Soul and Sieve," *University of California Publications in Classical Philology*, xii, no. 17 (1944) pp. 297-298.

Macchioro, V. *Orfismo e Paolinismo*. Montevarchi: Casa editrice cultura moderna, 1922.

———. "Curiosita canosine," *Apulia* 2 (1911) pp. 154-163.

Marconi, P. *Agrigento arcaica: il santuario delle divinità Chthonie e il tempio detto di Vulcano*. Roma: Società Magna Grecia, 1933.

Mayer, M. *Apulien vor und während der hellenisirung*. Leipzig and Berlin: Teubner, 1914.

Medawar, Sir Peter. *The Art of the Soluble*. London: Methuen, 1967.

Metzger, H. "A propos des images apuliennes de la bataille d'Alexandre et du conseil de Darius," *REG* 80 (1967) pp. 308-313.

Micalella, M. A. "Vasi italioti dei Messapi," *Apulia* 3 (1912) pp. 3-20.

Millin-Reinach — *Peintures de vases antiques recueillies par Millin (1808) et Millingen (1813) publiées et commentées par Salomon Reinach*. Paris: F. Didot, 1891.

Mylonas, G. E. *Eleusis and the Eleusinian Mysteries*. Princeton: Princeton University Press, 1961.

Neugebauer, K. A. *Berlin, Staatliche Museem: Führer durch das Antiquarium*. II, Vasen. Berlin: Mann, 1932.

Neutsch, B. "Archäologische Grabungen und Funde in Unteritalien," *AA* 71 (1956) pp. 194-450.

Nilsson, M. P. *Dionysiac Mysteries of the Hellenistic and Roman Age*. Lund: C. W. K. Gleerup, 1967.

Oliver, A. "The Lycugus Painter; an Apulian Artist of the Fourth Century B.C.," *BMMA* (Summer 1962) pp. 25-30.

Pagenstecher, R. *Unteritalische Grabdenkmäler*. Strassburg: J. M. E. Heitz, 1912.

Patroni, G. "Questioni Vascolari," *Rend Linc*, ser. 5, no. 21 (1912) pp. 545-600.

Parlangeli, O. *Studi Messapici*. Milano: Istituto lombardo di scienze e lettere, 1960.

Payne, H. G. *Necrocorinthia*. Oxford: Clarendon Press, 1931.

Pfuhl, E. "Das Beiwerk auf den ostgriechischen Grabreliefs," *JdI* 20 (1905) pp. 51-54.

Phillips, Kyle M. "Perseus und Andromeda," *AJA* 72 (1968) pp. 1-23.

Reinach, S. *Répertoire de reliefs grecs et romains*. Paris: E. Leroux, 1912. (See also "Millin-Reinach".)

⸻. *Répertoive de statuaire grecque et romaine*. 6 vols. Paris: E. Leroux (1897-1930).

Ribezzo, F. *La lingua degli antichi Messapici*. Napoli: Stab. tip. della R. Università, 1907.

Richter, G. M. A. and L. F. Hall. *Red-Figured Athenian Vases in the Metropolitan Museum of Art*. New Haven: Yale University Press, 1936.

Robinson, D. M. *Excavations at Olynthus*. 14 vols. Baltimore: Johns Hopkins Press, 1929-1952.

Rocco, A. "Il mito di Troilo su di un'anfora italiota della Biblioteca dei Gerolomini in Napoli," *ArchClass* 3 (1951) pp. 168-175.

Scarfi, Bianca Maria. "Gioia del Colle. Scavi nelle Zone di Monte Sannace," *Mon Linc* 45 (1961) pp. 144-331.

⸻. "Gioia del Colle (Bari): l'abitato peucetico di Monte Sannace," *NS* Serie VIII, vol. 16 (1962) pp. 1-283.

Schaal, H. *Griechische Vasen aus Frankfurter Sammlungen*. Frankfurt-am-Main: Frankfurter-verlags-anstalt, 1923.

⸻. *Abhandlungen und vorträge herausgegeben von der Bremer Wissenschaftlichen Gesellschaft* 7 (1933) Heft 1-2.

Schauenburg, K. "Pan in Süditalien," *AthMitt* 69 (1962) pp. 27-42.

⸻. "Zur symbolik unteritalischer Rankenmotive," *RM* 64 (1957) pp. 198-221.

Schmidt, Margot. *Der Dareios-Maler und sein Umkreis*. Münster: Aschendorf, 1960.

Schneider-Herrmann, M. "Apulische Schalengriffe," *BABesch* 37 (1962) pp. 40-51.

Schumacher, K. *Beschreibung der Sammlung antiker Bronzen*. Karlsruhe: Badisches Landesmuseum, n.d.

Séchan, L. *Études sur la tragédie grecque*. Paris: H. Champion, 1926.

Sestiere, P. C. "Metaponto — campagna di scavi (marzo-aprile 1939)," *NS* ser. 7.1 (1940) pp. 51-122.

⸻. "Trompietti funerari nelle vicinanze di Paestum," *NS* ser. 8.2 (1948) pp. 155-165.

Sichtermann, H. *Griechische Vasen in Unteritalien aus der Sammlung Jatta in Ruvo*. Tübingen: Ernst Wasmuth, 1966.

Simon, Erica. "Zagreus: über orphische Motive in Campanareliefs," in *Hommages à Albert Grenier*. Bruxelles-Berchem: Latomus, 1962. III, pp. 1418-1427.

Smith, H. R. W. "A Phlyax Vase in Rio de Janeiro," *AJA* 66 (1962) pp. 323-331.

⸻. "Deadlocks?," *BABesch* 45 (1970) pp. 68-85.

⸻. "Review of J. D. Beazley, Attic Black-Figure Vase-Painters," *Gnomon* 30 (1958) pp. 360-366.

Snell, B. *Scenes from Greek Drama*. Berkeley and Los Angeles: University of California Press, 1964.

Stephani, L. "Erklärung einiger Vasengemalde der Kaiserlichen Ermitage," *CRPetersburg* (1863) pp. 211-278.

⸻. *Die Vasen-Sammlung der Kaiserlichen Ermitage*. St. Petersburg: K. Akademie der Wissenschaften, 1869.

Tiné Bartocchi, F. *La Pittura Funeraria Apula*. Napoli: G. Macchiavoli, 1964.

Trendall, Sir A. D. "The mourning Niobe," *Revue archéologique* (1972) pp. 309-316.

    . "The Painter of BM F 63 and the new vases from Pontecagnano," *Apollo: Bolletino dei Musei provinciali del Salernitano* 1 (1961) pp. 29-52.

    . *Red-figured Vases of Lucania, Campania and Sicily*. Oxford: Clarendon Press, 1967. (= Trendall *LCS*).

    . *South Italian Vase Painting in the British Museum*. London: British Museum, 1966. (= Trendall *SIVP*).

    . *Vasi antichi dipinti del Vaticano – vasi italioti ed etruschi a figure rosse*. (= Trendall *VIE*).

Trendall, Sir A. D., and A. Cambitoglou. *Apulian Red-figured Vases of the Plain Style*. N.p. Archaeological Institute of America, 1961. (= Trendall and Cambitoglou, *APS*).

Vanacore, F. "I Vasi con Heroon dell'Italia meridionale," *Att Nap* 24 (1906) pp. 175-196.

Verdelis, N. M. "Χαλκῆ Τεφροδόχος κάλπις εκ Φαρσάλων," *AE* 89-90 (1950-1951) pp. 80-105.

Walters, H. B. *Catalogue of Greek and Etruscan Vases in the British Museum*, IV. London: British Museum, 1896.

Whatmough, J. *The Prae-Italic Dialects of Italy*. Harvard and the British Academy, 1933. (= *PID*)

Winkler, A. "Die Darstellungen der Unterwelt auf unteritalischen Vasen," *Breslauer Philologische Abhandlungen* 3:5 (1888) p. 19.

Wolters, P. "Relief aus Tarent," *Antike Denkmäler* 3.3 (1916-1917) pp. 35-36.

Wuilleumier, P. *Tarente des origines à la conquête romaine*. Paris: E. de Boccard, 1939.

Zanconi, D. "Una Stele funeraria Tarantina," *BdA* 20 (1926) pp. 15-25.

Index of Main Themes

206-207, 209-210, 211-214, 218, 231, 236, 248, 253-254: at Ostia, 203-209; on Attic vases, 213, 248; distinguished from food-box, 239; from trinket-box, 198, 204, 249

Fan: nuptial (attribute of wife), 5, 14, 24, 25, 28, 81, 83-84, 88, 90, 133, 163, 190, 197, 200-202, 211, 221-222, 254, 260, 263, 267, 276; held by nymph, 22: by Aphrodite, 173, 174, 225; "sex-insulting," 23, 42, 99; teletic, 7, 49, 268

Fillet: nuptial symbol, 61-62

Grapes, 28, 31, 33, 42, 73, 80, 230, 276; nuptial, 146-148, 152, 250-251; re-union presents, 149, 170; and "Happy Ending," 276; funerary, 81-82, 123; teletic in "Dismemberment," 93, 145, 149-151

Hydria: symbol of purification, 36, 59-61, 79, 90, 175-179, 189, 248; on Attic tombstones, 183

Jewelry Box, 14

Laver: symbol of purification, 22-23, 28, 36, 38, 59, 83, 86, 90-91, 127, 163 165, 173, 189, 207, 243

Mirror: nuptial symbol, indicates nubility, 5, 24, 59, 60, 68, 70, 99, 134, 143, 149, 152, 163, 180-181, 199, 230, 231, 236, 249, 267, 278-279; teletic in Dismemberment ritual, 7, 24, 30, 35, 58, 93, 98, 101, 110, 117, 149, 241, 255, 279; in mysteries of Demeter, 105; "sex-insulting," 23-24, 35, 43, 98, 195, 230-231; distinguished from washpan, 21-22, 59

Musical Instruments: symbolise genteel education, 137, 140-142, 272; of Apollo and Aphrodite, 137-139. See also Platage; Tympanon

Palm branch: symbolises "Happy Ending," 170

Parasol: identifies Aphrodite, 189-190, 207-208, 243; other, 111, 133, 245

Pentagram: Pythagorean symbol of health, 52, 61, 109

Phiale: nuptial symbol, 30, 76, 83, 90, 110, 132, 155, 196, 199, 213, 260-262, 271, 273, 275; for symposium, 111; as libation-pourer serves different purpose from washpan, 15, 17, 73

Phrygian bonnet: attribute of Mise, 51, 54

Pie (*popanon*, bump-cake, pastry): nuptial, for wedding-feast, 27, 30, 232-233; teletic, for funeral, 95, 125; Eleusinian, 97, 98, 101, 268, 270

Platage (*sistro apulo*, ladder of sounds, xylophone), 5, 30, 43, 127-132, 140-143, 145-146, 204, 253-254; nuptial or teletic?, 128-129, 135, 136, 215, 249; symbol of Aphrodite, 133, 136, 137-139, 164, 171, 204, 216, 225, 265

Rhombos: nuptial, as love charm, 49, 265; teletic, 99, 101, 102, 109, 118, 127, 129-130, 146, 265, 270

Rocks: symbols of underworld, 62-63, 65, 68, 70, 72, 74, 164

Spear: symbol of man's maturity, 61

Strigil (stlengis) symbol of male maturity, 5, 24, 54, 59, 60, 61, 68, 252, 261

Thyrsos: Dionysiac symbol, 22, 52, 61, 73, 80, 81, 84, 110, 147; denotes Dionysiac Aphrodite of Underworld, 165, 166, 168, 172-174, 225, 231, 238, 274, 275, 278-279; received by dead in antechamber of Paradise, 276

Torch: Demeter's, as nuptial symbol, 94-95; Dionysiac, 73, 165-166, 265; teletic, 199, 268, 270; and Mise, 28, 94, 133; doubtful symbolism, 244

Tympanon (Timbrel): nuptial, 25, 30, 38, 43, 46, 127-128, 234; Eros with, 230; Dionysiac, 21-22, 26, 32, 58, 60, 97; Eleusinian, 97, 101; in Naples "hellscape," 32, 112, 123, 234

Wardrobe: nuptial symbol, 194, 204, 225, 227, 230-231; sat on by Aphrodite, 175, 190

Washpan: form and function, 13-14, 15-17, 23, 58, 70; 207, 214-215; distinguished from mirror, 21; purifica-

Index of Vases in Museums

(See also Main Index for names of painters, and for vases from regularly excavated sites, names of sites).

Figures

a

b

c

Fig. 1. Neck Figures. (a) Obverse. (b) Reverse. From Volute Krater, Munich No. 3297. From Inghirami, *Pitture di Vasi Fittili,* IV, pls. 394, 395. (c) Neck Figure from reverse of Volute Krater, Naples H 3253. From FR II p. 145.

Fig. 2. Volute Krater, Leningrad, Hermitage St. 420. Figures from obverse. From *Mon-Inst* VI-VII (1862), pl. 66.

a

b

Fig. 3. Bell Krater, Leningrad, Hermitage St. 1427. (a) Reverse (b) Figures from obverse.
From *CR Petersburg* 1863, pl. 5, 1-2.

Fig. 4. Volute Krater, Leningrad, Hermitage St. 424. Figures from obverse. From *Wiener Vorlegeblätter,* Series E, pl. IV.

Fig. 5. Volute Krater "in Sir John Soane's Museum." Millin-Reinach II, pl. 25.

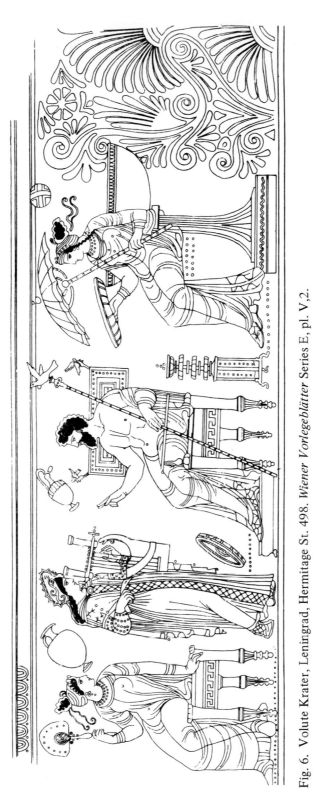

Fig. 6. Volute Krater, Leningrad, Hermitage St. 498. *Wiener Vorlegeblätter* Series E, pl. V,2.

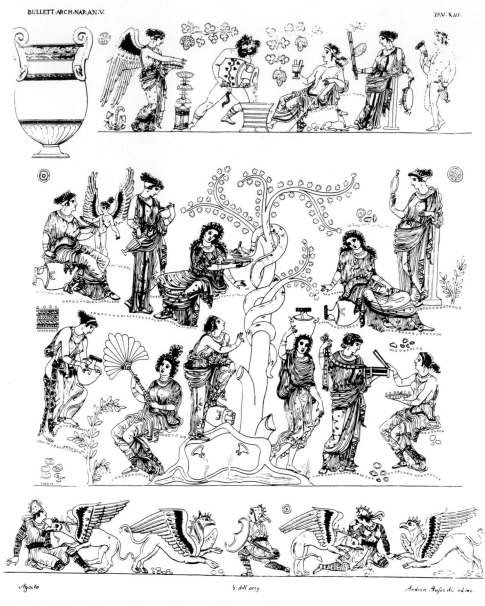

Fig. 7. Volute Krater, Ruvo, Jatta Collection No. 1097. Reverse. From *BullNap* NS. 5 (1857) pl. 13.

Fig. 8. Volute Krater, Naples, Museo Nazionale, H 3255. Reverse. From Inghirami, *Pitture di Vasi Fittili* IV, pl. 372.

Fig. 9. Volute Krater, Naples, Museo Nazionale, H 3255. Obverse. From Inghirami, *Pitture di Vasi Fittili* IV, pl. 371.

Fig. 10. Calyx Krater, New York, Metropolitan Museum of Art, No. 08.258.21 (Rogers Fund). From G. M. A. Richter and L. F. Hall, *Red-figured Athenian Vases in the Metropolitan Museum of Art,* pl. 135.

Fig. 11. Volute Krater, Naples, Museo Nazionale, H 3222. Reverse. From *Wiener Vorlegeblätter,* Series E, pl. II.

Fig. 12. Volute Krater, Leningrad, Hermitage St. 426. Figures from obverse. From *Wiener Vorlegeblätter* Series E, pl. VI.

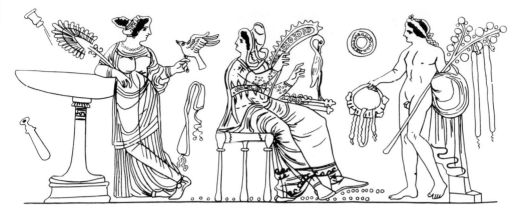

Fig. 13. Oenochoe, Ruvo, Jatta Collection No. 1554. From *BullNap* NS 6, pl. 11.

Fig. 14. Volute Krater, Naples, Museo Nazionale H 3256. Obverse. From *FR* II p. 152.

Fig. 15. Amphora, Berlin F 3241.

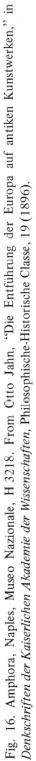

Fig. 16. Amphora, Naples, Museo Nazionale, H 3218. From Otto Jahn, "Die Entführung der Europa auf antiken Kunstwerken," in *Denkschriften der Kaiserlichen Akademie der Wissenschaften, Philosophische-Historische Classe*, 19 (1896).

Fig. 17. Volute Krater, Karlsruhe. From *Wiener Vorlegeblätter* Series E, pl. III, 1.

Fig. 18. Fragments in Fenicia collection. From *MonAnt* XVI, pl. III.

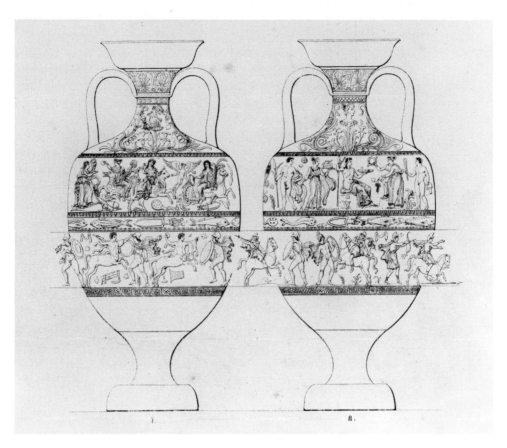

Fig. 19. Amphora, Berlin F 3241. From E. Gerhard, *Apulische Vasenbilder,* pl. A.

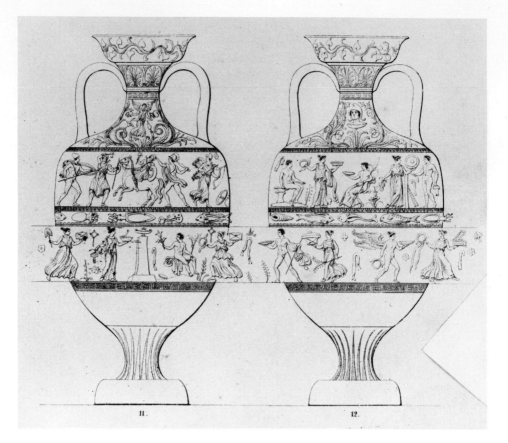

Fig. 20. Amphora, Berlin F 3242. From E. Gerhard, *Apulische Vasenbilder,* pl. A.

Fig. 21. Amphora, Berlin F 3244. From E. Gerhard, *Apulische Vasenbilder,* pl. A.

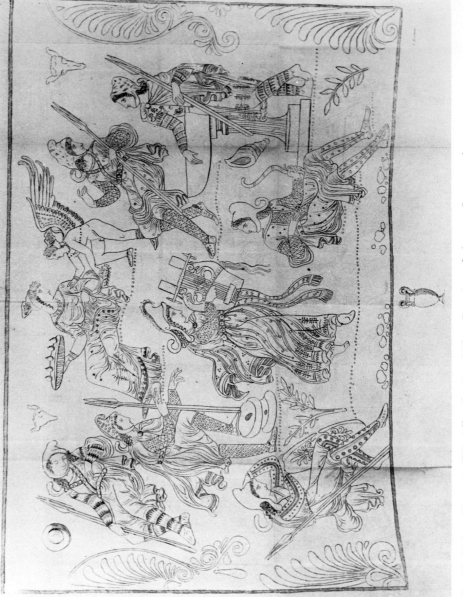

Fig. 22. Volute Krater in "H. A." collection, Milan. Drawing of obverse. Source unknown.

Plates

Pl. 1. Volute Krater, Munich, Antikensammlungen No. 3297. (a) Obverse. From *FR* I, pl. 10. (b) Reverse. From Inghirami, *Pitture di Vasi Fittili*, IV, pl. 393.

Pl. 2. Volute Krater, Leningrad, Hermitage St. 420 (reverse). By courtesy of the Hermitage Museum, Leningrad.

b

a

Pl. 3. Volute Krater, Leningrad, Hermitage St. 424. (a) Obverse. (b) Reverse. By courtesy of the Hermitage Museum, Leningrad.

b

a

Pl. 4. Volute Krater, Leningrad, Hermitage St. 426. (a) Obverse. (b) Reverse. By courtesy of the Hermitage Museum, Leningrad.

Pl. 5. Amphora, British Museum F 332. (a) Obverse. (b) Reverse. By courtesy of the Trustees of the British Museum.

b

a

a   b

Pl. 6. (a and b) Lekythos, Torino, Museo Nationale No. 4427. From *CVA* Italy 32 IV D, pl. 1. By courtesy of the Museo Nazionale, Torino.

a　　　　　　　　　　　　　　　　　　b

Pl. 7. (a, b, and c) Askos, British Museum No. 1928-1-17-68. By courtesy of the Trustees of the British Museum.

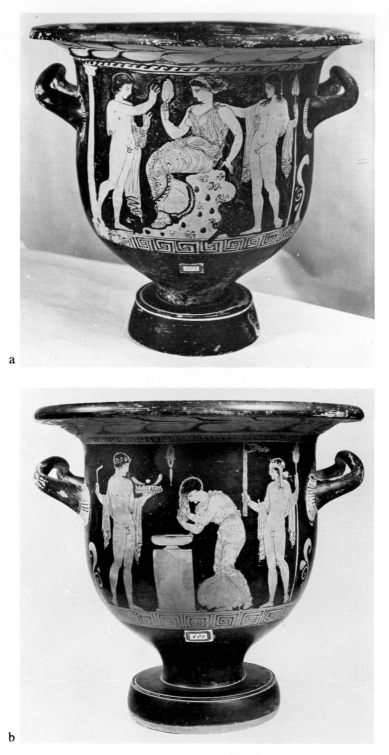

a

b

Pl. 8. (a) Bell Krater, Lecce, Museo Provinciale Castromediano
No. 623. By courtesy of Sir A. D. Trendall. (b) Bell Krater,
Lecce, Museo Provinciale Castromediano No. 620. By courtesy of
the Deutsches Archaeologisches Institut, through the kindness of
Sir A. D. Trendall.

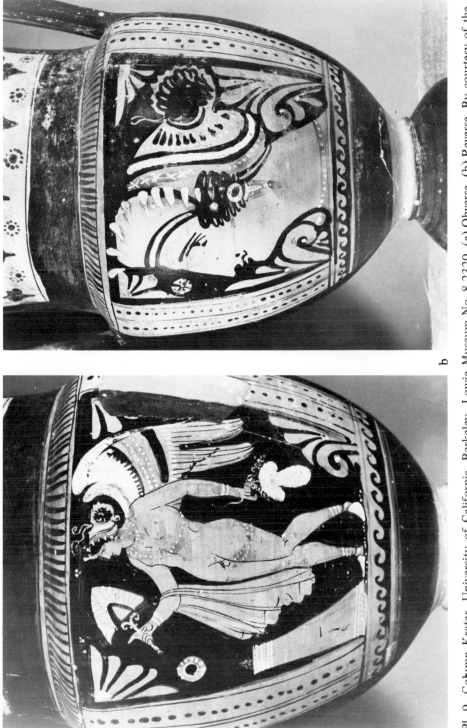

Pl. 9. Column Krater, University of California, Berkeley, Lowie Museum No. 8.2320. (a) Obverse. (b) Reverse. By courtesy of the Lowie Museum of Anthropology.

b

a

Pl. 10. Apulian Pan, Allard Persson Museum, Amsterdam. By courtesy of the Allard Persson Museum, through the kindness of Dr. Joost Crouwel.

b

a

Pl. 11. Volute Krater in "H.A." collection, Milan. (a) Obverse. (b) Reverse. By courtesy of Dr. Torno, Dr. H. Sichtermann, and the Deutsches Archaeologisches Institut, Rome.

Pl. 12. Same. Obverse, detail.

Pl. 13. Same. Reverse, detail.

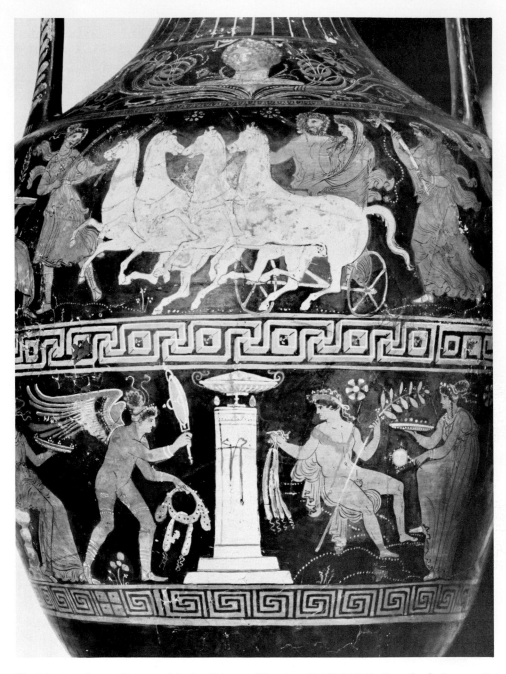

Pl. 14. Amphora, Geneva, Musée d'Art et Histoire, *MAH* 15043. Detail of obverse. By courtesy of the Musée d'Art et Histoire, Geneva.

Pl. 15. Volute Krater, Museo Nazionale, Naples, No. H 3255. Detail from reverse. By courtesy of the Museo Nazionale, Naples.

a   b

Pl. 16. (a and b) Pelike, Hearst San Simeon State Historical Monument, 5696. By
courtesy of Professor D. A. Amyx.

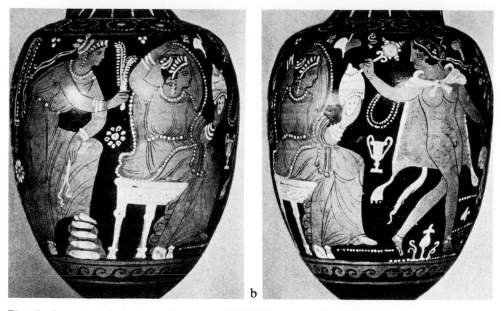

a   b

Pl. 17. (a and b) Oenochoe, Stuttgart, KAS 161. From *CVA* Germany 26, pl. 52, Figs. 3 and 4.

a   b

Pl. 18. Volute Krater, Jatte Collection, Ruvo, No. 1094. (a) Obverse. (b) Reverse. From
H. Sichtermann and H. Koppermann, *Griechische Vasen in Unteritalien aus der Samm-
lung Jatta in Ruvo,* pls. 52, 54. By courtesy of Dr. Sichtermann and the Deutsches
Archaeologisches Institut, Rome.

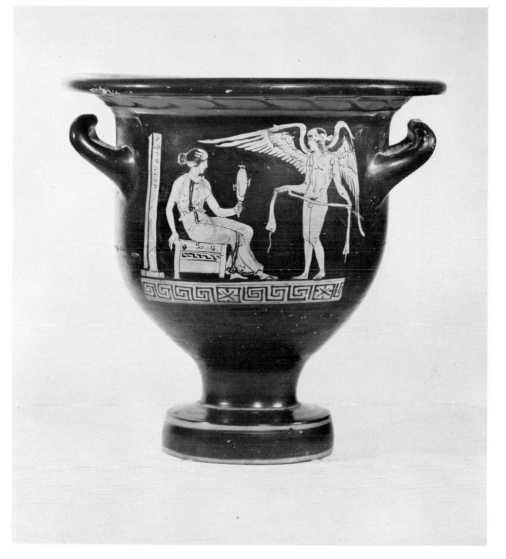

Pl. 19. Bell Krater, Cleveland Museum of Art No. 24,534 (Gift of J. H. Wade). Obverse.
By courtesy of the Cleveland Museum of Art.

Pl. 20. Hydria, Newark Museum No. 50.330 (The Eugene Schaefer Collection). By courtesy of the Newark Museum.

Pl. 21. Bell Krater, Vienna No. 182. Detail of obverse. By courtesy of Sir A. D. Trendall.

Pl. 22. (a, b, and c) Lekanis, Lipari No. 749A. By courtesy
of Sir A. D. Trendall.

Pl. 22. (d, e, and f) Lekanis, Lipari No. 749B. By courtesy of Sir A. D. Trendall.

Pl. 23. Amphora, Bari No. 873. By courtesy of Sir A. D. Trendall.

Pl. 24. Calyx Krater, British Museum No. F 272. By courtesy of the Trustees of the British Museum.

Pl. 25. a, b, c, and d) Amphora, Naples, Museo Nazionale No. H 3221. Details of frieze. By courtesy of the Museo Nazionale, Naples.

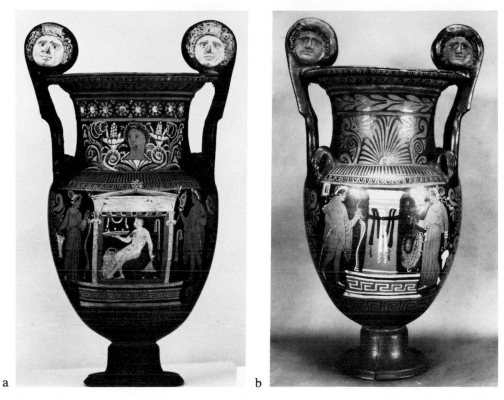

a   b

Pl.26. Volute Krater, University of California, Berkeley, Lowie Museum, No. 8.62.
(a) Obverse. (b) Reverse. By courtesy of the Lowie Museum of Anthropology.

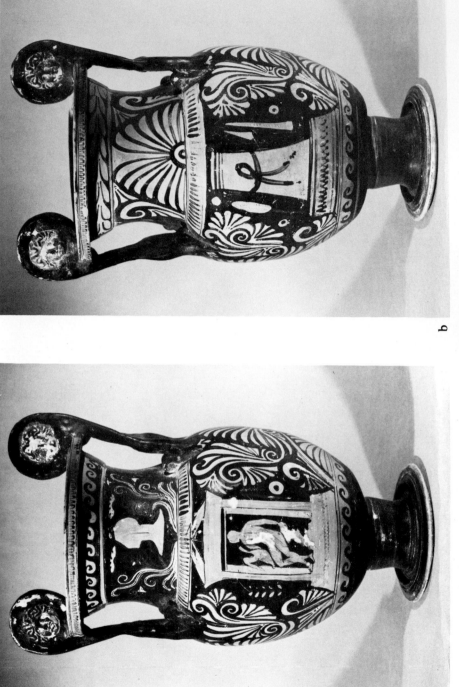

b

a

Pl. 27. (a and b) Volute Krater, British Museum No. F 286. By courtesy of the Trustees of the British Museum.

b

a

Pl. 28. Volute Krater, Milano, Museo Civico Archeologico No. 225. (a) Obverse. (b) Reverse. From *CVA* Italy 31 IV D, pl. 6.

a

Pl. 29. (a) Bucket, Bologna, Museo Civico, 631 (Palagi No. 708).
Obverse. By courtesy of Sir A. D. Trendall.

b

Pl. 29. (b) Bell Krater, Lecce, Museo Provinciale No. 774.
Obverse. By courtesy of Sir A. D. Trendall.